Old Hickory's War

"[Andrew Jackson] supposes that the volume of my opinions, and the force of my resentments against him really influenced my conclusions upon abstract questions of constitutional law. If he was capable of forming opinions upon such questions, no person would doubt the correctness of his conclusions, when applied to himself; but as he has not understanding enough to form such opinions, all the ideas he has upon all subjects are the result of his resentments, and of his vindictive passions."

—WILLIAM H. CRAWFORD
6 November 1820

SPEEDWAY PUBLIC LIBRARY
SPEEDWAY, INDIANA

Old Hickory's War

Andrew Jackson and
the Quest for Empire

David S. Heidler
and Jeanne T. Heidler

STACKPOLE
BOOKS

Copyright © 1996 by David S. Heidler and Jeanne T. Heidler

Published by
STACKPOLE BOOKS
5067 Ritter Road
Mechanicsburg, PA 17055

All rights reserved, including the right to reproduce this book or portions
thereof in any form or by any means, electronic or mechanical, including
photocopying, recording, or by any information storage and retrieval system,
without permission in writing from the publisher. All inquiries should be
addressed to Stackpole Books, 5067 Ritter Road, Mechanicsburg, PA 17055.

Printed in the United States of America

10 9 8 7 6 5 4 3 2 1

First edition

Portions of this book previously appeared in the *Journal of the Early Republic,*
13 (Winter 1993), 501–530, copyright © 1993 Society for Historians of the
Early American Republic. The authors are grateful to the editors for permission
to republish.

Library of Congress Cataloging-in-Publication Data

Heidler, David S.
    Old Hickory's war: Andrew Jackson and the quest for empire / David S.
Heidler and Jeanne T. Heidler — 1st ed.
        p.   cm.
    Includes bibliographical references (p.) and index.
    ISBN 0-8117-0113-1 (hardcover)
    1. Seminole War, 1818–1819. 2. Jackson, Andrew, 1767–1845. 3. Creek
Indians—Government relations. 4. Seminole Indians—Government rela-
tions. 5. Florida—History—Cession to the United States, 1819. I. Heidler,
David Stephen, 1955– . II. Title.
E83.817.H47   1996
973.5'4—dc20   95-32651
                                                                  CIP

For Our Parents

Joseph L. Twiggs
Sarah D. Twiggs
C. D. Heidler, Jr.
Jane Autry Heidler

"Chance does nothing that has not been prepared beforehand."

—Tocqueville

Contents

Acknowledgments

Many people helped us in our labors on this project, and we want to register our gratitude. Beleaguered and busy staffs at the National Archives and the Library of Congress in Washington, D.C., were always helpful and consistently cheerful. Those stalwart souls in the Military History Section of the National Archives merit special thanks for helping to track down, for one thing, elusive records of the Creek Indian Brigade. The men and women in charge of the reading room at the Library of Congress made our days there not only productive but also pleasant.

Norwood Kerr at the Alabama Department of Archives and History went, as always, above and beyond the call of archival duty to find us things that were pertinent, and Bruce Chappell of the P. K. Yonge Library at the University of Florida advised us about important Spanish sources that otherwise would have escaped our attention. Samantha Kahn Herrick proved to be so much help in our work with the Mitchell Papers at the Newberry Library that we owe her a special debt. The staff in the manuscript division of the University of Georgia Libraries was so attentive that we were never without something to do; only by stealing a few minutes from our work could we admire through the spacious windows of the reading room those spectacular thunderstorms that roll across north Georgia on hot summer afternoons.

We also extend thanks to Joyce P. Kobasa of the New York State

Office of Parks, Recreation, and Historic Preservation; Stephen E. Massengill of the North Carolina Department of Cultural Resources; Robert Behra of the Redwood Athenaeum; Gail Miller DeLoach of the Georgia Department of Archives and History; Barbara Katus of the Pennsylvania Academy of the Fine Arts; Andrew Kraushaar of the State Historical Society of Wisconsin; Joanna Norman and David Coles of the Florida State Archives; Paula Fleming of the Smithsonian Institution; Donald Frazier of Applied Academic Services; Wendy Haynes of The New-York Historical Society; and John McGill of the Historic New Orleans Collection.

A number of colleagues offered helpful suggestions, but none has matched the contribution of Dr. Kathryn E. Holland Braund, who read portions of the manuscript and offered exactly the kind of candid advice that makes her endearing as a friend and invaluable as a scholar. She is responsible for everything that is correct about Muskogee Indians in this book, and we admit exclusive culpability for that which is not.

Unstinting support and encouragement from those we work with made this project possible. Colonel Carl Redell and Colonel Mark Wells at the United States Air Force Academy and Dr. Ron Aichele and Dr. Bea Spade at the University of Southern Colorado have our thanks.

Sylvia Frank, as always, has been the picture of tact and equanimity. She and the other editors at Stackpole have improved this book with every suggestion. William C. Davis took the time from a busy schedule to read the draft and join in extended ruminations about the title. We are in their debt.

And we thank friends across the country, who welcomed us into their homes and to their dinner tables, in spite of our habit of frequently bringing with us a gaggle of ghosts, Old Hickory prominent among them. Timothy and Vicki Miller, John Shortt, Evelyn B. Holman, Jack and Tali Stovall, and Darrell and Kathy Hagar have always been there when it counted. Thank you, dear friends.

We most of all want to thank our family for its love and support. Our brothers, Dub, Joe, Jack, Bob, and Mike were always ready with a joke and always game for a drink. Our parents—C. D. Heidler, Jr., Jane Autry Heidler, Joseph L. Twiggs, and Sarah D. Twiggs—have been constant in their encouragement and unabashedly proud of all their children. We count ourselves among those children with love and gratitude.

Prologue

In May 1805, Rachel and Andrew Jackson entertained a famous guest at their home outside Nashville, Tennessee. Aaron Burr had visited many people during the previous months on a journey that was taking him from Kentucky to Louisiana. Now he pulled up at the Hermitage, Jackson's two-story, three-room blockhouse that sat in the midst of rolling hills just miles from the Tennessee capital and the Cumberland River. The former vice president would spend five days with the Jacksons, strolling the Hermitage's shaded grounds and ambling the streets of Nashville, always in the company of his host. The two presented quite a study in contrasts. Burr was short and compact, Jackson tall and angular; Burr's hair had begun to recede to leave a widow's peak while Jackson's resembled the tufted mane of a great lion; Burr spoke in the clipped, nervous phrases of a New Yorker, a counterpoint to Jackon's southern drawl; Burr the rake looked upon women as amorous opportunities while Jackson the backwoods cavalier regarded them as irreproachable angels.

Yet, in spite of all these differences, the two men had some important things in common. Just months before, Burr had fatally wounded Alexander Hamilton in a duel, earning a notoriety for the deed that was as widespread as it was disapproving. Jackson also would soon shoot dead a dueling opponent and would similarly suffer under the scorn of Nashville society. And now, as the two talked, Jackson learned that in addition to an inclination to shoot one's enemies, he and Burr also shared an entire range of opinions on other substantive matters. Jackson's guest had not come for a mere social visit. Aaron Burr had come to procure Jackson's help in a grand design.

Burr intended, he said, to oust the hated Spaniard from the Southwest and hence the North American continent. He characterized his journey as a preliminary stage of the enterprise to gauge and gather support. He also told his host that the United States government in the person of Secretary of War Henry Dearborn supported the project and would provide United States soldiers to help expel the Spaniards.

Nearly all westerners who heard the plan listened to Burr with broad smiles and eager eyes. Americans from the Ohio to the Mississippi River Valleys distrusted Spain. Some, like Andrew Jackson, openly detested Spaniards. It all stretched back to the years after the American Revolution when Spain had peevishly pinched off western trade and commerce by closing New Orleans to American shipping. In 1795 with the Treaty of San Lorenzo, Madrid had granted Americans navigation rights on the Mississippi, including the right of deposit at New Orleans, but only eight years later, the Intendent at New Orleans again closed the city to American traffic. As the Treaty of San Ildefonso was arranging the transfer of Louisiana to Napoleon's France, Jefferson's purchase of Louisiana in 1803 finally solved the West's traffic problem. Yet the fury over Spain's behavior remained unabated. People like Andrew Jackson had threatened to reopen New Orleans with force if necessary, and their blood, up for that task, stayed at the boil even after Spain had quit Louisiana.

Yet the Spaniards had not really departed. Although Louisiana belonged to the United States, Spanish Mexico still bordered it to the west. To the east, Spain still owned the Floridas, called such because the British had divided the peninsula into eastern and western sections when they owned it between 1763 and 1783. Americans believed that West Florida was, in fact, part of Louisiana and should have been included in Jefferson's purchase. Spain, angry with Napoleon for selling Louisiana in the first place, curtly disagreed.

In addition to these points of friction, the Americans in the West still chafed under Spanish control of waterways from the Gulf of Mexico into the Southwest. They saw this as an economic threat different only in degree from Spain's former control of New Orleans. Westerners also pointed out how the Spanish presence menaced their security. True enough, Europeans tolerated borders shared with sometimes fractious neighbors, but they were used to it; the American West felt its circumstance was different, and landlocked pioneers argued that if any power made war on the United States, the Gulf of Mexico would be a prime place for invasion precisely because of Spain. In West Florida, the Spanish presence—or really, the lack of it—seemed to prove the point. In 1805, Spaniards there peopled only a few frontier military posts, specifically at Mobile, Pensacola, and St. Marks. Even these garrisons were so small that Spain's authority did not reach much beyond the walls of their fortifications. Any power could mount an uncontested invasion of the United States by avoiding these three isolated sites. Few powers contemplating such an invasion, however, would have needed to bother. None of these garrisons could have resisted even a casual assault.

Spain's lax administration in the Floridas made the Indians there another security concern for neighboring Americans. Indians living in the United States could be controlled, with force if necessary. Florida Indians, however, attacked American frontier settlements, where they purloined livestock and snatched slaves and then took refuge on the other side of the Florida border. Also, the Floridas offered a sanctuary to runaway slaves fleeing an advancing cotton frontier. Either from indifference or inability, Spain did not even try to control these Indians or stop these fugitives. To Americans in the South, Spain's motive was immaterial; they saw only that Indians regularly crossed into the United States and slaves ran the other way to find freedom. So they did smile indeed over Aaron Burr's one solution to all these problems.

Andrew Jackson found the idea enthralling and jumped at the chance to join the project. Soon it became the opportunity to crawl out from under the censure of an angry Nashville and enhance his political reputation with a successful military campaign. So far, his major general's commission in the Tennessee militia had offered precious few prospects for martial glory, but Burr's venture could change that. Jackson agreed to provide boats and supplies for the expedition against Spain. Burr agreed to furnish Jackson with $3,500 in Kentucky banknotes to cover his costs. Jackson would have the Tennessee militia ready to march immediately once the plan was put into operation. The two men parted as partners, each having done for the other a great favor: Jackson's association with Burr restored him as a community leader in Nashville; Burr's association with Jackson had put the Tennessee militia at his service.

Soon, however, Jackson began to hear disturbing rumors. He heard that Burr did not intend to wage an undeclared war against Spain for the benefit of the United States. Instead, he planned to detach a part of the United States to combine with his conquered Spanish territory, thus to create a new country with himself at its head. Jackson panicked. He was willing to break his country's laws to advance his country's interests, but he would have no truck with traitors. Now believing he had connected himself with one, he fired off letters to the governor of Louisiana and President Thomas Jefferson. The letters were cryptic enough to veil his involvement in Burr's plans, clear enough in their warnings about what those plans possibly entailed.

Jackson shortly fell into a hazy confusion, however, about what Burr aimed to do. When Burr reappeared at the Hermitage, it took him only the shorter part of an hour to convince Jackson with an eloquent explanation that the plan held no harm for the country. Though Burr easily convinced Jackson of this, others alerted to the plan saw it as a conspiratorial plot. In New Orleans, General James Wilkinson, ranking United States Army officer, spy for Spain, and chief confederate of Aaron Burr, now turned on his fellow turncoats with enough enthusiasm to mask his part in the scheme. Burr was arrested and would stand trial for treason. Though he was finally acquitted, most people believed he had been up to more than appropriating Spanish territory.

Jackson, however, was not one of these. He attended Burr's grand jury hearing and trial in Richmond, Virginia, at the request of the defense. He testified to Burr's innocence before the grand jury, but he also delivered a spectacularly incoherent speech to a curious crowd clustered on the Virginia capitol steps, exculpating Burr and denouncing Thomas Jefferson and James Wilkinson. Burr's attorneys took the measure of this disturbing performance and decided to leave the hotheaded Tennessean off their witness list. The last thing they needed was Andrew Jackson throwing a temper tantrum under cross-examination.

Jackson believed that James Wilkinson was responsible for any illegalities in Burr's plan. Nursing a hatred for Wilkinson that stemmed from slights both real and imagined, Jackson was convinced that Wilkinson had done his nefarious work without Burr's knowledge. Jackson also blamed Jefferson for prosecuting the wrong man to cover up the administration's role in the original plan. Obsessively and tirelessly, Jackson would devote himself to proving these allegations years after the controversy had been put to rest. It was his way.

Perhaps he was also driven by a sense of what had been lost by the collapse of this plan. The West could have secured everything that it wanted and could have presented the new territory to the administration as a fait accompli. In the thick of excited planning, Jackson had on 4 October 1806 issued a proclamation to his militia to ready itself for a march on Spanish territory. If Burr had only given the word, Spanish Florida for starters would have been Jackson's for the taking, the gratitude of the nation his for the asking. But Burr had not given the word, and Wilkinson had then ruined everything. The haughty Spaniards were still in their forts, and the West had again been betrayed by the government in Washington. With contemptible politicians calling Burr a traitor for doing a patriot's work, who knew when another patriot would have another chance to do what needed to be done, in spite of the politicians.

It was frustrating just to nibble away at Spanish West Florida while cautious government policies stymied real expansion. Jefferson and his successor, James Madison, walked lightly around Spain, careful not to embroil the country in a war as relations with Great Britain rapidly deteriorated. The government's policy toward the Indians in the southern United States that encouraged white farming methods and sought only voluntary land cessions threatened to sequester from white settlement much of the best agricultural land. Meanwhile, Spain stubbornly clung to the Floridas.

Andrew Jackson and his neighbors saw their future prosperity in the opening of more land to speculative investment and farming. The Indians and the Spaniards who were in the way would have to be shoved aside and expelled; the politicians in Washington, as much as the courtiers in Madrid, would have to be convinced of this inevitability. As the country edged toward war with Britain, the chance for again doing a patriot's work was not lost on Jackson. In fact, that chance became his new obsession. It was his way.[1]

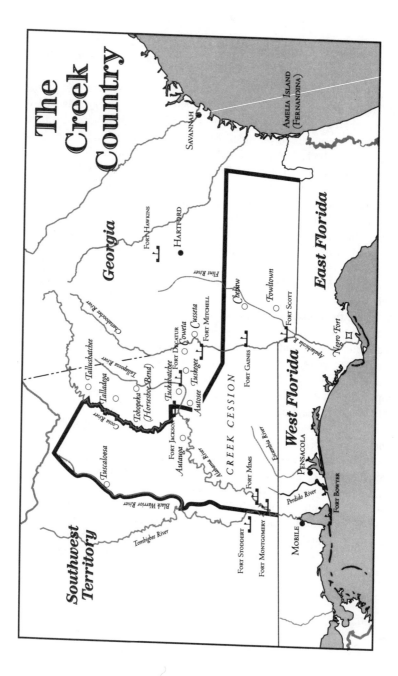

1

"The Cream
of Creek Country"

On 27 March 1814, Andrew Jackson won a staggering victory at Tohopeka, the Horseshoe Bend of the Tallapoosa River, nearly wiping out the hostile Creek Indians camped there. It was arguably the most stunning success of American arms over an Indian foe in the Southeast. Four months later that triumph culminated in a treaty to end, once and for all, the so-called Creek War, a struggle that had plagued the Mississippi Territory for nearly a year and a half. The treaty also would endeavor to end, once and for all, a major part of the Indian "problem" in the Southeast as the United States government perceived it. The War Department in Washington gave Jackson the first and final say of what the treaty would contain, a gesture most gratifying for him. After all, he might have taken "first and final" as a personal motto.

The growing number of Indians also gratified Andrew Jackson as they came from the piney woods into the small stockade built on the ruins of old French Fort Toulouse.[1] The Americans called this new structure Fort Jackson, and its namesake could pause now to measure the challenges confronted and the successes gained during the previous few months. Yet, some things vexed him. Jackson worried about potential obstacles thwarting the first and final arrangements he intended to make. He heard a rumor that Tustennuggee Thluco (called Big Warrior by whites), headman of Tuckabatchee and spokesman for the Upper Creek towns, had said the Indians need not take Jackson seriously. Big

Warrior said they would hear the real agreement from the White Father in Washington, President James Madison. Jackson angrily wrote to Creek Indian Agent Benjamin Hawkins that he should disabuse Big Warrior of any such notion. Where, Jackson wanted to know, had the Creek headman heard this? Was he deliberately trying to deceive his people? "I do not speak with forked tongue," Jackson snapped.[2]

Jackson thought that others habitually did, though. He distrusted Hawkins, and he suspected that the agent and United States Army Major General Thomas Pinckney so sympathized with the Indians that they put the whole compact at risk. The Big Warrior rumor illustrated exactly the "considerable difficulty in making the arrangement." Jackson suspected it stemmed from a letter Pinckney had sent to Hawkins outlining alternative, more lenient terms. This letter, for instance, contained promises about indemnities for Creek losses in the war. All such compensation was unauthorized, muttered Jackson, and thus would not appear in any treaty. Still, he judged the damage of such a letter, once known to the Creeks, already done.[3]

Jackson had a big surprise in store for all of these people, and Benjamin Hawkins had become by the summer of 1814 nothing more than another problem. For the Creek Indians, friend as well as foe, perhaps he always had been.

❧

By the War of 1812, Benjamin Hawkins, United States Agent to the Creek Indians, had spent nearly a generation trying to acculturate these Indians in white customs. He came from a prominent North Carolina family that had provided him with a good education to match his social status, but southeastern Indians enthralled Hawkins from the start. In the 1790s, he worked with the Muskogee Indians, whom whites identified as Creeks because of the many rivers and streams that capillaried the Creek territory.[4] Impressed by the young man's talent for negotiation, President George Washington appointed Hawkins agent to the Creeks in 1796. The Hawkins family regarded the appointment as nothing more than banishment among savages. Benjamin could not have been happier.

With high enthusiasm, Hawkins undertook to transform Creek society. Dispute still surrounds his motives. Was he trying to save the Creeks by making them less obnoxious to an overpowering white society? Or did he merely want to break down Creek cultural traditions to ease the way for American expansion?[5]

Perhaps Hawkins was nothing more than a good man working in a bad time, for it is hard to see any personal advantages he gained from his association with the Creeks. In fact, his career cast him into an odd, in-between world. He remained an alien in Creek culture and became an eccentric in his own. He steadfastly refused to take a Creek wife, though the Indians constantly pressed him to do so. Meanwhile, he maintained only a common law relationship with Lavinia Davis, possibly because she was beneath his family's social standing. In the winter of 1812 when serious sickness persuaded him he was dying, he finally married her. He had waited to what he thought was the last minute though, clinging to a primitive frontier marriage custom even as he tirelessly labored to "civilize" the Creeks.[6]

The Creeks were already civilized, of course; they had established complex governmental and economic practices decades before Hawkins's appointment, and the sedentary customs of town habitation—albeit mixed with hunting-gathering habits—preceded even the earliest European contacts. A Creek Confederation in some form had existed for a long time when Hawkins set up his agency. Europeans mingling in Creek society had resulted in mixed-blood descendants whose names—Alexander McGillivray, William Weatherford, Peter McQueen, William McIntosh—disguise for modern ears their influence in and ties to their Indian culture.[7] For Hawkins, however, Creek acculturation meant radically altering that culture by honing its agricultural skills and breaking down its tribal-clan kinship patterns. Hawkins had them sweating behind plows in one breath and privatizing their communal lands in the next. The agent encouraged Creeks to adopt the habits of the southern cotton culture, including black slave ownership.[8] Fields sprouted hybrid legumes outside Creek villages while the "capital" towns of Coweta and Tuckabatchee, one representing the Lower Towns and the other the Upper Towns, alternated as hosts to annual meetings of the Creek Council. A national police force of "law menders" exacted punishments for deeds proclaimed as crimes by this council, always under the guidance of Hawkins. With the council's authority, these policemen enjoyed exemption from the Creek tradition of clan blood vengeance.[9]

The problems inherent in such fundamental changes were tremendous. Creek gender roles specified that only women engage in horticulture, therefore efforts to transform Creek culture to one of agriculture and husbandry encountered resistance from many warriors who saw Hawkins's efforts as attempts to emasculate them. Whatever the good or bad of Hawkins's intent, his plan finally collapsed under geographical and political divisions that separated the Creek nation into Upper and Lower Towns. Hawkins intruded to widen this breach with attempts to force white conformity on both groups under the alien device of protonationalism. Primary differences between Upper and Lower Creeks became widening gulfs under Hawkins's tutelage. The Lower Creeks in the eastern part of the nation, mostly along the Chattahoochee River, lived closer to white society. Because the Lower Creeks experienced more cultural, social, and economic interaction with whites, they proved less resistant to white customs. The Upper Creeks, living almost due west of the Lower Towns, had less contact with whites, and so they suspected Americans and their acquisitive ways. Most of these Upper Towns intellectually resisted acculturation as resolutely as they opposed the running of American roads through their territory.[10]

The roads the United States cut through Creek country caused constant friction. In 1811, Hawkins went to Tuckabatchee to sell Big Warrior and the Upper Creeks on a road that would link Fort Stoddert near Mobile with Tennessee. Hawkins's exertions for Creek acquiescence were only a formality, of course; as engineers hewed the right-of-way, Americans ignored Indian grumbling, confident they could risk the offense. After all, the Federal Road, a route connecting the Creek Agency near Milledgeville with Fort Stoddert, benefitted even those complaining about it. When the United States completed the road in October 1811, Creeks began operating inns, stores, and ferries along its course. The 1805 Treaty of Washington authorized the activity as part of an economic incentive for Creek land cessions—a $12,000 per year annuity for eight years followed by $11,000 for another ten formed another part. Some of the younger warriors began collecting excessively high tolls, obviously considering it their due. Big Warrior, although far from young, did not miss the opportunity to enrich himself either.[11]

The violent reaction to these intrusions into Creek lands and the rejection of white corruptions of Creek culture explains the opening of the Creek Civil War. It began in July 1813 with a nativist attack upon

Tuckabatchee, the Upper Creek Town of Big Warrior. Tustennuggee Thluco's name signified his imposing stature, and in earlier days he had matched that big physique with big deeds: he succeeded Efau Hadjo (Mad Dog) as headman of Tuckabatchee on the Tallapoosa, outsmarted rivals to establish his unqualified leadership of all the Upper Towns in 1802, and afterward proved key in Upper Creek resistance to Hawkins's acculturation plans. Tecumseh visited Tuckabatchee in 1811 at almost the same time Hawkins was trying to obtain Upper Creek consent to American roads. This charismatic Shawnee, whose mother was Creek and hence was regarded as a Creek himself by this matrilineal culture, carried a message of aggressive nativism that threatened American expansionist plans from the Great Lakes to the Gulf of Mexico. When Big Warrior smoked with Tecumseh and learned the Shawnee's Lake Dance, Americans marked him as an enemy. Yet Big Warrior was growing old and cautious, and he eventually insisted that he had thought Tecumseh mad and his plans for a Niagara-to-Mobile Indian confederation bewildering. By then everyone, red and white alike, found the aging chief's behavior duplicitous. Hawkins did not like or trust him, and the nativists, spiritually inspired by their prophets and militarily led by mixed-bloods like the shrewd Red Eagle (known to whites as William Weatherford) and fierce Peter McQueen, loathed him. Weatherford would later say that only Big Warrior's cowardice prevented him from joining the nativists. After all, the headman despised whites as much as the angriest Red Stick did.[12]

The spiritual rebirth illuminating the Creek nativist movement did not point to Hawkins as the only deleterious influence on Creek life. Many Indians from the Great Lakes to the Gulf of Mexico had come to see native unity and native solutions to their growing problems as the only way to resist white expansion. Even before the agent's acculturation schemes, Creek trade in deerskins with Europeans had depleted the deer population, had broken down Creek tribal traditions, and had direly jeopardized the fabric of Creek society. Nativist prophets, whose murmuring voices became a steady chorus after Tecumseh's visit, urged a spiritual cleansing and a material purging that recognized the agent's activities as only the latest of many problems: the deer population had declined, they said, because white ways had encouraged farming and cattle raising. Domestic livestock should be killed, they intoned, and the white man's farm implements discarded.[13]

On the face of it then, the mere fact of white presence as well as the acculturation scheme sundered the Creek nation to pit nativist Upper Creeks against those who had accepted Hawkins's ideas, especially the Lower Creeks. But the lines of conflict never conformed to convenient categories such as location or nomenclature. The designation by many contemporaries of the nativist hostiles exclusively as "Red Sticks" came from the Creek practice of using bundles of sticks sent to towns as a measure of time before an important event. If red sticks were sent, it meant that war would commence after the number of days corresponding to the number of sticks in the bundle. Often Creeks would also leave behind a red war club at a battle site.[14] Never more than half of the Upper Creek towns joined the Red Stick nativists' holy war. None of the Lower Creek towns did, nor did the Creeks' Seminole relatives. If anything distinguished these belligerents, it was age. Many young Creeks, fired by the aggressive message of the prophets, took up arms against elders whose cautious response to white encroachment seemed weak and wicked.[15]

By 1813, the despised whites and their Creek collaborators in both Upper and Lower Towns were the only friends Big Warrior had. Some Upper Creeks, led by Tustennuggee Tuskegee (Little Warrior), had thrilled to the nativism of the Shawnee Tecumseh and his brother, the prophet Tenkswatawa, and had followed Tecumseh to Canada. There they joined the Shawnee in raids, so their blood was up when, as they were returning home, they killed several white men on the Duck River near Nashville. These nativists paid for the deed at the hands of the Creek law menders, who executed them under the authority of the Creek Council. To Creek nativists, the council's obvious fear of white retribution made it and its policemen appear as nothing more than white toadies. In retaliation, they flew into full fury against the traitors in their midst, the trucklers to the white men, Big Warrior prominent among them. They laid siege to Tuckabatchee with the idea of destroying it and him.[16]

Thus started the Creek Civil War. Big Warrior begged Hawkins for help, and the Indian agent sent it, though with misgivings. More than anything he wanted to contain these hostilities because he suspected how they would end. The Indians, all of them, would suffer dire hardships, and in the end they would lose more land to the United States.[17] Yet Hawkins sent Creeks from the Lower Town of Coweta to relieve

Tuckabatchee. They did so by mid-July, but amid a good deal of be-
wilderment about what it all meant. The Cowetas, who suffered
losses in the rescue, offered Big Warrior sanctuary in their town, but
they planned nothing more until they could determine the intentions of
the other Upper Towns. They would have a meeting to decide what
to do.[18]

Hawkins himself pondered what to do. He wanted to isolate the conflict from the whites, so he used Lower Creeks to rescue Big Warrior.
Yet that decision itself hopelessly divided the Creek nation into full-
blown civil war. Complicating everything was the War of 1812 between
the United States and Britain, now in its second year and threatening in
Hawkins's part of the world to involve these hostile Indians and the
Spaniards in Florida. Those Spaniards, hoping to use the Creeks and
their southern cousins the Seminoles as a buffer against American
expansion, regularly promised them guns and ammunition. It was a
risky gamble for Spain. If these Indians became so strong that they
recklessly attacked Americans, it could compel the United States to
invade Florida, something completely counter to what the Spaniards
wanted to use the Indians for in the first place.[19]

British plans, directed by the strategic needs of the War of 1812,
were more aggressive. An agent of Bahamian Governor Charles
Cameron of New Providence proposed arming Creeks and Seminoles
and placing them under British officers. An estimate of fifteen thousand
such armed Indian warriors meant that Americans would have to transfer a comparable number from the Canadian front. In London Earl
Bathurst, the secretary of state for war, approved the plan, and in the
spring of 1814 Admiral Alexander Cochrane would order Captain
Hugh Pigot of H.M.S. *Orpheus* to start recruiting the Indians on the
Apalachicola River in West Florida.[20]

So the situation taking shape in 1813 meant that Hawkins could not
have stopped American involvement in the Creek War, regardless of his
exertions. Because the Creek conflict occurred during the War of 1812,
it could not but profoundly influence United States–Creek relations
both in the short and long term. Immediately, the United States correctly feared that the British and Spanish would use the Creek contest to
their advantage in the Southeast. The United States intervened to prevent the Spanish in Florida from supplying the nativist Red Sticks and
thus coincidentally allied with those Creeks who opposed the nativists.

The vague nature of this arrangement has caused confusion over who those Creek allies were and what to call them. Some have classified them as Lower Creeks, although many came from Upper Towns. Also some have called them "friendlies," although their ties with the United States had to do more with self-preservation than sentiment. Probably it is best to call them Allied Creeks to denote their bond with the United States as one of mutual necessity rather than mutual affection, a tie prompted by a shared occasion rather than any shared principles. Nativist Red Sticks, railing at the opportunism, snarled that these Allied Creeks had lost their souls; nobody suspected that the Allied Creeks in fact would lose their country.[21]

Under the weight of varied concerns, Hawkins grew testy. While waiting for the agent's response to pleas for help, Big Warrior, his people in distress, sought help from the Georgia governor, David B. Mitchell. Hawkins finally answered with an impatient admonishment that the headman's political problems with Peter McQueen's people had nothing to do with the Creek Agency. Hawkins reminded Big Warrior that he had urged him to address his differences with these nativists long ago. Hawkins meant, of course, that Tuckabatchee should have attacked the nativists first. He said he would do what he could to send weapons and ammunition. He bluntly told Big Warrior to use them this time.[22]

On the same day Hawkins promised this assistance, an event near the Florida line made American military involvement in the Creek Civil War inevitable. At Burnt Corn Creek on 27 July, whites ambushed nativists under Peter McQueen coming from Pensacola, one hundred miles south, where they had procured powder and ammunition. The whites did little more than capture the nativists' supplies, and McQueen's warriors made the encounter so hot that the whites soon fled the field. McQueen returned to Pensacola, where he and his comrade High Head Jim intimidated Spanish Governor Mateo González Manrique into providing them with one thousand pounds of powder and the shot to go with it. Soon reports told of McQueen having as many as 350 men and 100 horses under his command.[23]

Having agitated the hornet's nest, the whites retreated to Fort Mims, a rude stockade north of Mobile inhabited by about four hundred militiamen, white settlers, Indian allies, and mixed-bloods, and more than two hundred slaves. On 30 August, about one thousand nativists under William Weatherford descended on this place at high noon with such frenzy that even had the militia been prepared and the gates closed, it would not have made much difference. After the first rush into the open stockade demobilized most resistance, the Indians continued a thorough job of butchering everybody they could find, whether man, woman, or child. Few escaped.[24]

The Fort Mims Massacre completely revised American attitudes about the Creek Civil War. To the north, Big Warrior had spent much of August ensconced in Coweta joining his voice with that of his host, Coweta chief and Lower Town headman Tustennuggee Hopoi, known to whites as Little Prince. Both importuned David Mitchell and Benjamin Hawkins for help, claiming that the nativists menaced Coweta. True, an alarming number of towns were falling in with the nativist campaign. On 4 August, the two chiefs guessed that twenty-five hundred Red Stick warriors were amassing against the sixteen Allied towns they could depend on.[25]

By the end of September, Hawkins had armed Coweta with powder and lead. After Fort Mims, however, the American response to the Creek Civil War immediately grew more resolute and aggressively interventionist. Soon United States military forces moved into the field to take over the campaign rather than merely to supply it. Nativists lifted the scalps of Allied Creeks into October while the American military prepared to intervene from several directions; the United States was about to change the Creek Civil War into the Creek War.[26]

Andrew Jackson and his West Tennessee militia would wreak the most destruction in the coming campaign, but they would not be the only elements engaged. In sympathetic outrage over the Fort Mims Massacre, Tennessee's governor and legislature sent Jackson into the field. By the time Jackson brought his people the considerable distance south, the Red Stick nativists had already suffered at the hands of their new American foes allied with their Creek enemies. Hawkins, apparently worried about Jackson's arrival, sent the Creek Council's principal law mender and foremost warrior among Creek Allies, William McIntosh, to meet him. McIntosh took about twenty mounted warriors and four runners on the errand, but they all became linked to Georgia General John Floyd's militia expedition advancing from the east. They and 450 other Allied Creeks fought with Floyd against the nativists at

Autosee on 29 November. The Georgians and Allied Creeks destroyed the town, but the Red Sticks managed a fierce retaliation in a surprise attack on the Georgians' camp. McIntosh's Allied Creeks, said Floyd, were largely responsible for his success.[27]

Known to Creeks as Tustennuggee Hutkee (White Warrior), McIntosh's father had been a Tory officer named William McIntosh, his mother a member of Coweta's powerful Wind Clan. Since the Creek matrilineal tradition conveyed influence through the mother's family, McIntosh was an important man in Creek society by birth, while his father provided influential family connections to Georgia's white community. One half brother sat in the Georgia legislature and another was the customs collector in Savannah. Future governor and powerful political leader George M. Troup was a cousin. McIntosh expanded these birthrights with talent and ambition. Of considerable oratorical ability and from an important Creek family and clan, he had come to prominence in 1805 while only in his late twenties. He became the "speaker" for Little Prince, a duty that required him to present the views of the headman. As Little Prince and Big Warrior declined with age, McIntosh grew in importance. He headed the National Council's police, leading the detachment that executed Little Warrior and his raiders in the summer of 1812. McIntosh was nothing if not opportunistic, and he habitually gave his interests more weight than those of fellow Creeks. Big Warrior, who does not seem to have cared much for anyone, especially despised William McIntosh.[28]

Americans now found the wily mixed-blood indispensable. McIntosh's Cherokee wife afforded him friends and in-laws among the Cherokees, so he traveled in the summer of 1813 to Oostanaula in the Cherokee nation to ask for aid against Red Stick nativists. The Ridge, an influential member of the so-called pro-treaty faction of the Cherokees—that group intent upon conciliatory cooperation with whites—escorted McIntosh back to Coweta. There the Ridge received a talk (the Creek term for a significant communication) to carry back to his people, a talk that he delivered with strong personal recommendations that the Cherokees aid the Creeks against their Red Stick enemies. The Cherokee Council ignored such urging to remain neutral, but the Ridge personally called for volunteers. Many young Cherokees responded by heading south.[29]

Andrew Jackson was heading south as well. Driving his militia with especial vigor, he battled terrain and his men's flagging enthusiasm as much as he did Red Stick nativists. In spite of horrifying carnage, with the nativists taking the worst of it, Jackson's relief of Talladega from the besieging Weatherford in early November had proved as indecisive for concluding the war as had General John Coffee's terrible victory at Tallushatchee. Red Sticks matched Floyd's destruction of Autosee several weeks later, at the end of November, with a nasty counterattack that augured the greatest danger of Indian warfare: its tendency to devolve into inconclusive forays in which tactical triumphs served as poor substitutes for definitive victory.[30]

Jackson would have no substitutes for victory. His behavior in the Creek War created the image of the hard-bitten Indian-hater, and contemporaries, who could see nothing wrong with that, and historians, who naturally do, have argued over the Tennessean's real motives and actual beliefs regarding Indians ever since.

Some have suggested that Jackson did not hate Indians. Instead he hated the British, whose pawns he believed Indians to be. After all, following the massacre at Tallushatchee, he adopted the infant Lyncoya, orphaned by the battle and friendless among his own people. This interpretation sees Jackson concentrating his actions against Indians to vanquish their British manipulators and achieve American security.[31]

Others, however, have speculated that Jackson's violent frontier days in young Tennessee planted in him a rigid opinion of Indians as savage and untrustworthy. "Why do we attempt," Jackson wrote in 1793, "to Treat with Savage Tribe [*sic*] that will neither adhere to Treaties, nor the law of Nations."[32]

He still felt that way in 1813 when Tennessee Governor Willie Blount called him to lead the Tennessee militia against the Red Stick nativists. By then Jackson was forty-six years old, propertied and prominent. He owned a large estate near Nashville and had won eminence in political and legal venues. Yet, mature deliberation and rational thought were always brittle facets of this man's turbulent personality. His marriage to already married Rachel Donelson Robards provided grist for the mills of scandal most of his adult life, and Jackson reacted to the chronic gossip with gestures that were frequently undignified. When Governor John Sevier suggested impropriety in Jackson's courtship of Rachel, Jackson tried to force the governor to a duel; on another occasion young Charles Dickinson, a Nashville attorney, reportedly maligned Rachel's virtue. Dickinson claimed he was drunk, had meant no harm, and apologized; nevertheless, he and Jackson continued to quarrel over other matters until Jackson shot Dickinson dead in a duel. Of course, such behavior only muted sniggering talk about Rachel while spreading it farther; moreover, such behavior portrayed Jackson as a murderous bully.[33]

Jackson took a bullet in his chest in the Dickinson duel, a painful wound that would plague him for the rest of his life, but it was only one of a growing list of corporeal injuries that matched his spiritual scars. His involvement in politics saw him using physical intimidation almost as often as persuasive debate, and he numbered his enemies in the dozens, making certain that they knew where he and they stood and what fate might await them should they risk a chance encounter.

Meanwhile, the man who insisted upon scrupulous patriotism in others could not resist the sordid scheme of Aaron Burr. The former vice president told Jackson that his plan to detach Mexico from Spain was secretly approved by the United States government, when in fact the wily Burr was probably planning to detach a discontented West from the United States. The whole episode revealed Jackson's apparent belief that he was a law unto himself and his willingness to engage in dubious activities if they promised to advance a program of which he personally approved.[34]

From the conspirators' den to the campaign stump to the dueling field, Jackson moved as a tempest, a force capable of killing everything but the odious talk and the vicious rumors. All of it, after all, was sprinkled with fine, ghastly grains of truth. In spite of defenses mounted and explanations made by admirers then and since, nothing can alter the evidence that Andrew Jackson was an angry young man who became an angry old man. He might have contrived for effect the rages that peppered his life, as some suggest, but the quieter tantrums sprang from his insides and sculpted his defining, exterior character. His mother had died of cholera during the American Revolution, making young Andy an orphan at fourteen. As far as he could reckon, the British had done that, had created the hardships of pestilence and destruction that killed his mother, his brothers, and the gentler edges of his nature. He had been duped into Aaron Burr's half-baked plot because he detested swaggering Spaniards—"greasers" as Jackson called them—whose contempt for the United States Jackson brooded over and fulminated against.[35] He would destroy them and any of their friends. He would take their land, dash the standards of His Most Catholic Majesty to the ground, crush the British Lion and Unicorn; he would stand before their red allies as he had before young Dickinson, even after taking the bullet, his absurdly narrow shoulders drawn back, his long head tilted down to stress the snarl, to shade his blue eyes from the sun. He would carefully draw aim. He would kill them all.

⤜⤛

At Horseshoe Bend in March 1814, Andrew Jackson nearly killed them all. He came to Tohopeka on the Tallapoosa wearied by a series of engagements that had left the Americans frustrated and frightened. Jackson tried to quell mutiny with intimidation, force, and scorn, but much of his army trickled away to Tennessee during the winter of 1813–14. William Weatherford and Peter McQueen proved resourceful and elusive, adopting Fabian tactics to taunt the Tennessee Hannibal to distraction. By March, though, a new muster of Tennessee militia reinforced Jackson with twenty-five hundred men, and he again marched forth to destroy the Indians. At Horseshoe Bend, he nearly killed them all.

One thousand Creeks from the nativist towns camped there, taking false comfort in the protection the curving river gave their backs, placing mistaken faith in the elaborate breastworks they had placed in their front. Jackson immediately saw the opportunity, because the Horseshoe was more a barrier to the Indians' escape than a shield against his attack. The Red Stick nativists put themselves into a corral that on 27 March Jackson turned into a slaughter pen.[36]

First, he sent John Coffee and the Indian allies across the Tallapoosa to cut off the Red Stick flight. On the morning of the twenty-seventh, Jackson's guns opened on the Red Stick front while the men he had sent across the river caught those in flight. After the five-hour battle, 557 Creeks lay dead on the land in the bend with as many as 300 bobbing lifelessly in the Tallapoosa. The Americans and their Indian allies continued the killing until dark stopped them, but they would renew what amounted to systematic execution the following morning. Jackson at first did not think that more than 20 had escaped, and he exulted in the completeness of the victory. The Red Stick prophet Monahoee lay among the dead, his face shattered by grapeshot that had torn off his jaw—"as if," Jackson mused, "Heaven designed to chastise his impostures by an appropriate punishment."[37]

The high toll of Horseshoe Bend effectively concluded this stage of the war. At a cost of 49 dead from his own force (almost half of whom were Allied Creeks and the Ridge's Cherokee volunteers), Jackson had killed at least 800 hostile Creeks, some of them women and children, but almost all of them the best of the Red Stick warriors. Attesting to Red Stick evisceration, among the 350 prisoners taken at the Horseshoe virtually all were women and children. Not more than 4 warriors remained on the ground alive.[38]

Yet some had gotten away, and in only a few days Jackson began to doubt the conclusiveness of his victory. Rumors spoke of nativists gathering to the south as Jackson's army, confident of victory, began to melt away again to the north as it had the previous winter. Coffee doubted that the nativists had enough food to wage another campaign, but Jackson intended to finish them, even if he had to do so with diminished forces. By the first week of April, he was moving against whatever Indian forces remained to his south. He expected to collide with them soon, perhaps by the eleventh at Haithlewalle. Suspecting there were more Red Sticks there than previously estimated, Jackson complained that he was short of supplies and men.[39]

Jackson's anxiety stemmed from the illusion that his victory at the Horseshoe had not broken the physical power of the Red Sticks. Hawkins knew better and sent Allied Creeks into the countryside to persuade nativist refugees to surrender. The Allied Creeks knew more about their Red Stick enemies than either Jackson or Hawkins did, however. Horseshoe Bend had broken the nativists' backs, but not their wills.[40] So the Allied Creeks, although doing Hawkins's bidding, did not think that the Red Sticks would stop fighting. Hawkins's Creeks were willing to keep fighting with Sharp Knife, as the Indians called Jackson after Horseshoe Bend. They were of one mind with Sharp Knife about finishing this job.[41]

Actually, Coffee was right. The refugees from Horseshoe Bend were starving to death. The ravages of more than one year of almost constant war now bore only the bitter harvest of gaunt faces and bloated bellies. Stragglers who fell into Jackson's hands told of how their nativist brothers were streaming to Pensacola in Spanish Florida, hoping to rearm themselves in Spanish arsenals and nourish themselves at Spanish larders. Jackson believed it, but he also believed that enough active hostiles still peopled the nearby thickets to warrant another campaign.[42] Major General Thomas Pinckney promised Jackson assistance, but as Sharp Knife tried to run the Indians to ground, reinforcements were tardy, and he could do little more than rage at his colleagues' sloth and incompetence.[43]

The advent of British plans in the Gulf added special hazards to a possible Red Stick resurgence. In line with the Cameron plan approved in 1813 by Lord Bathurst, Captain Hugh Pigot's *Orpheus* arrived at the Apalachicola River on 10 May to find bedraggled and beleaguered Indians there, many of them refugees from Horseshoe Bend. Nevertheless, Pigot told Cochrane that with only two thousand to three thousand additional soldiers the whole lot could capture Mobile and New Orleans. The British government had already been eyeing the Gulf coast, and Cochrane now provided them with a scheme that would not strain resources already taxed by the war on the Canadian border and against Napoleon in Europe.[44]

The British would recruit as many Creeks, Seminoles, and runaway slaves as possible to the cause. Diversionary attacks directed by the Royal Navy would harry the Georgia coast. The British also counted on (haplessly, as it turned out) the help of Jean Lafitte's notorious pirates in the Gulf. The various elements of British strategy in the Southeast appeared organized, effectual, and menacing.[45]

The Red Stick nativists, however, were not to be a telling factor in the few months remaining to British efforts, soon made irrelevant by the Treaty of Ghent. Hunger drove them harder than revenge, and to the north they began wandering into Andrew Jackson's camps begging for something to eat. As American carpenters laid the first timbers for Fort Jackson, captures swelled the ranks of those surrendering. Peter McQueen briefly fell into American hands, but he soon escaped. William Weatherford, however, strolled into camp one April day and calmly surrendered himself to Jackson.[46]

Dramatic myth rings the Weatherford surrender, as though the event resolved all uncertainties surrounding the muddled Creek War. The surrender provides a convenient conclusion marked by Weatherford's heroic dignity and Jackson's high magnanimity, for Jackson let

Weatherford go in a display of charity as uncharacteristic as it was shrewd. Weatherford did not become a martyr that day because Andrew Jackson would not oblige him.

Rather than dramatically closing the Creek War, however, Weatherford's surrender illustrated its troubling ambiguities. According to the traditional account, Weatherford stood before a fuming Jackson and made a brave speech about the integrity of warriors that gradually melted Old Hickory's anger into more than grudging respect. Indeed, before the afternoon was out, Weatherford, commander of the massacre at Fort Mims, was sharing a brandy with Jackson, commander of the massacre at Horseshoe Bend, though one can hardly imagine that either would think this a point to stimulate a conversation. Yet Jackson—the man who had killed and would kill better men than Weatherford for lesser offenses—was so moved by the Indian's dignity and courage, we are told, that he raised a glass with him and then let him go. More, Jackson simply released Weatherford; he did not parole him upon any formal promise that the Red Stick would never again raise arms against the United States or its friends. Much to the contrary, Weatherford actually stated that if he could have, he would have continued fighting. Jackson rarely rewarded the candor of his enemies, but this time inexplicably he let Weatherford go.[47]

It might also seem strange that the most notorious Red Stick nativist would not figure in any treaty ostensibly ending the war with the Red Stick nativists—strange, at least, until one considers the conditions evolving after Horseshoe Bend. Enemies of the Americans—the tattered and dispossessed Red Sticks—did not have anything that the United States wanted. American friends—the Allied Creeks—were another matter.

∽

Just weeks after Jackson shattered the Red Stick nativists at Horseshoe Bend, Secretary of War John Armstrong wrote Major General Thomas Pinckney that at the least the United States should secure a land cession from the Creeks to cover American expenses in the Creek conflict. Beyond that, the terms would sequester the Creeks from all European influences by prohibiting trade with Spaniards and permitting it exclusively with licensed American merchants. The United States would have the right to build roads through and use waterways on Creek land

and would put trading posts there, erecting forts to protect them. Armstrong wanted Pinckney and Agent Hawkins to negotiate such a settlement as soon as they could persuade Creeks to accept it.[48]

Having said that, Armstrong began to think about it, and finally he thought better of it. The treaty, he wrote to Pinckney three days later, should "be in the form of a capitulation." This striking resolve, so different from previous intentions, marked a major shift in Washington's posture on Indian relations in the Southeast. Pinckney would now exclude Hawkins from negotiations so the military could completely control dealings with the Creeks. The general could consult Hawkins, but officially the agent was to have nothing to do with the treaty's formulation or consummation.[49]

From that moment, the treaty, negotiations attendant to it, and the people involved for both sides ceased to make any sense. Negotiating trade and construction privileges with the Creek Confederation became hopelessly blurred with punitively ending the war with the Red Stick nativists. Friends would capitulate while enemies remained at large, unpunished and unrepentant.

The desire for the Creek's land caused the shift. Westerners—especially Tennesseans—joined militia leaders to squint suspiciously at Benjamin Hawkins as a negotiator. Many thought that Pinckney would be soft on the Indians as well.[50] Actually, Pinckney also thought Hawkins too lenient, but as late as mid-May, the general did not envision large Allied Creek land losses; only the hostiles should suffer heavy cessions, he thought, leaving them enough land for agricultural subsistence.[51]

In April, Pinckney and Hawkins, the latter in his new role as a consultant, arrived at Fort Jackson to begin the negotiations. The Creek War appeared over, so Pinckney told Jackson to take his men north to Fort Williams on the Coosa River, from there to send many of them home. Most notably then, the Tennessean was to have nothing to do with the final settlement of the Creek War; Pinckney had nothing more for Jackson to do than supervise the construction of a chain of forts from Tennessee to Fort Jackson.[52]

As Jackson and his Tennesseans marched through Huntsville, the town's cheers rang in their ears.[53] He had only just returned to Nashville when his exploits against the Red Sticks earned him official recognition to match popular acclaim. On 22 May, Secretary of War Armstrong wrote to give Jackson the command of the Seventh Military District with a regular line rank of brigadier general, brevetted to major general. When six days later William Henry Harrison resigned his major general's commission and thus created a vacancy at the grade, Armstrong filled it with Jackson's name. President Madison approved the promotion straightaway.[54]

By then, the government had decided to change yet again the team negotiating with the Creeks. Jackson was to return to Fort Jackson and assume complete and exclusive control. Armstrong told him that the Allied Creek presence in the area would ensure the peace and thus preclude Jackson's reassembling the Tennessee militia.[55] Considering what would happen at Fort Jackson, relying on the Allied Creeks to preserve the peace was a high irony.

"The friendly Indians have entire confidence in the justice of our government," Benjamin Hawkins informed Armstrong in the first week of June. Hawkins busied himself providing food and shelter to the Allied Creeks, especially some seven hundred displaced from Tuckabatchee, the first town attacked by the nativists.[56] Possibly the agent did not yet know that Andrew Jackson was on his way from the Hermitage to assume control of the negotiations. The news would have done nothing but distress him. Jackson's appointment as sole negotiator simply changed everything. Even if Benjamin Hawkins did know about Jackson's impending appearance, he apparently did not want to admit it to the Allied Creeks. While they awaited Jackson's arrival from Nashville, Hawkins assured them that no treaty would injure them.[57] Yet Jackson had already expressed his belief that the *entire* Creek nation should be "confined to very small limits."[58]

This sentiment explains Jackson's appointment as sole negotiator. He and his men had expressed outrage over the government's original plan to allow all of the Allied Creeks to keep their land. Furthermore, Jackson believed that his men had earned first claims on any ceded territory.[59] They likely agreed. Jackson intended to treat all Creek lands as spoils of war, although doing so introduced ethical questions on both personal and public levels. Whether or not Jackson's habit of land speculation guided his actions in the summer of 1814 is still disputed.[60] But the United States government did not appoint him as the sole negotiator so he could increase his personal land holdings. The government wanted to separate Creeks from all foreign territory by creating an unbroken frontier from Georgia to Mobile.[61] Such a cession happened to provide the United States with excellent land, the best in the area. The public policy required a measure of Allied Creek disquiet; Jackson's personal policy would bloat the cession to punish them as well.

When Jackson arrived at Fort Jackson on 10 July, the Allied Creeks did not yet know what his involvement meant. The following day Jackson told Hawkins that he wanted a general meeting with surrendered hostile Creeks at Fort Jackson on 1 August. Ominously, he instructed Hawkins to convene all the friendly chiefs too.[62] At the 1 August meeting the Allied Creeks first heard how the United States would acknowledge their contribution to the Creek War. Until that meeting they had harbored the illusion that the Pinckney-Hawkins terms would form the gist of any agreement. Now they sat slack-jawed to discover that Jackson intended to take their land as well as that of the Red Sticks. In fact, Jackson would take almost half of all land remaining to the Creek nation, doing so with a document entitled "Articles of Agreement and Capitulation."[63]

It was more than they could bear. Their stunned response to the terms included numbed protests. Jackson snarled at Big Warrior's suggestion that the White Father in Washington would have the last say. The general told the aging warrior that he could by rights take every acre of Creek land if he wanted to because the Creeks had been deceitful, talking to the devil Tecumseh and keeping secret that enemies of the United States moved among smiling Creek towns.[64] On 7 August, the Allied Creeks appealed to their mentor, Benjamin Hawkins, for help. Jackson demanded terms far in excess of those they had expected as solemn promises, and they stuttered in disbelief that Sharp Knife would punish them more than he would the Red Sticks, only one of whom was even present.[65]

Jackson saw such protests as a sniveling whine, and he took little pains to hide his contempt for these nonplussed Indians when they met with him and Hawkins on the following day. His mood mirrored what he did not say but felt in his heart. They were despicable creatures, showing no loyalty to anything. That they had turned on their own people to befriend the United States did not oblige him to show any generosity.[66] When they asked him to soften the terms, Jackson flatly refused. They then offered Jackson and Hawkins each three square miles of land as a gift. Jackson said that if the president consented, he would accept it. (Madison approved of the grant, but Congress did not.) Indeed, Jackson wanted the land, even though it was probably an Allied

Creek attempt to shame him for what he was doing to them in the treaty. Jackson was beyond shame. The size of the cession remained unchanged.[67]

Hawkins watched all this unfold with helpless resignation. On the afternoon of 9 August, Andrew Jackson formally presented the Allied Creeks with the Treaty of Fort Jackson. The document began with statements about how the Creeks had violated the peace between the United States and the Creek nation. It made no distinction between enemies and allies among the Creeks, instead explaining that two thirds of all Creeks fought in the war. The treaty resolved that because of this majority's involvement, the United States could expect substantial recompense from the entire nation. Thus Jackson rationalized the extraordinary lines of the land cession. He gloated to Governor Blount that the area comprised "the whole of [the] Alabama [River] and the valuable part of [the] Coosa and Cohaba [Rivers], in all containing about 22 Millions of Acres."[68] Even Jackson did not know how much land he was taking from the Creeks. He had undercalculated it by about a million acres.[69]

"I finished the convention with the creeks on yesterday," Jackson wrote his Tennessee friend John Overton on 10 August. "At 2 P.M. it was fully executed, and ceded to the U.S. 20 million of acres of the cream of creek country." To Jackson, how much land he was taking from the Allied Creeks mattered less than that it was their best land. In more muted terms he assured Armstrong that the terms of the treaty would easily cover American expenses from the late war while effectively interdicting any communication between Creeks in the United States and Spaniards in Florida.[70]

Hawkins counseled the helpless Indians to sign the treaty. There was little else he could do at the time. The agent disapproved of the terms, however, and the day after the signing he scathingly attacked Jackson in a letter to Secretary of War Armstrong. Had it not been for the friendly disposition of these Indian chiefs, Hawkins bluntly said, Jackson could never have secured such excessive terms. The alleged objects of the treaty, the Red Sticks, "were fugitives in Pensacola or the Floridas" with "but one chief present of the hostile Indians."[71] The Treaty of Fort Jackson indeed bore thirty-six marks, only one of which belonged to a Red Stick. It was a punitive treaty of capitulation that actually included none of the belligerents.[72]

Hawkins doubtless knew the futility of his gesture. Not only did the

War Department ignore his objections at the time, but apparently Jackson supporters, eager to create an unblemished record, later removed most of Hawkins's condemnatory letters from the secretary of war's files.[73]

The dictatorial land cession of Fort Jackson was also inconsistently applied among the Allied Creeks. Although many Allies suffered capricious injury, others prospered. William McIntosh, who emerged from the Creek War a colonel, was one of the few Creeks who did not lose a large amount of land. The terms of Fort Jackson distressed most Creeks, however, whether they were Allied, neutral, or Red Stick. Jackson's primary stated purpose—to separate the Creeks from foreign influences in Florida—did not explain to American friends why they should lose so much of their lands in the bargain. The humiliated Allied chiefs, intimidated into placing their marks on a document entitled "Articles of Agreement and Capitulation," must have stung with regret over their decision to ally their people with the United States.[74]

Moreover, the treaty did not end the conflict. Because its terms were so unreasonably harsh, the treaty inspired Creeks in Florida to continue the war.[75] About one thousand hostile warriors remained in the field at the close of the summer of 1814, led by the warrior Peter McQueen and the prophet Hillis Hadjo (Josiah Francis). They began reacting to the treaty with raids south of Georgia's most frontier town, Hartford (near modern Hawkinsville), within weeks of its signing. Allied Creeks watched silently, their enthusiasm for fighting the Red Stick nativists considerably dimmed. Some might have joined their former foes had the nativists had any food.[76]

The United States Senate meanwhile took the Treaty of Fort Jackson under deliberation. It roused so much opposition that many feared it would fail ratification. Not until word reached Washington that Jackson had defeated the British in New Orleans did the opposition fade to the point that managers felt sure the treaty would succeed. The Senate ratified it on 16 February 1815.[77]

By then Jackson had fulfilled the last vow he had made to the Allied Creeks in August at Fort Jackson. If they did not like the terms of the treaty, he had said, they should go to Florida. He told them that soon, however, he would be going there too.[78]

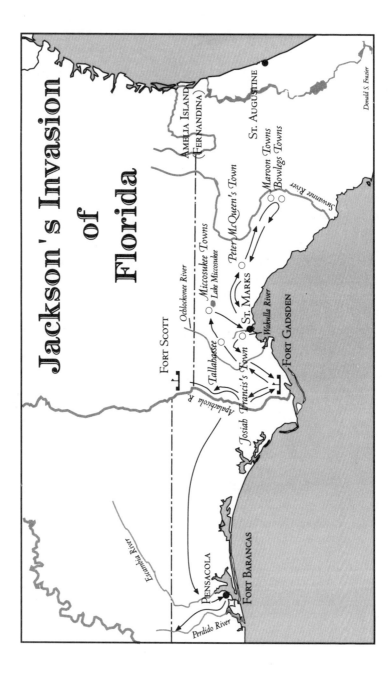

Jackson's Invasion of Florida

2

"Children of Nature"

Jackson relied heavily on Allied Creeks in the summer of 1814, using them to protect the frontier, and he was not happy about it. His militia gradually abandoned the border posts, leaving Fort Mitchell by the end of July and eventually Fort Hull, Fort Bainbridge, and Fort Decatur as well.[1] Jackson grumbled that the government should hold the militia in the ready to enforce his treaty. He repeated to Secretary of War Armstrong rumors about McQueen joining Seminoles in Florida, and he remarked darkly about British mischief there. Armstrong replied that neither the British nor any of their potential Indian allies would likely be active in the hot summer months. He also speculated that since the Seminoles had not helped the Red Sticks before their defeat, they probably would not do so now. Jackson, however, persisted with admonishments to the War Department. He reported the rumor that the British had delivered twenty thousand muskets to Apalachicola. What if the rumors about British activity were true? If the Creeks were taking refuge in Florida, Jackson mused, would Washington allow him to cross the Spanish line? If so, he promised to make short work of the matter and terminate the war quickly.[2]

Such talk must have perplexed Armstrong. Since the spring, he had thought the Creek War already concluded, a fact signaled after all by the initiation of the treaty negotiations. Jackson's suggestion about invading Spanish Florida spurred the secretary to reply quickly and unequivocally. Jackson was not to go into Florida unless he could clearly prove that Spain was voluntarily aiding the Indians and the British. This letter reached Jackson after he had already seized Pensacola. Armstrong claimed that Madison delayed the letter's dispatch, intimating that the government in Washington acted disingenuously by instructing Jackson not to do something it fully expected him to do. But the War Department was in disarray during the fall of 1814, and Washington, D.C., also suffered in August the disruptive British attack that had ended in occupation and arson.[3]

Anyway, Jackson fumed that Spaniards in Florida were abetting American enemies. During the summer, he sent Captain John Jones to Pensacola on a surreptitious mission to scout the town's defenses. Because Spain termed itself neutral in the War of 1812, Americans could come and go to Spanish Florida as they pleased.[4]

It was only one of many bothersome American habits, so Spanish authorities tried to help the defeated nativists by arming and feeding them after Horseshoe Bend. Because of the war in Europe against Napoleon, Madrid could not afford to send more men to West Florida, so in Pensacola Governor Mateo González Manrique had to rely on Indians and blacks to keep the United States from gobbling up any more of Florida than it already had. These Indians could hardly function as the buffer, let alone as auxiliaries, in the shape they were in.[5]

So McQueen and the prophet Hillis Hadjo (Josiah Francis) received Spanish aid. Soon other Red Stick nativists, such as Homathlemico and Savannah Jack, came to Florida as well. Americans, fretting over the help given to these Indians by Spanish Pensacola, first barked alarms at each other and finally aimed threats at the Spaniards. The Spanish town, Jackson explained, was critical to British success in the Gulf. When Governor Manrique meekly explained that he had no jurisdiction over Indians, Americans howled. "Pensacola should belong to the United States," Governor Blount bellowed at Armstrong. And Jackson described as brazen the Spaniards' plan to use hostile Indians to defend Pensacola, unwittingly raising the question of whom they would have to defend it from.[6]

Jackson knew the answer, just as he knew that the Treaty of Fort Jackson would push many Indians to new extremes. He told the government to feed and clothe the Allied Creeks he had just humiliated because otherwise they would prove susceptible to British overtures.

For example, he heard that the British were giving Indians on the Gulf red uniforms, an activity that enraged Jackson as much as it frightened him. The Spaniards were insulting, but the British were dangerous. He again protested Madison's decision to discharge the militia as premature, heatedly explaining that the weather in September and October made them the best months to conduct campaigns on the Gulf. He fretted over rumors that Spain had secretly ceded Pensacola to the British. Rather than discharge the militia in service, Jackson wanted to call up more—unless the government wanted a defenseless eight hundred-mile frontier. By the first week of September, he was pestering James Monroe, now acting secretary of war, with the same alarms. Why did the United States not order the occupation of Pensacola? Spain was obviously acting the part of enemy. The time to take the city—and by implication, the province—was now![7]

Because Armstrong's letter was delayed, the administration did not rein in Jackson. But, contrary to Armstrong's implications, events rather than design caused the delay. That is not to deny the overwhelming temptation in Washington to let Jackson have at Florida. The United States government had wanted Florida for a long time, stretching back to the Louisiana Purchase. Thomas Jefferson at the time regarded the Floridas as even more important than Louisiana and regretted that the Purchase did not explicitly include them. He feared that England or France might acquire the peninsula to endanger the approaches to Louisiana, especially the Mississippi River.[8] Yet a stubborn Spain, already incensed that Napoleon would alienate Louisiana to grasping Americans, blocked both Jefferson and his successor James Madison in their efforts to extend the Purchase eastward into Florida. Finally an 1810 disturbance in Baton Rouge inspired Madison to authorize secretly the occupation of West Florida to the Perdido River. Little could conceal that Madison had, in fact, taken advantage of Napoleon's distracting ouster of the Spanish government in Madrid. Nevertheless, the president prepared a lame rationalization for taking Spanish territory by citing the ambiguities of the Louisiana Purchase boundary. Congress stood by the president, in spite of troubling assertions from Federalists, such as Delaware's Outerbridge Horsey, that Madison was making war on Spain without congressional authorization. Henry Clay, however, supported the administration. Illustrating the growing power of Clay's War Hawk expansionists in the House of Representatives, so did Congress.[9]

In this rarified atmosphere of incipient nationalism Congress grew dizzy with expansionism and sought to adjust constitutional punctilio to fit an aggressive agenda. Less than a year after the seizure of West Florida to the Perdido, Congress authorized Madison to take the Floridas east of the Perdido, in whole or in part, if local authority concurred. For Madison, there lay the rub. The initiative for taking Florida, such as it was, stalled on the phrase "local authority." If that meant Spain, the United States could forget it.[10]

But Georgians and settlers in the Mississippi Territory could not forget it. They saw the Floridas as a potential trophy in the impending war with Britain. If Spain allied with England, these expansionists would have their excuse, and Spanish weakness in Florida would give them the chance. American offensives in the Floridas had occurred before the war with much less justification.[11] In 1814, Jackson's insistence for an invasion of Florida was new only in that it emanated from the American military. As such, Jackson's temperament would set the tone of American military behavior for the next four years. Hostilities with the Creeks did not end with the battle at Horseshoe Bend or the Treaty of Fort Jackson. Instead, they made for convenient turbulence on the Spanish border. The United States Army, at times acting as though it were an independent branch of government, would habitually exploit the situation. Red Stick nativists absent from Horseshoe Bend and the few who escaped it were entirely correct when they saw the war as merely shifting southward. They did not realize, though, that they had become an excuse for pursuing a larger objective.[12]

The one thousand Red Sticks who migrated to Florida during the spring and summer of 1814 were actually part of a larger exodus to Florida, a migration that spanned from 1813 to 1820. The 1814 influx of defeated Red Sticks was the most important of the migrations, because it disturbed a roughly stabilized equilibrium between the eastern and western groups of Seminoles, the former in the Alachua lands and the latter on the Suwannee River and Lake Miccosukee. A rapidly expanding Indian population put strains on food supplies already imperiled by white encroachment and destruction. Indeed, the lands the Seminoles inhabited, especially the Apalachee region south of the forks of the Chattahoochee and Flint Rivers, did not offer bounteous agricultural potential. The Seminoles instead subsisted off a large hunting ground with the help of European gifts and trade.[13]

The Seminoles, like their Lower Creek neighbors below Fort Hawkins on the Chattahoochee, had not participated in the recent Creek War. Nevertheless, the Seminoles felt the same way Red Sticks did about whites to the north. The Florida Indians were as nativistic as Red Sticks and had rejected the authority of the Creek National Council. Therefore it was easy for them to join the Red Sticks in opposing Americans and their Creek allies. Indeed, for the Seminoles such an alliance served as a melding of purpose already determined; they too had fought the United States when the American army and navy had trespassed on Seminole land. It had happened almost simultaneously to the outbreak of the Creek conflict. Whites called it the Patriot War. The Seminoles did not think that it was over either.[14]

⚬⚬⚬

The Seminoles were for the most part originally Creeks who had left their traditional lands to settle southward in a series of migrations begun in the mid-eighteenth century. Nobody is altogether sure about why these migrations occurred, but most likely they were spurred by the search for fertile land, game, and refuge from expanding frontier settlements in Georgia.[15]

Of Creek origin, Seminole society and culture held to many of the clan and kinship traditions of their northern neighbors. The Seminoles were matrilineal, for instance, just like the Creeks, with a chief inheriting his title from his mother's brother.[16] Nevertheless, the Seminoles illustrated the ambiguities and differences that mottled the loose pre-Hawkins Creek Confederation, an arrangement that Seminoles found too binding.[17] Their earliest language was mainly Mikasuki, derived from Lower Creek Hitchiti (rather than the Muskogee common to Upper Creeks), but this linguistic similarity fell to a myriad of complexities and variations brought on by new migrations into the area. By the turn of the nineteenth century, a dozen different dialects, including Muskogee, were spoken by dozens of independent towns from the Alachua lands near St. Augustine to the Apalachee lands near Lake Miccosukee.[18]

One of the few whites to comprehend the Seminoles called them "children of nature," a tender and some would say naive tribute to their autonomy, self-reliance, and guilelessness.[19] Understanding the Seminoles came hard almost to everyone they encountered, from the Apalachee and Timucuan predecessors they had annihilated to the English who quixotically sought to govern Florida between 1763 and 1783 by dividing it into eastern and western provinces. When the Spaniards returned in the latter year they did not try to promote the fiction of governance at all, so they and the Seminoles got along rather well. The Seminoles did not live an easy life, however, and they remained more mobile than other southeastern cultures because they were afflicted by fairly constant warfare.[20] Clashes with traditional enemies and occasional involvement in the squabbles of the European powers marked much of their time in Florida. Amidst all of that, they hunted and raised their cattle and crops while carrying on an easy, informal trade with the Spaniards, maintaining at every turn their independence from them and even each other. The origins of the name Seminole point to the habit, for although there is dispute as to its entomological ancestry, it most probably meant something like "those who live apart."[21]

In the second decade of the nineteenth century, they inhabited towns discretely situated and self-governing, little city-states planted in the Florida wilderness. Aliens who came into their midst either as traders or refugees found a people no more aloof or friendly than others, no shrewder or more deceitful than people are anywhere. Yet, their isolation from the Creeks gradually caused them to reject the authority of the Creek Confederation and brought about an evolving culture quite distinct from that of the Creeks. Their relations with their slaves, perhaps more than any other aspect, point to one of these major differences. The Seminoles came by slaves either by purchase or gift from the British and Spanish governments; some they stole, and others came to them as fugitives. These slaves almost always lived apart from the Seminoles— or more accurately and true to their habit, the Seminoles lived apart from their slaves—so the blacks established so-called Maroon communities that easily fit into Seminole culture because of that society's inherently diverse ethnicity. The Maroons practiced a rudimentary form of tenancy, working their own fields and paying tribute to their Seminole "masters" by giving a portion of their crops at harvest or meat after slaughtering. These blacks, so much happier than the wretched slaves in the cotton culture of Georgia and the Mississippi Territory, bestowed upon their hosts a loyalty commensurate to the relatively benign treatment they enjoyed at Seminole hands.[22]

In fact, the lenient arrangement attracted runaways from American bondage and invited the anger of both red and white slaveholders in the southeastern United States.[23] Sometimes that anger took tangible form in slave raids. Some incidents were serious, but mainly occurrences were confined to local rows on the Georgia border, where cattle rustling, slave raiding, and reprisals disturbed the peace more than they threatened systematic war. In 1812, however, all that changed.

From the turn of the century, Protestant Americans had made up the largest number of immigrants into His Most Catholic Majesty's Florida. Most were Southerners, although many came from northern states. During the first years of migration, most came with considerable property, including slaves and commercial goods. These immigrants became an important link between East Florida and the southern United States, and when combined with the poorer American squatters who came into the area after 1808 they altered the political complexion and national loyalties of the population.[24]

By 1812 southern congressmen and newspapers commenced a steady pressure to annex East Florida and what so far remained unclaimed of West Florida. Tennesseans especially coveted the river routes to Mobile and the Gulf, and Jackson went on record in the summer of 1812 to say that the Tennessee militia was ready to invade Florida if necessary.[25] The impending war with Britain made Spanish sensibilities less an obstacle, and soon enough the Creek War would make the Indian presence a reason for invasion rather than a restraint against it. Georgians strained at their southern border's leash.

With only the slightest encouragement, some of these Georgians slipped the leash and fomented an insurrection against Spanish authority in St. Augustine. Elderly George Mathews, a former Georgia governor and spirited adventurer, managed at the outset to raise nearly eighty "Patriots," most imported from Georgia with a sprinkle from the indigenous Florida immigrants. Hoping to gain East Florida with no official fuss, Madison approved the scheme, but only if the United States would appear to have no connection to it. Nevertheless, American military and naval forces made themselves covertly available to Mathews: United States ships helped in early actions to take Amelia Island, claiming as they did so that they were not acting as part of the United States Navy; Lieutenant Colonel Thomas Smith, commanding the United States garrison at St. Mary's, would allow the involvement of American regular soldiers.[26]

It was the spring of 1812, about a month before the American declaration of war against Britain, and Mathews with his men appeared on the verge of success against the frail Spaniards in East Florida. St. Augustine entreated the Seminoles at Alachua for help against the Patriots, but Mathews managed at first to secure Seminole neutrality. The Seminole Maroons, however, were another matter. These blacks understandably fretted over what an American victory in East Florida meant to their casual demislave status. Soon Mathews abandoned friendly gestures to level dire threats at any Seminole who inclined toward the Spaniards. Such behavior betrayed his desperation. The entire Patriot scheme quickly came unraveled, a victim of climate, poor planning, and lack of supply.[27]

On 25 June, in the wake of declaring war on Britain, the House of Representatives authorized Madison to annex Florida.[28] The president, however, publicly disavowed the Patriots even as Secretary of State James Monroe told Governor Mitchell of Georgia to prevent any foreign occupation of East Florida; in fact, Monroe told Mitchell that if the British were likely to occupy East Florida, he could complete the conquest begun by Mathews. Georgia's most tireless political operator, William H. Crawford, forewarned the governor about the State Department's desire that Georgia make some exertions in "this delicate affair."[29] Mitchell took the hint. Georgia militia arrived in East Florida in June, but General John McIntosh was soon correctly warning Mitchell that they did not have enough provisions and incorrectly predicting that a British occupation of St. Augustine was likely.[30] Meanwhile, the Seminoles smarted under the interruption of their trade with St. Augustine and grew fearful over so many armed Americans suddenly meandering around their lands. As an incentive, the Spanish governor in St. Augustine offered a thousand dollars for John McIntosh's scalp, ten dollars each for those of his minions. Perhaps some young Seminoles acted because of these economic inducements, but most warriors apparently helped the Spaniards because they were less obnoxious than Americans.[31]

On 25 July, Seminoles attacked American settlements on the St. John's River. Those Patriots who had stuck it out so far now lost even the dwindling enthusiasm that had increasingly marked their participation in this floundering debacle. They deserted Mathews in droves to protect their homes.[32] The Seminoles attacked a party of United States

Marines on 12 September, causing Governor Mitchell to echo the wails of his constituents that the southern border was aflame. Madison, rethinking the entire project, contemplated deserting Mathews too.[33]

Neither Georgia nor Tennessee would have it. General John Floyd led Georgia militia against the Seminoles to hand them a defeat on 3 November.[34] Jackson and some of the Tennessee militia sallied forth, ostensibly to protect New Orleans, but really and secretly as part of the larger American design on the Floridas.[35] Colonel John Williams, adjutant general of the Tennessee militia, raised 240 east Tennesseeans to go into East Florida, striding through Georgia to do so, deaf to the objections of both Hawkins and Mitchell. Mitchell worried about the political credit Tennessee would gather as protectors of the frontier; Hawkins worried about an expanding circle of hostilities threatening his acculturated paradise. The Seminoles, so weary of the war that they had asked for peace, retreated in alarm.[36]

In spite of Seminole peace overtures, Williams's Tennesseans joined Georgia militia and General Thomas Flournoy's United States soldiers for the campaign in Florida. In February 1813, they destroyed two abandoned Seminole towns by burning nearly four hundred homes. They stole seven hundred horses and cattle; ate, carried off, or burned nearly two thousand bushels of corn; and pilfered two thousand deerskins.[37]

Other than destroying winter food supplies for most Indians and blacks in central Florida, this raid accomplished little more than to provoke the Alachua Seminoles. Those Indians hid in the swamps before the greater military menace of Flournoy's regulars. They then scattered, some toward Tampa. Many followed their headman Bowlegs westward to escape starvation, eventually stopping near Lake Miccosukee on the west bank of the Suwannee River. There they came into contact with the western Seminoles, who, because of American aggressors, were now closer in spirit as well as location.[38]

The ragtag remnants of the Patriots strutted into the Alachua lands to demand annexation by the United States. With the Creek War fully under way and the belief that the Spaniards in Pensacola audaciously were helping Red Sticks, a variety of voices described such annexation as only just. But the war with Britain compelled Washington to caution. In early 1813, antiadministration Republicans joined Federalists in the Senate to vote down the House resolution to seize East Florida. Madison would not recognize the Patriots, and the United States would not risk Spanish anger or Senate censure by annexing East Florida. In March, the government recalled Jackson's West Florida expedition from its gathering point in Nashville. It was over.[39]

Over, but not dead. The little project had failed, but Georgians continued their slave-stealing raids into Florida, a bad habit they could not break.[40] And the little war that faded to nothing had contained memorable incidents of violence and destruction. It had put Seminoles at the throats of settlers in bloodied south Georgia cabins; it had put United States soldiers in ransacked, smoldering Seminole villages. Neither the white survivors on the Georgia frontier nor the children of nature in Florida would forget.

⊱⊰

Both exiled Red Sticks and native Seminoles took hope when Captain Hugh Pigot's frigate *Orpheus* and Lieutenant David Hope's *Shelbourne* arrived at Apalachicola Bay on 11 May 1814. The Creeks had been in contact with the British in the Bahamas throughout the Creek War, but no real help had resulted from these communications. Now, after Horseshoe Bend, the Indians were so physically distressed that it remained questionable whether they were salvageable.[41] Pigot, however, brought arms, ammunition, blankets, and promises of more aid. Now Americans had cause to worry not only about the "defeated" Red Sticks, but about neutral and even Allied Creeks, too. Reports circulated in Georgia that the British had brought five thousand muskets to Florida and were attempting to include Big Warrior in their plans. News that the British intended to arm escaped slaves and encourage others to rebellion scared Americans witless.[42]

The British plan for attacking New Orleans began forming up in June 1814. It called for using the southeastern Indians and runaway slaves as a diversion to the east of the Crescent City. The British aimed to take Mobile first and use it as a base from which to strike at Baton Rouge and thereby cut off New Orleans. They then expected the city to surrender. In all of this, the importance of diversionary forces to tie down troops along the Carolina and Georgia coasts became paramount. The Indians were to provide a pivotal contribution in this strategy.[43]

The first man on the ground for England in this project was Captain George Woodbine of the Royal Marines, who stepped ashore that May afternoon from Pigot's ships at Apalachicola with Sergeant Samuel Smith and Corporal James Denny. Woodbine first established a base on St. Vincent Island but soon moved up the Apalachicola River to Prospect Bluff. At the end of May he began building a fort there, and soon the Americans were not the only whites disturbed about it.[44]

Half a mile from this site, William Hambly and Edmund Doyle had been running a store for Forbes and Company, a British mercantile concern that engaged in a prosperous trade with the Indians. At first, Hambly and Doyle cheerfully helped Woodbine and agreed to move their store to the new fort. They provided him with supplies and served as interpreters to the Seminoles. Woodbine consistently neglected to pay for supplies, however, and Forbes's inventory began to suffer under what were actually confiscatory requisitions. It got worse: some of Forbes's slaves joined Woodbine apparently because he promised them their freedom. The Indians collecting around Woodbine became suspicious of Doyle and Hambly, whose increasingly gloomy mood was made more ominous in Indian eyes by an intercepted letter from John Forbes that described the Americans to the north as invincible.[45]

Woodbine might have believed the same thing. The meager number of Indians at Prospect Bluff presented sparse opportunity for offensive action. He dealt exclusively with Seminoles for several weeks, making an agreement with the principal Miccosukee Seminole chief, Capachamico, also known as Tom Perryman and sometimes called Kinache.[46] To augment these forces, he sent a messenger to Pensacola to recruit Red Sticks, the warrior McQueen and prophet Francis among them. Soon more Red Sticks, Seminoles, and fugitive slaves flocked to the fort at Prospect Bluff. By August, as Jackson was humiliating old friends to the north, the Royal Marines were making many new ones in Florida. Woodbine estimated his numbers at one thousand warriors on the Apalachicola and two thousand more in the interior.[47]

Though Jackson maintained the fiction that the Creek War was over, he knew that the British alliance posed a new danger. He also undoubtedly knew that the hostile British and Indian force in Spanish Florida provided him with an excuse to invade it, a move his friends and neighbors had been encouraging for years.[48] Yet Jackson, charged with protecting the Gulf coast, had to exercise caution. Big Warrior's habit of duplicity spawned rumors about his contacting the British. Jackson had to be careful.

British offers of help undoubtedly tempted many Creeks, although Woodbine consistently underestimated the hostility that still divided the Red Sticks and American Allied Creeks.[49] British recruiting efforts at Prospect Bluff on the Apalachicola alarmed both Benjamin Hawkins and Andrew Jackson from the outset and certainly after the Treaty of Fort Jackson. It was not immediately apparent how successful the British would be in exploiting Indian indignation caused by Jackson's terms. Woodbine unquestionably thought an alliance with disaffected Lower Creeks became more likely in the wake of the treaty.[50]

Big Warrior troubled the Americans. In late August, Jackson heard that some of the headman's subordinates had met with Woodbine in Pensacola. Could the United States, a friend asked Jackson, trust the headman?[51] Big Warrior admitted to Hawkins that some Creeks had gone to Florida to see what the British were up to, but he insisted that they had not succumbed to British blandishments nor believed British promises of friendship. Instead, Big Warrior said that British plans to lure slaves to Florida troubled him and other Creeks.[52]

This much was true. Of all British activities in Florida, the recruitment of fugitive slaves struck both whites and reds as the most consistently obnoxious. British promises of slave emancipation went far in thwarting British overtures to Allied Creeks in the crucial summer and fall months of 1814. The apparent strength of American forces also prevented other southern tribes, such as the Chickasaws, Choctaws, and Cherokees, from entertaining British propositions.[53]

Admiral Cochrane, however, appraised the project so far as successful. He believed that three thousand British soldiers aided by the Spanish and allied with Indians and blacks could wrest the Gulf coast from the United States. He sent more arms and equipment to Apalachicola while urging Indians and blacks to increase recruiting. By July Cochrane, anticipating the day when these Indians and blacks would be ready for the Gulf offensive, sent Major Edward Nicholls to Florida to take command of the irregulars. Captain Sir William H. Percy's H.M.S. *Hermes* and Captain P. Spencer's *Carron* ferried the Royal Marine and a brace of supplies from the Bahamas to Florida in early August. By the tenth, Nicholls had arrived at Prospect Bluff.[54]

The scene did not offer much encouragement. Severe food shortages so plagued the base at Prospect Bluff that it resembled more a refugee camp than a military bivouac. Still, the numbers impressed Nicholls—

more than fifteen hundred Indians and blacks—and even more impressive was their hatred toward the United States.[55] News of the Treaty of Fort Jackson soon amplified that rancor and further cemented the Red Stick–Seminole–British alliance in Florida. The treaty that took most of the exiled Red Sticks' lands also took territory in southwestern Georgia from Seminoles whose eastern cousins had already seen some of their towns gutted by American soldiers. Neither Red Sticks nor Seminoles had been represented at Fort Jackson, and both refused to recognize the treaty's validity. Nicholls stoked the resentment to swell recruitment.[56]

Woodbine was not at Prospect Bluff when Nicholls arrived there. At the end of July, he traveled to Pensacola to procure food for the hungry post at Prospect Bluff and to reassure Governor Manrique that Britain could repel an American invasion. The British presence in Florida alarmed Manrique, because he correctly believed it invited American aggression. Spanish authorities had tried to distance themselves from the British by disapproving of British soldiers in Spanish settlements such as St. Augustine, St. Marks, and Pensacola. For a time they apparently had not worried about the British popping up anyplace else, such as at Prospect Bluff, but Manrique was beginning to have second thoughts about that, too.[57]

Woodbine sent several hundred Seminoles overland to Pensacola while he went there by ship.[58] Soon Nicholls at Prospect Bluff received Woodbine's summons to come to Pensacola with reinforcements. On 14 August, the *Hermes, Carron,* and *Sophy* arrived off Pensacola with at least two hundred men under Nicholls's command. Manrique must have viewed these developments with sick anxiety. An anonymous correspondent in Havana had warned the governor about Nicholls, describing him as "an impatient blustering Irishman . . . apparently brave and cruel."[59]

Plainly the British planned to assault Mobile as much as protect Pensacola. Nicholls issued a bombastic proclamation to Louisianans and Kentuckians, promising the former to liberate them from "a faithless, imbecile government," luring the latter with money and free navigation of the Mississippi.[60] Whether or not Nicholls really expected help from discontented Creoles and bluegrass frontiersmen, he certainly expected it from Forbes and Company in Pensacola. Yet the Forbes men there, John and James Innerarity, mirrored Doyle and Hambly's disillusionment with the Royal Marines. The Inneraritys, in fact, regarded

Nicholls and Woodbine as little better than their new Red Stick friend Peter McQueen, whom the British factors considered a swindler. Nicholls found the Inneraritys' patriotism so wanting that he suspected the Forbes representatives were in league with Americans, and he was right. John Innerarity sent a warning to the Americans about the impending British attack on Mobile.[61]

When the British and their Indian allies began their first offensive campaign in the Gulf, Nicholls told his Royal Marines "to exhibit to them [the Indians] the most exact discipline, being a pattern to those children of nature," exhorting his soldiers to do so primarily by staying sober. It was all futile. Colonel William Lawrence's 158 Americans at Fort Bowyer outside of Mobile were ready for them. Woodbine had spent the entire summer boasting about his successful recruiting efforts, and Nicholls had echoed the brag, but of the 2,000 Indian warriors the British claimed to have at Pensacola, fewer than 200 accompanied about 100 Royal Marines to assault Mobile. The attack on Bowyer by four British ships supporting landing parties ended on 15 September in bloody failure. The British lost the *Hermes,* and Nicholls suffered wounds that cost him his right eye. There was no way of putting a good face on it, especially for the Indians who had made up most of the expedition, and most especially for Woodbine and Nicholls, who had invested so much confidence in the Indian alliance.[62]

Ugly recrimination and lawlessness marked the retreat. A Forbes store at Bon Secour lay along the route back to Pensacola, and the force that could not take Mobile sacked this emporium instead, stealing its inventory and carrying off ten Forbes slaves.[63] Perhaps the looters felt they had gotten back some of their own.

✑

As early as May 1814, Allied Creeks under William McIntosh out of Coweta had volunteered to invade Florida to destroy the Red Sticks. Big Warrior repeated the offer to Hawkins in late August.[64] Up to a point, Jackson resisted the plan because it would have revealed the Treaty of Fort Jackson's inconclusiveness. When the British shifted from Prospect Bluff to Pensacola, however, Jackson wanted to enroll every southern Indian warrior he could to join all the militia he could muster.[65] Then after the British attack on Fort Bowyer, Jackson reversed his policy of separating the warring Creek factions and finally approved the Allied Creek foray into Florida. He expected William McIntosh to destroy enemy strongholds on the Apalachicola and capture any blacks in the area.[66]

McIntosh left for Florida with about two hundred warriors on 23 September 1814. He expected between one hundred and two hundred more to join him on the way. Jackson obviously expected this large force to do more than reconnoiter the Florida landscape, yet when McIntosh returned in three weeks, that is all he had really done. He had met with Seminole leader Tom Perryman on the Apalachicola to confirm that the British were now concentrating in Pensacola. Moreover, the Seminoles told him that many Red Sticks, disheartened by the British failure to capture Mobile, might turn themselves over to American authority.[67]

By the end of October, however, events gave the lie to this optimistic intelligence. By then Seminoles and Red Sticks worked so congruently on plans to assail the Georgia frontier that Americans could hardly distinguish between the two groups. Seminoles ranged as far north as the Creek Agency to steal horses, and they remained an active presence on the Georgia frontier. Slaves fled their masters to head south, apparently after receiving prearranged signals from the British. Hawkins reported that the Seminoles were eating "war food" while planning attacks south of Fort Hawkins near Hartford. Since the Florida Indians obviously had joined with the enemies of the Allied Creeks, Hawkins persuaded the Allied Creeks to police the Georgia frontier.[68]

The British move from the Apalachicola to Pensacola signaled for Jackson either Spanish perfidy or weakness (he suspected both), and he claimed it required the American occupation of West Florida. Americans heard that the British were sending talks to Creeks around Fort Decatur just across from Tuckabatchee and that many planned to go to Pensacola. Monroe warned Jackson to expect a major British invasion in the Gulf and to recruit Choctaws and Creeks to resist it. Monroe said he would send blankets and other goods to help recruiting.[69]

Military preparations accelerated as the frontier braced for Indian invasions from Florida bases. All evidence pointed to British support for such Seminole–Red Stick attacks. Benjamin Hawkins frantically tried to prepare Allied Creeks and the Georgia government for the assaults. Andrew Jackson meanwhile focused on Spanish Pensacola, hundreds of miles away. Jackson had not believed Seminole promises of friendship, but he insisted that if Americans took Pensacola, all Seminoles and Creeks would then be friendly.[70]

For its part, Pensacola was in a dither. Jackson and Governor Manrique exchanged heated messages in which Jackson demanded that Spaniards neither help the British nor harbor fugitive Red Sticks. Manrique was initially belligerent, because he believed that armed and fed Red Sticks under Peter McQueen and Josiah Francis would deter any aggressions the Americans contemplated. But when many Red Sticks began migrating to the better-supplied British camps on the Apalachicola, Manrique became nervous. Woodbine's reassurances of British support offered increasingly less comfort, and finally no comfort at all. By autumn the governor resolved that cooperation with the British simply invited American invasion. Indeed, Jackson was preparing his thirty-four hundred regulars and militiamen to join seven hundred Choctaw warriors for an assault on Pensacola. Meanwhile, Secretary of War James Monroe was writing Jackson to avoid "measures which would involve the government in a contest with Spain." Jackson claimed that he was sure the government would back his actions.[71]

While Manrique fretted about Jackson, Edward Nicholls tried to prepare a defense for Pensacola. Some Americans did not overlook the pecuniary plum that Pensacola represented. A district paymaster named Pemberton instructed Captain Waters Allen to accompany Jackson to Pensacola to calculate how much money could be made from "the articles you mention"; such articles were almost certainly slaves. Allen was to send such articles to the right people for sale. "I would like," said the paymaster, "to make five or six thousand dollars."[72]

Nicholls received little cooperation from fearful townspeople who believed Jackson had promised a seven thousand-man force twenty-four hours of looting upon the capture of a resistant city. Low on supplies, the British fumed when local merchants refused them credit. Finally, Spanish objections about Nicholls's recruitment of slaves to help with defenses pushed him beyond patience; he threatened to level the town if anyone tried to surrender to Jackson.[73]

Jackson had moved out of Fort Jackson shortly after signing the Treaty of Fort Jackson. By the third week of August, he was at Mobile taking stock of his situation. He could count within the Seventh Military District five infantry regiments for a total of 2,378 men, but the figures were misleading.[74] Morale plummeted with the onset of autumn, and desertions began to dwindle his army as they had a year before. One September morning, 26 of 66 men at Fort Williams simply picked up to head for home; the remainder of the Fort Jackson garrison threatened to do the same, and reports told of an all but abandoned Fort Strother. Attempts to round up these deserters offered only mixed results.[75]

Jackson suspected that the meager forces in Pensacola would soon be augmented. As it stood, only about one hundred British officers and enlisted men made their headquarters at Fort San Miguel, guests of an increasingly querulous Spanish government and sullen merchants. Jackson chose to move on the city with what forces he could muster, a mixture of regulars, militia, Choctaws, and Chickasaws. He did what he could to seal Mobile as well as Pensacola and sought to enroll on his muster rolls all free men, including blacks, to whom Jackson explained, "Through a mistaken policy you have heretofore been deprived of a participation in the glorious struggle for national rights." Having himself corrected the policy and thus variously reinforced, he arrived at Pensacola on the evening of 6 November and immediately renewed his communications with Manrique.[76]

This was not the first American invasion of Spanish Florida, but it was the first one led by Andrew Jackson. The Indians knew about Sharp Knife firsthand, the British from the stories that preceded him, and the Spaniards from a generation of living near the squire of the Hermitage. His reputation for violence and rigid resolve had already unnerved Pensacola's inhabitants, their edginess apparent when the garrison at Fort St. Michael fired a twelve-pounder at Jackson's messenger, Major Peire. Lividly denouncing the cowards who had fired on a flag of truce, Jackson sent a Spanish prisoner with a second message repeating the demand of his first, that Manrique surrender the city. Jackson insisted that he was not making war on Spain, but Manrique, refusing to yield the city, contended it was hard to see otherwise, especially considering that only nations at war saw the need for flags of truce.[77]

If the Spanish governor took any solace in winning this debating point with Jackson, it was short-lived. On the following day, as the Americans began to move in for the attack, Manrique began a stammering equivocation: the British had violated Spanish neutrality, he claimed, without his knowledge; in fact, he had nothing to do with the

British currently manning the fortifications.[78] As hard as this was to believe, Manrique's eleventh-hour written defense proved as inconsequential as the military one mounted by the British. When Jackson moved on the city on the morning of the seventh, Manrique surrendered within minutes. Realizing the impossibility of a defense, the British organized the retreat of their Indian and black allies while their ships—the *Sophy, Childers,* and *Sea Horse*—destroyed the town's fortifications and the harbor's defenses.[79]

Jackson explained to Washington that he took Pensacola to stop Spanish collaboration with the British. By the second week of November, he had received Monroe's letter instructing him to leave Spanish Florida alone, but Jackson remained blithe about disregarding his superior's orders.[80] "Should you have made the proposed attack," Monroe wrote Jackson in early December, "you will on receipt of this letter, withdraw your troops from the Spanish Territory, declaring that you had entered it for the sole purpose of freeing it from the British violation."[81]

Fortunately for American diplomacy, the British destruction of Pensacola's fortifications had already solved the problem of what to do with the town. Naked Pensacola was as indefensible for occupying Americans as it had been for the beleaguered British, so Jackson returned it to the hapless Manrique after only a few days. The general had anticipated Secretary Monroe's instructions, but for entirely different reasons. The Floridas would have to wait.[82]

∽

Jackson rushed his army toward New Orleans, the new focus of British strategy in the Gulf. Meanwhile, in spite of the British failures at Mobile and Pensacola, Nicholls and Woodbine continued their activities on the Apalachicola, though with diminishing success. These undaunted Britons became their own worst enemies. The Innerarity brothers in Pensacola angrily marked the Royal Marines as thieves and brigands, slave stealers, in whose hands property got used up or simply disappeared. The belly of Nicholls and Woodbine's beast was at Prospect Bluff, where they returned after evacuating Pensacola. They took with them as many slaves, boats, and provisions as they could transport, most of the property belonging to Forbes and Company, all irretrievable according to Innerarity agents sent to the Apalachicola to reclaim it. Woodbine ranged eastward to St. Augustine, where Governor Sebastian Kindelan bluntly told him to leave; Woodbine gloomily complied, though not before rounding up eighty East Florida slaves to labor at Prospect Bluff. American soldiers briefly occupying Pensacola, grumbled John Innerarity, had been models of propriety in contrast.[83]

The Spaniards might have agreed. Perhaps their cheer over getting rid of Nicholls and Woodbine muted their diplomatic protests about Jackson's behavior.[84] Manrique had the British to thank for blasted fortifications at Santa Rosa Island and the gutted fort at San Carlos. When Nicholls abandoned Pensacola, he had taken black Cuban-Spanish troops to labor at Prospect Bluff (instead of in Pensacola) for the remainder of the war. Constant rumors that pirates planned to attack the town chased many civilians from their unprotected homes. Manrique left Pensacola a year later, presenting the defenseless city to his successor, Mauricio de Zuñiga. Zuñiga tried to strengthen Fort Barrancas, all that really remained of the town's shields, constructing a floating battery to guard the approaches from the Gulf. It would hardly be enough when the time came.[85]

Benjamin Hawkins knew this helpless feeling as well. He also knew a great deal about British plans in West Florida, thanks to information provided by disgruntled Forbes agents.[86] Even as Jackson's sights had narrowed on Pensacola, Allied Creeks had to repulse two British-armed Seminole war parties on the Flint River. "The king of the Miccasookees does what he Can to restrain his young people," reported one observer, ". . . but they are impudent & eager for Mischief."[87] It was Woodbine's work, the British officer having visited the Miccosukees to offer them the astounding bounty of $100 per American scalp.[88]

Andrew Jackson had twice declared the Indian war in the Southeast ended. Yet when Jackson took the military to New Orleans, Benjamin Hawkins immediately detected the renewed British-Indian preparations along the Apalachicola. Some recounted tales of violence in the vast stretches of piney woods. In frustration, Hawkins tried to organize Allied Creeks and Georgia militia for an assault on the British stronghold at Prospect Bluff. Defensive measures on such an extensive frontier would be futile, he said; Americans would have to trace hostiles to their towns of origin and attack them there. Hawkins expected the British to subvert any temporary peace, so he wanted to do it right. At least five hundred mounted infantry under "an officer of ability" provided by the Georgia militia could "crush these people."[89]

In mid-November as he headed for New Orleans, Jackson tried to arrange such a blow. Major General John McIntosh of the Georgia militia was to direct Major Uriah Blue of the Thirty-ninth Infantry to take a force of Tennessee militia, Choctaws, Chickasaws, and Allied Creeks along both sides of the Escambia River, killing or capturing all Red Sticks he could find, rounding up straggling women and children, and destroying every town. Allied Creek Samuel Manac would be Blue's guide and interpreter, the settlement at Prospect Bluff his primary target.[90]

General McIntosh's carpenters began building boats to take the Georgia complement down to the Seminoles, and Hawkins quickly rounded up the Allied Creeks under William McIntosh, but they need not have hurried. American forces remained scattered and ineffectual. Soaked by torrential rains, Blue waited for supplies while hunkering down at Fort Montgomery. David Mitchell's successor, Governor Peter Early, apprehensive about possible British attacks on the Georgia coast, sent the bulk of Georgia's militia there, precisely in the direction opposite to Blue's proposed campaign. When Blue and his soggy command did leave Fort Montgomery to venture along the Escambia, it was not until the first week of a miserably cold December. He learned that the Red Sticks who had evacuated Pensacola before Jackson's arrival now occupied an island in the Gulf. With two Creek-speaking Choctaws, Blue lured a couple of these Red Sticks to the mainland, using cattle as bait. Blue's men captured the two Creeks, questioned them, and then allowed the Choctaws to scalp them. Exploiting his information, Blue caught the Red Sticks unaware, collaring eighty-one and allowing only eight to escape. By then, though, he had exhausted his food and had to return to Fort Montgomery. He had never gotten close to Prospect Bluff. Hawkins meanwhile sat with McIntosh and a thousand Allied Creeks at the confluence of the Flint and Chattahoochee Rivers, battle dressed but with no particular place to go. They amused themselves with a few larcenous raids into Florida where, according to some, they behaved even less decorously than Blue's people had.[91]

Thus at Prospect Bluff Woodbine and Nicholls to this degree succeeded. In spite of the glaring insufficiency of the Indian auxiliaries, in spite of the near starvation that stalked the British camp, the numbers of Indians and blacks had swelled to nearly two thousand by the end of the year. They appeared more menacing than they really were—these people were hungry, cold, and weary—but appearances counted for everything on this nervous frontier. The British presence on the Apalachicola kept twenty-five hundred Allied Creeks, Georgia and Tennessee militiamen, Choctaws, and Chickasaws from helping Jackson fight the British at New Orleans.[92]

They also terrified Georgia. Tuckewikee, a Miccosukee Seminole, led a band into Georgia to kill five whites, later to brandish their scalps before the British at Prospect Bluff. At the least, Hawkins wanted to establish a fort at the confluence of the Flint and Chattahoochee Rivers to discourage such forays. Meanwhile, Nicholls, Seminole chiefs, and the Red Stick prophet Francis returned from New Orleans at the end of January, the Royal Marine apparently undaunted by the defeat in Louisiana. Hawkins, for instance, heard that the British continued to recruit runaway slaves, and he could believe the information because he had reliable sources, something that made the substance of these reports even more chilling. Apparently unaware of the level of the Forbes Company's discontent, Nicholls continued to trust the company's agent, William Hambly; Hambly provided information to the disgruntled Inneraritys, who gave it to the Americans. Big Warrior's people, who regularly visited Prospect Bluff, also provided intelligence about conditions there, although that Big Warrior's people were anywhere near Prospect Bluff at all must have given Hawkins pause.[93]

Indeed, several things gave Hawkins pause. He believed the stories about starvation stalking the camp at Prospect Bluff, and he also believed that consistent British military failures must have dispirited the Indians. And yet Nicholls brought food from Admiral Cochrane to bolster the sagging morale on the Apalachicola; on the Atlantic coast, Admiral Sir George Cockburn landed on Cumberland Island promising freedom to all slaves who joined him against the Americans. Before January was out, other British forces descended on St. Simon's Island on the Georgia coast and moved up the St. Mary's River.[94]

Jackson mistakenly thought that Uriah Blue or John McIntosh had dispersed British-Indian forces on the Apalachicola, and he concluded that his victory at New Orleans would convince the Red Sticks of their complete defeat. And yet Hawkins heard that Peter McQueen and Josiah Francis wore British uniforms at Prospect Bluff as they listened to Nicholls's promises of land reclaimed and Americans annihilated.[95] On 11 February, a British force separate from that under Nicholls and Woodbine mounted a successful assault on Fort Bowyer as a prelude to attacking Mobile; and yet, this British victory came almost at the same time that Nicholls called together the Indians on the Apalachicola to tell them that the Great British Father in London had ended his war—and thus theirs too—against the Americans. The agreement ending the war, he assured them, provided for the return of their lands.[96]

Nicholls referred to Article Nine of the Treaty of Ghent, and he apparently took its substance as a literal promise: in concluding the war between the United States and British Indian allies, the United States would restore all lands taken from the Indians during the war.[97] The implications for the Treaty of Fort Jackson's cession would have been devastating. The Liverpool ministry never intended to commit permanent British support to the Creeks, however; London always regarded the British-Indian relationship as one of occasion, not affection. The British inclusion of Indian rights and privileges in the treaty actually marked a retreat from an earlier position calling for an Indian barrier state and more elaborately defined Indian rights. The more modest British proposal that resulted in Article Nine, delivered to the American delegation on 19 September 1814, urged that the Indians have their rights, privileges, and territories restored as they had existed in 1811. Yet British Foreign Secretary Viscount Castlereagh never proposed to outlaw American acquisitions in a war caused, as Americans claimed, by Indian aggression. The British delegation at Ghent complained that Americans always described their wars as defensive, but by October 1814, the British government had virtually abandoned its Indian allies in the negotiations to end the War of 1812. In London's view, the occasion and hence the relationship was over.[98]

$\approx$

Edward Nicholls, the Seminoles, and the Red Stick Creeks did not know they had been abandoned, so the Royal Marine took it upon himself to see that Article Nine of the Treaty of Ghent became more than an empty negotiating point traded by wigged envoys in a chilly Belgian town. Dispute surrounds Nicholls's motives for trying to secure Indians' rights. Some claim that he wanted to become the British Indian superintendent in Florida simply for the perquisites. He apparently also expected grateful Seminoles to reward him with a generous parcel of land.[99]

Whatever his motives, Nicholls pursued Indian advocacy with a will.

He first bolstered the military situation at Prospect Bluff, continuing throughout the spring to supply the camp with food and stock the fort with weapons. British ships secured the approaches to the Apalachicola and brought artillery and stands of arms to the encampment. The numbers of blacks, many stolen in Louisiana, continued to swell. All the while, Nicholls repeatedly told the Indians that the Treaty of Ghent would return the land they lost at Fort Jackson.[100]

He also repeatedly told this to Benjamin Hawkins, but neither the Creek agent nor his government in Washington was buying. When Hawkins first heard about the Treaty of Ghent, he expected it to signal the end of Nicholls and Woodbine in Florida. Instead, he received from Nicholls a brusque interpretation of Article Nine as nullifying the Treaty of Fort Jackson's cession. Hawkins immediately began planning an operation against Prospect Bluff, hoping to exploit the short supply situation by starving the inhabitants out. In Washington, the War Department also grew impatient with the continued British presence in the Gulf, but not so much as to authorize another invasion of Spanish Florida. At the most, Jackson received instructions to remove the British from any part of West Florida claimed by the United States.[101]

The delicious ambiguity of these instructions had barely dented the American military's understanding when Seminoles and Georgians began a new cycle of violence and retaliation. At Fort Mitchell, wagon drivers made a sport of whipping Creeks who came to the fort for food. In the first week of March, three Indians crossed the Georgia line from Florida, attacked a wagon train, and killed a wagoner to steal the wagon and its team; in the succeeding weeks three other attacks by Indians suggested a distressing pattern. Hawkins insisted that these Indians were Seminoles, but no hard evidence could prove that they were not Red Stick nativists still at war. Bowlegs's Seminoles, however, bore the brunt of retaliation, with one of his nephews dying and another falling to capture. Worse, it all seemed to mean that should Article Nine be moot, the rest of the arrangements for peace would be as well.[102]

In exasperation, Hawkins sent Nicholls a copy of the Treaty of Ghent as if an actual reading of the document would clear up all the problems. Lacking a better point for argument, Hawkins pointed out the provision that proscribed the taking of slaves. Allied Creeks trudged to Prospect Bluff to retrieve their slaves, but nobody, including Hawkins, expected much success from the effort. Nicholls in fact proved incorri-

gible about this matter as well as all others. He blithely told Hawkins
that he had sent the American and Allied Creek slaves to other British
colonies to assure their continued freedom. He also wanted Hawkins to
investigate the murderous, thieving activities of Georgians against
Chief Bowlegs's Seminoles. In the meantime, he said, the Seminoles
had decided to cease all discussions with any Americans to end the fric-
tions between their peoples. The implication was as clear as it was mad-
dening; Nicholls would henceforth act as the speaker for these Indians
with the Americans. To drive home that point, the Royal Marine
reminded Hawkins again that Article Nine returned all ceded land to the
Indians.[103]

Next Nicholls wrote Hawkins that he had seen his Indians punish
their people for disturbing the American peace; would the Americans
do the same to those who had assailed Bowlegs's people? Nicholls said
that he had instructed the Creeks not to cross the line into the United
States anymore; he wanted the United States to do the same favor for
the Creeks. Where this line lay—the one that nobody would in the
future cross—was, of course, at the heart of the controversy. Nicholls
expressed dismay that the Americans planned to build forts in land that
had been, by Article Nine, returned to the Creeks. But it was the information that he had just completed a treaty of alliance with the Creeks—
a treaty that cemented trade relations between Britain and the Indians,
withdrew Forbes land grants, and promised grants to British subjects
who helped the Indians' cause—that sent Americans spinning. Nicholls
expected London to ratify the treaty soon.[104]

The United States Army now took stock of the menace to the south.
A full four months after signing the Treaty of Ghent, the British still
supplied the Indians on the Apalachicola, and the Spaniards remained
powerless to stop the enterprise. Nicholls had some eight hundred to
nine hundred warriors, the army reckoned, about half that many blacks,
the former motivated by Nicholls's endless reassurances about Article
Nine, the latter by the preservation of their freedom. The American
military regarded it a bad combination.[105]

For Hawkins, it was a damnably infuriating one. Practically in one
breath he demanded that Nicholls return the slaves and excoriated his
dealings with the Indians. In the first place, Hawkins said, of the three
chiefs Nicholls put forward as speaking for the Creeks, at least one was
a Seminole. Indeed, those chiefs were Homathlemico (whom Hawkins

said was a Seminole), Hopoi Micco, and Caupichau Micco. The last of these could have been the aged Miccosukee King (Capachamico), definitely an Apalachee Seminole, but the point Hawkins tried to make got tangled in the jurisdictions claimed by Americans from the Treaty of Fort Jackson and Indian land rights under the Treaty of Ghent. Hawkins began arguing in illogical gibberish. The Seminoles never had any authority to usurp the Creek National Council, he insisted, thus they had nothing to do with the terms of Fort Jackson; if the Seminoles had a complaint, Hawkins insisted, they should take it to the Spanish government. Otherwise, he speculated that Bowlegs probably had mistaken for Georgians the shadowy remnants of the Patriots who inhabited the banks of the St. John's River, people Hawkins said were only seeking revenge for the vicious assaults earlier endured at the hands of the Alachua Seminoles.[106]

What any of this had to do with Article Nine was anybody's guess. Hawkins revealed the depth of his frustration by referring the matter to Andrew Jackson.[107] The Indian agent now firmly believed that some military force would have to reduce the fort at Prospect Bluff. In Washington, a less impulsive mood governed the American reaction. A new acting secretary of war, Alexander Dallas, advised Hawkins that the president hoped the British government would stop sponsoring Nicholls and Woodbine and reiterated the official American position that the Treaty of Ghent did not promise the Indians anything other than peace.[108]

Whether it promised that was doubtful. Displaced Creeks—by now a mixture of some neutrals, a few Allies, and Red Stick nativists—moved down along the coast as far west as Mobile to hunt and practice subsistence agriculture. Their own overhunting had long since depleted the wild game that had provided skins for trade, so these Indians frequently raided north for cattle, driven by frustration and anger as much as hunger. Americans often mistook these Creeks for Seminoles.[109]

Josiah Francis led his people eastward to settle near the Spanish fort at St. Marks. They were all nativists, mostly Upper Creeks, mainly from the Tallapoosa region and the Coosa River towns. Now they sought refuge in Spanish Florida, hewing out among the pines and mangroves a series of villages west of where the Suwannee River flowed into the Gulf. Because they no longer had the capacity to act as a buffer between the United States and the Spanish, it was unlikely that His

Most Catholic Majesty would help them reclaim their land. Yet the British might still champion their cause. Nicholls repeated as rhythmically as any prophet a chant about the import of Article Nine of the Treaty of Ghent, the arrangement made to protect the red brothers of the redcoats.[110]

Francis, prophet of his people, had no alternative but to believe, had no choice but to take Nicholls at his word, to follow the Royal Marine to London, there to remind the Great English Father of his Red Stick friends. In the summer of 1815, they left aboard a vessel of the Royal Navy for England, Nicholls one-eyed from the wound at Mobile, prophet Francis possessed of presumably boundless vision. Yet both were strangely blind to the fresh forces at work in the New World to their backs, ignorant of the ancient intrigues at play in the old one to which they sped.

3

"A Blow in Another Quarter"

The British government wanted nothing to do with either Edward Nicholls or Josiah Francis. Worn down by two decades of war, Britain had no intention of disputing the United States' interpretation of Article Nine, an interpretation that rendered that part of the treaty meaningless. Lord Castlereagh's foreign office soon viewed the Red Stick's presence as an embarrassment, and it winced over Nicholls's insistence that he had negotiated a Creek alliance. The United States's protests about Nicholls and the so-called treaty with the Creeks forced Castlereagh's office into the breach: Nicholls, London instructed, was to have no further communication with the foreign office. For good measure, the foreign office officially described Nicholls's Indian treaty as unauthorized. In late summer, while the Royal Marine and the Red Stick prophet were under sail for Britain, Washington's minister to Great Britain, John Quincy Adams, informed the State Department that all evidence depicted Nicholls as a diplomatic renegade, acting with no instructions from the Liverpool ministry. To make sure, Adams began a long (and initially unsuccessful) effort to secure an official disavowal of all of Nicholls's activities. Castlereagh, however, would not do that. After all, he was not contrite, merely cautious.[1]

The foreign secretary could be uncommunicative when it suited British interests. The foreign office never informed the Indians in Florida that it had disavowed Nicholls and deserted them. Those

Indians must have noticed though that during the late spring and summer of 1815, nothing really impeded Georgian raids into Florida settlements. When the Indians retaliated, the frontier became querulous rather than chastened, shouting alarms that Seminoles, Creeks, and runaway slaves in Florida plotted another Indian war. Benjamin Hawkins remained alarmed and angry, fearful on the one hand about his unprotected southern marches, irritated on the other by Edward Nicholls's provocative behavior in Florida. Yet, Hawkins had to admit that when Chief Bowlegs complained about Georgians stealing cattle from Suwannee settlements, the Seminole had a point. The Indian agent did not fear Red Stick resurgence in Georgia—too many of them were surrendering for a bowl of meal—but Peter McQueen in Florida scared him. The Spaniards were so very weak, and McQueen so very determined. Could the implacable Red Stick warrior wrest the peninsula from Spain?[2]

❦

It must have been very hard for Benjamin Hawkins in the months after the War of 1812, when he saw the work of two decades unravel into the untidy mess on the Florida border. No matter where he looked, whether at the mischief-making British to the south or at the thieving Americans in his own midst, everything seemed headed for calamity. He had taught his charges to farm like whites. Now over half of them wandered in the wilderness starving. He had counseled his countrymen to patience. Now they howled in panic over Indian depredations real and fabricated. Finally, events reduced him to promoting something he did not support to sustain a position he could not abide.

It is otherwise difficult to explain Hawkins's actions regarding the Treaty of Fort Jackson, an arrangement he opposed from the start and found indefensible in the interim. Suddenly, he concocted contorted explanations of why Fort Jackson should stand and Article Nine of Ghent could not. He came to believe by the middle of 1815 that the whole controversy hinged on the Red Sticks not signing Jackson's dictate. As a solution to this predicament, he now contended that those who had signed the treaty represented all the Creeks, whether nativists, Allies, or neutrals. Demonstrating a remarkable capacity for self-deception, Hawkins believed that Creek exasperation centered on the paucity of Creek representation at the negotiations. Actually Creeks, grumbling that no negotiations had occurred, objected to the treaty itself. The government, Hawkins insisted, only had to recognize Allied Creek leaders as representatives of the entire Creek Nation. Such recognition would nullify British claims that the ceded land fell under the terms of Ghent. He proposed such a course to Washington and remained manifestly ignorant that even the Allied Creeks chafed under the treaty's terms. Conforming to a growing pattern of ineffectiveness, he also described white attacks on Seminoles as the work of dissociated Patriots from the St. John's region. The explanation did not vindicate Bowlegs's victimized Seminoles any more than his interpretation of Fort Jackson and Ghent soothed cheated Allied Creeks.[3]

So Hawkins heard his voice gradually drowned out by the din of frightened frontiersmen, squabbling politicians in Milledgeville, and grim-faced army officers. This last group had the job of protecting the survey teams that would mark the Fort Jackson cession, a job as dangerous as it was difficult. In the business of the survey, Hawkins received the latest of many slights. The original survey commissioners were former Tennessee Governor John Sevier, William Barnett, and Colonel John Kershaw. When Kershaw resigned and Hawkins replaced him, it seemed a boost for the Indian agent's prestige and a blow to Jackson's influence. Sevier, also, was a member of a rival Tennessee faction and had years before conducted a bitter quarrel with Jackson. Yet in September, Sevier died and Hawkins later suffered dismissal. God had apparently interceded for Old Hickory with Sevier, but the general had done his own work to get rid of Hawkins. In both cases, however, Jackson won signal victories. His chief subordinate in the area, Brigadier General Edmund Pendleton Gaines, took Sevier's place; his close friend John Coffee replaced Hawkins. The survey commission simply became an extension of Andrew Jackson's will.[4]

Even before his appointment to the commission, Gaines had the job of protecting the survey crews. Born in Virginia during the Revolution, Gaines came from a family prominent in politics—he was his Great Uncle Edmund Pendleton's namesake, his mother was a Strother, and his father, James, had been a member of the constitutional ratifying convention in North Carolina—but Edmund inclined toward the military life at an early age. His family finally settled in 1794 in what would become Tennessee, and it was there at the age of eighteen that he first served in the militia to fight Indians. In 1797 he entered the United

States infantry as an ensign and quickly won promotion to lieutenant. Gaines lived in exciting times, and he usually found himself in the middle of important events: he arrested Aaron Burr and was a prominent witness at Burr's treason trial. He flirted briefly with another career when he practiced law in the Mississippi Territory, but the War of 1812 drew him back to his first love. He rose rapidly through the ranks to become a colonel by 1813, and conspicuous bravery and herculean endurance, first at Chrysler's Farm and then as the commander of beleaguered Fort Erie, won him not only a brigadier's rank but the accolades of Congress as well. A nasty wound forced him to sit out the rest of the war, but he had made his mark already, and the government marked it well with the award of a gold medal. A ringing chorus of thanks stretched from states as diverse as New York to North Carolina.

Gaines perhaps counted his new job a bit of rotten luck. The running of the Fort Jackson cession line promised to be hazardous. Gaines knew the work; he had led the surveying team that cut the road from Nashville to Natchez twelve years before. But that had been different. No Nicholls preceded him then to stir the Indians with inflammatory talk about stolen lands and broken agreements. Gaines heard how the Royal Marine, just before leaving for England, had told the Indians to resist the running of the line. As the teams clanked into the wilderness to rattle chains and gaze through transits, their soldier escorts nervously watched the sullen Indians who followed, silent but menacing. Red Stick and Seminole anger surprised no one. The nativists' flight into Florida burdened Seminole resources, but it also infused the Seminoles themselves with a rejuvenated desire to resist white encroachment. More disturbing, the Indians who shadowed the survey expedition were neither Red Stick nativists nor Seminoles; they were Allied Creeks, mostly from the Lower Towns. Promised supplies when they signed the Treaty of Fort Jackson, they never received them. The government had withheld their annuity for three years and had failed to pay many Allied Creek soldiers for their service during the Creek War. On top of all that, they now saw what the Treaty of Fort Jackson meant. They were losing as much land as the nativists.[5]

By September, Allied Creeks had moved from indignation to anger. Gaines snugged his soldiers closer to the surveyors, and Andrew Jackson threatened his old allies with extermination if they interfered with the teams. In reply, Big Warrior sharpened his protest by describing

Jackson's intimidating tactics during the proceedings at Fort Jackson. Jackson, the aging headman said, had forced them into signing away their land. In a statement both poignant and ominous, Big Warrior remarked that he *had* considered Jackson his friend.[6]

The Seventh United States Infantry and the readiness of two thousand Georgia militiamen shielded the survey crews from physical assault in the fall of 1815, but nothing prevented the Indians from vowing that they would never allow settlers on the land.[7] The Indians did not mean it as an empty threat, but the tide of white immigration soon flooding the Fort Jackson lands made it seem one. As soon as the surveyors and their entourage moved on, squatters inundated the area. The new secretary of war, William H. Crawford, himself a Georgian, nearly exploded over this premature incursion by those he described as the "worst part of our citizens." He wanted them removed, not so much to preserve Indian amity as to assure that this rabble did not diminish the property values in the cession.[8]

The rabble was more like a swarm, amorphous and ubiquitous, at once there and everywhere. The army now had the double duty of protecting both surveyors and squatters, because both Creeks and Seminoles soon had many reasons for violent retaliation. The squatters raided into Florida to steal livestock and slaves, while soldiers winked at or openly abetted them. The soldiers could be as odious when they put their minds to it. Survey Commissioner William Barnett was sickened by the violence, especially by one contemptible incident in which soldiers wantonly murdered a Creek woman. At year's end, the survey expeditions reached the east bank of the Chattahoochee River. Now the most provocative part of the job was behind them, they thought, and many expected peace to return to the Georgia frontier.[9]

The army knew better. Intimidating the Allied Creeks within American boundaries was one thing. Frightening hostile Indians and runaway blacks in Spanish Florida was something else altogether. In December, the War Department moved the Fourth Infantry under Lieutenant Colonel Duncan Clinch from Charleston, South Carolina, to Fort Hawkins to reinforce the Seventh Infantry there. A native of North Carolina, and hence aware of the way Indian fighting could go, Clinch was young enough to be worried—he would turn twenty-nine in April—and experienced enough—he would mark his eighth year in the army in July—to take counsel of his fears. Soon he received instruc-

tions to move his men farther south to Fort Gaines on the Chattahoochee River, a scant one hundred miles north of the Florida line.
Jackson wanted the southwestern part of the survey to proceed unmo-
lested, but Jackson's civilian superior in Washington, Secretary of War
Crawford, wanted the army to remove the hundreds of squatters swarm-
ing over the ceded territory. Clinch had reason to worry, and not just
because of the enemies in his front.[10]

Gradually, others realized what the army knew. Hawkins had
remained hopeful about maintaining peace on the Georgia frontier, but
Seminole and nativist Red Stick anger eroded such optimism. And then
there were the runaway slaves. As early as August 1815, Hawkins had
heard that about eighty blacks occupied the fortifications abandoned
by the British at Prospect Bluff. Nicholls had called the post Fort
Apalachicola, but Americans had gotten into the habit of calling it
Negro Fort. Nicholls's nomenclature made it sound imposing; the
American name made it frightening.

It was both. A six-sided structure with twenty-five- to thirty-foot
walls, the fort boasted an arsenal of twelve artillery pieces, about
twenty-five hundred muskets, and enough powder and lead to make
them formidable. Woodbine had chosen the site on Prospect Bluff, a
commanding vantage about fifteen miles up the Apalachicola, and
Nicholls had helped to design the works, so the best of British military
science had contributed to the fort's defensibility. More important, its
location had made it a beacon for slaves fleeing their masters from all
over, whether from Allied Creek towns on the Chattahoochee, or American plantations in Georgia, or Spanish towns in Florida. By early 1816,
about three hundred blacks and two dozen Choctaws lived around the
fort, a refuge of freedom for a growing number of restive slaves, a dark
lantern of economic ruin and violent defiance to slave owners, white
and red alike.[11]

Jackson wanted his own forts, and he pestered the War Department
for engineers to build them on the border. Ostensibly, he wanted to bolster frontier defenses, but rumors said otherwise: talk in the army had it
that soon Jackson would be "fighting for the Floridas."[12] Hawkins,
already worried about the slaves lured away from Allied Creeks and
Georgians, fretted over news that had Seminoles and blacks in Florida
performing the Red Stick dance. Worse, Hawkins heard that Red Stick
nativists expected British help in reclaiming their lost land. The Innerar-

ity brothers in Pensacola remained his reliable source for information, but they offered little comfort with such gloomy and unsettling bulletins. The frontier remained ugly and dangerous. Hawkins heard that near Fort Claiborne Indians had murdered two white men named Johnson and McGaskey practically under American soldiers' noses.[13]

Was a war of conquest, a fight for the Floridas, the answer? Spain feared that the United States would come to think so. Concerned less with Indian and runaway slave activity than with what it might provoke, Spanish administrators watched increasingly aggressive American behavior with growing alarm. Madrid still staggered from the disruptions of the Peninsular War, and soon it had to cope with nascent Latin American revolutions that threatened to destroy Spain's New World empire. The option of strengthening Florida militarily and economically withered before the demands and challenges laying claim to dwindling Spanish resources. From Madrid to Havana to St. Augustine to Pensacola, the sensitive antennae of scribbling governors, supernumeraries, clerks, and couriers sensed the same thing. Sooner or later, the United States intended to take Florida.[14]

◈

Jackson probably thought the taking would occur sooner. For the time being, though, he was busy. He persisted in his plans for building forts on the Georgia frontier. The posts would protect inhabitants from the Florida Indians, but they also could serve as staging areas for an invasion. He told Gaines to raise two such establishments, one on the Escambia and the other at the confluence of the Flint and Chattahoochee Rivers where they form the Apalachicola. The Seventh Infantry would build and garrison the Escambia fort; Clinch's Fourth Infantry would construct and man the Apalachicola post. Perhaps most important, their placement would put them on an axis with West and East Florida, respectively. In preparation for these two important forts, Gaines moved out of Fort Hawkins at the end of March to construct what would become Fort Gaines. This post would provide an important link between Fort Hawkins and the other new fort to the south near the Florida line. Jackson also directed Gaines to bar all Creeks except a few specified Allies from entering the ceded territory until Johnson and McGaskey's killers were in custody. Gaines should treat all other Creeks found there, Jackson said, "as enemies."[15]

The construction program and the sequestration of potential hostiles had the look of war preparations. Gaines proceeded with this program while Jackson conducted an inspection tour of the Southern Division that took him to New Orleans. During Jackson's absence, Gaines altered the defensive aspects of the plan. Gaines, knowing Jackson as well as he did, would not have done so on his own initiative. Although the Johnson and McGaskey murders had occurred a considerable distance away from it, Negro Fort became the exclusive focus of Gaines's activities. Duncan Clinch's people fashioned seven flat-bottomed boats, shallow enough in draft to descend the Chattahoochee. Gaines told Jackson and Crawford that the supply route for the new Georgia fort could originate in New Orleans or Mobile and use the Apalachicola from the Gulf. The route would provide an opportunity to keep an eye on Negro Fort, under whose ramparts such expeditions would have to pass. Gaines bluntly told Jackson that as long as Negro Fort existed, the United States would have slave troubles from Georgia to the Mississippi River.[16]

This novel idea of a supply route up the Apalachicola struck William Crawford as risky at best, perhaps overly perilous in fact. Too many anger-tinged things were happening too quickly to suit the secretary. For instance, Jackson had interpreted the Fort Jackson cession so liberally that it presumed Creek lands extended northward well into land traditionally claimed by the Cherokees. Crawford tried to calm anxious Cherokees by instructing Jackson's friend and new commissioner John Coffee to stop the survey on the Tennessee border. The government, Crawford believed, would have to offer some accommodation to the Cherokees before proceeding. The secretary wanted to avoid a fight on the Tennessee River as well as on the Florida border, but Jackson regarded Crawford's action as a personal affront. He had a long memory for such things.[17]

As if this were not enough, Crawford wrote to Jackson that the governor of West Florida had the responsibility to control or reduce Negro Fort. If the governor refused, then the president, and only the president, had the authority to determine what action to take.[18] Crawford was about to discover what previous secretaries had learned, from Armstrong to Monroe, and what a future secretary, John C. Calhoun, would soon realize: Andrew Jackson was a difficult man to control.

Hawkins could tell them all about that. The agent had spent nearly all of his time lately trying to obviate problems with Allied Creeks created by the Treaty of Fort Jackson. He simultaneously tried to persuade the Allied Creeks to reduce Negro Fort. He sent a deputation of Allied Creeks to the Seminoles hoping to persuade the Florida Indians to remain neutral in a fight with Negro Fort and to return any runaway slaves they found. Yet he encountered a chilly mood among his Allied Creeks. He told Big Warrior and Little Prince that the United States would view the destruction of Negro Fort as a gesture of extreme good faith, but the two old leaders found any faith at all in the United States a scarce commodity. Rankling under the terms of Fort Jackson, both of them were in contact with the British, Big Warrior renewing communications, Little Prince establishing them. Neither could see that the British who really counted—specifically, the Liverpool ministry in London—had no intention of interceding on the behalf of any Creeks, but the depths of Allied Creek disaffection made talking to former enemies of the Americans seem not only sensible, but liberating.[19]

Hawkins probably realized how angry the headmen were, but he kept the information to himself. Big Warrior was not so discreet. In mid-April, he sent a talk reminding Jackson of warnings spoken by himself to the general in August 1814. At Fort Jackson, Big Warrior had cautioned that the nativist Red Sticks remained undefeated. The headman's signature on the treaty had made him a pariah among certain Upper Creeks who regularly threatened his life, so he was "unusually serious" when dictating this talk to Jackson. Big Warrior denied he had any jurisdiction over the land where Johnson and McGaskey had been killed, a point that must have vexed Jackson because it was precisely the point that the United States had been insisting upon for almost two years. Big Warrior asserted that the lack of jurisdiction deprived him of any authority to punish the killers. In any event, he pointed out, four of his people had been slain and no one had taken the trouble to find their murderers, especially those soldiers who had killed the "very respectable" Creek woman.[20]

Hawkins had better luck with Little Prince, at least at first. Little Prince said he would try to persuade the Seminoles to help Allied Creeks destroy Negro Fort. He proved indolent in the effort, however, and then became alarmed about the construction of the two forts in the ceded territory. When Little Prince demanded an explanation, Hawkins revealed his frustration and impatience in an angry reply. The agent threatened the Allied Creeks with the loss of more land if they did not assist in returning all the slaves at Negro Fort to their owners. Meanwhile, the agent lied to Gaines to keep secret Little Prince's disaffection. The Creeks were meeting Seminoles on the Apalachicola, Hawkins said, with the object of a joint operation against Negro Fort.[21]

Gaines probably did not believe this. If he did, he likely did not think the Allied Creek–Seminole project would come to anything. He ignored Little Prince's objections and continued to supervise Clinch's construction project on the left bank of the Chattahoochee. As the post, originally called Camp Crawford but eventually renamed Fort Scott, took shape, its possible contribution to an offensive campaign became more apparent. Meanwhile, Jackson agreed with Gaines that somebody, preferably Allied Creeks, would have to destroy Negro Fort if it contained any runaway slaves from the United States.[22] Jackson's nod to the Indian allies marked a grudging agreement with William Crawford: the governor of West Florida was the line of first resort regarding Negro Fort. Yet, if the Allied Creeks did the deed, Americans could always disclaim involvement.

As the sawing and hammering on the forts echoed through the south Georgia woods, however, Jackson pursued the direct approach as well. At the end of April, he sent Captain Ferdinand L. Amelung to Pensacola with a message to Governor Mauricio de Zuñiga. Amelung was to await the governor's response. If that response was anything but hostile, the mails could carry it to Jackson in Nashville; any hint of belligerence, however, would require dispatch by express courier. Amelung's instructions did more than plan for Zuñiga's petulance; they practically predicted it, and with good reason, because Captain Amelung carried a written grenade to the Spaniard: Jackson told Zuñiga that he knew about Negro Fort, that it contained 250 runaway slaves, and that if the governor did not do something about it, the United States would.[23]

Such was hardly what William Crawford had in mind. He had told Jackson to deal with the governor, not threaten him. But Zuñiga resisted the provocation. Actually, the Spanish governor would have liked nothing better than to eliminate the fort because it had become a magnet for Spanish slaves too. At one point, Spaniards had contemplated sending an unofficial force to infiltrate the fort and blow it up, but they had abandoned the idea under the concern that it might alienate the Indians, some of the few friends Spain still had in Florida.[24] Nonetheless, Jackson neither cared about what the governor wanted nor waited for what he had to say. Part of Amelung's mission called for a reconnaissance of Spanish forces in Florida and the strength of Negro Fort. Jackson had already sent orders to Gaines to arrange the attack on Prospect Bluff.[25]

Only one day after Amelung's departure for Pensacola, supposedly to persuade Spain to destroy Negro Fort, Jackson wrote to Crawford expressing the hope that Gaines had already dealt with Negro Fort and the "Land Pirates" it contained. He casually mentioned that he had given Gaines discretion in the matter.[26] The news must have disconcerted Crawford. He had explicitly told Jackson that any decision would rest exclusively with the president.

Gaines hesitated with his discretionary power, but only because he wanted to make sure that Clinch had enough strength to hold his position on the Chattahoochee before starting any offensive. While the Americans mulled, the Seminoles suddenly acted. By early May, all signs pointed to a growing Seminole resentment over the terms of Fort Jackson, now compounded by the survey teams tramping through their land and the soldiers laboring away at the fort on the Chattahoochee. Two soldiers and the cattle they herded outside the fort simply disappeared, snatched by the Seminoles and taken into Florida.[27]

Duncan Clinch took out after them, but soon he received news that set him back on his haunches. The Seminoles congregating at the confluence of the Flint and Chattahoochee Rivers reportedly had between fifteen hundred and three thousand warriors ready to strike not only Clinch but also Hartford, Georgia, for good measure. Hawkins scornfully dismissed the numbers as grossly exaggerated. Even before the kidnapping of the two soldiers, the agent had declared that the time for talk was over; he proposed to lead an army of Allied Creeks under William McIntosh to destroy Negro Fort. Little Prince had told Hawkins that only three hundred Seminoles clustered to the south, and Hawkins believed that they were belligerent only because outsiders riled them up. Now was the time to strike them.[28]

Accepting that baseless rumors had counted three hundred warriors as three thousand, Clinch took heart from the adjusted numbers to renew his chase. Only two days after his startled pause, he announced that he would move south as soon as he had provisions. He would do Jackson's bidding to clear the cession area of all unauthorized Creeks. That meant he would destroy all towns on the Flint that had not lodged

special requests to remain until their harvests were in. After he had finished that chore, he said, he would move downriver to "strike a blow in
another quarter." [29]

Clinch, usually plainspoken, began to show an uncharacteristic
appreciation for euphemism. Gaines, the bulk of whose instructions to
Clinch do not survive, possibly urged his subordinate to use evasive
language when discussing the proposed invasion of Spanish Florida.
Jackson, however, felt no need for restraint, as his correspondence with
the War Department amply shows. On 12 May, he wrote to Crawford
expressing the hope that the secretary would not object to Gaines's discretionary orders. Both those orders and the letter to Crawford about
them preceded any knowledge Jackson had of the kidnapped soldiers. [30]

Crawford must have been as perplexed as he was angry in the spring
of 1816. Mail pouches to the War Department contained letters describing events weeks old and filtered through Jackson in Nashville. His and
Jackson's letters sometimes crossed, but on the crucial points, the secretary's messages remained so consistent that anything Jackson reported
would not likely have changed their substance. Nobody in the Southeast
had yet heard from the Spaniards about Negro Fort, something Crawford (and President Madison) insisted was the first step toward resolving the matter. In fact, Crawford in late May told Jackson to slow down
on the forts because there was no need for hurry. The United States was
not on the verge of war with any nation, the secretary reminded the general. [31] The general might have mused that he would possibly have some
news for the secretary on that count.

Crawford also countermanded those of Jackson's instructions to
Gaines that he knew about, specifically the order to treat all Indians in
the ceded territory as enemies. Blaming all Indians for the actions of a
few would not only be unjust, it would sanction attacks on innocents.
That would be "an unequivocal act of war," Crawford lectured, "which
cannot be waged without legislative sanction." Crawford added that
Jackson could better preserve the peace by ousting squatters from the
ceded territory and settling disputes with the Creeks by negotiation. [32]

The secretary's and the general's letters crossed, but both made policy, the secretary under constitutional provisions and the general under
personal prerogative. Gaines and Clinch moved ahead with the plans to
attack Negro Fort, and Jackson continued to send announcements to the
War Department, announcements that apparently were impervious to

anything coming the other way from Washington. Before receiving Crawford's suggestions for preserving the peace, Jackson declared that he hoped Clinch had already destroyed Negro Fort. He also repeated his long-held conviction that Seminoles and nativist Red Sticks planned a full-scale war (though he had twice declared such a war concluded) and that the British and Spanish encouraged them to the task. Jackson told Crawford that because war was so imminent, he was transferring the First Infantry from New Orleans to join the Fourth and Seventh, effectively reinforcing Gaines. As an aside, he also mentioned that he had directed the quartermaster to put more funds at Gaines's disposal so he could destroy "this den of wolves."[33]

The general's and the secretary's letters crossed. As this latest from Jackson moved toward Washington carrying the news that Jackson predicted war and was maneuvering men and appropriating funds to wage it, Crawford's admonition about preserving the peace came to Jackson's hands. The general exploded, diverting for the moment the focus of his fury from Indians and Britons and Spaniards to the administration in Washington. He wished, he disdainfully told Crawford, that President Madison was "as well acquainted with the depravity, intrigue, cunning, and native cruelty of the Indians" as Jackson was. If Madison had a better way of dealing with Indians, Jackson wanted to hear it.[34]

Of course, Jackson did not want Madison's opinion any more than that of Crawford or, for that matter, Zuñiga. When these exchanges between the military and the War Department occurred, at least two different plans aimed to attack Negro Fort. Gaines moved ahead with his plans, and Hawkins proceeded with his as well, but the Gaines plan held the most promise because it was the craftier of the two. Gaines intended to provoke a conflict with Negro Fort rather than just attack it outright, as Hawkins proposed. He would accomplish this by conducting the experiment in supplying Camp Crawford by water. He wrote Commodore Daniel T. Patterson in New Orleans to broach the idea, requesting that the navy provide him with two gunboats to escort a supply convoy up the Apalachicola to Camp Crawford. Almost as if it were an afterthought, Gaines mused that if Negro Fort menaced the convoy in any way, Patterson could destroy it.[35]

While Hawkins considered leading Allied Creeks against Negro Fort, Gaines swiftly organized a combined operation that would have Duncan Clinch moving down from Georgia while naval forces navigated up the Apalachicola from the Gulf. Gaines felt he had to do something. The survey teams had announced that they would halt their work until somebody did something about the Indian menace.[36]

Yet it was hard to say what Negro Fort had to do with the Indian menace. Indeed, it was hard to say what Indian menace existed in the summer of 1816. When neither Hawkins nor Gaines could accurately gauge the resolve for hostility among Seminoles and nativist Red Sticks, they formed separate plans focusing on Negro Fort because both regarded it as the one certain provenance of hostilities. But different motives guided the two men to this same object. When the abductors of the two soldiers released them, Hawkins became convinced that the Indians wanted peace. The agent feared another civil war among the Creeks, so he seized upon the soldiers' release as representing more than a sign; it was a signal, a peace offering. Better to attack Negro Fort than ignite again the retaliatory cycle among the Indians of Florida. Gaines, however, cared less for signals than for the axioms of military operations. If Clinch had any chance to destroy Negro Fort, he would have to concentrate his forces. That was why Gaines told Clinch to destroy only those Indian villages in his path toward Negro Fort. He relied on the Georgia militia to assist Clinch in his endeavors. Gaines only had so much to go around, and better that it should go at Negro Fort than be scattered in the Florida wilderness.[37]

Obviously then this blow in another quarter had less and less to do with Indians in Florida. When the two kidnapped soldiers turned up, bewildered and blinking but really none the worse for their ordeal, preparations for the invasion of Florida did not even pause. Meanwhile, Zuñiga's reply to Jackson's ultimatum, a month in the making but bearing the manner of a cool head, did not bluster at all, but instead agreed with Jackson that something had to be done about Negro Fort. Zuñiga said, however, that he hesitated to act without instructions from his superiors in Havana. While he awaited those directions, he urged Jackson to wait as well.[38]

Mauricio de Zuñiga acted calm, but actually American activities continued to alarm Spanish officials everywhere. During the spring and summer of 1816, Spanish minister to the United States, Don Luis de Onís, railed at the United States's apparent indifference toward pirates and adventurers outfitting in United States ports to assail Spain's crumbling Latin American empire. Such indifference belied American neutrality, he chided. The State Department habitually replied with renewed assurances of American goodwill while adding its own lectures about Spain's inability to police the Florida border. On one point, however, Zuñiga told the absolute truth: the Spanish government would have gladly destroyed Negro Fort if only it had possessed the resources to do so. Now, the Spaniards watched helplessly as the United States Army advanced its plans to destroy the fort, hoping that was all the Americans intended to do.[39]

For the moment, Zuñiga was safe in that hope. The courier-spy Amelung estimated that the Spanish garrison in Pensacola could not number more than one hundred men and contended that the town would be easy to take, but Jackson kept his sights narrowed on Prospect Bluff. He informed Crawford that the Spanish governor would not mind if the United States destroyed the fort.[40] The observation surely overstated the case as it ignored a host of questions about sovereignty and international relations. It also overlooked the central point that all officially promoted reasons for going into Florida had disappeared. The two kidnapped soldiers had returned, and rumors of war dances between Indians and runaway slaves had ceased. Indians turned in two of the accused killers of Johnson and McGaskey to military authorities at Fort Jackson, and former nativist prisoner Paddy Welch fell again to capture. The border enjoyed a calm it had not seen in years. Yet as Clinch's men finished the fort on the forks of the Chattahoochee and Flint Rivers, Commodore Patterson issued orders to Sailing Master Jarius Loomis to command a gunboat escort for the supply convoy leaving New Orleans. Gaines's plan for an experiment in supply proved as impervious to changing events as Jackson's attitude was to new instructions from his secretary of war.[41]

The return of peace to his Indian frontier must have pleased Benjamin Hawkins. He still fretted over the haven for runaways at Prospect Bluff, and he hoped to the last that his Allied Creeks with himself at their head would eliminate that problem, thereby to gain the gratitude of their neighbors and restore the waning prestige of his agency. In early June, however, as the weather turned fetid and hot, Hawkins took suddenly ill. Such bouts had occurred with growing frequency in the previous few years, but this one came fiercely and never relented. On 16 June 1816, Benjamin Hawkins died.[42]

They buried him at the Creek Agency, putting him in the ground he had told his Creeks to cultivate, reading over him in the shadow of rusting Creek plowshares and shattered Creek parliaments. He had never meant them harm, but for twenty years he had tried to do good by making them white, and his legacy had become war, famine, and disgrace. Benjamin Hawkins of good heart was dead, and the time of dark hearts had begun. It was the tragedy of his life that it would be hard to tell the difference.

∝

Philemon Hawkins, nephew of the deceased agent, temporarily took over the Creek Agency until the administration would name a permanent replacement. The Allied Creeks, for the first time in twenty years, would enjoy in the next few months unfettered freedom. The path many would follow took them to the door of army officers who saw the opportunity to turn Hawkins's death to their advantage. He had been so proprietary regarding the Creeks that his agency had come to resemble a foreign embassy; the army viewed the Allied Creeks as merely an extension of Hawkins's will and hence as unreliable. Now William McIntosh leapt at the army's promise of booty in return for help against Negro Fort. Only two years after the humiliation at Fort Jackson, Allied Creeks again would march with the United States Army.[43]

The War Department remained ignorant of Jackson's extensive preparations for war. Clinch lingered only because he had not yet received word that the supply transports had arrived off the Apalachicola. Meanwhile, Crawford wrote to Gaines that before undertaking any efforts to supply the forts through Spanish territory, it would be necessary to secure Spain's permission. Before that letter arrived, American ships were moving up the Apalachicola River into Spanish Florida, and an American army was moving south into Florida from Georgia.[44]

On 10 July, Loomis arrived off the mouth of the Apalachicola with United States Gunboats 149 and 154 escorting the schooners *General Pike* and *Semilante*. Lafarka, an Allied Creek who had crept to the coast, came aboard with a message from Clinch: Loomis was to stand off the Apalachicola until Clinch brought his men down to accompany the transports upriver. As the four ships swung on their anchors that lazy July afternoon, a small boat glided out of the mouth of the river. To Loomis's thinking, here was a chance to inquire about the lay of the land around the fabled Negro Fort, so he sent some men in a small skiff to hail the strangers. Loomis watched from the deck of No. 149 as the sailors rowed out toward the craft, watched the little puff of smoke billow from it, heard the report crackle across the water. The strange boat turned and headed swiftly for the safety of the river. Loomis unlimbered his guns, but the best he could do was to splash some shot around the boat as it moved quickly beyond his range. If nothing else, the American naval expedition off the coast of West Florida had been spotted.

Loomis waited—and waited. A week passed with no sign of Clinch. On 17 July, chafing under the delay, Loomis sent a midshipman named Luffborough and four sailors ashore for fresh water. Luffborough had resigned his commission just before the expedition's departure from New Orleans, so his presence on Gunboat 149 was more a personal favor to the United States Navy than the fulfillment of any duty. Now, he and his party left No. 149 at 5:00 in the morning, rowing off in the dawn to the gray shore. Loomis would never see him again.

As the sun rose through midmorning, someone spotted a dark shape bobbing in the swells between the ships and the beach. A boat from No. 154 collected it, bringing it alongside No. 149 for Loomis to see. It was John Burgess, one of Luffborough's sailors, shot through the heart. As the day wore on, it got worse. Forlornly stranded on a sandbar, another sailor, John Lopaz, waited until late afternoon, when a boat from the convoy finally picked him up. He was the only survivor of the Luffborough party.

Lopaz described what had happened. As they neared the mouth of the Apalachicola, the men spied a black man on the beach. Luffborough ordered the boat ashore so he could inquire about fresh water. The midshipman had only just begun to approach the stranger when several additional black men and Indians appeared from the brush. Wordlessly, they lowered their muskets to fire a volley that killed Robert Maitland, Burgess, and Luffborough. Lopaz ran thrashing into the water, swimming for his life, glancing back only briefly to see the fifth member of the party, Edward Daniels, taken prisoner.[45]

So now Loomis waited with a pall over his ships. With three men dead, another taken captive, and his crews nervous, he could only wait. After three days, a canoe emerged from the shimmering river. The five Indians that slid next to No. 149 were from Clinch, at last, with directions to proceed upriver. Yet Loomis hesitated and then stopped. Who were these people? Where was Clinch? His crews, remembering Luffborough's luck, must have been grateful that Loomis decided to sit tight.

Actually the Creeks did come from Clinch. The army commander had left Fort Scott on the same day Luffborough and his men were killed, 17 July. Clinch had 116 men divided into two companies under Major Peter Muhlenberg and Captain William Taylor. They traveled mostly by boat. That night, William McIntosh led 150 Allied Creeks into Clinch's camp, and on the next night Mad Tiger brought in additional Allied Creeks. Clinch sent some of these Indians ahead of his main force, hoping that with their stealth they would capture any blacks reckless enough to be outside Negro Fort upon their approach. Clinch took up the journey into Florida with high confidence; not only did he have these Allied Creeks under accommodating commanders, but he also had an excellent guide in William Hambly, the very man who ran the Forbes Store at Prospect Bluff, now upon the departure of the British openly in league with the Americans. With such reliable guidance, Clinch and the main part of his command arrived about a mile north of Negro Fort on 20 July two hours after midnight. As soon as the rising sun began to silhouette the trees of the piney woods, he immediately sent the five Creeks to fetch Loomis.[46]

Yet Loomis was not budging. He squinted at these Indians who tried to convince him that they served Clinch as messengers. They related information from a black man captured outside Negro Fort, information that detailed the attack on the Luffborough party, information made credible by this black man's carrying the scalp of one of the victims. The story did not allay Loomis's fears; likely it raised them a notch. He was not budging.[47]

For the next three days Clinch and his Creeks reconnoitered the area around Negro Fort. When Allied Creeks edged toward the fort under a flag of truce, the commander, Garçon, shouted that the fort would never surrender. To give proof to their defiance, the fort's inhabitants raised a British flag next to a red banner and periodically fired their artillery at Clinch's forces.[48]

Clinch needed Loomis's artillery, and he knew it. On 23 July, he sent another group of messengers—two Creeks and a white man, possibly William Hambly—down to the mouth of the river to hurry Loomis along. Yet the sailing master still would not budge. After all, here were just three more people with a verbal message to come up a winding, sometimes narrow river where he had already lost four men to ambush. He kept the white and one Creek, sending the other back with a message that he wanted to see an American officer right away. Clinch complied the next day with a will. A lieutenant and thirteen men stalked down to the coast to convince Loomis finally that all the prior people had indeed been American emissaries. The convoy immediately started upriver and on 25 July arrived at Dueling Bluff four miles below Negro Fort. Clinch was there waiting.[49]

Because of Negro Fort's obvious belligerence, there was no question about the need to protect the transports as they passed Prospect Bluff. Clinch and Loomis looked over the ground and that night concluded that they would use the dark to have the *Semilante* bring two eighteen-pounders upriver. The guns would compose a battery set on the west bank of the Apalachicola to cover the transports' passage. On the following day, 26 July, Clinch's men began clearing the chosen ground for the guns.[50]

Suddenly Clinch wavered. Admitting his ignorance of artillery, he nevertheless insisted that the battery's position was too far from the fort. Loomis was at first bewildered—what kind of lieutenant colonel knew nothing about artillery?—and then nonplussed. With growing exasperation and probably ever more willing to take Clinch at his word about his ignorance, Loomis heatedly pointed out that the fort was "within point blank range." Clinch remained adamant, and finally he ordered his men to stop clearing the site. That did it for the navy. Loomis curtly announced that he would take his vessels past the fort without any help from the army. Now that the campaign had come to its crux, the navy would handle it by default.[51]

At 4:00 the next morning, Loomis got his two gunboats underway. Within the hour they were drawing abreast of Prospect Bluff, hugging the west bank of the river, when pink spikes of light flashed from the fort's cannon ports. The fort's unpracticed gunnery could not find the gunboats' range, and naval gunners began to take the scope of the fort with cold shot. Loomis ordered some balls heated, and by the time they were ready, the last of eight cannon shots had found the mark. The ninth was hot, shimmering red when it went in the muzzle, sparkling across the dawning sky as it arced into the fort to smash squarely into its powder magazine. A muffled concussion fed upon itself with larger, louder, sharper explosions until, with a spectacular burst of light and sound, Negro Fort disintegrated, blowing into high-flung splinters that mingled with dismembered bodies. As parts of the fort and the people fell back into the trees or splashed hissing into the Apalachicola, the army, navy, and Allied Creeks paused in startled awe. Nobody had ever seen or heard anything like this. People in Pensacola, a hundred miles away, had heard Negro Fort explode.[52]

The blast instantly killed some 270 out of the estimated 320 people in the fort. Most of the survivors writhed on the ground in and around the fort's smoldering ruins. As it got lighter, the full scale of the disaster came to view, as did other things. The Americans and Allied Creeks who moved among the moaning wounded soon shook from these survivors the fate of Seaman Edward Daniels, the captive taken from Luffborough's party: a grisly ceremony of torture, they were told, had ended with his tar-smeared body set on fire. Clinch, who had stopped scalptaking by the Allied Creeks, now turned over to his Indians the two commanders of Negro Fort, the black Garçon and a Choctaw chief. Incredibly, both had survived the explosion. McIntosh's people now stabbed, shot, and scalped them. Loomis did not object.

The sailing master, however, was not so agreeable when he saw the Allied Creeks looting the fort's unscathed outbuildings. Clinch's explanation—that in return for their help, he had promised the Allied Creeks all of the small arms and ammunition seized at the fort—left him unmollified. In fact, Loomis did not know the half of it: Gaines had made a similar promise weeks before that possibly had attracted the Allied Creeks to the expedition in the first place. Clinch later sweetened that deal by also pledging to pay $50 for every runaway slave who did not belong to the Creeks.

Negro Fort kept most of its small arms in sheds outside the main stockade, so they survived the explosion. Loomis informally marked an inventory that provided Americans with a chilling testimony to the abundant supply system assembled by Nicholls and Woodbine. There were twenty-five hundred stands of muskets, five hundred carbines, five hundred swords, four hundred pistols, three hundred gunpowder casks, and various other military stores. Considering the conduct of the actual contest, such as it was, all of this should have gone to the United States Navy as a prize of war, but after the Allied Creeks seized what they wanted, Clinch took the next turn selecting items. Loomis sulked but held his tongue; from what he had seen in the last few weeks of Indians, friend or foe, he thought it wise to avoid a misunderstanding with the Allied Creeks. Clinch at least allowed the navy to take to New Orleans what nobody else wanted. The sailing master guessed that Clinch and the Creeks made off with items worth about $200,000.[53]

As soon as Negro Fort blew up, nothing could disguise Gaines's supply experiment as anything more than a ploy to put Americans near Prospect Bluff. Supplying the new American forts by water was impossible because the Apalachicola just above the ruins of Negro Fort proved virtually impassable. The *General Pike* drew too much water, so all supplies had to be removed from her; lightening the smaller *Semilante*'s load allowed that schooner to float upstream, but only just barely. On such unnavigable waters, the navy became an encumbrance, so Loomis, after destroying the remnants of the few settlements in the area, departed for New Orleans. No doubt he was as glad as his crew to do so.[54]

Clinch's people now had the unhappy task of completing the experiment alone. They escorted the *Semilante* upriver as they piled the excess materiel from the *General Pike* in small boats or dragged it overland. The men were edgy, and everyone thought they had reason to be. Campfire talk pictured stalking Seminoles in the flickering shadows just beyond the firelight, waiting for the chance to avenge their black allies. Soon daylight was doing nothing to shake the nightmare, so Major Muhlenberg took one hundred nervous men, the surviving blacks, and the supplies ahead while the remainder of the command, including the Allied Creeks, scoured the area for the Seminoles. The Creeks looked upon the sweep as another opportunity to collar more runaway slaves, but the search yielded neither Seminoles nor fugitive blacks. On 2 August, the American army headed for Georgia as well, another invasion of Spanish Florida scored in its annals.[55]

⁜

When the news of what had happened in Florida reached Washington, the administration reacted with silence. The invasion could not have surprised William Crawford too much, because by then he had received all of Jackson's letters penned during the spring and early summer. Those letters had made perfectly clear that Jackson planned some kind of aggression, and now that it had happened, Crawford decided to put the best face on it. Privately, the secretary hoped that Negro Fort's destruction would restore peace to the frontier, but public utterances were another matter. Spain incredibly had not made an issue of the invasion, so the Madison administration, only months away from retirement, decided that prudent silence was the best tactic.[56]

And yet significant concerns were at stake here. The failure to address these concerns left not only international but domestic questions unresolved, from the sovereign integrity of foreign territory to civilian authority over the military establishment. Not everyone overlooked the gravity of an invasion that raised "various and interesting points of national jurisdiction, jurisprudence, and national policy." Simply put, the army's action should have involved a "legislative decision."[57]

President Madison very likely agreed, but his only official action was to issue an order that from now on nobody was to cross into Florida to kill Indians. The gesture, benign as far as it went, incensed Duncan Clinch, who got it in his head that the lack of public approbation from Washington amounted to tacit condemnation. Clinch took to brooding over the perceived slight. Soon he was pressing to publish his report on the action, thereby to win vindication. His superiors—a chain that stretched from Gaines to Jackson to Crawford to Madison—said no. Nobody wanted it broadcast that Gaines had directly ordered Clinch's invasion. At one point, Clinch wrote directly to Andrew Jackson seeking support for a public exoneration. Jackson did not answer, but his adjutant did. Everyone knew that Clinch had acted under orders, said Old Hickory's mouthpiece, but publishing the report would not be politic since the invasion had targeted a "Fort . . . in the Territory of a neutral power." In about as many words, though more tactfully crafted, Jackson's adjutant told Clinch to shut up and accept Madison's silence as tacit approval.[58]

For the government, Clinch silent was more important than Clinch justified, especially because so far the military's little adventure had drawn neither domestic fire nor foreign protest. It remained to be seen, of course, what would happen on the Florida border. Everyone on the frontier, even Spanish Floridians, expected the Seminoles to retaliate for Negro Fort. Meanwhile, to the consternation of red and white slave owners, the destruction of Negro Fort did nothing to stem the flow of runaway slaves into Florida. Most of the runaway slaves at Negro Fort lived in towns and on farms some distance from Prospect Bluff, so the fort's destruction had left them still in place. As Georgians and Allied Creeks continued their predatory raids into Florida throughout the fall of 1816, however, many of these fugitives fled to the Maroon settlements on the Suwannee.[59]

Washington remained blind to it, but slowly Milledgeville came to realize that these white bandits posed as great a threat to the peace as the Seminoles did. They were only a small part of Georgia's population, but as Crawford had pointed out, they were some of the worst part. They operated out of the region around the St. Mary's River, bunching together in small bands of about a dozen each but making such mayhem that they threatened to hurl the Georgia frontier into a full-scale Indian war. In one typical incident, three of these outlaws ambled down to St. Augustine, where, eight miles outside of town, they abducted a free black family to sell in Georgia. Of course, Florida planters complained about such activities, but the decrepit Spanish administration could provide no real defense against the raiders, and American authorities seemed indifferent. At the end of September, a large gang of raiders openly outfitted themselves in Camden County to maraud deep into the Alachua lands. They returned with deerskins and what they claimed were Seminole scalps, but one of them in fact belonged to an Allied Creek known to whites as Indian George. The outlaws had found him alone near St. Mary's. They shot him dead for six horses.[60]

These and other obnoxious activities—especially slave-stealing and illegal homesteading in the ceded territory—increased after the United States destroyed Negro Fort. The people committing these acts correctly assumed that many of the runaways in the area of Negro Fort had not been in it. They also assumed—though not so correctly—that the fort's destruction had made the frontier safer. One assumption encouraged them to erect isolated sheds in the wilderness, and the other invited them to supplement their sparse standard of living by raiding into Florida for slaves and livestock. Even when authorities caught these thieves, efforts to prosecute them stumbled over legal points such as their having committed their crimes in Spanish Florida.[61]

Technical impediments to law enforcement along with the physical inability to patrol the lengthy border helped widen a circle of corruption. As the cotton frontier expanded, labor shortages increased the value of slaves, and the temptation of profit became harder to resist. Even people who would have never thought of slave-raiding in Florida sometimes stretched the truth about their own runaways. In the late summer of 1816, letters inundated Governor David B. Mitchell's office, all from people with an exaggerated estimate of how many slaves Clinch had recovered at Negro Fort. Each of these correspondents insisted that the vague newspaper descriptions of Clinch's captives matched those of their own fugitives.[62]

Yet even under the weight of large abuses and little corruptions, the frontier remained persistently peaceful in the fall of 1816, as though nothing could shake it to violence. White raids caused no serious reprisals, and when one Georgian turned up dead near Fort Gaines in mid-October, Clinch declared the murder an isolated act committed by one Indian and turned the matter over to the Allied Creeks. Crawford's private prediction of peace seemed so accurate that he prepared to assign the frontier garrisons to roadwork elsewhere. By the end of the year, the army, without telling Washington, would abandon its new Fort Scott even before its timbers had weathered. The army said that south-western Georgia had become so tranquil that the outpost was a pointless extravagance.[63]

The quiet also allowed the commander of the Southern Division to attend to some items wanting attention. Andrew Jackson grumbled over the negotiations Crawford had ordered between the Creeks, Cherokees, Choctaws, and Chickasaws to delineate each tribe's domain. The talks went slowly. Jackson blamed Big Warrior, who, the general said, had become a habitual obstructionist. Showing the commissioners how to conduct treaty negotiations, Jackson bypassed the Creeks to make a treaty with the Cherokees and Choctaws that acquired the disputed land touching to the northern part of the Creek cession.[64]

The agreement at least had the advantage of conforming to what William Crawford had wanted in the first place, but Big Warrior and Little Prince had felt uneasy engaging in another treaty negotiation with Andrew Jackson. Now they did not even have Benjamin Hawkins to commiserate with—in truth the only real function the ineffectual agent had served at the end—nor did they have any evidence that their annu-ity, interrupted by the Creek War, would ever be resumed. The aging headmen agreed: they would send a delegation directly to Washington. William McIntosh, increasingly influential and hence eminent, would lead the group to convince the Great White Father that the Creeks would no longer listen to outsiders. McIntosh's golden tongue, they hoped, would win back the annuity they had lost while they and the Red Sticks were at one another's throats.[65]

The Creeks still had no permanent agent, Philemon Hawkins continuing as a temporary replacement. Creek leaders grateful for Duncan Clinch's generosity on the Negro Fort expedition wanted him to succeed Hawkins. They did not know that the Madison administration had already offered the job to the Georgia governor, David B. Mitchell.

The upcoming November presidential election assured an uncontested triumph to James Monroe, and William H. Crawford left the War Department to take over the Treasury even before Madison left office. Crawford, always mindful of his political future, labored to cast his patronage net in a wide arc before leaving his post, placing supporters in as many positions as possible to increase his hold over Georgia politics. State politics in Georgia had sunk into a nasty rivalry between two parties: the Crawford–Troup faction led by Crawford and his ally George M. Troup, cousin to William McIntosh; and the Clark faction, headed by John Clark, son of the Revolutionary War hero Elijah Clark. The contention between these two groups derived not just from the desire to exclude one's rivals from office. Class consciousness and all the visceral reflexes inspired by it came into play as well. The Crawfordites represented old-style republicanism of erudite and gentried families, a reflection of Crawford's Virginia roots. Clark men comprised the denizens of piney woods, the day laborers of towns and villages, the subsistence farmers, and the squatters in the ceded territory. They were the poorer elements of the population, the people Crawford lumped into a large mass and described as the worst part of the citizenry. In a few years, they would be describing themselves as Jacksonians.

David B. Mitchell belonged to the Crawford faction in Georgia politics. He had come from his native Scotland to Georgia when only seventeen to claim property he inherited from his uncle. Mitchell studied law, entered politics, and became solicitor general of the state in 1795. He served in the infamous Georgia legislature of 1796 that had been corrupted by bribing land speculators to pass the Yazoo Act, land legislation that virtually gave away millions of acres and thus became the most notorious scandal of its generation. David Mitchell would gain a reputation as an honest politician by voting against the Yazoo Act. He supported the declaration of war in 1812, and at Madison's behest in that year, he engaged in a futile effort to mediate between Spanish East Florida and the Patriots. Governor of Georgia until Peter Early replaced him in 1813, Mitchell reclaimed the office in 1815. Now Crawford eagerly surveyed the prospect of having Mitchell become the Creek agent while another Crawfordite succeeded him in Milledgeville. William Rabun could be that man if Crawfordites could arrange the tricky shuffling of offices. Rabun would become the president of the Georgia senate, second in line for a vacated governorship, but not until the next legislative session. Governor Mitchell would have to delay his resignation and postpone his assumption of the Creek Agency until Rabun could take his place.[66]

It was a complicated but not impossible plan, especially for seasoned professionals. The initial problem was that Mitchell did not want to become the Creek agent. At least, he did not want to live in the Creek Nation the way Benjamin Hawkins eccentrically had. Crawford balked at that. Madison, he said, would never consent to such an arrangement because it would reveal the appointment as a straight political sinecure. Perhaps, the secretary cajoled, Mitchell could set up a residence in the Creek Nation and then rarely visit it. At least the appearance of living with the Creeks would help prevent blame from settling on Mitchell for Creek misdeeds. With such letters that alternated between describing the agency as a plum and Mitchell's taking it a duty, Crawford maintained a steady pressure that finally paid off. Mitchell accepted the position, and Crawford set in motion the machinery that would place Mitchell and Rabun in their new positions the following March. The secretary was not the top dog in Georgia politics for nothing.[67]

Meanwhile, Andrew Jackson wasted no time contacting James Monroe, the president-elect. Initiating the correspondence in November, Jackson provided advice about the policies of the impending administration, and Monroe warmly responded, aware of the power and popularity of the Hero of New Orleans. By the end of the year, the two had come around to the subject of Florida. Monroe revealed to Jackson his belief that the United States's occupation of Florida was inevitable. The surge of Americans into the land around Florida would put such pressure on the Spaniards that not only would they not want Florida, no one else would either.[68]

It was an odd letter, at once consultative and predictive, offering opinions that from the mouth of the chief executive were impolitic and

brazenly undiplomatic. And it was odd that Monroe, the new commander in chief, would send such a letter to Jackson, his military commander of the Southern Division. Whether the two of them realized it or
not—and likely both to some degree realized it well enough—they had
begun a journey that would become most memorable, starting with this
letter that Jackson would never forget.

∝⌁

General Andrew Jackson hated Secretary of War William H. Crawford,
and the secretary returned the favor with pleasure. Although no clear
evidence for the origins of the mutual animus exists, it is easy enough to
discern its causes, some obviously petty. Crawford's political ambitions
would have made the politically popular Jackson a rival under the best
of circumstances; Crawford's power in Georgia and at the federal level
made him a natural enemy for Jackson, the aspiring politician. Yet other
causes ran deeper and made the enmity even more malicious. Crawford
probably regarded Jackson as poor white trash who had come into
money, and Jackson likely thought Crawford a supercilious fop.

In a less personal vein, Crawford caviled over Jackson's increasing
independence from civilian control, and he tried to limit Jackson's
influence in a variety of ways, at each turn inviting a deeper loathing
from the Tennessean who saw any such attempts as maligning his
honor. When Jackson ally and chief subordinate Edmund Pendleton
Gaines tried to ignore Crawford's recommendation of a contractor to
supply troops on the Georgia frontier, Crawford told Governor Mitchell
to gather evidence demonstrating that the general did not have the country's best economic interests at heart. Crawford also opposed Jackson's
suggestion that the government quickly place the Creek cession on the
market. Jackson took the opposition personally, dismissing Crawford's
reason—the secretary said that too much land at one time would glut
the market and deprive the government of land office revenue—while
he accused Crawford of trying to stall the depopulation of Georgia by
intentionally hurting land-hungry westerners. Jackson, in fact, believed
that Crawford disputed the quick sale merely because Jackson had suggested it.[69]

With rationalizations, the two tried to disguise their individual prejudices and ambitions while meanly sniping at the character and motives
of the other. While that game heated up, the calm on the Georgia fron-

tier showed signs of ending. The cattle and slave raids from Georgia into Florida continued as Seminole frustration spread. Since Nicholls had left, the Indians had no one to complain to and no one to speak for them; that changed in the fall of 1816. Americans above the Florida line did not know it, but the British had returned.

True enough, the reappearance of the British had not occurred amidst great fanfare and celebration, for the Royal Navy did not materialize to bring supplies and advice. Yet to the disheartened Indians, anyone appearing with a British flag signaled the return of their friends. One they knew. George Woodbine, now a soldier of fortune, had returned with a new companion: a Scottish trader named Alexander Arbuthnot, whom the Seminoles would come to admire.[70]

By the end of 1816, Forbes and Company almost exclusively concentrated on developing an American market. Edmund Doyle reopened the store at Prospect Bluff, but many of his goods went to another store run by William Hambly thirty-five miles to the north. The Hambly store sold to Americans above the Florida line. After November 1816, the new Spanish governor in West Florida, José Masot, demanded that Forbes pay customs on goods coming from or destined for the United States. But the Inneraritys in Pensacola ignored the complaints, sometimes shipping goods directly from American ports such as New Orleans to the stores on the Apalachicola. Moreover, when the Forbes people cultivated the American market, they disregarded the less profitable trade with Florida Indians. Arbuthnot, a canny and experienced businessman, saw profits waiting in this void, and he intended to claim the one by filling the other.[71]

He was old—seventy by the time he stepped ashore at Florida—and he was wise in more than the ways of business. When Woodbine pledged renewed aid to eager Seminoles and claimed to represent the British government, Arbuthnot suspected it for the lie it was. Arbuthnot had come from the Bahamas, where decades of watching British administration had taught him what to believe and what to discount. Woodbine and His Britannic Majesty's government were no more connected than was Arbuthnot's trading sloop *Chance* affiliated with the Royal Navy.

To the Seminoles, however, Woodbine remained a Royal Marine, and the Union Jack snapped atop Arbuthnot's *Chance* just the way it did from the mastheads of English warships. So they talked to the two, pouring out the litany of abuses and injuries. Chief Bowlegs of the Suwannee talked, and so did Peter McQueen of the Red Stick settlements near St. Marks. They related the thefts of their cattle and horses and described the murders of their people. Either Woodbine or Arbuthnot agreed to draft a letter from Bowlegs to Governor José Coppinger of East Florida. It asked for Spanish help against the Georgians. Likely, neither the Indians nor their two British guests expected anything to come of the letter—Coppinger's limited resources could offer no real aid—but there was comfort in having done something. It was rapidly becoming cold comfort, though, especially for younger Seminole and Creek warriors, impatient with the inactivity of their elders and smarting under mistreatment unavenged and thus unending.[72]

The United States Army's behavior at this critical time can only be regarded as a mystery. At the dawn of 1817, neither Milledgeville nor Washington could ignore the growing unrest in Florida, but efforts to do something about it, mainly by curbing the illegal activity of some Georgians, inexplicably faltered. To a point, Jackson and Gaines can be excused for misreading the false peace to remove virtually all the soldiers from southern Georgia, sending most of them to what would become the new territory of Alabama. Yet when it became apparent that the situation had changed and the frontier faced renewed threats, neither Jackson nor Gaines responded. Mitchell, still sitting in Milledgeville as governor, wailed when he heard that Woodbine had returned to Florida and was attracting runaway slaves and Indians to the Suwannee River.[73]

Yet that reaction paled in comparison to the one that greeted news of the soldiers' withdrawal. Incredibly, no one told the governor of Georgia about the transfers, and Mitchell did not know that the army had quit Fort Scott until February. He found out about the undefended frontier because Seminoles, raiding into south Georgia for horses, fought a sharp engagement with about eight Georgians, killing one of them. Mitchell had bluntly declared that the squatters in the ceded lands antagonized these Indians, and he pleaded with the army to remove the illegal settlers before a general Indian war erupted. Now he discovered that the army had not only left the squatters in place but had left them alone.

For once, communications were swift. In early February, Gaines in Milledgeville traded several letters with the governor across town, marking a correspondence that took hours instead of days. To

Mitchell's dismay, however, it made no difference. Gaines offered to move two artillery companies from Charleston to the Georgia frontier, but Mitchell considered that a poor substitute for the Fourth Infantry. Reports from Fort Gaines told of how Seminoles had looted Fort Scott as soon as the soldiers departed, burning its buildings and evicting its caretakers, the mixed-blood Perryman family. Neither Jackson nor Gaines, however, saw the need to return the Fourth Infantry to the forks of the Flint and Chattahoochee; neither had they seen the need to inform the War Department about the regiment's withdrawal, a transfer that Duncan Clinch, aware of the hostility growing in the woods to the south, found frankly odd.[74]

So did Mitchell. Gaines explained that the regulars were needed in south Alabama because reliable reports placed Pensacola and West Florida under danger of imminent attack by Latin American revolutionaries. Georgia outlaws alone did not threaten Florida's security. The revolutions in the balance of Spain's American colonies threatened to spill over into Florida. Although Florida's Spaniards had no thoughts of revolution, insurrectionaries and adventurers farther south saw Florida as an ideal base of operations to launch forays into South and Central America. Complicating the international situation further, many such freebooters outfitted their expeditions in United States ports from New Orleans to Baltimore, occasioning an increasingly voluble protest from the Spanish government.[75]

The Spanish administration in the Floridas could no more resist freebooters in the peninsula than it could prevent Seminoles and Red Sticks from retaliating against Georgians. Everyone in St. Augustine, Pensacola, Milledgeville, and Washington knew this, so the Fourth Infantry's shift to Fort Montgomery, Gaines said, would allow it to better protect that American frontier from such insurrectionaries. Gaines warranted that Indian unrest still plagued the Georgia frontier, but he believed the two artillery companies would calm the area. He added that the calming effect would be especially enhanced if the companies had permission to pursue the Seminoles into Florida.[76]

Mitchell, unassuaged and unconvinced, continued to insist that the illegal squatters were the primary problem. The army only evinced interest in the Georgia frontier when passing through it on the way to invade Florida. Yes, he said, the Indians should be punished for illegal activity, but he also held "it a good rule to do as I would be done by."[77]

The Seminoles would agree. As George Vingant, his brother Stephen, William Hogan, William Lain, and William Young roamed along Black Creek in St. Mary's County, they saw an Indian on horseback. Just that quickly, Stephen Vingant killed him so they could steal his horse. When news about the murder spread, the whole countryside feared reprisal.[78]

On 24 February in St. Mary's County, shots rang out at the isolated homestead belonging to the Garrett family. As a neighbor ran toward the cabin, a dark shaft of smoke already billowed up from the woods. Obadiah Garrett, planter Israel Barber's overseer, was not at home, so his wife and two children were alone when some fifteen Seminoles came to the cabin. The Indians no doubt saw property in the Garrett clearing that looked familiar, items resembling those that Georgians had taken in a recent Florida raid, but such a discovery probably just excited them for a deed already planned. Their revenge was quick and thorough.

When the neighbor reached the clearing, what he saw must have taken his breath away. He found Mrs. Garrett—shot twice, stabbed, scalped. The two Garrett children lay dead as well. The neighbor did his best to put out the fire and clean up the mess, but it was a hard, sad job. The older child, scalped, had been a three-year-old boy; the younger, too young to give hair, had been a baby of only ten months. The charred cabin sent pungent smoke skyward, and the Seminoles silently moved through the brambly woods southward to Florida, in their minds at least now having done as they had been done by, trading a blow for blows in all quarters.[79]

ANDREW JACKSON

William H. Crawford spoke of Jackson as guided exclusively by "vindictive passions," and others noted the alarming propensity for Old Hickory to place personal prerogative above national policy or constitutional law. "One man with courage makes a majority," he would say, and thus defined democracy in terms that both vindicated and liberated him from the constraints of lesser men. Jackson never doubted the rectitude of his opinions nor the propriety of his behavior. *(Courtesy of the New York State Office of Parks, Recreation and Historic Preservation, Clermont State Historic Site)*

BENJAMIN HAWKINS

A native North Carolinian of good family, Hawkins spent the bulk of his adult life among the Creek Indians, holding the office of United States Indian Agent to those Muskogee people for twenty years. During that time, he instituted a white acculturation program for the Creeks. *(Courtesy of the North Carolina Division of Archives and History)*

WILLIAM MCINTOSH

He was the Creek National Council's principal law mender, in essence the chief law enforcement officer for the Creeks, and he also served as the speaker for powerful Lower Creek headman Little Prince. His mixed blood derived from his Wind Clan mother and his Scottish father, thus making him important in both red and white worlds. *(Courtesy of the Alabama Department of Archives and History)*

EDMUND PENDLETON GAINES

He had earned a hero's reputation during the War of 1812 for exemplary behavior under fire. Given the job of protecting the survey crews marking the Treaty of Fort Jackson cession, he brought to the southern frontier a sense of dogged persistence and single-minded determination much resembling that of his superior, Andrew Jackson. *(Courtesy of the State Historical Society of Wisconsin)*

WILLIAM H. CRAWFORD

rst the minister to France and then acting
cretary of war during the War of 1812,
rawford finally landed at the head of the
reasury Department in the closing months
f the Madison administration. He kept the
ost during Monroe's presidency, hoping
 use it as a springboard to a Crawford
residency. *(Courtesy of the Pennsylvania
cademy of the Fine Arts, Philadelphia,
ift of Charles Roberts)*

DAVID B. MITCHELL

He was a member of the Crawford faction
in Georgia and was tapped to succeed Benjamin Hawkins as Creek Agent shortly after
Hawkins died in 1816. His career in Georgia
politics had taken him from the legislature
to the governor's chair and finally to the
Creek agency, which he occupied during
the crucial time before Jackson's invasion of Florida. *(Courtesy of the Georgia
Department of Archives and History)*

NEAMATHLA

eadman of Fowltown, he had remained
loof from the turbulence of the Creek War
nd had presided over a village whose neu-
·ality resulted from its geographical situa-
on that made it more Seminole than
·reek. Yet Fowltown's location also placed
 in the vicinity of newly constructed Fort
cott, the building of which displeased the
eretofore unoffending Indians. *(Smithson-
in Institution)*

JAMES MONROE

He is credited with a conciliatory manner that helped to usher in the so-called Era of Good Feelings, the period following the War of 1812 when Federalists were fading and Republicans rose virtually unopposed. Monroe was lucky, if nothing else. In spite of chronic indecisiveness and remarkably ineffectual leadership, he emerged as a successful president because, for one thing, his administration acquired Florida and the Pacific Northwest from Spain. But it was Adams who did much of his thinking, and it was Jackson, whom Monroe feared, who did much of the acquiring. *(National Portrait Gallery, Smithsonian Institution)*

JOHN C. CALHOUN

Emerging from the War of 1812 as an ardent nationalist, this son of South Carolina finally went to Monroe's War Department as the president's third choice. Calhoun worked hard and did good work, but he bristled at Jackson's obstinate disregard for civilian authority and that, in the wake of the Florida invasion, eventually would be his undoing. John Quincy Adams thought Calhoun was brilliant but too principled for his and the country's good. Adams, as usual, was right. *(Redwood Library and Athenaeum)*

MILLY FRANCIS RESCUES DUNCAN MCKRIMMON

Nobody knows why the daughter of Red Stick prophet Josiah Francis pleaded for the life of the hapless Georgia militiaman that spring day in 1818, but her intercession saved him from a gruesome death. Either her beauty (described as startling) or her innocence (she was only sixteen) blunted the rage of McKrimmon's captors, and they let him go. The signal act of kindness caused her to be compared to Pocahontas, and indeed she, like her Virginia counterpart, was to die far from home. *(Courtesy of the Florida State Archives)*

CHRISTOPHER GADSDEN

In spite of his callow appearance, young Gadsden was a capable and conscientious junior officer who came of age in the Florida invasion of 1818. He not only drafted plans for Jackson's supply depot at Prospect Bluff, he also placed Old Hickory's artillery at Pensacola for the brief siege of Barrancas. His labors earned him a field promotion to captain. *(Courtesy of the Florida State Archives)*

CAPTURE OF JOSIAH FRANCIS AND HOMATHLEMICO

At St. Marks, the Red Stick prophet and chief were lured to an American warship flying a British flag. When Jackson seized St. Marks, Francis and Homathlemico were brought ashore in chains, their fates sealed. *(Courtesy of the Florida State Archives)*

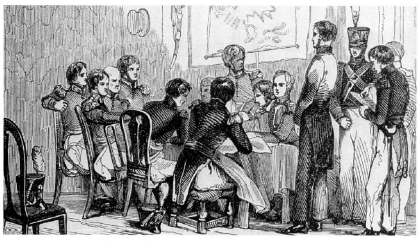

TRIAL OF ARBUTHNOT AND AMBRISTER

Neither age nor circumstance could save the elderly Alexander Arbuthnot or the youthful Robert Chrystie Ambrister. Captured separately during Jackson's March 1818 invasion, the two British subjects stood trial together at St. Marks as Jackson prepared his march on Pensacola. The court convicted both men of aiding the Seminoles, but sentenced only Arbuthnot to death. Jackson insisted, however, on Ambrister's execution as well. *(Courtesy of the Florida State Archives)*

JOHN QUINCY ADAMS

Monroe appointed Adams his secretary of state, much to Henry Clay's annoyance, but the scion of the prominent Massachusetts family proved to be talented, aggressive, and diligent in the office. Realizing the diplomatic leverage Jackson's invasion provided the United States, Adams bullied and maneuvered Don Luis de Onís into one of the most successful treaties the United States has ever signed. Virtually Jackson's lone defender in Monroe's cabinet after the 1818 invasion, Adams ironically eventually would number among Old Hickory's most despised enemies after having the temerity to challenge him for the presidency. *(The National Portrait Gallery, Smithsonian Institution)*

HENRY CLAY

"Great Harry of the West" had already accomplished great things by 1818, even though this Kentuckian's most lasting fame as the Great Compromiser still lay on the horizon. He was a consummate politician who, as Speaker of the House, had steered much of the nation's policy toward Britain before the War of 1812. He was ambitious, and he could be prickly when denied, so his fractious behavior toward the Monroe administration was guided by his disappointment over not getting the State Department. Although an ardent expansionist, he opposed Jackson's invasion of Florida—some said from self-interested motives—and he delivered a blistering denunciation of Old Hickory on the floor of the House in January 1819. Jackson would never forget it. *(Collection of The New-York Historical Society)*

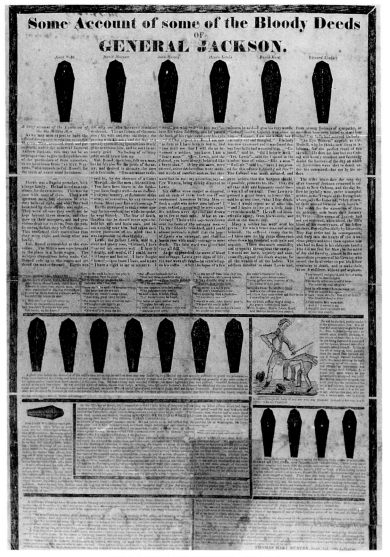

THE COFFIN HANDBILL OF 1828

Jackson's behavior during his southeastern campaigns provided ample ammunition to his political opponents. One of the most infamous and damaging examples appeared a decade later during Jackson's 1828 campaign for the presidency. Jackson partisans regarded the stark message of the Coffin Handbill so effective that they published an elaborate defense of Old Hickory that nevertheless could not escape the essential truth of the broadside's point. They had to make do by attacking the motives of the handbill's authors. *(Courtesy of the North Carolina Division of Archives and History)*

4

"Shall We Be Permitted to Visit the Spaniards?"

Nobody important paid much attention to the Garrett murders and what they meant. Military forces remained concentrated at Fort Montgomery to guard against the rumored Latin American revolutionaries, and Allied Creeks focused their attention on what was left of their northern border with the Cherokees. The Creek delegation in Washington tried to convince the lame duck Madison administration and the incoming Monroe administration that the Cherokees were peddling Creek land. If the Cherokees wanted to exchange their land in the East for land west of the Mississippi River, it was their business. The Creeks wanted to make sure that nobody confused them with such designs.[1]

The delegation wanted to correct other problems as well. McIntosh managed to wring a grudging concession from the government to make a greater effort to remove whites from Creek land, but the effectiveness of anybody doing that had become dubious. The steady trickle of white migration had become a Niagara. Alabama Fever, they called it, after the new territory created in March 1817 with Crawfordite William W. Bibb as its governor.[2]

The Seminoles sent no formal delegations to Washington, so their anger went unnoticed. In fact, it remained so until it became useful to stop ignoring it. Authorities dismissed reports that a thousand Seminoles and blacks marched and drilled near King Bowlegs's towns on the Suwannee; they paid no heed to warnings that these people planned additional retaliations against Americans and Allied Creeks for the destruction of Negro Fort. Even David Mitchell became complacent. While governor, he loudly protested the withdrawal of soldiers, but once installed as Creek agent in early March, he calmed down. The Garrett murders, he said, were an isolated incident of revenge. He still thought that regulars should be posted on the frontier, but only because their absence gave the impression of American vacillation. Better, he thought, to have those troops on hand to regulate whites. Mitchell did not expect any attacks on whites north of the Florida line, although news filtering up from Florida about Alexander Arbuthnot bothered him some.[3]

Arbuthnot had begun bothering everybody almost from the start, including the British government. Great Britain's minister to the United States, Charles Bagot, refused not only to correspond with Arbuthnot but to pay the postage due on Arbuthnot's letters. Bagot's behavior reflected Castlereagh's desire to maintain cordial relations with the United States. British indifference toward their former red allies had found expression in the chilly reception given to Josiah Francis and the rejection of Nicholls's treaty. Yet Castlereagh was not uninterested in Florida, and he had spoken out of turn on the matter. When rumors circulated in early 1816 that Spain had secretly ceded Florida to Great Britain, Castlereagh emphatically denied it to John Quincy Adams. But he also had stated that Britain would not countenance American aggression in the peninsula. Then the foreign minister made his mistake. In a casual conversation with the Spanish ambassador, Castlereagh described his remarks to Adams. The ambassador reported them to Madrid, where His Most Catholic Majesty's government seized upon them as though they were a talisman. From then through 1817, Spain labored under the illusion that Britain would protect Spanish Florida from American attack. Feeling empowered by the Royal Navy, Spain dismissed American efforts to negotiate the matter of the United States's southern border with Spanish territory.[4]

Yet the United States troubled Spain, even if a friendly Britain stood in the wings. Too many people in the United States chortled over Spain's Latin American difficulties, looking upon the distracting revolutions as providing the opportunity to seize Florida. Credible reports described filibusters outfitting in the southwestern United States to snatch Mexico, and abundant evidence still showed that American citizens helped pirates and revolutionaries equip ships to prey upon Spanish vessels. Growing popular sympathy with the philosophy of Latin American revolution threatened the equilibrium of United States diplomacy; perhaps it would force Monroe's recognition of rebel governments. On 3 March 1817, one day before Monroe's inauguration, Congress passed a neutrality act prohibiting preparation of ships that preyed on countries with which the United States was at peace, but ominously some Congressmen suggested eliminating that restriction.[5]

Don Luis de Onís worked under hard disadvantages in this climate, but he was used to it. He arrived in the United States in 1809, an emissary from a government unsettled by the Napoleonic Wars in Europe generally, in Spain specifically. Aloof but professional, Onís nevertheless barely managed to hide his disdain for the upstart Americans, and his resentment blossomed under the sun of a dozen indignities. A six-year delay before the United States recognized his government and hence accepted his credentials as bona fide did not help. Worse was Madrid's seeming ineptitude. Even by early 1817, Onís's government had not given him authority to negotiate anything involving Florida. The Spanish minister, taking the measure of American frustration, feared war.[6]

He need not have for the moment. In early 1817, James Monroe tackled the difficult business of organizing his cabinet without alienating the various factions of the Republican Party. He had already offered Treasury to William H. Crawford (who had held the post for Madison since October) and the attorney general's job to William Wirt. Monroe offered the State Department to John Quincy Adams, much to Henry Clay's chagrin, who considered the post his due and now Monroe his enemy. Clay had served with Adams on the delegation to Ghent that had ended the War of 1812 and had not liked him very much either, so with high pique he flatly turned down Monroe's offer of the War Department. Clay instead would remain in the House of Representatives as its speaker, influential and troublesome, always watchful for chances to embarrass the Monroe presidency.

The War Department seemed to be the first such opportunity. It was proving annoyingly difficult to assign and in the interim annoyingly difficult period. After Clay, Isaac Shelby refused it too. Monroe, apprising Jackson of his search for a secretary, casually mentioned that he would have offered the general the job except a mutual friend had said Jackson would not accept it. The friend was right—no doubt to Monroe's relief—but that only pointed to another problem. Everybody judged the War Department an inferior cabinet post, especially when it was without a war. The best Monroe could do for the time being was to leave the department under George Graham, long its chief clerk and since the fall of 1816, its acting secretary.[7]

Graham had his hands full in this supposedly dead-end job. When Crawford resigned in 1816, he left a messy controversy centering around Andrew Jackson. In fact, Crawford had set the stage for the dispute by transferring Major Stephen H. Long from Jackson's command without sending the order through Old Hickory. By the time Crawford left the department weeks later, the general had reached full fury over what he railed was an intrusive meddling by politicians. Graham caught the brunt of the rage. Failure to adhere to the chain of command hurt military discipline, Jackson lectured the acting secretary, leaving little doubt about where he thought that chain's first and last links lay. On 22 April 1817, Jackson ordered his officers to obey orders from the War Department only if they first passed through him.[8] He explained that to do otherwise "would be a tame surrender of military rights and etiquette."[9]

Jackson saw nothing wrong with this opinion, nothing untoward in his behavior. He would not have listened to the observation that George Washington had conceived the tame surrender of military rights to civil authority as the principal bulwark of republican liberty. Nobody in the civil authority mentioned it to him. Indeed, Acting Secretary Graham stood helpless before such an attitude. No doubt he counted the days until Monroe could find a permanent secretary.

⸘

Americans finally came to believe that Alexander Arbuthnot was possibly more dangerous than either Nicholls or Woodbine ever had been. As he set up his trading business with the Florida Indians, Arbuthnot took the novel tack of making these customers his clients. He would look after their interests as well as sell them what they needed. He wrote letters to everybody, continuing the futile attempts to contact British diplomats in Washington while listing Indian grievances in letters to Georgia officials. He naively expected the Georgia government and United States military officers to help recover Peter McQueen's slaves, and he protested about white settlements in the ceded territory. Like Nicholls before him, Arbuthnot insisted that the land belonged to the Indians because of Article Nine in the Treaty of Ghent.[10]

Gaines knew about Alexander Arbuthnot's activities among the Indians. In early April, he described Arbuthnot as "one of those self-styled philanthropists, who have for a long time past contrived to foment a spirit of discord among the Indians."[11] People on the Georgia frontier never doubted that trouble stewed on their doorstep. They saw Arbuthnot as another British agent among the Red Sticks and Seminoles, and they believed the stories about Indians and blacks dancing on the Apalachicola. As news of the Garrett murders spread, the region edged toward panic, blaming the army for removing soldiers. The few soldiers who remained huddled with settlers at Fort Gaines, under-supplied and just as unnerved by the rumors of the British on the Apalachicola, rumors that had the British distributing powder, lead, and tomahawks.[12]

Gaines, however, remained focused on Spanish Pensacola. He continued his plans to build up forces on the frontier and renewed his request to take the fight into Florida. As part of his efforts to strengthen Fort Crawford (built in 1816 near modern Brewton, Alabama), Gaines opened negotiations with José Masot, the governor of West Florida, and soon worsened already strained relations. Gaines wanted to use the Escambia River to supply the fort from New Orleans, so he sent Colonel David Brearley to Pensacola to secure Masot's permission to pass through Spanish territory.

The Brearley mission immediately went wrong. In a series of acrimonious letters, Masot said, in gist, that he had no authority to waive customs duties for foreign vessels. Only the Captain General in Cuba had such power, and Masot suggested Brearley treat with him. Brearley bristled at what he regarded as an imperious and dismissive tone, but there was more. An American supply ship had already arrived in Pensacola accompanied by a naval escort. Apparently Gaines had anticipated no objections from the Spaniards. But if Americans had regarded Brearley's request a mere formality, Masot did not. He demanded that the United States Navy quit Spanish waters. Gaines would have probably used Masot's demeanor as a pretext for a serious American response, but supplying Fort Crawford was more than a pretext—it was a real and expensive problem. Gaines knew paying a duty to Spain for the use of the Escambia was still cheaper than carting provisions overland.[13]

None of this made frontier Georgians feel any better. The two artillery companies Gaines had pulled from Charleston protected the eastern frontier of the state, but the region around the Chattahoochee remained undermanned. Fort Gaines continued to suffer chronic supply shortages even with most of its garrison transferred to Fort Crawford. Meanwhile, as though to test the limits of Seminole patience, squatters in the Fort Jackson cession continued their cattle stealing deep into Seminole enclaves in Florida. The Garretts' fate had not taught these people anything.[14]

All along, the military in the Southeast and the government in Washington worked at crossed purposes. While Congress passed a neutrality act and the president tried to prevent filibustering expeditions from launching into Spanish territory from American ports, Gaines relayed to Graham his regret that Allied Creeks and white settlers in the Alabama Territory had not run the Spaniards out of Florida. Jackson too revealed his disregard for the government's policies when he ordered Gaines to punish the Garrett murderers any way he could. In so many implied words, Gaines had Jackson's approval to take a punitive expedition into Florida.[15]

Neither officer felt the slightest trepidation about making up policy. They openly resorted to their habit of the previous year to interpret the United States government's policy as fundamentally in agreement with theirs. Jackson made no secret of this practice. At the end of April, he wrote to Graham, "As long as I have the honor to command I will enforce justice from our neighbors, whether Indian, British, or Spanish."[16]

That covered just about everybody. Georgians, though, wondered who was first on Jackson's list for the enforcement of justice, because it did not seem to be any of Georgia's neighbors. The military's ostensible indifference put the new governor, William Rabun, in a political bind. Constituents on the frontier clamored for protection. Clark supporters to a man, they were suspicious of the Crawfordite Rabun anyway, and it did not help that the new governor came to his office just a week after the Garrett murders. Major General John Floyd, commanding the Georgia militia, had castigated David Mitchell for his apparent lack of concern for the frontier—unfairly, as it happened, for Mitchell actually had tried to move the army to action. When Rabun seemed to ignore

Floyd's request for reinforcements—the governor's response miscar-
ried—the frontier believed it had evidence of Rabun's callous disregard. An angry Floyd on his own initiative mustered Major William
Bailey's Camden County militia, an impetuous and unfortunate act
matched only by Floyd's blistering letter to Rabun upbraiding him for
neglecting the needs of citizens. It all became very embarrassing for
Floyd. More than half of Bailey's men were the very thieves who had
been marauding into Florida; now, acting as militia, they attacked a
camp of Indians who had not done anything to anybody. News of this
wanton assault accompanied the revelation that far from ignoring
Floyd's earlier request, Rabun had answered it with a letter vehemently
expressing his desire to help the frontier.[17]

It would have been foolish for Rabun to do otherwise. David B.
Mitchell's vacating the governor's chair to become Creek agent made
Rabun only the acting governor, and he was left with little choice but to
act like it. He would stand for election before the legislature in November, his opponent the frontiersmen's darling, John Clark, so his solici-
tude for the frontier's plight was politically crucial. Down in the piney
woods, that meant a hard line on Indians. Rabun worried that these
stubbly-bearded men with their gaunt wives and spindly children would
harbor lingering skepticism that he, William Rabun, was a man of the
people. Instead they might think that he was the kind of citified fop who
would leave them to their fate at the hands of the Indians. Rabun agreed
with Floyd—with whom he had cleared up his misunderstanding about
undelivered letters—that people like Bailey's militia caused many of
the frontier's problems, but he dared not say so. Instead, he told Floyd
in regard to Indians "that the only method to keep them in awe, will be
to chastise them severely whenever they may be caught, until they cease
to intrude on the persons or property of our citizens." Thus Rabun con-
doned Bailey's attack on unoffending Indians and told Floyd to distrib-
ute their property among Bailey's men as captured booty.[18]

The governor's mailbag regularly arrived stuffed with offers to join a
march against the Florida Indians.[19] Yet as Rabun learned more about
the squatters along the southern border, he reconsidered the entire situation. In early summer, Georgia authorities traveled the Fort Jackson
cession with the aim of evicting interlopers, and what they found
had them gaping in disbelief mixed with disgust. These backwoods
denizens lived without manners or morals, cheerfully divulging that

they had legal rights to settle on these lands because they had traded their daughters to the Indians as payment. Mulling that, Rabun finally reversed his instructions about distributing peaceful Indians' property to elements drawn from such stock. They would only view it as an encouragement to go forth and do more of the same. Things were complicated enough without borrowing trouble.[20]

✌

Actually, the frontier had already become more complicated than either Floyd or Rabun knew, and a variety of forces threatened its fragile tranquility. On the Apalachicola, Alexander Arbuthnot feuded with his rivals, Hambly and Doyle, while General Gaines continued to trade angry words with Governor Masot. The Gaines-Masot argument was immediately the more serious because the general could, if pressed, elevate it from shouting match to shooting war. Reduced to the simplest point of contention, Gaines wanted to transport goods on the Escambia River to Fort Crawford, duty free, and Masot would not let him.[21]

Gaines took the refusal petulantly, ignoring what he knew as truth: paying the duty was the cheaper alternative if supplying the fort really was the primary goal. But there was much more to it than the simplest point of contention. Gaines adopted a provocative tone toward Masot with a condescending lecture on the proper hospitality between civilized nations. Responding to Masot's insistence that the eight-man navy escort leave Pensacola, Gaines told Masot that these men were not "authorized to menace your excellency."[22] In the War Department, George Graham gauged Gaines's response as unwarranted and told him to pay the duties. By the time Graham's letter had arrived, Gaines had already decided to bow to Spanish customs, but he could not erase the angry words he had exchanged with the Spanish governor. That damage was already done.[23]

Another complication on the border also worked to damage Spanish-American relations. When rumors again circulated about Spanish revolutionaries planning to seize the Floridas, some Americans openly endorsed the idea. After all, they reasoned, these adventurers would likely turn to the United States for aid, probably in the form of annexation. These expansionists, however, had not envisioned the advent of someone like Sir Gregor McGregor.

McGregor was of a type uncommon even for his time, when the

soldier-revolutionary in Latin America was more ubiquitous than the missionary. After serving in the British army in Spain during the Napoleonic Wars, he had hired himself out to various Spanish American independence movements. These connections ultimately inspired McGregor's ambitious plan to strike Spain in the Floridas, thereby to divert already distracted Spanish counterrevolutionary resources. A few Americans did more than savor the plan; they apparently supported McGregor by providing him with men and supplies. Striking forth from Charleston and Savannah, McGregor planted himself, 150 men, and a revolutionary ensign on Amelia Island. It was 29 June 1817, the first day of the reign of Gregor McGregor.[24]

He might have chuckled over the ease of his first conquest. Even if it had been stronger (and it was not nearly strong enough to control West Florida), Pensacola was too far away to do anything about McGregor. St. Augustine had no such geographical excuse. Spanish authority in the capital of East Florida was simply weak, unable to administer much beyond the walls of the Castillo de San Marcos, and thus reduced to watching the strutting Scot with his friends claim Amelia Island and set up shop in its town of Fernandina without firing a shot, except in celebration. Governor Sebastian Kindelan at least took comfort that McGregor and 150 men could not menace the imposing Castillo. But the character of McGregor's people posed another threat. Soon enough this operation revealed what some had suspected all along. These men were pirates, either in aspiration or fact, confirming that by immediately assailing ships along the Florida coast. McGregor called it a blockade, and though he intended to waylay only Spanish vessels, nobody could assume that his "navy" would be so particular.[25]

William H. Crawford spoke for many when he declared McGregor's invasion as just the trigger to invoke Congress's long dormant authorization of the president to seize Florida should it appear on the verge of occupation by a power other than Spain. But even Crawford realized that the ragged edges of the current situation might not fit the congressional resolve of 1812. One hundred fifty men of varied nationality, including some Americans, could hardly fulfill the legal definition of a "foreign power." Clearly Congress had meant England; clearly Gregor McGregor was something else. Monroe chose caution. At most, he contemplated sending a few regulars to eastern Georgia, placing them at Point Petre, from where they could keep a watch on Amelia Island.[26]

It was not an uncharacteristic response from the Monroe administration. Cautious deliberation with plenty of opportunity for disclaimer and denial marked the Monroe presidency in all but a few instances. Here the administration was new at being forceful (or timid), so it was less artful than it would become later as it moved with indecisive decisiveness, feeling strongly both ways, formulating a passively aggressive policy that threw the dice while buying time. There was always the chance that a rebel takeover of Florida would, as some said, result in the offer of the peninsula to the United States. Better to wait and see, because then again the rebels might fail miserably. Spain had not stopped McGregor's modest forces, true, but neither had McGregor inspired Florida's inhabitants to rebellion. When John Quincy Adams returned from Britain to take up the State Department, perhaps he could negotiate Florida's cession with the owl-like Onís. Yes, it was much better to wait and see. And thus Monroe consigned his administration's Florida policy to a firmly wavering hand on the helm. It was what Jefferson, with a happier facility for rhetorical rationalization, had called awaiting the chapter of accidents. Monroe did not call it anything at all.

In any event, moving regulars from Charleston was not an easy proposition. The administration had to consider Jackson's order of 22 April 1817. The controversy spawned by Old Hickory's insistence that all orders from Washington descend through him had not died. In fact, it had only awaited another opportunity to surface. Crawford at Treasury complained privately about Jackson's prideful tail wagging Monroe's policy dog. To satisfy Jackson's personal protocol meant that men sent from Charleston to Point Petre would not arrive in southeastern Georgia until October. Crawford blamed Monroe as much as Jackson for the lingering controversy. "The silence of the Executive," he mused, "has no doubt been construed into acquiescence in the order."[27]

Monroe had not acquiesced; he merely had not intervened. Though he should have known better, he thought that given enough time the issue would go away. His letters to Jackson consulting him about policy and cabinet appointments illustrate the president's belief that ignoring the popular Hero of New Orleans was politically perilous. Time, however, was of the essence when events accelerated in Florida, and Monroe could not disregard the need for rapid communication between the War Department and all officers on the Florida border. On 4 August, the president sent Jackson a gentle but unequivocal message: all orders from the War Department must be obeyed, no matter their provenance or destination. Jackson sizzled toward another explosion, and Monroe, sensitive to the pungent scent of trouble, tried to snuff the Tennessean's short fuse with lavish praise. In October, the president again told Jackson that War Department orders were presidential orders and would have to be obeyed. Yet, he framed this remonstrance with such lofty assurances of everyone's esteem for Jackson that, for the time being at least, he averted a convulsion. Monroe would leave the matter to his permanent secretary of war—once he found one.[28]

While Jackson stood on principle, Gaines finally awakened to the perils developing on the frontier. Rabun continued to call for a greater military presence in south Georgia, and piney woods dwellers themselves wrote to Gaines that their lives and property were in constant danger. Meanwhile, the scattering of men Gaines did have on the frontier were still running low on supplies. The best he could do was encourage the settlers' patience and implore them to restrain themselves from tangling with potential hostiles.[29]

The full impact of the Garrett murders and another murder in July persuaded Gaines that Florida Indians, rather than rampant Latin American revolutionaries, posed the primary problem. Indeed, Gaines came to believe that these Indians would have to be chastised. The details of the July killing capped it. A fellow named Glass heard a shot near his homestead in the Fort Jackson cession of the Alabama Territory. He trekked into the woods to investigate and found a lone Indian woman who refused to answer any of his questions. As Glass approached her, an Indian warrior jumped from the bushes and shot him. Glass stumbled away, firing his gun aimlessly. A traveler found him, but the wound was serious and within a day proved mortal. Neighbors poked about the shooting scene to find a dead cow (doubtless from the shot that had summoned Glass in the first place), and others followed tracks to deduce that the two Indians at the Glass shooting were from a raiding party of fifty, perhaps sixty others. Soon enough, speculation had these people responsible for the Johnson and McGasky murders the previous year.[30]

It was little more than speculation. Hunger and desperation drove many Florida Creeks and Seminoles into the American frontier for food and plunder. Meanwhile, the Creeks of Hawkins's old Confederation exhibited little concern both for the plight and behavior of their Florida cousins. Meeting with David B. Mitchell during the first twelve days of July, all they wanted to talk about was the restoration of their annuity. They were willing, they said, to cooperate with white neighbors; they were even willing to abandon ancient laws prescribing clan vengeance for murders. Instead the Confederation would adopt laws that called for the direct punishment of actual perpetrators rather than indiscriminate killing of their kin. Benjamin Hawkins had labored more than twenty years for just such a cultural breakthrough. For the Creeks, of course, it marked a major cultural breakdown, a significant departure from their traditions that was sure to alienate them even more from Seminoles and Red Stick nativists, even as it would possibly fail to ingratiate them with white neighbors. In the immediate sense, however, their tactic literally paid off: the government restored the annuity.[31]

⚮

Gaines followed through with his alarm about recent raids from Florida by lodging requisitions for Georgia militia and planning the reoccupation of Fort Scott. Gaines intended to awe the Florida Indians with such moves. The garrison at Fort Scott would also recreate the conditions of the previous year, when the military had routed supplies from the Gulf up the Apalachicola. The same conditions might produce the same result, meaning they might provoke a confrontation with inhabitants of the region, whether Creek, Seminole, or Spaniard.[32] Anticipating such an incident, Gaines asked Tennessee Senator John Williams, "Shall we be permitted to visit the Spaniards?"[33]

That was in July. By the end of the month, soldiers of the Seventh Infantry had reoccupied Fort Scott, vacant since late 1816. The new commander was Major David E. Twiggs, a native Georgian and the son of Revolutionary war hero John Twiggs.[34] Twiggs immediately sent word to neighboring Indian villages that it was time to talk. Six chiefs answered his call to meet on 4 August. Though technically members of the Confederation, these six had not attended the July meeting at Fort Hawkins. They told Twiggs that it had been too far to travel, assuring him that geography rather than disaffection had kept them away from Mitchell's talks. They seemed happy to talk now and cheerfully consented to all the agreements reached at Fort Hawkins.[35] For Twiggs, anyway, it was so far, so good.

With the Indians presumably pleasant and placated, that left the querulous Fort Jackson cession squatters as the perennial bane of frontier peace. George Graham reminded Jackson in August that the army had the authority to remove these people. Of course, Graham implied with this that the army had the obligation to evict the squatters, but he had learned to issue suggestions rather than orders in Jackson's department. Gaines, concerned about Indians in Florida, did finally realize that white interlopers also posed as a major obstacle to peace. They certainly had begun to annoy him, mainly with complaints about stolen livestock. Gaines snapped that they should seek redress with the civil government. The army had no obligation to overlook the squatters' illegal residence while protecting their property rights. Perhaps Gaines was especially bothered by their presence lately because the first sections of ceded land were scheduled for auction in August. Jackson had been telling potential buyers about the land's richness; he had not mentioned its unauthorized inhabitants.[36]

The squatters were annoying, but the Florida Indians were much the more convenient target for blame, both politically and militarily. Gaines, after all, wanted an excuse to invade Florida, and taking the side of wronged Seminoles offered only a reason to discipline squatters. Gaines knew the truth of it, that what Alexander Arbuthnot was saying had merit, but it accomplished nothing to admit that. Much more productive for the army's aims was to blame Arbuthnot for encouraging Seminole obstinance rather than listen to their complaints that American rustlers had murdered five of their people. So Gaines interpreted the Seminole failure to produce the Garrett and Glass killers as bad faith. He saw Tom Perryman's refusal to permit slave hunters to meander Miccosukee land as an invitation to war.[37]

The Miccosukee Seminoles did not want war, and they sent talks to Gaines stating it. They only wanted whites to stop stealing their cattle and killing their people. They assured the Americans that the blacks residing on the Suwannee River were the residuals of British activity during the late war and had no connection with Seminoles. These words came from the headmen of the ten Miccosukee towns and as far as they went, they were doubtless true, but they did not go far enough. The headmen were old men, tired of running and wary of fighting, fearful of losing everything and destroying their people. When they promised peace, they spoke the truth. Yet they could no more promise peace for their part than James Monroe could for his. The Miccosukee headmen could not control their young men who chafed under the timid tendencies of their elders. Just as Jackson was wont to insist that his government did not understand the barbarity of Indians, young Seminole warriors grumbled that their government did not know the barbarity of whites. The attitude made both angry and ultimately ungovernable.

Indian frustrations only increased when the United States Army clearly planned to dwell on Indian transgressions and ignore American violations. The army singled out Fowltown for its highest suspicion, choosing to pester a town on the American side of the Florida line, just a scant fifteen miles north of Fort Scott.[38] After all, dealing with such an enclave would be relatively easy.

Gaines scoffed at the ten towns' assertion that because ten Indians had died at the hands of whites and only seven whites at the hands of Indians, the United States actually owed the Indians three more lives. Disregarding the arithmetic (precisely logical to the Seminole mind), Gaines advised Jackson that the Seminole tally simply meant that the Indians would not turn over the Garrett and Glass killers. Gaines concluded that the only recourse was force. At almost the same time he reached this conclusion, Fowltown raised its back over the treatment it had been receiving. Though situated on the United States side of the Florida line, Fowltown was isolated from Lower Creek enclaves on the Chattahoochee and hence closer in spirit to the Florida Indians than to the Georgia Creeks. The separation helps to explain Fowltown's neutrality in the Creek War and its growing fear of the expanding United States military presence. The village informed Twiggs that his Fort Scott garrison was no longer welcome on the Fowltown side of the Flint River, even to gather wood.[39] It was an impetuous display of territoriality taken by heretofore inoffensive Indians. More important, it was a significant act of resolute independence and implied sovereignty that Edmund Pendleton Gaines would not let pass.

∽

Preparing his show of force, Gaines began moving troops in the fall of 1817 from Forts Montgomery and Crawford in the Alabama Territory to Fort Scott. In Washington, George Graham approved the movements, but he apparently remained unaware of Gaines and Jackson's actual plans. Gaines said he hoped reinforcing Fort Scott would deter further Indian attacks and might awe the Seminoles into turning over the Garrett killers. At the close of October, Graham told Gaines to remove Indians from the ceded lands, excepting those who had been guaranteed certain parcels. Graham did tell Gaines that under no circumstances was he to pursue Indians into Florida.[40]

Graham was more than suspicious about the military plans forming up down south. He had to know that Gaines wanted to invade Florida. After all, the general only reflected the attitude of much of the Southwest and especially that of his immediate superior, Andrew Jackson. Spain knew this, knowing too that she would not be able to resist southwestern designs on the Floridas now that numerous revolutions and internal intrigues mortgaged her resources.[41]

Indeed, by the autumn of 1817, revolutions in Latin America thoroughly occupied Spanish officials. Filibusterers organizing in the southwestern United States and Latin American insurrectionaries threatened West Florida generally and Pensacola specifically. Meanwhile, St. Augustine grimly watched the situation in East Florida take on an ever worsening caste. Brigands and pirates flocked to Amelia Island, much to Gregor McGregor's dismay. The ubiquitous George Woodbine, still untethered and so even more game for adventure, arrived in Fernandina to show his friend McGregor some plans, the nature of which remains unknown. Whatever they contained, they did not include the deteriorating circumstances on Amelia Island. McGregor resigned what had become an illusory authority over this gaggle of thieves, departing on 4 September. Pennsylvanian Jared Irvine temporarily assumed "command," his most signal act of leadership being to dismantle all remaining vestiges of restraint on privateering. Irvine opened the island to pirates of all nations to prey upon the shipping of all nations. McGregor and Woodbine went to Nassau full of schemes, those also yet to remain cloudy but perhaps aimed at West Florida, where the year before Woodbine had talked to Bowlegs on the Suwannee. In the coming spring they would send a compatriot to the Suwannee. He was one of Woodbine's acquaintances from the Royal Marines, a youthful former lieutenant named Robert Chrystie Ambrister.[42]

On Amelia, Irvine's carefree reign soon had a rival regime upon the arrival of Luis Aury, who sauntered into Fernandina on 21 September. Aury was a French pirate who claimed to operate under the auspices of the Republic of Mexico in spite of the inconvenient fact that the Republic of Mexico no longer existed. Such a small detail was of little concern to Aury, for he was no ordinary pirate; he was a man of such force to exercise control over the previously uncontrollable criminals ranging out of Amelia. He intended no better fate for Atlantic shipping than they did, but he planned to concentrate more intensely on Spaniards. While making matters worse for the Spaniards—Aury cut off St. Augustine from the rest of the Spanish Empire—he also made things bad for the Americans. United States forces across the border in southeastern Georgia had to notice St. Augustine's distress, which could not have bothered them too much, and to detect an increase in smuggling into the United States, which had to bother them a great deal. Slaves formed the bulk of the contraband as the pirates took advantage of the unprotected and fluid Georgia-Florida border. The Monroe administration finally responded to the worsening problem because it had to. The president consulted with his cabinet on 31 October and decided to authorize the United States Army and Navy to clean out the nest of pirates on Amelia Island.[43]

Neither Monroe nor George Graham knew it, but the United States Army already had plans for Florida, but in another direction. While revolutionaries, mercenaries, and thieves moved with impunity throughout the eastern part of the peninsula, Gaines and Jackson diligently worked in 1817 to put the United States military into the western part. They intended to revert to the successful provocation of the previous year, attempting again Gaines's experiment in supply up the Apalachicola to Fort Scott. In October, Gaines ordered Major Peter Muhlenberg to bring troops and provisions by water from Fort Montgomery near Mobile, using the Gulf route to the Apalachicola. Gaines promised Muhlenberg that boats out of Fort Scott would come down the river to help bring up the men and supplies. It all sounded very familiar.[44]

Gaines sent a threatening message to any potentially hostile Indians. Instead of the women and children they had killed in the past, he said, they would now be confronting men; this time the British would not be there to help them. Gaines also wrote to Governor Rabun and General Jackson, both letters the same with minor variations. He told Rabun that reoccupying Fort Scott and reinforcing the frontier had not intimidated the Indians after all, so the regular army would need Georgia militia for the upcoming campaign. To Jackson, Gaines reported this request with the news that Twiggs had heard reports that twenty-seven hundred

Miccosukee Seminole warriors were gathering below Fort Scott. Gaines sent Graham this intelligence also. In letters to both Jackson and the War Department, Gaines conceded that nearly three thousand warriors seemed a high estimate of Seminole strength, but to Graham he quickly justified his call for Georgia militia. Fort Scott needed such reinforcements, he said, although with his adjusted estimates of enemy strength, it was hard to see why.[45]

Agent David Mitchell could not see why at all. The army's activities troubled him, especially because he was beginning a new round of negotiations for another Creek land cession in Georgia. Also he was trying to coax in more Red Sticks using the carrot of restored annuities, rather than the stick of war. Mitchell, who would be caught in a worse trap soon enough, found himself stumbling into a recurrent one in late 1817. United States–Indian relations put menacing military commanders and conciliatory agents on the same side to send contradictory messages to increasingly distrustful Indians. Here it threatened to conjure a full-scale war in the Southwest. In November, Mitchell heard from Graham that the administration only wanted to separate Indians and settlers, news that must have reassured him. Gaines had wanted to take war to the Seminoles in Florida, Graham noted, but the War Department had ordered him not to.[46]

Actually, the War Department by then had ordered Gaines to clean up Amelia Island. On 12 November, Graham issued orders to Gaines to proceed immediately to Point Petre and assume command of an expedition to seize the island. Graham asked Rabun for five hundred Georgia militia to assist the campaign. Before either of these letters reached their destinations, Gaines had already started his plan to chastise Fowltown. Georgia militiamen already moved toward a rendezvous at Fort Hawkins.[47]

Gaines moved his headquarters from Fort Gaines to Fort Scott to wait for the supply transports coming up the Apalachicola. Arriving there on 19 November, he immediately sent a message to Neamathla, the headman of Fowltown. Gaines said he wanted to talk, but there was more to it than that. Fowltown had issued that territorial directive to the Fort Scott garrison, and Gaines had decided to make it a point of issue. He had also decided to embrace to the letter Graham's permission to remove all Indians but a few specified Allied Creeks from the Fort Jackson cession. For their part, the Fowltown Indians, not represented at Fort Jackson, did not recognize the treaty's terms as applying to them. Neamathla did not have any reason to go to Gaines. He had less reason to talk with him. He refused the general's invitation.[48]

Gaines hardly paused before making his next move. On 20 November, he ordered Twiggs to take a force out of Fort Scott to Fowltown. Gaines authorized Twiggs to use force to bring in Neamathla and his warriors, but he was not to harm women and children. The major left that day with about 250 men. A forced march through the night covered the fifteen miles to Fowltown, bringing Twiggs to its environs as the morning sun came over the horizon. In the growing light, the Indians spotted the soldiers and foiled their attempt to surround the town. Taking fire on his left flank, Twiggs ordered a pursuit of fleeing Indians into the nearby swamps, and suddenly the whole venture turned messy and disorganized with two—perhaps four (nobody was sure)—warriors and a woman killed. Twiggs searched the town and found in Neamathla's house a scarlet British tunic and a letter attesting to British friendship for the town. Twiggs reported the discovery to Jackson, Graham, and Rabun. Oddly enough, he did not mention it in his report to Gaines.[49]

It did not matter. In only a few days another army expedition trudged toward Fowltown, this time with orders from Gaines to destroy it. Colonel Matthew Arbuckle commanded the soldiers who found an eerie silence at Fowltown, evacuated upon the Americans' return by the warriors who alone remained. They had taken refuge in the surrounding swamps and gamely fired on Arbuckle's men, losing five (maybe six—again, it was hard to tell) warriors for their trouble, but at least killing one soldier before scampering deeper into the wetlands around the Flint River. By then the smoke of their burning village was fogging the countryside.[50]

David Mitchell was horrified. Two years later in the Senate hearings on the First Seminole War, Mitchell accused Gaines of starting the war with this attack on Fowltown. True enough, by 1819 Agent Mitchell had reasons to gratify a personal animus against Gaines, but all contemporary evidence shows that before and after the attack on Fowltown, Mitchell tried to prevent the escalation of hostilities. In late 1817, however, events were rapidly spinning out of David Mitchell's control.[51]

William Rabun exulted over this show of force as a tangible demonstration of military preparations for a bigger campaign. Calls for the

Georgia militia variously from Gaines and Graham reassured rather than alarmed him. He did not see these clearly uncoordinated requests as disjointed. Instead he thought they were a sign that Monroe intended to take more from Spain than Amelia Island. The War Department, if taken at its word, intended no such thing, but Rabun was not exclusively guilty of self-delusion. Gaines was helping. In spite of Graham's instructions, Gaines blithely prepared an invasion of West Florida from Fort Scott by setting up supply depots for the expeditionary force.[52]

The escaped Fowltown warriors could not forget the smoldering ruins of their village, and their anger was freshly raw as the advance boats of Peter Muhlenberg's supply convoy started up the Apalachicola. Gaines kept his promise to provide support for the trip upriver, sending Lieutenant R. W. Scott to act as a guide. When Muhlenberg received word that the Apalachicola was high enough for the trip, he sent Scott back to Fort Scott in a boat containing forty men, seven of their wives, and several children. Twenty men of Scott's party were ill and apparently so needful of medical attention that his boat ranged far ahead of the others.

Lieutenant Scott knew the dangers of the journey. William Hambly warned him that Indian warriors were congregating at the confluence of the Flint and Chattahoochee Rivers. No doubt they would try to prevent boats from passing up the river. Scott paused at Spanish Bluff to dispatch a message to Gaines that because so many of his men were sick, he would not be able to resist any attack. Nevertheless, he told Gaines he was proceeding upriver immediately—again, his men's illness evidently would not permit him to tarry.

Within two days a carrier brought Scott's letter into Fort Scott, and on 30 November Gaines sent a force downriver to cover Scott's passage. Although this detachment also had orders to move further downriver to help the main convoy under Muhlenberg, a sense of urgency revealed it as nothing but a rescue party sent to save the intrepid but nervous Lieutenant Scott. It would be too late.[53]

⚬✄

James Monroe finally found his secretary of war. South Carolinian John C. Calhoun accepted the post and arrived in Washington in early December to begin his duties. He was at least Monroe's third choice and perhaps his fifth, but that did not mean that Monroe doubted Calhoun's abilities. In fact, Monroe's failure to lure a qualified westerner for the War Department allowed him the luxury of selecting the most talented man he could find. Few of his contemporaries would have disputed that Calhoun was one of the most talented men in public life. Tall and angular, he was also a youthful thirty-six years old with a capacity for work that astonished friends and foes alike. A native southerner, Calhoun displayed none of the South's fabled charm and easygoing nonchalance. He rarely paused for idle chatter and remained aloof from all but his closest family. He had always been all business, old beyond his years, graduating from Yale when twenty-two, more inclined to efficiency than affability. His sharp mind and forceful character made him an indispensable part of Clay's War Hawk faction immediately upon entering the House of Representatives in 1811, and Speaker Clay had nodded at Calhoun's talent by making him chief lieutenant among the War Hawks colleagues and had made him the chair of the Foreign Relations Committee. Calhoun was ambitious, and he made up for what he lacked in popularity with persistence.

There would come a time when his political power in South Carolina would be virtually undisputed and unchallenged, but in 1817 he was a young man in a hurry, determined to earn a reputation for unalloyed nationalism and supreme competence. That was why he accepted Monroe's offer. The War Department was not the usual proving ground for future presidents—State was and hence Clay's pique at Monroe's slight—but Calhoun did not intend to be an ordinary secretary of war. Monroe would value his new secretary's energy and enthusiasm, and initially so would Secretary of the Treasury Crawford and Secretary of State Adams. The eager, young South Carolinian was about to discover, however, that doing a superb job in a competitive political environment is a quick way to make enemies.[54]

Calhoun's entrance at the War Department signaled a dramatic change in policy because he believed that the government should allow American forces to cross the Florida line to destroy Indian towns on the Spanish side. Monroe too had come to that conclusion, though with great reluctance and indeterminate resolve. As late as 2 December, he informed Congress in his annual message that the frontier did not need a large military presence because the Indians there were too frightened to make trouble. And on that same day, the weary George Graham dispatched his last orders to Gaines before leaving the War Department, orders explaining that because of the delicate negotiations with Spain for the Floridas, Europe would probably condemn an American army traipsing into the peninsula. In any event, Gaines by then had received Graham's earlier instructions to repair to the Georgia coast for the Amelia Island campaign. Gaines did so, but not before writing to Washington about what had happened on the Apalachicola River.[55]

After sending the runner from Spanish Bluff, Lieutenant Scott true to his word had immediately proceeded upriver. The river's current ran strong, especially near bends and bluffs, so the boat in such places became difficult to control and impossible to keep away from the river's banks. The group made progress, though, and Scott likely had begun to watch the wooded shoreline less apprehensively. Indeed they were almost home when it happened.

The current drove the boat toward a throng of Indians hidden in the foliage, perhaps commanded by Homathlemico, very likely intent upon avenging the destruction of Fowltown. They probably had stalked Scott's boat, waiting for the current to bring it close. When it slipped into point-blank range, the Indians wasted no time. Their first volley knocked down thirty-four of the forty men, including Scott. Many were too ill to flee, let alone resist, so the attackers made a thorough job of it, killing six of the seven women, sparing as a captive a Mrs. Stewart—no one knows why. They killed all the children, however, swinging some by their heels to smash their skulls against the side of the boat. It all happened only a mile below Fort Scott.[56]

Gaines wrote this news the same day Calhoun arrived in Washington, the same day Monroe's Annual Message described a tranquil frontier. He addressed the letter to George Graham, chiding the acting secretary for his and Monroe's insistence that no American military forces could cross into Florida. Surely the attack on Lieutenant Scott changed all that, Gaines said; and he continued saying it while en route to the Amelia Island campaign, promising that he would not go far into Florida if allowed to cross the line.[57]

Graham received the letter in mid-December and promptly handed it over to Calhoun, no doubt with a sense of emancipation. Just a week before, Calhoun already had modified the administration's position to allow action a few miles inside Florida. Now, as Gaines had predicted, the Scott massacre changed everything. The military had searched for an excuse to invade Florida for nearly two years. Now with Gaines's description of the massacre in hand, Calhoun gave the general even more liberty, authorizing him to pursue Indians anywhere except into Spanish posts. If any hostile Indians took sanctuary with the Spaniards, Gaines was to notify the War Department immediately and wait for instructions. Presumably, he would watch the Spanish post while awaiting those instructions, apprehending or fighting any Indians who tried to escape.[58]

Some might have wondered what the government in Washington was thinking about. George Graham had dispatched Gaines to Amelia Island, and no one at Fort Scott felt empowered to act on Calhoun's latest instructions. The general left behind him a nervous frontier. Angry Seminoles and Red Sticks roamed the woods, and Fort Scott remained beleaguered and isolated because incessant Indian attacks along the Apalachicola had stalled Muhlenberg's supply convoy. James Monroe took counsel and finally made a decision. It was time to do something about this. It was time for Andrew Jackson.

5

"The Supreme Law of Nature and Nations"

David Mitchell was livid. The reason for Indian attacks on the Scott party and Muhlenberg's transports two weeks later held no mystery. The destruction of Fowltown had pushed Indians over the edge. The only doubt concerned how many Indians had snapped, and Agent Mitchell intended to find out. Almost everyone assumed—correctly, as it happened—that Fowltown's warriors were involved in the attacks, but Mitchell could not wholly condemn them. The inhabitants of Fowltown had wanted peace, he believed, and Edmund Pendleton Gaines had deprived them of any reason for preserving it. Now Mitchell met with Allied Creek leaders to determine who else had joined Fowltown refugees so he could send negotiators to prevent a major Indian war.[1]

Mitchell took haste because of Gaines's parting letter to him. The general described the Scott massacre and informed Mitchell that some Allied Creeks had already offered to help fight Seminoles. That sounded like William McIntosh planning to collaborate in another unauthorized invasion of Florida, and Mitchell would have none of it. Unaware of the new War Department policy, the agent saw Gaines's plans as a clear violation of the instructions Graham had provided Mitchell in early November, instructions that emphatically prohibited any American forces from crossing the Florida line. Mitchell had no intention of allowing Gaines or anyone else to muster his charges into service. Meanwhile, if he could negotiate a return to peace, he could remove the need for Allied Creek military service. Knowing how head-strong the military could be, Mitchell saw that course as the one most likely to succeed.[2]

First, he had to remove any trace of potential Indian provocation. To that end, Mitchell had the Allied Creeks send Hopoi Haijo, headman of the Osochis (Allied Lower Creeks), into the Fort Jackson cession to per-suade any Creeks remaining there to leave. The headman was then to travel to Florida to take the measure of Indian belligerence there. Soon Little Prince reported to Mitchell that Hopoi Haijo had started for the Miccosukee towns only to encounter large numbers of Miccosukees who swore they had nothing to do with the Scott massacre. They repeated their insistence that all they wanted was to be left alone, and they described the Scott ambushers as Red Sticks.[3]

Hopoi Haijo and Little Prince believed the Miccosukees, but the Osochi headman had some troubling information to report. He saw two white men, the traders Edmund Doyle and William Hambly, with the Miccosukee Seminoles; obviously by their manner, they were captives. The Miccosukees had snatched them from their store on the Apalachi-cola on 13 December, and over the next few weeks had dragged them on an anxious odyssey through West Florida, a trek edged with the threat of torture and death. Little Prince assured Mitchell that Allied Creeks would take care of it, and indeed they did. Rescued by a party under Tustennuggee Chasco, Hambly and Doyle found themselves deposited by the Allied Creeks at the Spanish fort in St. Marks. This was not until 12 February 1818, however, and by then their ordeal had left them considerably worse for wear. More, it made them willing to believe what they heard at St. Marks; their capture had been plotted by their rival, Alexander Arbuthnot.[4]

⁂

Arbuthnot and his Forbes competitors feuded from the moment the Scot arrived in Florida. The level of argument naturally was tied to the suc-cess of Arbuthnot's store at the mouth of the Ochlockonee River, but there was no reason to believe that it would come to Hambly and Doyle's kidnapping and possibly their murder. In fact, Arbuthnot had received more threatening messages from William Hambly than the other way around.[5] In any event, Arbuthnot did not need to incite Indian resentment against Hambly and Doyle. They had managed that themselves with no help from anyone.

Miccosukee Seminoles and Red Stick Creeks knew that William Hambly had guided Duncan Clinch's expedition to Negro Fort. The Indians grumbled about the traders' increasingly cozy relations with the United States, and how those relations excluded them. Arbuthnot filled the trade void, but Hambly and Doyle remained as painful reminders of Indian hopes dashed by, in part, their betrayal at the hands of Forbes and Company. When the Forbes store openly sold supplies to squatters who raided Indian towns, Red Sticks and Seminoles had seen enough. In the summer of 1817, they called for the execution of Hambly and Doyle.[6]

Forbes's new marketing strategy did not work well on the Apalachicola, and as finances suffered, Doyle contemplated moving on. Arbuthnot increased the competition and further encroached upon Forbes's profits by opening a second store on the Wakulla River and taking over the lucrative trade with the Spanish fort at St. Marks. Furthermore, Seminoles made clear that the Forbes men had worn out their welcome by revoking the company's land grants on the Apalachicola, effectively expropriating not only the stores run by Hambly and Doyle, but their farms as well.[7]

Arbuthnot probably engineered this ouster. Certainly after it he became more visibly active in Indian affairs. In June 1817, he acquired power of attorney from twelve Seminole and Red Stick headmen, and soon he was dispatching another spate of letters every which way. He mainly pleaded the case of Florida Indians as victims of American aggression, especially to Bahamian Governor Charles Cameron and Seminole friend Edward Nicholls.[8] Also in June, Arbuthnot provided transportation aboard his schooner to Josiah Francis, who had returned from England to the Bahamas. Meeting the friendly Scot was the first hopeful thing that had happened to the Red Stick prophet in two years. His sojourn in England had proved fruitless, marked at first by an occasional empty ceremony and the bestowal of the customary baubles, but nothing more, and then not even that. Returning home via Nassau, Francis stayed there with George Woodbine only to have Woodbine confiscate the silver and gold tomahawk His Most Britannic Majesty had, through subalterns, presented him at one of those empty ceremonies. He returned to Florida after a two year absence without even ephemeral promises of help from any Briton who mattered. Arbuthnot, whether he mattered or not, was willing to help, so Josiah Francis clutched another diminished alternative as he slid down a spiral of diminished opportunities. He was very dispirited, as Arbuthnot described him in a letter to Nicholls in August. He had wanted to accompany Arbuthnot to Nassau until persuaded that his people needed him in Florida. The dilapidated Red Stick settlements must have been very depressing for the prophet in that summer of his homecoming. That he would have preferred the company of George Woodbine, who mixed hospitality with avarice, shows the depth of his despondency. Perhaps he missed Edward Nicholls, who had labored for the Red Stick cause in England, doing so no less ardently because of its futility. Nicholls had stayed in England when Francis left. They would never see each other again. Arbuthnot alone now remained in Florida as the last vestige of the British friendship—an old man peddling dry goods who owned a schooner and some pens and ink. Hambly and Doyle remained, too, but Francis made no secret of his contempt for them. He had not forgotten the way Forbes and Company had acted during the Creek War, and no doubt his people fully apprised him of the way the two traders had behaved while he was in England. Neither Josiah Francis and his Red Sticks nor the Seminoles needed encouragement from Alexander Arbuthnot to hate Edmund Doyle and William Hambly. Everybody knew that one of the last transactions out of their store had been to help supply the American soldiers who attacked Fowltown. By such deeds, they had vied for a place among the enemies of the Florida Indians. They had not been disappointed.[9]

✂

In the wake of the Scott massacre, whites on the Georgia frontier created chaos and called it military preparation. The state militia, already answering Gaines's previous call, now converged on Fort Hawkins by the hundreds and with added fervor. There they did little other than sit or mill around. Whatever they did, it was while hungry because the crude and corrupt contract system that was to supply their rations completely broke down in the winter of 1817–18. Also rumors drifting up from the south conjured disturbing images for these men: Seminoles had surrounded Fort Scott, said one; they had cut off Hartford, already vulnerable as Georgia's most isolated settlement, said another. But the militiamen did not need gossip to make them edgy. William Strother and Thomas Miller, two otherwise unremarkable fellows, gained instant if brief celebrity in that miserable winter by getting themselves killed and scalped within walking distance of Fort Hawkins itself. Wild stories in the newspapers about Alabama Creeks and North Georgia Cherokees joining Florida Seminoles to exterminate everything white in between notched up the anxiety. All the while, nothing put a speck of food in Fort Hawkins, let alone the reportedly besieged Fort Scott.[10]

Fort Scott was not quite as imperiled by Indians as rumor had it. Starvation posed a more immediate danger. Bringing men in from the Alabama Territory had nearly exhausted the garrison's already meager larders, and that Gaines had put supply solely at the mercy of the Apalachicola route did not promise much relief. Muhlenberg could not move up the river, and soon the garrison could not leave the fort because of constant, withering fire from across the Flint River. On 19 December, Lieutenant Colonel Arbuckle grimly noted that his stores had only twenty rations of meat remaining per man. He sent a runner to Fort Gaines.[11]

Arbuckle correctly suspected, though, that it was Muhlenberg or nothing. As of 20 December, Muhlenberg's convoy still stood thirty miles from Fort Scott and had resorted to kedging upriver against the strong current. With reinforcements and supplies, Arbuckle reckoned he could send a detachment to speed Muhlenberg's passage. That meant to help Muhlenberg he needed the militia, and he was not sure when or if the militia was coming. It also meant, nonsensically, that to help Muhlenberg's convoy, he needed Muhlenberg's cargo. When he received word that the transports had come to a dead stop and would proceed no farther—kedging became impossible while taking fire from Indians on the riverbanks—Arbuckle had no choice but to send down a relief boat under Major Twiggs. The relief party left under the shadow of Lieutenant Scott's fate, but the prospect of sending Muhlenberg back to the Gulf overshadowed everything else. If that convoy did not deliver muskets, ammunition, and food to Fort Scott, Arbuckle did not know what he would do. Likely he preferred not to think about it.[12]

Twiggs got through and soon returned, for what it was worth. He brought back to Fort Scott Muhlenberg's wounded—more mouths to feed was just what Arbuckle needed—and Muhlenberg's written complaints that Arbuckle had not been any help at all. Following quick upon this cheery communication came Captain Robert Irvin's response to the plea sent to Fort Gaines. It seemed unlikely, reported Irvin, that the Georgia militia would march to Fort Scott's assistance. The captain also told Arbuckle not to count on seeing any Allied Creeks, either. Agent Mitchell had criticized Gaines's attack on Fowltown, said Irvin, describing it to Allied Creeks as equal in perfidy to anything perpetrated by the Seminoles. When McIntosh and his warriors arrived at the agency, Mitchell had sent them home, telling them not to come back for a month. Captain Irvin, by now worked into high dudgeon, blamed peace feelers to the Seminoles for creating a false security among settlers. Many were leaving the forts, and even Hartford's citizens complained that the militia sent to protect them was as unnecessary as it was bothersome.[13]

Washington was more agitated than Hartford because the Monroe administration had no information about either Fort Scott or the Amelia Island campaign. The War Department had sent the original orders to seize the island to Major James Bankhead at Point Petre. The army was to cooperate with Captain J. D. Henley's naval force out of New York City. Calhoun and Monroe could only wonder if Bankhead and Henley had joined forces, could only speculate that Gaines had received his orders to join them and had departed western Georgia to do so. The whole operation seemed makeshift and hence its success unpredictable, so Monroe fretted. Having sent United States forces into action, the president yet remained apprehensive about the American military clashing with foreigners and what that might mean. He hoped the United States could take Amelia with persuasion instead of force—persuasion was so much more flexible, so much more tractable. The president got his wish. Nobody needed to shoot at Luis Aury to show him his time was up. Henley and Bankhead scared him off the island on 23 December. Amelia, even if it did not belong to her, was at least now in the possession of the United States of America.[14]

Gaines arrived three days later with a complement of Georgia militia and immediately made plans to return to the Georgia frontier. The entire Amelia business had proved an annoying distraction, and he was eager to carry on with his plans to the west.[15] The War Department, however, had learned of Gaines's departure from Fort Scott, and viewed from the War Department's vantage there was every indication that Seminole attacks would worsen. At least, that was the reason Monroe and Calhoun brandished for making a fateful decision: they ordered the commander of the Southern Division, Major General Andrew Jackson, to take direct charge of the campaign against the Seminoles.[16]

❦

On the day after Christmas, the same day Gaines arrived at Amelia Island, Calhoun sat down at his desk to write yet another set of instructions on how to respond to the Seminole situation on the Georgia frontier, but this time he addressed them to Andrew Jackson. The secretary apprised Old Hickory of the eight hundred regulars and one thousand Georgia militiamen in the area and authorized Jackson to call on neighboring governors for more militia if he needed them.[17]

John Calhoun's political career would afford him numerous successes in the coming years, but it would also be marked by a number of colossal mistakes. Accepting the cabinet post for the War Department at this critical juncture in the nation's affairs was perhaps the first one. Few would dispute that Calhoun ranks with another southerner, Jefferson Davis, as the finest secretaries the War Department would have before the Civil War. Like Davis after him, Calhoun would bring his department into the modern age by instituting reforms in diet, supply, and general organization of the military. In every instance, his changes resulted in greater efficiency and reduced cost, ever the holy grail of government. With such successes, Calhoun hoped to elevate the War Department to a level in the executive branch to rival the importance of State and Treasury. Monroe, who liked basking in success, shared his young secretary's visions for improving the department. It all looked very promising—up to a point.

That point emerged in the midst of the Florida crisis and would continue after it. Political jealousies prompted by presidential ambitions turned colleagues into rivals, especially in the case of William H. Crawford, always vigilant for threats to his ascendancy in a post-Monroe Washington. Calhoun's most immediate and enduring problem, however, was and would be his relationship with Andrew Jackson. By becoming secretary of war, Calhoun became Andrew Jackson's superior. Jackson did not have superiors; at least, he would not brook anyone acting like one. Alexander Dallas, Crawford, George Graham, even Monroe during his brief time at Madison's War Department—all had learned this, frequently the hard way. Constitutional prescriptions establishing who was in charge of the military did not take into account the mantle of glory (and hence the presumably infallible patriotism) bestowed by a few days of resolute work outside New Orleans at the end of the late war. Those prescriptions did not take into account the tremendous popularity of a man who, in addition to being a major general, was also becoming a political icon for a vast new constituency eager to flex political muscles in state houses, Capitol Hill, and the Executive Mansion.

As secretary of war, Calhoun would not have the luxury of constitutional nonchalance for political expediency, at least without running the risk of grave injury to republican government. Another type of man—what in that day would have been called a dodger or a trimmer, a scoundrel by timeless definition—could have swallowed the constitutional requirement and risked the republic, but not Calhoun. Taking his job seriously, Calhoun would simply have to take positions during his first year and a half that would sooner or later place him at odds with Andrew Jackson. It was a sure way to ruin one's career, sooner or later.

Actually, Calhoun had two problem officers. Jackson, the commander of the Southern Division, was in some ways no more difficult than was Major General Jacob Brown, the commander of the Northern Division. Naturally, these two detested one another. Jackson was junior in rank to Brown but refused to act like it. Both jealously guarded their authority over their respective departments.[18]

Jackson, however, made an especial effort to quarrel with the War Department. The dispute over how orders would be issued in the Southern Division had started under Crawford, had continued under Graham, and now fell to Calhoun. Jackson remained stubborn about his way of doing things, probably because he suspected Crawford as deliberately contriving the whole affair to embarrass him and diminish his authority. Monroe, who had hoped to let the issue die by inattention, now faced the necessity of completely resolving the matter before Jackson took the field. The president could not figure out how to conciliate Jackson without subverting the principle of executive authority, so he told Calhoun to take care of it. Monroe wanted the matter settled and Jackson happy, so he more than implied that Jackson should be pacified by making it appear he had won the point. In office less than a month and about to commit his department to a military offensive, Calhoun swallowed the government's pride and did the president's bidding.

On 29 December 1817, he wrote to Jackson to say that in most cases, the War Department would send orders to officers through division commanders; when circumstances made that impossible, the department would simultaneously dispatch copies of orders to division commanders. Calhoun actually could take solace that this note did not signal any great shift in policy, for it merely described a practice in place for some time, especially in the recent Amelia Island affair. Indeed, it was hardly what Jackson had declared as his minimum demand in his general order the previous April—that all orders would come through him or not at all. Nonetheless, Old Hickory now crowed that at last he had brought Washington to heel. When Calhoun's letter arrived, the general scribbled on it that the secretary had outlined the very policy for which he had argued all along.[19]

∽

Calhoun's 26 December 1817 orders to Jackson to assume command presumed that he understood them to carry a reiteration of previous instructions to Gaines, meaning specifically the restrictions about whom and whom not to attack in Spanish Florida. The War Department had copied all such communications to Jackson, allowing him to keep abreast of the Florida situation. Jackson knew about the early restrictions contained therein, a fact illustrated by his echoing Gaines's complaints about not being allowed into Florida. Acting the specialist in international law, Jackson had lectured the government that Spain's failure to control Indians within her borders violated the Treaty of San Lorenzo. The United States therefore had the right to fight the Seminoles wherever they might be—Florida, especially.[20]

Presented with that insistence and Jackson's reputation, Calhoun probably should not have been so casual about what restrictions still did apply, even with the wider latitude the government had provided to Gaines and now to Jackson. United States forces in Florida were specifically forbidden to assail any Spaniards, even if Indians took refuge in Spanish posts. Given Jackson's touchiness about overly elaborate messages from Washington, Calhoun's reticence is understandable. He let the matter slide by telling Jackson that he was forwarding (again) all of Gaines's orders pertinent to the campaign. Jackson, who had always noticed restrictions before, received this packet in Nashville on 11 January 1818. By then, however, he already had some ideas of his own.[21]

Five days before this pouch arrived from Calhoun, Jackson decided on the best solution to the Seminole problem. The United States military should seize Florida. Of course, this idea was not unique to or new with Jackson; he had wanted to take the Floridas for years, and the desire placed him among the majority of his neighbors and on the side of a large portion of the political establishment in Washington. Monroe wanted the Floridas, and he had told Jackson, in a letter shortly after his election, that he thought sooner or later the United States would have them. Secretary of State Adams busily tried to negotiate Florida's cession with the obdurate Onís, and Crawford also was on record as wanting the territory in American hands. What made Jackson different was that he had the power, if not the legitimate authority, to do something about taking Florida. What made him different, even from fellow soldiers like Gaines, was his unshakable certitude that the military could scratch this itch without inviting international disruptions and provoking domestic protests. Jackson apparently did not think anything would happen or, if it did, that it would amount to anything.[22]

The Spanish response to the seizure of Amelia Island and the Monroe administration's behavior regrettably seemed to support Jackson's speculation. Everything about Amelia Island was more complicated than it appeared, however. Military preparations in Georgia that amassed soldiers just north of the Florida line had become by the end of 1817 only one source of alarm for Spain. The American State Department also had sent unofficial envoys to Buenos Aires to meet with Spanish revolutionaries, seeming thereby to threaten Spanish possessions everywhere in the hemisphere. Indeed, the fear that the United States planned to organize and supply revolutionaries wherever it could find them drove Spanish policy for the next three years.[23] Encountering anything less than that level of American behavior allowed Spain to temporize that matters could always be worse.

Because Spain actually had misread the situation, the United States enjoyed a greater leeway than it deserved. United States relations with revolutionaries were never cozy, and they threatened to sour quickly, depending on the proximity of revolutionary activity to American borders. McGregor's behavior and then Aury's antics had seemed part of a British or French scheme to take Florida, and Florida was too close to the United States to allow that. Adams's unofficial delegation to South

America in November 1817 had not traveled to organize Latin American rebels. It had warned them that the United States would not tolerate such operations so close to American borders.

That done, however, Adams then marveled over the tantalizing opportunity for expansion provided by the easy seizure of Amelia Island. He labored to convince Monroe to keep the island, but cabinet discussions on this matter troubled the president. East Florida authorities had protested the seizure to United States officers on Amelia, and the issue could easily expand into a larger international incident, possibly involving the British. In early January, Calhoun joined Adams to argue for keeping the island, but Crawford adamantly opposed it. Adams believed Crawford's dissent sprung solely from his desire to diminish Adams's influence with the president, and he churned with worry when Attorney General William Wirt sided with Crawford. He had done so, Adams groused, only because it looked as though Crawford had won over Monroe. A few days later, however, Monroe swung back to Adams and Calhoun, deciding, in characteristic fashion, not so much to hold on to Amelia Island as not to give it up—at least for the time being. He would wait until other matters in Florida were settled.[24]

In short, and for whatever reason, the cabinet divided on the issue of Amelia Island and came only uneasily to a presidential resolve that yet remained tentative for the long term. Monroe would wait for the settlement of a broader Florida policy that so far the government had failed to formulate. On 6 January, the same day that the cabinet began wrestling with what to do about Amelia, Jackson sat down in Nashville to formulate his own Florida policy. He would propose it directly to Monroe. After all, they had communicated candidly about the matter before. Now, Jackson pushed candor to its limits and thus created one of the most controversial misunderstandings in American history.

Jackson wrote to Monroe to argue again against the restrictions in Gaines's orders that prohibited attacking Spanish posts even if Indians took refuge in them. Jackson wanted to attack Spanish posts in any event, and he revealed his true intentions about the campaign. He claimed he could take possession of Florida in sixty days and suggested that if Monroe wanted this to happen, he should send word quietly to Jackson through Congressman John Rhea of Tennessee. Jackson apparently saw no inconsistency between his yearlong insistence that the War

Department strictly observe the chain of command in its orders to his subordinates while he appealed over the head of the secretary of war for permission to attack a foreign country.[25]

Whatever the case, Monroe never answered Jackson either directly or through John Rhea. At the end of the 1820s, Jackson revealed what he claimed was a communication elicited by his 6 January letter. A decade after the alleged event, Jackson said that Rhea had sent him the requested authorization, which, after reading, he had burned. This most certainly never happened. When the controversy over Jackson's invasion broke out in the winter of 1818–19, Monroe remembered Jackson's 6 January letter. According to his later recollection, he had been ill when the letter arrived, so he had given it to Calhoun. In early 1819, he asked John Rhea if somehow he had unwittingly by some remark given approval for the seizure of Florida that Rhea had misinterpreted as an instruction intended for Jackson. Rhea assured the president that no such remark had ever occurred and that he had never written to Jackson about Florida. Monroe did not mention the matter then, and neither did Jackson; not until 1827 did Jackson say he received the Rhea letter giving Monroe's permission to attack Spanish posts.[26]

Jackson was lying. His most magnanimous biographer, Robert Remini, does not think that Monroe contacted Rhea or sanctioned annexation; he does believe, however, that Monroe wanted Florida and sent Jackson there knowing he would take it. It is a view shared by other students of the period.[27] Monroe's biographers—William P. Cresson and Harry Ammon—also believe there was no communication through Rhea to Jackson.[28] In a brief biographical sketch of John Rhea, Marguerite Hamer suggests that the whole matter arose from a misunderstanding in which Rhea conveyed Monroe's consent to Jackson about another matter.[29]

In a private letter in December 1818, just as Congress was about to begin its investigation of Jackson's conduct in Florida, Rhea told Jackson that after reading all the evidence submitted by Monroe to Congress, he believed he could support Jackson's actions. Rhea did not mention that he had transmitted to Jackson Monroe's approval for the campaign against Spain. In late January 1819, when Rhea spoke before Congress to defend Jackson's invasion, he of course made no mention of any letter conveying a message from Monroe to Jackson. He might have mentioned executive approval of the invasion in some fashion, however. Others certainly did, but not John Rhea. In fact, Rhea explicitly stated that "Jackson was authorized by the supreme law of nature and nations, the law of self-defence [*sic*]," rather than Monroe.[30] Other Jackson supporters also thought he had acted without orders.[31]

Little doubt exists about Monroe wanting Florida. He had told both Jackson and Crawford that Spain was troublesome and would be trouble, and he had mentioned in writing that Indians would fare better under the United States.[32] Yet Monroe never had John Rhea tell Andrew Jackson to seize Florida. Jackson did not mention the Rhea letter as a defense of his actions when Congress threatened to censure him in early 1819 because it never existed until he invented it almost ten years later. By then, political circumstances required that he discredit Monroe, and one day he would feel the same way about Calhoun. It was something more easily accomplished with a lie than the truth.

Monroe should have responded to Jackson's letter. That he did not do so was extravagantly negligent. Yet it also was entirely consistent with Monroe's management style of ignoring unpleasant or potentially troublesome tasks in the hope that they would go away or resolve themselves. The most disturbing facet of the Rhea letter controversy, however, is that an American general felt no compunction about starting a foreign war without congressional consent and an American president felt no urgent need to tell him not to. Jackson lied about Monroe's authorization, but Monroe had actually done worse by the country than unleashing the military for a foreign adventure. He had done nothing.

❧

Calhoun's new orders to Gaines, also sent on 26 December, not only instructed him to join Jackson as soon as possible but also suggested that if he thought he had enough men, he should return to southwest Georgia through north Florida, attacking Seminole villages along the way. Gaines, however, had already left Amelia Island to take the easy route through Georgia, sending word ahead to the Allied Creeks that he would need their services.[33] This was in keeping with the administration's intention to use available Indian allies to bolster Jackson's force. Monroe and Calhoun wanted to reduce forever the Seminoles and refugee Red Sticks as fighting forces, thus they authorized the use of any militia and Indians, too. Governor Rabun busily complied to pre-

pare his state forces for the march into Florida. Calhoun told Governor
Willie Blount of Tennessee to help Jackson recruit Cherokees. This
would be a major campaign.[34]

Gaines did not know until his return to Hartford, Georgia, that Jackson would take command of the campaign. While Old Hickory planned
strategy in Nashville, however, the military's situation on the frontier
rapidly deteriorated. Gaines learned that Muhlenberg was still fighting
his way up the Apalachicola to Fort Scott.[35] When that relentless journey finally ended with his arrival in mid-January, Muhlenberg found
that Fort Scott offered little refuge. Officers were resigning their com-
missions, rations were almost exhausted, and no reinforcements seemed
likely to appear. At Hartford, Gaines took heart, though, after finally
receiving Calhoun's instructions of 9 and 16 December that authorized
him to invade Florida. The rations he had ordered from Mobile had not
yet arrived at the mouth of the Apalachicola, but he had a contingency
plan to collect food in Hartford and Fort Hawkins and concentrate his
forces at Fort Scott. He reckoned that by 24 January, he could begin the
campaign. The Georgia militia's term of service was about to expire,
but Gaines intended to ask Rabun for replacements.[36]

The Georgia militia, in fact, posed several problems beyond the
lapse of their terms, but the militia's commander was not one of them.
Brigadier General Thomas Glascock assumed command of the militia
when John Floyd resigned at the end of 1817. An Augusta native, Glascock was all of twenty-six years old, but he made up for his lack of
experience with enthusiasm and a strong sense of honor. All the enthusiasm in the world, however, could not make up for his men's lack of it.
The militia's low morale no doubt resulted from short rations in part,
but recruiting practices also contributed to the malaise. Militia in the
early republic comprised a rambunctious lot at best, drawn from districts designated by geographical areas of about one hundred able-
bodied men between the ages of eighteen and forty-five. These men
trained in battalion musters held twice a year at their county seats. Such
affairs frequently became rowdy festivals in which training consisted of
consuming corn whiskey, peach brandy, and homemade beer while conducting some drills and sportively discharging firearms.[37] Aside from
such twice-yearly carnivals, extended militia service was an oner-
ous distraction for gainfully employed men with families to support, so
ranks tended to fill with the jobless, frequently emptied from jails and

gathered from taverns. Such men rarely had ties to the community and little sense of personal honor. Still, Gaines hoped the next batch of militiamen would be better.[38]

Jackson wanted a force large enough to do whatever he found necessary to do. As he prepared to leave Nashville, he wrote to Rabun asking for at least one thousand militia. Yet Jackson suspected the reliability of these Georgians, so he planned to take along men he felt were more trustworthy. Writing from the Hermitage, Jackson informed John Coffee, "I have made an appeal to your Vollunteer [*sic*] Brigade through the officers that commanded the Reg't for one thousand mounted gunmen—and flatter myself, that twelve hundred will be found ready." Jackson planned to meet the officers on the next Monday, 19 January, in Nashville to find out if two regiments could be raised. "If I can get 1200 mounted gunmen from Tennessee with my regular force," he concluded, "If the Georgians mutiny, I can put it down, and drive into the Gulf all the Indians and [their] adherents." Thus within twenty-four hours of receiving his orders to take over command in Georgia, he had summoned one thousand volunteers from west Tennessee.[39]

Gaines had already called the Allied Creeks, and Jackson was counting on their services as well. David Mitchell had prohibited their use before, but once he learned of the War Department's new position on invading Florida, he allowed McIntosh and his warriors to enter United States service, giving his blessing to Allied Creek participation after a 9 January meeting between Creek leaders and Colonel David Brearley at Fort Hawkins. McIntosh's brigade would eventually number between fifteen hundred and two thousand warriors.

Mitchell still hoped that war with the Seminoles would not happen, and on his instigation Big Warrior had sent runners to the Miccosukee Seminoles. Convinced that these people wanted peace, Mitchell persisted in the naive hope that talks could avert hostilities and make unnecessary an American invasion of Florida.[40] Mitchell's mission already had attracted the scornful disapproval of Captain Irvin at Fort Gaines and soon it would make for him thoroughgoing enemies of Gaines and Jackson. It did not matter if the Seminoles wanted peace, did not matter that, according to a traveler through Indian territory, the Indians were terrified, not hostile. Anyone who bothered to dwell on such facts to oppose the impending invasion ran considerable risks, as Mitchell was to discover. In early January, Gaines heard unsubstantiated stories that African slaves were being smuggled into Georgia (in violation of the 1807 prohibition of the foreign slave trade), and some had been spotted at the Creek Agency. Gaines did not pause a minute before reporting the story to Calhoun.[41]

Mitchell had no idea how ugly this accusation would become nor how serious its consequences would be. As he worked for a peaceful resolution of the Seminole problem, he remained pathetically unaware of his enemies and how far they would go in their tactics. When word of Gaines's allegations reached him at the end of January, he seemed genuinely puzzled. By letter, he asked Gaines why he was still so obviously angry about the delay in mustering Allied Creeks; Mitchell reminded Gaines of their conversation at the Creek Agency in December when the general had stopped on his way to Amelia Island. Gaines had evidently accepted Mitchell's reasons for withholding the warriors then, and so Mitchell could not understand the renewed anger. After all, the Allied Creeks were now in United States service. Not realizing what any of this was about, Mitchell recklessly admonished Gaines for not considering the peaceful intentions of the Seminoles.

Just how blind Mitchell was to the sticky web spinning around him was revealed by his mistaken belief that the imputation about his hampering military preparations was the much more serious charge. He explained briefly that a white leader of the Cherokees named Gideon Morgan had brought some slaves to the agency with the aim of selling them in the Alabama Territory. Morgan had since returned to the Cherokees to raise warriors for Gaines, but Mitchell suggested that since Gaines knew Morgan, he could ask him personally about the slaves. Mitchell also said that Brearley had been at the agency when Morgan arrived and could explain where the slaves had come from.[42]

The way the whole business had come up nagged at Mitchell, though, and in a few days he decided to take some precautions by telling his side of the story to Calhoun. Once again, he explained that when Gaines first called on the Allied Creeks, Mitchell withheld them because he thought Gaines's intentions toward Florida violated Graham's instructions. As soon as it was clear to him that those instructions had changed, Mitchell said, he had immediately prepared the Allied Creeks for United States service. Again, obviously unaware of the relative seriousness of the complaints lodged against him, he briefly explained the presence of the slaves at the agency.[43]

In February, Jackson joined in the accusations about slave smuggling, and as Mitchell began to piece things together, a sense of alarm gradually spread over his responses, especially when Jackson cited David Brearley as one of the sources of information against him. Why, asked the agent with some exasperation, would he report to the administration the presence of slaves he was trying to smuggle? Deducing now that his initial action regarding the Allied Creeks had sparked these other allegations, Mitchell again explained his previous position and denied that he had prevented Allied Creek participation in an authorized campaign.[44]

Finally realizing he had reason to be, Mitchell was scared. He turned to his mentor, William H. Crawford, casually asking for advice in a note whose timbre revealed more anxiety than calm. The treasury secretary replied that certainly Mitchell's enemies were behind the accusation about the slaves; Crawford said he could do little to help, however, especially now that the popular Jackson had joined the accusers.[45] It must have been a troubling letter for Mitchell to receive. In sum, it meant that whether he was innocent or guilty of the charges made no difference. Because Jackson had made the charges, Mitchell would be lucky to have few, if any defenders. Crawford also knew that although the whole matter would apparently disappear in the first rush of the Florida campaign, perhaps giving Mitchell the hope that it had been forgotten, Jackson would eventually revive his charges. Crawford knew Andrew Jackson.

∽

The problems of supply that had afflicted the military on the frontier in late fall now became a logistical nightmare as preparations commenced for the invasion. The men who would fight in Florida would leave hungry and stay that way. Some problems stemmed from bad frontier roads that made transportation acutely difficult and sometimes impossible. Also, the small population endemic to the frontier meant that normally only small amounts of food were produced near forts suddenly containing hundreds of extra soldiers. The major problem, however, was the government's contract system. Washington awarded supply contracts to the lowest bidder, advancing these entrepreneurs substantial sums of money to provide rations of usable quality. Frequently these contractors, already paid for something, supplied nothing at all.

That practice precisely describes the conduct of the two contractors commissioned on the Georgia frontier. In the first two weeks of January, the government gave O. W. Callis several thousand dollars to supply food to the regulars at Hartford and Fort Scott as well as to Glascock's Georgia militia. Callis never produced an ounce of rations, and soon officers at these places were reduced to scrounging for food wherever they could find it. The War Department fired Callis, replacing him with Benjamin Orr, whose negligence became legendary by the end of the campaign. Orr combined Callis's corruption with ineptitude. The few rations he delivered to Fort Hawkins wound up among Creeks camped nearby.[46]

Such misadventures had become part of military lore, so Jackson anticipated them. He had experienced the same problems during the Creek War. Before leaving Nashville, he suggested to the War Department that it abandon the use of civilian contractors and instead deposit money in local state banks. Army quartermasters could then purchase supplies from local farmers and merchants. Callis and Orr's failings had, in fact, forced Gaines to resort to just such a system or let his men starve. He borrowed $10,000 from Georgia's treasury and put it at the disposal of his quartermaster. Calhoun later endorsed Gaines's resourcefulness and came to agree with Jackson that the contract system should be eliminated.[47]

In the meantime, the system's shortcomings nearly starved men who huddled in and around forts on the Georgia frontier. By 13 January, Fort Scott had completely exhausted its meat. All the horses at the post snorted and shivered with distemper. Adding to the grim mood, rumors from downriver told of Seminoles and Red Sticks at the mouth of the Flint planning attacks on the fort and Chattahoochee River settlements. Arbuckle sent word to Glascock pleading that the militia share its supplies, but Glascock's skimpy larder was being daily depleted by his men, who, as their terms expired, headed for home with snacks for the road. The new muster of Georgia militia and any supplies with it would not arrive until mid-February. Arbuckle desperately tried to buy forty head of cattle from nearby farms, but their owners would not sell. Convinced his men would die otherwise, Arbuckle confiscated the cattle. He would let the devil, who was probably a civilian, take the hindmost.[48]

❧

Nobody in the south of Georgia and the Alabama Territory took lightly the rumors of impending Indian attacks. Throughout January and February reports warned about Seminole offensives against virtually every frontier fort and settlement. Responding in mid-January to an expected attack on lightly defended Fort Gaines, the Georgia militia dispatched a twenty-two-man relief mission. It stopped at Chehaw, an Allied Creek village, where fourteen warriors joined the journey to Fort Gaines. The constant stories of imminent Seminole attack had them so edgy that when they arrived at Fort Gaines, they took the calm there as a sign that they were too late. They watched from outside, not sure what to do. After dark, someone summoned his courage to approach the fort. Instead of dead soldiers, scalped and mutilated, the scout saw the Fort Gaines garrison routinely going about its evening activities. The relief party entered the fort more relieved than the regulars it was supposed to rescue. In a few days, more regulars arrived. Things were looking up.

Others, however, were not so fortunate. On 22 January, Glascock sent six men to Hartford to escort a supply train back to Camp Experience, the rendezvous point for Georgia militia outside the town. Once they had met the train, their number had grown to about thirty, and about that many Indians were stalking them. As the militia crossed a creek, the Indians made their move, killing two men bringing up the rear. The rest of the militia dug in on the far side of the creek, and there they remained, pinned down until Glascock sent reinforcements to bring everyone and the wagons into camp.[49]

Little wonder then that few Georgia militiamen wanted to renew their terms when they expired on 31 January. The effort to raise a new contingent of militia likewise suffered, and when counties were asked to fill a specified quota, they had to resort to conscription when no volunteers answered their summons. Many draftees promptly deserted. With some chagrin, Georgia authorities might have noted that the first muster in the fall of 1817 had assembled the comparatively conscientious and martial; the second in January was apparently congregating the unwilling and fleet-footed.[50]

Andrew Jackson believed that Georgia's recruiting problems stemmed from the state's stunted patriotism. He proudly regarded his enthusiastic west Tennesseans.[51] The predicted mutiny of the Georgia militia never happened, but Jackson's animus against Georgians would persist. It was an aversion as unexplained as it was unfair. Perhaps his hatred of Crawford colored his attitude toward the whole state. In any event, the attitude overlooked those men of Georgia's militia who had not shirked their duty or, once called, had not run away. They had shivered and starved with young Glascock on the frontier for months while Jackson's eager Tennesseans had tended their farms and families.

Gaines waited anxiously at Hartford, delaying a march to the beleaguered Fort Scott until he heard from Jackson. Old Hickory, meanwhile, organized his staff, gathering officers who had served under him in the last war. He designated Fayetteville, Tennessee, as the rendezvous for the two regiments of mounted volunteers, all to meet there on 31 January for their ride to Florida. He arranged for supplies and rations along the route. Jackson took care with these preparations because he planned to travel ahead of the volunteers and wanted no small impediments to slow their ability to catch up. Reasonably satisfied, he retired early on the eve of the twenty-second. He would leave for Georgia at dawn.[52]

In addition to his military preparations, Jackson had also attended to some personal business during the days before his departure. As bad luck would have it for him, while he conducted the Florida campaign much of the northern section of the Fort Jackson cession would come on the auction block in Huntsville, Alabama. As good luck would have it for Jackson, though, close friend John Coffee had become surveyor general of Alabama Territory and thus had supervised the survey of the northern section. Coffee provided the descriptions of the surveyed land to a select group of friends and speculators, the latter of whom paid a fee for the favor. This group alone privately saw public records so they could earmark the most valuable parcels of land. Jackson gave Coffee the task of placing bids on selected tracts while the general went to march with and fight against Creeks who had lost that very land in the last war.[53]

❧

Jackson, once started, moved swiftly into western Alabama. Five days saw him in Huntsville, where he paused to write to Calhoun. The secretary no doubt was grateful for the letter, for he wanted to follow the progress of preparations as closely as distance would permit. This 27 January letter told about Jackson's recruiting efforts and carried some advice. Jackson suggested the immediate establishment of a federal armory and arsenal for the Southwest. Calhoun agreed but felt that first things should come first, and the very first thing was the impending campaign against the Seminoles. Maps, or more precisely the scarcity of reliable ones for Florida, worried the secretary. The War Department had come up blank in its search, and Calhoun apologized for it. Perhaps Gaines, said Calhoun, would know the topography well enough to plot an invasion route. Jackson would discover, however, that Gaines knew little more about the lay of north Florida's land than he did.[54]

President Monroe also followed events developing in the Southwest, and they were beginning to make him nervous. Jackson's recruiting success pleased him, but by late January, Monroe's memories of Jackson's unpredictable nature troubled him. He told Calhoun to remind Jackson not to attack any Spanish posts; the international repercussions from such a rash act might ripple out from Madrid to include any or all of Spain's European friends. In short, Monroe did not see this campaign as one of conquest, did not envision it as a direct means of acquiring Florida, and still believed that Adams's efforts with Onís provided the most promising avenue for cession and settlement.[55]

The United States had apparently avoided any diplomatic difficulties surrounding the seizure of Amelia Island. To be sure, the Spanish back had bowed slightly, but Britain and France had not stirred, possibly because the American military's campaign on Amelia Island had been so unmilitant. Afterward, Spain played a delicate diplomatic game, one that by early 1818 had begun to tax an already nervous Spanish diplomatic corps. Foreign Minister José de León y Pizarro had concluded that Florida made for more trouble than it was worth, but he also feared that to give it to the United States would remove the only check restraining American aid to Latin American rebels. It is possible that had the United States promised not to recognize rebel republics, Spain would have ceded Florida in early 1818. But Monroe could not have made such a promise because of, for one thing, Henry Clay. The speaker had already scored political points by castigating the administration's reluctance to recognize and help brother republics to the south. If Monroe had disowned these republics, Clay would have brought the House of Representatives down around the president's ears.[56]

Monroe feared that Spain would provoke an incident with the United States, hoping to draw in another power, especially England. Monroe was not necessarily quaking before ghosts: Spain did hope that inviting British mediation of its American border disputes would involve the British as a Spanish ally against upstart Yankees. The United States so tactfully declined the British offer, however, that the Anglo-American rift Spain hoped for did not happen. Pathetically then, Spain fell to relying on a chimerical British presence in this controversy, pinning hopes on overanalyzed and misinterpreted remarks by Castlereagh while ignoring colder, harder evidence. The British government had disowned Edward Nicholls, had ignored Josiah Francis, and would not read Arbuthnot's letters. England had plenty of opportunities to take an interest in Florida, but it would gradually become apparent that Britain simply was not interested.[57]

Yet it became apparent so gradually that Monroe did not see it right away, and he wanted to make certain that no war broke out with Spain that might involve Britain. Hence, he told Calhoun to repeat explicitly the restraints on Jackson in Florida. Monroe might have rested easier believing that his military commanders knew not to attack anyone but Indians in Florida. For some reason, though, Calhoun never sent the repeated instructions. Why he neglected to do so remains unclear, especially considering the significance of Jackson's 6 January letter. It could be that the secretary was so busy pushing a military reorganization bill through Congress that writing to Jackson simply slipped his mind.

Perhaps Calhoun took comfort in the appearance that Jackson did not intend to do anything other than chastise Seminoles. Arriving at Fort Hawkins on 9 February, Jackson read a disturbing litany of messages from Gaines describing Fort Scott's supply shortage and much of the Georgia militia's departure. Jackson's immediate worry that a frontier without militia asked for trouble was confirmed on 19 February. Indians attacked a party of whites outside Fort Mitchell, killing one man and injuring a woman and a child. Jackson moved quickly to arrange what he believed would be a sufficient ration supply for his army's journey to and from Florida, and he raced to Hartford to meet finally with Gaines in person. Arriving there on 12 February, he finally had some good news. The new muster of Georgia militia was already collecting at Hartford and would be ready to march in a few days.[58]

Other matters, however, did not offer much encouragement. As he traveled the state, Jackson learned from officers stuck on the frontier for months just how desperate the supply crisis was. From Hartford to Fort

Early, a small supply depot on the Flint River, the situation was simply dispiriting, and when Glascock brought in some of the second muster of militia on 19 February, the mood did not improve. In fact, a letter from Arbuckle to Gaines added a sense of urgency. If he did not receive supplies soon, Arbuckle said, he would abandon Fort Scott. Gaines fired instructions to the Creek Agency to ship some rations downriver to Forts Early and Scott immediately. He could only hope they would tide everyone over until the long awaited transports from Mobile arrived. In any event, Fort Scott simply could not be abandoned; it was too important as a staging area for the upcoming campaign. Gaines hurried to Fort Scott to bolster the garrison's resolve. Jackson, prepared to do some bolstering of his own if necessary, planned to follow close behind.[59]

Gaines did not outrace his commander to Fort Scott. Speeding downriver from Hartford, his boat capsized. An officer and three enlisted men drowned in the swift current while Gaines and the remainder of his entourage pulled themselves to the banks. They clawed out of the frigid water to crouch wet and shivering, marooned in a roadless wilderness. They wandered, probably as much to stay warm as to cover ground, and finally staggered into Jackson's camp, half naked from the brambles tearing their clothes.[60]

They were lucky to find Jackson at all because his progress had been slow. He arrived at Fort Early on 26 February, the same day as the rest of Glascock's militia. It had taken everyone over a week to travel the forty-eight miles between Hartford and the fort because heavy rains had so swelled creeks that they swamped baggage wagons and sent bobbing columns of men scattering. Jackson stayed at Fort Early only a day before heading south, but the militia rested an extra day before following Jackson on the twenty-eighth, catching up with him at Chehaw village on 2 March. The Creek town was only ten miles from Fort Early, but Jackson paused there to buy food and wait for Glascock's militia. It was the last interlude approaching anything pleasant for this army, for the Chehaws were friendly, generous, and eager to help, even providing about forty warriors to augment Jackson's numbers. When everyone set out again on 3 March, the weather had turned colder, freezing ponds and streams, and even dropping big snowflakes out of a dirty cotton sky. The entire party—swelled by an additional six hundred when some of the Allied Creeks joined the column on 6 March—pulled into Fort

Scott on 9 March, having already waged a terrific battle against weather, terrain, and hunger. They had yet to see a hostile Indian.[61]

That they had seen Allied ones, especially in the significant numbers that joined them on the march from Chehaw, probably surprised Jackson. Gaines had persisted in claims that Mitchell would stop Allied Creek participation in the campaign. Jackson willingly believed it, although all Mitchell had actually done was to repeat his wish that disputes could be settled short of war. A letter from Alexander Arbuthnot had briefly encouraged Mitchell's hope, but once he realized the administration's resolve to defeat the Seminoles, he had actually helped Brearley muster somewhere between fifteen hundred and two thousand Allied Creek warriors.[62]

If anything had delayed recruiting Allied Creeks, it had been the need for Mitchell to fulfill an official duty. While preparations for the campaign got under way, Mitchell and Creek leaders negotiated another land cession to the United States. The previous October, Acting Secretary of War George Graham had commissioned Mitchell to purchase all Creek land remaining east of the Ocmulgee River. The agent labored throughout most of January to conclude a treaty on the twenty-second that acquired all Creek land from the Altamaha to the St. Mary's to the Oconee Rivers. The Creeks thus ceded approximately 1.5 million acres for a $20,000 initial payment and a $10,000 annuity for ten years. Mitchell told Calhoun that continuing resentment over the terms of Fort Jackson had prevented securing all the land the government wanted.[63]

Immediately after completing those negotiations, Mitchell turned his attention to recruiting the Allied Creek warriors for Jackson's campaign while defending himself against Gaines's accusations. Far from practicing obstructionism, the agent proved resourceful in his recruiting efforts. Adding to those Creeks raised by William McIntosh, Mitchell enrolled one company of Uchees under Timpoochee Barnard (son of Creek trader Timothy Barnard and his Uchee wife) and another company of Creeks from Cusseta. While additional Allied Creeks marched out of Fort Early to join Jackson, Mitchell sent others to secure the routes between the frontier forts. If Mitchell thought these worthwhile contributions to the campaign would make him part of Gaines and Jackson's team, however, he was mistaken. His troubles, while so far dormant, were only beginning.[64]

⚮

Not until he arrived at Fort Scott did Jackson know the full measure of the garrison's deprivation and fear. Having made do on half-rations and sometimes nothing at all for months, they had become prisoners in the fort. On 9 February, a boy and a soldier had ventured too far from its walls and died for their trouble not more than five hundred yards from the garrison. Constant hunger had intensified the harrowing supposition that Josiah Francis was collecting two hundred warriors at the mouth of the Flint River.

The state of Fort Scott's garrison only made Jackson more impatient to begin the campaign. Shortly after his arrival on 9 March, he sent his Allied Creeks to patrol the area. He issued a small portion of pork and a few handfuls of corn to each Georgia militiaman. He made plans to move. Those legendary supply boats from Mobile simply had to be near the mouth of the Apalachicola by now. The food had been slow in coming to this place, and Jackson knew how to fix that. He would take his starving army down to the food.

At 9:00 A.M. on 11 March, Andrew Jackson led his men out of Fort Scott, marching down the east bank of the Flint River. The following day, 12 March, twenty miles south of Fort Scott, Andrew Jackson crossed into Spanish Florida for the second time in his life. His army, famished and tattered, was a sight, but that was all right. As long as these men kept following him south and did what he told them to, they looked just fine to him.[65]

6

"The Consciences of Some Men"

Andrew Jackson's 1818 Florida campaign is generally referred to as the First Seminole War, yet this contest was neither a discrete incident of belligerence nor an isolated event of hostility. This war was actually a continuation of the two conflicts prosecuted by the United States against the Seminoles in Alachua in 1813 and against the Red Stick nativist Creeks in 1813–14. The flight of Red Sticks to Florida had not ended that war; instead it had merely carried that war south to meld with the other one. The massive land cession stipulated by the Treaty of Fort Jackson had encouraged disaffected Indians to continue fighting, and the depredations of white squatters both within the disputed cession and against Seminole and Red Stick enclaves in Florida had invited violent retaliation. In the two years following the close of the War of 1812, the United States military had conducted two aggressive campaigns either against Seminole allies (Negro Fort) or against unoffending neutrals (Fowltown).

Both sides claimed to want peace. Undoubtedly many on both sides were sincere. Yet the fighting had continued, sometimes pausing, sometimes spreading, but never completely stopping. When Jackson crossed into Florida, the war did not begin; it entered yet another phase. And instantly its objectives became different things to different people. The Monroe administration saw the campaign as a punitive expedition to convince with force Florida Seminoles and Red Sticks that the United

States would not tolerate attacks across its border no matter their provocation. The Allied Creeks saw the campaign as another chance to kill old enemies and plunder their cattle and slaves. Slave-owning southerners saw the campaign as a solution to the runaway slave problem: Florida Indians had long provided a refuge for fugitive slaves, and southerners hoped this military foray would at once retrieve runaways and destroy what they had been running away to. Andrew Jackson, however, saw the campaign as something else altogether. His objectives would be clear to everyone in a few weeks.[1]

Jackson's march into Florida was swift by nineteenth-century standards, but it was disorganized by any century's. Jackson's entire Southern Division had fewer than thirty-five hundred men fit for duty. The vast frontier that stretched from Missouri to the coast of Georgia made it impossible for Jackson to use half of these. Jackson supplemented his force with Tennessee and Kentucky Volunteers, Georgia militia, and Allied Creeks; soon he found himself coping with a haphazard coordination between regulars, the disparate auxiliaries, and difficult civilian contractors. Making matters worse, the military command had to wrestle with the logistical and communications problems caused by trying to traverse broad expanses of territory while maintaining the security of the rest of the Southern Division.[2]

One such area suddenly vulnerable to Indian attack—and about to succumb to panicky fantasies that saw danger even from Spanish Pensacola—was the Alabama Territory. Governor William Bibb watched the departing soldiers with mounting alarm. Soon he complained about how Jackson's campaign had left his territory defenseless. If Jackson wanted to fight Indians, Bibb snapped, there were plenty of them just two miles below the Alabama line, much closer than down the Apalachicola. Few regulars remained in the territory, mainly at Fort Crawford. Pensacola's Governor Masot again threatened to raise objections over the fort's Escambia River supply route. He had better not, wrote Jackson, who was clearly looking for any excuse; if Masot hampered in any way Fort Crawford's supply, Jackson told him, it would be interpreted as an act of war.[3]

The bare threat was, for the time being, empty. Jackson's immediate attention focused on the Indians south of Georgia and anyone helping them, but getting the army something to eat actually superseded even that objective. Jackson had to move rapidly downriver to meet supply transports he hoped were pulling their way up the Apalachicola. Indeed, he so spurred his regulars and the Georgia militia to this task that they ran far ahead of the Tennessee Volunteers and most of the Allied Creeks. The supply transports simply had to be there.[4]

Jackson had every reason to believe they would be, and he expected his little army to find them any day. Colonel George Gibson, the division quartermaster, had told him that the supply convoy would be leaving New Orleans on 12 February, now more than a month ago. For once, something went right. Within a day of crossing the Florida line, the hungry, dispirited men spotted the first of the supply boats rounding a bend in the Apalachicola. Captain Isaac McKeever of the United States Navy had brought Andrew Jackson his dinner.[5]

The food worked a tonic on everyone. They rested, and for the first time in weeks, everybody ate his fill. It was grand to camp and eat. Erecting a bivouac and cooking over open fires might have made them feel like an army, but an incident during this first encampment on hostile ground proved otherwise. Some of the men captured three Indians and assumed them to be belligerent, but within a day they had become so inattentive to their prisoners that one tried to run away. At least fifty muskets blasted away at the fleeing Indian, the scope of the barrage overcoming excited marksmanship to kill him. The volume of fire also aroused the rest of the army, convincing many they were under attack. After the pandemonium subsided, officers got everyone bedded down, and the army slept, after a fashion. The men would resume their march the next day, undoubtedly more sheepish than jaunty. In their first battle, they had killed one unarmed Indian who had been trying to run away.[6]

❧

On 16 March, the army arrived at what had been Negro Fort. Charred remains and scattered debris still bore witness to the explosion in 1816. Jackson had to give grudging admiration to Woodbine and Nicholls, though; this was by far the best location he had seen for a fort on the river. Liking the site and the terrain around it, he decided to build a fortified supply depot there, instructing his aide, Lieutenant James Gadsden, to draw the plans. Young Gadsden had a flair for the work, and Jackson so liked the drawings that he christened the new structure Fort Gadsden.[7]

Building the fort became a holiday for part of the army. Fed and idle—the men would camp at Prospect Bluff for the better part of two weeks—those of the Tennessee Volunteers who had managed to make the trip this far passed the time with sporting contests, an occasional fistfight, and other forms of high jinks that mark the activities of young men with nothing to do. Regulars, Georgia militia, and Allied Creeks spent their daylight building Fort Gadsden, but the Tennesseans who accompanied Jackson with the air of a Praetorian Guard roamed the camp making mischief. Some suspected Jackson favored the Tennesseans with light duties because he held them in higher esteem than the Georgians. While possible, the higher esteem probably resulted from the old political habit of catering to one's own state forces to secure a loyal political constituency.

In any event, Jackson did not much like Georgians anyway. One day while everyone else worked, a few rollicking Tennesseans undertook to give a Georgia militiaman a bath, hoisting him up to throw him in the Apalachicola. Jackson watched with amusement until Georgian Thomas Woodward intervened to stop the dunking. Woodward, part Indian himself, commanded some of the Indian troops accompanying the campaign, and he was menacing enough to make these boys know he had seen enough Tennessee antics for one day. An uncomfortable pause ended finally with their sullenly releasing the Georgian, but Jackson stood scowling. Finally he stalked away, cursing Woodward as an "Indian looking son-of-a-bitch."[8]

During the army's pause at Prospect Bluff, another Georgian fell into a far more serious predicament than rough joshing by some Tennessee rowdies. Sergeant Duncan McKrimmon of the Second Regiment of Georgia militia misread the uneventful nature of the campaign to believe the woods away from Fort Gadsden held no perils. With fishing rod in hand, he slipped away for a pleasant day far from the hammering, sawing, lifting, and carrying. The water was restful and the pastime soothing. McKrimmon probably never saw them until they were on him.

They were Red Sticks, patrolling the area and, to McKrimmon's good fortune, more interested in what he knew than anything else. That at least kept him alive and relatively untouched as the Indians dragged him into Josiah Francis's town on the Wakulla River. He told them everything he knew about Jackson's plans, but it could not have been much more than they already suspected, so poor McKrimmon quickly exhausted his usefulness. His captors stripped him naked, blackened his face, and tied him to a tree. They began dancing as a preparatory ritual for his torture and execution. Not far away, on the banks of the Wakulla, two teenaged girls heard the commotion and came running to see what was causing the excitement. They were sisters, both daughters of the prophet Francis, the older named Milly. She was only sixteen but already, it was said, a great beauty who took girlish pleasure in wearing the odd but fine garments her father had brought from England. Arriving in the square, she saw the dancing warriors circling McKrimmon and knew instantly what was about to happen. She ran to her father to beg his intervention, but he reminded her that tradition prohibited his interference in such matters. Only the men who had captured McKrimmon had the power to kill or spare him; yet, said Francis, he would not stop her from talking to the warriors.

When she did, they stopped their dancing while one exploded into an enraged explanation of why McKrimmon had to die. Whites had killed two of his sisters, he shouted. Milly said that killing the young white man would not bring back the sisters. She persisted. Gradually, the anger drained away from the scene to leave the warriors still in their tracks, no more to dance, and finally to cut down McKrimmon. Soon, at St. Marks, they would ransom him to the Spaniards for seven and a half gallons of rum, probably thinking they had gotten the better of the bargain.

After the war, after Milly with her sister and mother had lost everything, they surrendered to the army at Fort Gadsden. Duncan McKrimmon heard about this, so he traveled from his home in Milledgeville to Prospect Bluff, where so many months before he had gone fishing almost for the last time. He found the Francis women destitute, so he was happy to bring Milly a modest gift of money from the citizens of Milledgeville, a remembrance for her gallant, graceful intercession on his behalf. Duncan McKrimmon also asked Milly Francis to marry him. She gratefully took the money, but gently refused him. "I did not save you for that," she said, and indeed she had not done it for any reward. Neither for marriage nor money had Milly Francis saved the terrified white boy that spring afternoon on the banks of the Wakulla. She had just done it.[9]

At Prospect Bluff while finishing up Fort Gadsden, the army again counted its meals. The route up the Apalachicola had yielded only that first schooner, and Jackson had to draw on the meager supplies at Fort Scott. There was no need to tarry at Prospect Bluff if the wait was to be without food, so Jackson sent out a scouting party on 20 March to see whether supply boats were on the way from the Gulf. Three days later the regulars and some sixty Indians returned with the news that one gunboat and three supply vessels were coming, but they thought a storm had claimed the rest of the convoy. Two days later on 25 March—the army had been at Prospect Bluff now for nine days—one of the transports appeared, but only one. It carried eight days' rations. Jackson figured that would be enough. In any case, it would have to be. He would put the army on the march.[10]

Jackson intended to move on the Seminole towns around Lake Miccosukee, but he planned eventually to swing down toward the Spanish fort at St. Marks. Before leaving Fort Gadsden, Jackson wrote Calhoun that he had heard a rumor that Indians had taken St. Marks. He did not say when or from whom he had heard it.[11] Actually, Jackson had clearly issued instructions to Captain McKeever that revealed his prior resolve to take St. Marks, no matter what its disposition. Jackson told McKeever to take his boats out to the Gulf of Mexico and stand off St. Marks. The army, he claimed, had reliable information that Josiah Francis, Peter McQueen, Alexander Arbuthnot, and George Woodbine were at the Spanish fort. Jackson wanted to cut off all avenues of escape for these people. While the army approached St. Marks, McKeever could block their flight by water. Jackson expected the navy to be in place in eight days—exactly the number of days' rations he had.[12]

On 26 March, the American army struck eastward for the Miccosukee towns. Jackson's outward confidence belied his uneasiness: most of the mounted Tennessee volunteers still had not yet caught up with the army's race down the Apalachicola two weeks earlier. Furthermore, the bulk of the Allied Creeks still patrolled the countryside away from the main body. That had resulted from Jackson's instructions to William McIntosh, now a brigadier general commanding the sixteen-hundred-men-strong Creek brigade, to scour the west banks of the Chattahoochee and Apalachicola Rivers.

McIntosh accordingly had moved out of Fort Scott to do the only real fighting of the campaign so far. Things had started out slowly when, in early March, days of combing the woods had resulted in the capture of three Red Stick men, dutifully delivered to Fort Gaines. The commander there had no use for Indian prisoners—after all, they would have to be fed—so he gave them back to the Allied Creeks. McIntosh's warriors killed them. Rolling across the wilderness now with a purpose, the Allied Creeks fell upon the town of Red Ground on 19 March to capture 53 warriors (2 of whom were killed trying to escape) and 180 women and children. After a brief return to Fort Scott for supplies, McIntosh set out to meet Jackson on the Ochlockonee River.[13]

When Jackson's army pitched its camp on the Ochlockonee on 29 March, most of the Tennessee Volunteers had still not appeared and McIntosh was still en route. The heavy rains had swollen the river, so the army made canoes for the crossing. In only a few hours, they had nineteen vessels ready to begin the ferrying operation to the other bank, but their 8:00 P.M. start delayed everything. Not until 11:00 the next morning did Jackson have everybody across the river and ready to move out. Even this delay did not produce his Volunteers or McIntosh. Going into camp that night, the best Jackson could do was send Major Twiggs ahead with two hundred Allied Creeks, hoping he could surprise the Miccosukee town of Tallahassee. It was a fugitive hope. At dawn on the thirty-first, Twiggs and his Creeks entered a ghost town. Beating the surrounding bushes scared up only two Indians, and one of these escaped before anyone could question him. The other would not talk.[14]

Twiggs burned the town and waited for Jackson to come up with the main body. When it showed up late in the day, Old Hickory's patience was worn more than thin. No Tennessee Volunteers, no McIntosh with his Allied Creeks, and rations only for a few more days—and these were being consumed even as he fumed that he had seen precious few hostiles. He let his people rest only a few hours before rousting them out at midnight. They were going to march on the main Miccosukee town right away and kill some Seminoles.

Indians had abandoned Tallahassee, but Miccosukee might fight, so when a rider galloped into camp at first light the next morning to tell Jackson the Tennessee Volunteers had at last arrived, he paused and decided to wait. Yet the arrival of the Volunteers was a mixed event because they were a mixed bunch. Not all the Tennessee Volunteers had made the journey from Fort Scott. Indeed, these boys had had a generally dreadful time ever since arriving in south Georgia. First the supply system had done its best to starve them, and then measles had carved through those who remained, making many unable to continue. The Tennessee column approaching Jackson's camp was as big as it was only because some eager Kentuckians had tagged along. It was probably about as much as Andy Jackson could bear. Nobody mentioned it was April Fool's Day.[15]

At least he now had some people to fight the Indians. When McIntosh's Creek Brigade also showed up that day, Jackson felt confident in his strength, even if it was mainly composed of Indians, Kentuckians, and Georgians. He would attack Miccosukee itself, one of the largest towns in the area, but Old Hickory was taking no chances. He sent the Tennesseans he had—three companies worth—to scout the army's advance. When they had moved within two miles of the town, they spotted Indians herding cattle along Lake Miccosukee. When Jackson heard about the sighting, he sent several more companies forward as reinforcements while he formed the balance of the army into columns to envelop the town. The scouting party acted as a vanguard, charging the Miccosukee to push them toward the American right. With the American right and left converging from both sides, Jackson stood a chance of capturing everyone in the town. At least he stood the chance before the American attack disintegrated. The right wing mistook McIntosh's Creeks on the left as the enemy, opening fire on them and causing enough confusion to allow the flowing tide of Miccosukees, once nearly dammed, to squirt through the openings and escape to swamps near the lake. They left at least a dozen dead behind, and four women fell to capture. American losses were light—one regular killed and four Tennessee Volunteers wounded.[16]

But the loss of the chance to score a major triumph was the heaviest blow. And then the Americans made the kind of discovery that drains away all exuberance. Entering the environs of Miccosukee, the men in sobered silence found a pole thickly adorned with scalps. Many had belonged to women, and some were fresh enough to have been taken from the Scott party. Yet there were too many for that number of victims. The pole held the grisly trophies of countless, earlier conflicts, trophies that not one of the Americans entering the village that day was likely to forget.[17]

The next day, scouting parties to the other towns on Lake Miccosukee turned up more evidence of Seminole hostility. Gaines commanded one party that included McIntosh's Creeks. After fording the shallow lake, they attacked a small group of Miccosukees, killing one black man and three Seminole warriors, one of whom was wearing an American uniform. It had belonged to a private killed in December on a relief boat bound from Fort Scott to Muhlenberg's convoy. Personal belongings and letters of American soldiers also turned up. Yet in the midst of these grave discoveries, Americans also found hundreds of cattle, horses, hogs, and chickens in and around the towns. That, with over a thousand bushels of corn, made the next few days splendidly memorable. The army burned the towns while it intermittently rested and ate.[18]

Jackson let them tend to this task for three days, but he pushed them to little else. He never mounted a systematic search for the large number of Seminoles who had evacuated the towns but obviously remained in the area. Instead he left, taking most of the army with him, detaching only McIntosh and his warriors to stay behind amid the ruins of the Miccosukee towns to harry the Seminoles displaced by their villages' destruction. Jackson meanwhile headed for St. Marks.

He arrived at the Spanish fort on the evening of 6 April and sent in a white flag. The Spaniards sent out a white flag of their own and extended their hospitality beyond this mere greeting to an open-armed welcome—or at least an open-gated one. During the night, American officers went in and out of the fort as they wished. One of these officers was Jackson's aide, Lieutenant Gadsden, who carried a letter to the Spanish commander, Don Francisco Caso y Luengo. It was a demand that Luengo surrender St. Marks to the United States Army.[19]

The demand might have astounded Luengo. After all, he had demonstrated by his actions that for Spain white flags meant something. With Alexander Arbuthnot as his guest, the Spanish commander had followed the progress of Jackson's army since it entered Florida. He so far had scrupulously followed his orders not to provoke any conflict with the United States, but this latest demand was a different matter. Luengo, like any of His Most Catholic Majesty's general officers, was a proud man faced with the prospect of humiliating not only himself but his king's standard. He must have cringed when reading Jackson's letter, especially the part that reasoned the fort's surrender would benefit Spain because the Americans could better prevent its capture by

Indians. Later, Jackson's supporters, citing this passage, would claim his initial desire to take over the fort was born of his friendship toward Spain. They, however, eventually would have to adjust their defense to match his later (and accurate) representation of his motives at St. Marks. After he arrived, they said, Jackson concluded the Spaniards were willingly helping the Indians, so he took possession of the fort, not to protect Spaniards from Indians (as he first said), but to remove a source of succor for the Indians (as he later explained).[20]

Luengo tried to save what honor he could with abasement. He answered Jackson's demand with a letter congratulating the general's successful campaign. He adamantly but deferentially denied accusations that he had supplied munitions to Indians. On the contrary, he said, hospitality extended to Jackson's officers and the ministration of the fort's infirmary to his sick surely demonstrated Spain's friendship toward the United States. In any event, Luengo's letter mumbled, finally getting to the point, he could not permit even a friendly occupation of the fort without his government's permission. He urged Jackson to wait until he could seek that consent.[21]

Luengo had done the best he could. His garrison was too small to resist, and his position before the American army too untenable. His letter, reminiscent of the one crafted by Mauricio de Zúñiga almost two years before about Negro Fort, was just as ineffective in diverting American plans. Jackson did not even respond. He ordered Major Twiggs to take possession of the fort. With three companies of the Seventh and one from the Fourth Infantry, Twiggs marched through the fort's open gates and so surprised the garrison's seventy soldiers that their attempt to man their cannon was more comical than threatening. American regulars easily stopped them. With the fort thus secured, Jackson strode into it to lower with his own hands the Spanish flag. He handed it to Luengo, whose humiliation and chagrin reached high exasperation as the American Stars and Stripes was hoisted above his command. Andrew Jackson had waited a long time, but at last the conquest of Florida had begun.[22]

⌘

From his vantage in St. Marks Bay, Isaac McKeever saw the United States flag snapping over St. Marks. His little fleet had arrived on 1 April, standing off the fort whose occupants had no idea these were ships of the United States Navy because McKeever was flying the British Union Jack. While sailing under false colors was certainly outside the protocols of the sea, it proved splendidly successful at St. Marks. When a Spanish officer rowed out to McKeever's flagship to ascertain his business, McKeever explained the ships had come to help the Indians. McKeever later said the Spaniard seemed pleased. And well he might have been. An American army had meandered into Spanish territory with purposes unclear and so seeming doubly sinister. Spain could not resist if it had to, and Spain doubted the Indians would. Spain had always counted on Britain should this particular nightmare unfold. Now it had, and Britain was here.

Even if the inquisitive Spanish officer was not transparently cheerful about the "British" arrival, he certainly was either singularly unobservant or woefully unschooled in what Royal Naval vessels and British uniforms should look like. Assured by this initial investigation that the British had returned, Josiah Francis and Homathlemico crawled into a boat and rowed out to their friends, so long absent, but now back at this most propitious, needful moment. The Red Stick prophet and chieftain had hardly touched the deck of McKeever's ship when they realized their awful mistake. Their people ashore took longer to worry that something was wrong, but their two leaders' lengthy absence finally concerned them. They approached the ships in canoes, but the Americans dropped all pretense to fire on them, so they withdrew. One of the canoes perhaps held Milly Francis. She would not have been able to see her father, though; the Americans had him and Homathlemico below in irons.[23]

Now, with Jackson in possession of St. Marks, a landing party from McKeever told him about the prisoners. Jackson instructed the navy to deliver the two Red Sticks to him the next morning. As soon as their feet touched ground, Jackson ordered them both hanged. One story has Francis requesting a meeting with Jackson so that the prophet could kill Sharp Knife with one hidden up his sleeve. Jackson would not meet with Francis, however, and he refused his request to be shot rather than hanged. And so Homathlemico, chieftain, and Josiah Francis, prophet, died that April morning at the end of hemp ropes.

There were no last words, but perhaps Francis thought of Nicholls and England, the silver tomahawk, his wife and daughters, especially Milly with the scared white boy on the Wakulla, that Wakulla not

unlike the gentle waters of the Coosa, which was home. And Jackson—
of course, Jackson, and the American ship with the British flag; now the
upturned faces, the April sun, the glittering bay, the sharp horizon and
what lay beyond—prophet, to see forever; finally to sleep.[24]

⤬

Jackson would wait to deal with another prisoner. Alexander Arbuthnot,
visiting Luengo when the Americans arrived at St. Marks, had now
fallen into Jackson's hands. Jackson's critics would later allege that he
had captured Arbuthnot with a subterfuge as dishonorable as that which
had lured Francis and Homathlemico. Jackson, they claimed, had
requested an interview, and Arbuthnot had innocently consented.
Others said Jackson captured Arbuthnot while he was trying to escape
from the fort. Whatever the circumstances of his capture, the elderly
Scottish trader now found himself under guard to await Jackson's return
from his campaign on the Suwannee.[25]

Jackson impatiently wanted to start for the Suwannee immediately,
but disposing of an entire Spanish garrison, no matter how small, was
more complicated than hanging two Indians and locking up an old man.
Luengo, with nothing left to lose, had swapped chagrin for outrage to
protest violently the American affront. Because he could not spare
enough men to guard these restive Spaniards, Jackson agreed to
Luengo's demand for the garrison's removal to Pensacola. Eager to be
on his way, Jackson also promised to inventory all property in the fort
and guarantee its security. With such small and largely meaningless
demands Luengo tried to reclaim some of his and Spain's dignity. He
departed for Pensacola to begin explaining for the rest of his life how he
had lost St. Marks without firing a shot.[26]

It took two days to tidy up all his problems, but at last Jackson readied his army for the march against King Bowlegs's towns on the Suwannee River. These Seminoles knew Americans of all stripes too well, and
their associations had been consistently unpleasant. Bowlegs's people
were perhaps descended from the first Indians called Seminole, those
who had emigrated from the Oconee River as followers of the
Cowkeeper in the eighteenth century, settling finally on the Alachua
Prairie near the St. John's River. There they had raised livestock until
the American invasions of the Patriot War in 1812–13 pushed them
westward. King Payne's death during the Patriot War left them to

follow his brother, Bowlegs, to the Suwannee, where they hoped their isolation would shield them from white America, uniformed or otherwise. That very isolation had ironically heightened their peril because it made the Suwannee towns ideal refuges for runaway slaves. After Negro Fort's destruction, the Suwannee became the destination of choice for such fugitives. It also became the target of slave raids originating in south Georgia. Refugees from Negro Fort and additional runaway slaves lived in separate towns north of distinctly Seminole ones, working under an informal servitude typical of Seminole slavery. Vassals more than slaves—and because of this, more allies than vassals—blacks living near Bowlegs's Seminoles had a large stake in maintaining the security of the Suwannee towns.[27]

The large black presence on the Suwannee certainly concerned Andrew Jackson and the many other southerners on the campaign. Jackson likely believed accusations that Bowlegs's cattle herds depended on rustling rather than husbandry for their fat numbers, although Seminoles had descended from the people of the Cowkeeper, known for his stock-breeding acumen. In any case, these factors at least gave a reason for Jackson's moving east; they conveniently coincided, however, with this apparent goal of establishing an American presence in as much of Florida as he could.

On 9 April, with eight days' rations and minus the two hundred men detached to garrison St. Marks, the army began marching toward Bowlegs's towns one hundred miles east. The next day, McIntosh's Creeks and the rest of the Tennessee Volunteers (finally) joined the main army, but not before stumbling on some Seminoles. The Creeks and Tennesseans had charged, killing one man, wounding another and a woman, and shooting the lower jaw off a child. These offending Indians—all three men, one woman, and two children—had been preoccupied with cutting down a tree to collect a honeycomb, so the attack was fairly light work for the American forces. It was much lighter work than that of a few days later when they would encounter the warriors of Peter McQueen.[28]

McIntosh joined Jackson, and the enlarged army trudged eastward for another day without seeing a single Seminole. On the night of 11 April, though, pickets could hear lowing cattle and barking dogs, distant but unmistakable. Jackson warmed to the task the next day, moving McIntosh's Creeks from their rearward camps to act as advance scouts while the rest of the army moved in behind. The Creek brigadier cautiously sent ahead a small scouting party of his own and soon had a message from Major Kinard, its commander. Kinard had found Red Sticks rather than Seminoles, but he had found them in such abundance that he was barely holding his own and needed help right away. No one knew it yet, but this was Peter McQueen's town on the Ecofina River. The warriors there had been surprised by the American approach, but not paralyzed by it, so they fought their way to cover in a nearby swamp. All along, they hurled such a furious fire as to stall Kinard and then convince McIntosh, soon on the scene with most of his warriors, that he would need reinforcements to hold the Red Sticks in place for capture. Jackson hurried his Tennesseans to the fray at McIntosh's prompting, but they arrived too late. McQueen and his warriors had melted into the swamps, leaving the Volunteers again disappointed. Most of them had yet to see a hostile Indian, Red Stick or Seminole, let alone kill one. Kinard's scouts could have told them a few things.[29]

Indeed, they did have one interesting thing to tell, but not about the fighting. Through the sputtering muskets and hissing bullets, the Allied Creeks could hear a woman shouting in English from one of the village's houses. Fighting their way through the town, they finally found the house and the white woman in it. It was Mrs. Stewart, the only captive taken from the Scott massacre, spared for reasons that neither she nor anyone else on the American side would ever know. The ordeal had left her bedraggled, but little else marked her time in captivity, and she claimed later that the Indians had not treated her badly. The same men who had opened the skulls of children had inexplicably bundled her back to their country, where absolutely nothing had happened to her until 12 April, when some other Indians had found her. It must have made little sense to Mrs. Stewart.[30]

The American attack on their town probably made even less sense to the hundred women and children now rounded up by the Allied Creeks. Forty of their husbands and fathers lay dead, and the rest were refugees again with those of their sisters who also had scampered into the swamps. As McIntosh counted his casualties—he had only lost three Allied Creeks—and collected the town's livestock and stores—hundreds of cattle and large caches of corn—what remained of McQueen's once dreaded Red Stick band again took flight. Only about two hundred could find each other to emerge south of the swamps and head even farther south, eventually to settle around Tampa Bay, hoping that finally it was far enough away, probably knowing that eventually it too would not be.[31]

Jackson hardly paused over this last of his victories against the Red Sticks. Farther east, Bowlegs's towns remained his objective, and Jackson worried that refugees from McQueen's town would warn the Seminoles of the American approach, allowing them to escape. McIntosh's Creeks fanned out in pursuit, but instead of fleeing Red Sticks, they stumbled on a Seminole family. They killed the husband and wounded his wife and three children, but in doing so they raised such a ruckus that Jackson believed McIntosh was under attack. Finding out the truth did not relieve Old Hickory so much as it abraded his frayed nerves. McIntosh had started annoying Jackson, especially because of the way he kept the lion's share of captured cattle for his own warriors. Jackson's men had again depleted their meat rations, and here were Allied Creeks herding hundreds of cattle. The general lashed out at his Creek brigadier: how dare he engage the enemy without informing his commanding officer? Jackson said he immediately wanted that beef and a full report for good measure.[32]

This happened on 14 April. A reasonable pace would have placed the army within two days of the Suwannee, but Jackson thought he could reach it in one. He still fretted that forewarning would allow the Seminoles there to escape, and he wanted to make sure that nothing like the fiasco at McQueen's town happened again. He planned to catch the Suwannee towns unaware and make a thorough job of it.

Jackson's plan, however, was already undone. Before his capture, Arbuthnot had written to his son at their store on the Suwannee. Arbuthnot did not know Jackson's intentions, but he could suspect that eventually they would include a trip to the Suwannee. He warned his son to watch the west for the American approach. Also McQueen's messengers flew through the swamps in advance of the American pursuit, and Jackson could not hasten his people forward with the same dispatch. Ordinarily, the advantage of having many of his force mounted would have made the difference, but in the north Florida wilderness a horse became an encumbrance. Lacking adequate forage, many animals soon fell, snorting and wheezing, to die. The dismounted men floundered in water and muck through pungent reeds and stark cypress, dragging themselves dripping through the scrub and piney flatlands. Usually hungry, always tired, and increasingly edgy, the three-thousand-man army had become a lumbering behemoth, plodding along and shooting at everything that moved. A blind and deaf Indian would have noticed its approach.[33]

Bowlegs's towns, both Seminole and Maroon, were hardly either. Situated on the western bank of the Suwannee, the Maroon towns lay just north and west of the Indians' settlements. On the afternoon of 16 April, Jackson's army was still six miles from the outlying Maroon villages when he decided to camp the men on the banks of a large pond. Six mounted Seminoles watched from a distance as the American force began settling in. Still clinging to the illusion that he would surprise anyone on the Suwannee, Jackson ordered these Indians chased down before they could alert their villages. Yet what horses he had left were no match for the Seminoles' fresh mounts.

With the frantic urgency of a man already late, Jackson tried to use the little measure of remaining daylight and ordered his shambling men into three lines of attack. He set them into motion toward Bowlegs's towns, whipping them along so that by sunset they reached their objective just as it began to dim in the fading light. The Second Regiment of Tennessee Volunteers and Kinard's Allied Creeks formed Jackson's left column and readied to attack the left of one of the towns. Meanwhile, Old Hickory put into motion an elaborate ballet intended to reprise Horseshoe Bend: his center would quickly advance to support the general attack while the right column of the remaining Tennesseans and McIntosh's Creeks would swing around the towns to block escape routes across the river. The dance, however, was played to an empty theater. Jackson's army marched against deserted towns, whose inhabitants had already crossed the Suwannee.[34]

Kinard tried to make the day count for something as it gradually gave way to night. Some Maroons remained on the west bank of the Suwannee to cover the evacuation. They stubbornly stuck to their position while making anyone sorry for trying either to collar them or to shoo them along. Finally, and just as Kinard was about to pin them to the river, they splashed across it. Once on the other bank, though, they proved in no hurry, pausing to nettle their pursuers before falling back a little way to pause again, always staying between Kinard's Creeks and the Seminole women and children scattering in the brush. When dark finally closed the dangerous chase, this sharp little action had left thirteen of Kinard's warriors wounded in payment for the two Seminoles and nine blacks killed on the other side.[35]

Foiled again, the army regrouped. Jackson sent Gaines in pursuit, but neither officer expected any success against prey far more familiar with the terrain. The best Gaines could do was collect the livestock and gather the corn the Seminoles trailed behind them as they lightened their flight. At least it was something, and Jackson, short of an actual victory, touted this as an indirect one. The Indians had left so much behind, he wrote to Rachel, that surely they would starve. He picked out a nice cow to bring home to her as a present.[36]

While Gaines turned his people into drovers and green grocers, the rest of the army made a leisurely job of burning all the homes and outbuildings in Bowlegs's towns. In off moments, they ranged the countryside for loot. One such excursion took some Georgia militia along the river, where they found Arbuthnot's store. They made short work of looting its inventory of corn and deerskins.

And thus they spent two days collecting all the spoils they could carry and burning the rest. On the night of 18 April, the men had settled around their campfires to swap stories when four strangers strode purposefully into the camp. It took only a moment for the startled Americans to realize these fellows did not belong. It took only an instant for the strangers to realize they had made an awful mistake. One wore a British uniform, two were black, and the fourth, another white man, wore civilian clothes. They had expected to find Seminoles clustered around the fires. Now they found their legs and worked them for all they were worth, darting into the dark woods with shouting Americans pounding right behind them. It took a few minutes, but the soldiers finally caught all four and shoved them back into the firelight. They then discovered who had dropped into their laps: the white civilian was Peter Cook, an employee of Alexander Arbuthnot; the military man was Robert Chrystie Ambrister, late of His Majesty's Royal Marines. The prisoners needed no introduction to their captors. Ambrister knew trouble when he saw it.[37]

❧

Robert Chrystie Ambrister had packed a lot of life into his twenty-one years. A native of the Bahamas, he had served as a young midshipman in the Royal Marines under Edward Nicholls, following him to Florida during the last war. Lore describes him as adventurous and dashing, partly perhaps because of the story that an illegal duel cost him his commission after the war. Whatever the truth of that, he was looking for employment when George Woodbine offered him a way back into the service of arms. Thus Ambrister became involved in Woodbine's and McGregor's plans to use blacks and Indians to undermine the Spanish Empire. In fact, Ambrister became the project's point man when Woodbine sent him to Tampa Bay in March 1818. There he was to train blacks and Seminoles in the military arts, eventually for use in Florida and possibly elsewhere in Latin America.[38]

Ambrister had involved himself in an opportunistic enterprise that was no less ramshackle because it was dangerous. For transportation along Florida's west coast, he had struck some kind of bargain with the captain of Arbuthnot's schooner, and it had not taken long for this deal to sour. The captain, having brought the young mercenary up the peninsula, refused to take him back down to Tampa Bay until Ambrister provided him with more supplies. The quest for these supplies was what brought Ambrister with Peter Cook to Bowlegs's towns on the Suwannee at just this inopportune moment. According to Cook, Ambrister had read for Bowlegs the letter Arbuthnot had sent to his son warning that Jackson might be on his way. Now he and Cook had become American prisoners, and they proved most cooperative. They told Jackson exactly where to find Arbuthnot's schooner, and the general immediately sent a detachment under Gadsden to commandeer it to transport his sick and wounded to St. Marks.[39]

Gadsden left on his mission that night; two days later, Jackson decided that the campaign against the Seminoles was over. That evening he summoned Glascock to tell him that his militia would no longer be needed. Eager to get home, the Georgians assured Jackson they had enough rations to head directly for Hartford without returning to St. Marks. Instructed to muster out his men at Hartford, Glascock also carried Jackson's letter to Rabun asking that Georgia pay its militia and promising that Washington would reimburse the state's treasury.[40] Jackson also told McIntosh to take the Allied Creeks home by way of Fort Scott, where the United States officers there would muster them out of national service. Jackson said he planned to march what was left of the army—the Tennessee Volunteers and the regulars—back to St.

Marks as soon as he heard from Gadsden. From St. Marks he would begin the evacuation of most of the army from Florida. At least, that is what he told the War Department.[41]

Later that night, word came from Gadsden that he had Arbuthnot's ship at the mouth of the Suwannee. Jackson wasted no time. He sent his sick and wounded downriver, where Gadsden loaded them on the *Chance* for the trip back to St. Marks. The rest of the army bedded down for some rest before beginning their march the next morning. Jackson, however, sat up late writing a long letter to Calhoun. He detailed the campaign and outlined his next moves. He said he would move quickly to St. Marks and from there send or lead a reconnaissance of the region west of the post. He would look for Red Sticks, he said, because he had heard that Pensacola had supplied some in the area. Jackson did not mention from whom he had heard this information; he did say that neither his nor his men's health would permit much more activity than such a search. He intended to go home after conducting it. At least, that is what he told the War Department.[42]

Despite his observation about their feeling poorly, Jackson pushed his people to a rapid pace through the Florida wilderness on the return to St. Marks. They made the trip in only four days. McIntosh and his Creeks went part of the way, but soon they branched away to Fort Scott, leaving only the Tennessee Volunteers and United States regulars to race back to St. Marks. Gadsden arrived there on board the *Chance* just hours before Jackson. By the end of April, Andrew Jackson had managed to place himself in Florida exclusively with men he could trust completely. They could be counted on, either through professionalism or personal loyalty, to do whatever he told them to.

The campaign he had envisioned from the outset was not over by any means, and Jackson knew it. Yet, in this brief interlude before he began its next and concluding phase, he attended to some unfinished business. As soon as he reached St. Marks, he set into motion the wheels of his personal justice system to punish Alexander Arbuthnot and Robert Ambrister for crimes against the United States.[43]

Jackson appointed a military court of twelve voting officers, Edmund Pendleton Gaines presiding, to hear charges that Arbuthnot and Ambrister had aided and abetted the enemy of the United States in the Seminole War. Of the panel, five were Volunteer officers whom Jackson had personally recruited for the campaign.[44] Even though partially stacking the board and conducting the proceeding as a court-martial in the Florida wilderness obviated the need for precise legal punctilio, Old Hickory ruminated over just how to go about the business. His original idea of charging his two prisoners with piracy had appeal because it allowed him to take action against these subjects of a neutral power for aiding one nation against another nation. Yet, the similarities of such a circumstance to that of the Marquis de Lafayette's Revolutionary War service nagged at Jackson as an embarrassing comparison. By the time he convened the court-martial, Jackson had hit upon the solution. "The laws of war did not apply to conflicts with savages," he solemnly intoned, and thus was he able to dispense with not only the laws of war, but virtually all laws altogether. The court would charge Arbuthnot and Ambrister with assisting and encouraging the Seminoles. In Jackson's legal universe, these were capital offenses.[45]

The specific charges accused Arbuthnot of inciting the Creeks to make war on the United States, of spying for the Seminoles, and of inciting the Seminoles to kidnap, torture, and kill William Hambly and Edmund Doyle. Charges against Ambrister stated that he had aided and abetted Seminoles and had led Seminoles against the United States.[46]

Arbuthnot requested counsel, and the court obliged him by appointing one, but he apparently managed most of his own defense. Some describe his efforts as eloquent, but both he and Ambrister must have realized that their part in this show was already scripted to its conclusion. Ambrister, in fact, finally abandoned all pretense of due process simply to throw himself on the mercy of the court. Gadsden said he had found letters aboard the *Chance* implicating both men as tireless helpers of the Seminoles. William Hambly (unkilled and untortured) and Peter Cook (Arbuthnot's disgruntled employee) agreed to testify for the prosecution. The court would not allow Arbuthnot to call Ambrister in his defense.[47]

Prosecution witnesses recited all their lines perfectly. William Hambly gave vivid testimony of how Arbuthnot had urged the Seminoles to conduct raids into Georgia. That Hambly was Arbuthnot's competitor, that he and his partner had threatened the old Scot in writing, did not impeach his testimony. Peter Cook testified against his boss, possibly to settle some grudge, certainly to save his own neck. That Cook's previous employer in the Bahamas had fired the clerk after accusing him of theft never clouded Cook's probity for the court; that some believed

Cook was involved in the Scott massacre never was posed to question his motives on the witness stand. Another witness, John Winslett, said he had carried and had read a letter written by Arbuthnot to Little Prince urging the Lower Creek headman to ally with the Seminoles. Arbuthnot denied writing such a letter, and it was never produced. Checking with Little Prince or others to corroborate or discredit Winslett was out of the question.[48]

Actually, any extant documentary evidence regarding Arbuthnot—especially his letters to David B. Mitchell and the 2 April 1818 letter to his son John—shows a man determined to preserve peace between the Seminoles and the United States. If only working from a practical level of self-interest, Arbuthnot the businessman stood to gain much more from peace than war. The Scot knew that the Seminoles could never win a war against the United States; he also knew from personally encountering their indifference that the British would not help the Indians should such a war come. Actually, the most damning evidence in the eyes of Jackson and the court's presiding officer, Edmund Pendleton Gaines, was very likely one of Arbuthnot's letters Gadsden had found aboard the *Chance*. Intended for Edward Nicholls, the letter accused Jackson and Gaines of manufacturing the crisis on the border so they could acquire possession of all Indian land. Arbuthnot said that Hambly (one of the primary witnesses testifying against him) and the Innerarity were cheerful accomplices in this project, but the Scot absolved the United States government of any role. In fact, he specifically praised David Mitchell's peace initiatives, something that could not have enhanced the agent's reputation with Jackson and Gaines.[49]

Although it did not matter, Ambrister at least had the consolation of knowing he had partly done what the court alleged. He had been most indiscreet, writing letters begging for supplies to Governor Cameron in the Bahamas and Nicholls in England, letters that had now fallen into American hands. Perhaps young Ambrister had really believed Woodbine's boasts about raising an army of Indians and blacks to seize Spain's colonial empire. That plan must have seemed a distant and alien thing to Ambrister that April evening in St. Marks as he watched the court frown over information about his arming and drilling fugitive slaves in Florida. The panel left little doubt that this crime was about the most horrifying one Ambrister could have committed.[50]

A verdict and subsequent sentence required a two-thirds majority of the court. Exactly that number found Arbuthnot guilty of everything but spying, and that was more than enough in their eyes to hang him. The court found Ambrister guilty of all charges and, bowing to a fellow soldier, sentenced him to a firing squad. Yet, having done that, the military court paused, and at least one member of the panel not only changed his vote but also called on his colleagues to reconsider theirs. Ambrister was so young, so clear-eyed, so unlucky, and so like any one of them at any given time when things could have gone wrong to put them before hard-faced men behind drumheads, handing out death to the sound of guttering lamps and chirping crickets. So the court paused, and then it voted to reconsider Ambrister's sentence. Then it imposed upon Robert Chrystie Ambrister a fine of fifty lashes and a penance of one year at hard labor. The boy had, after all, thrown himself on the mercy of the court at the end, and the court could, in the end, be merciful. Arbuthnot, old and proud, protesting his innocence and asking for no pity, would get none. Ambrister was different.[51]

Except to Andrew Jackson. The court had done exactly what he wanted, and then it had gone soft and ruined everything. More, the members of the panel had actually deluded themselves that their hearings, rulings, verdicts, and sentences meant anything. Receiving his military tribunal's decisions on 28 April, Jackson simply chose the sentences he wanted, approving Arbuthnot's execution and reinstating Ambrister's. The next morning, soldiers led the old man from his confinement to his own schooner. A noose dangled from a yardarm of the *Chance,* and with little ceremony it was soon around the seventy-year-old neck and pulled up taut, hoisting Arbuthnot above the deck to twist in the breeze and serve as an example to anyone else bold enough to write letters for Indians. Only a brief pause marked some preparations, then the staccato pop of muskets dropped Robert Chrystie Ambrister dead before an American firing squad.[52]

Some men would remember the day with a barbed intensity. Others who had been hundreds of miles away would coldly question the legality of executing two British subjects in Spanish territory while at peace with both nations, but men who were there had a different kind of judgment. Four decades later, the old Indian fighter Thomas Woodward was still turning it over in his mind and in his stomach. "Could their lives have been spared," he said, "their families at least would have been more benefitted, our country would have sustained no loss, and the consciences of some men, on mature reflection would have rested easier."[53]

☙

Most of the army did not see Arbuthnot hanged and Ambrister shot, having departed even before the court handed down the verdicts. Jackson did not intend to be far behind. While watching the trial unfold, he had written to Calhoun that he would station a garrison at Fort Gadsden and then leave for Nashville. Claiming his campaign had scattered the Seminoles so they could no longer communicate with foreign agents, Jackson proclaimed the frontier secure. Even while thus assuring the secretary of war, however, Jackson prepared a letter for Governor José Masot. He accused the Spaniards in Pensacola of harboring hostile Indians, including the perpetrators of the Scott massacre.[54]

As Jackson rode out of St. Marks, his stated plans and his real intentions simply did not match. He arrived at Fort Gadsden on 2 May, conveniently catching up to his marching army that had pulled into Prospect Bluff just hours before. There he spent two days, finally writing to Calhoun on 5 May that he had decided to take Pensacola. As justification, Jackson cited reports of large numbers of hostile Indians camped around the Spanish capital from whence they were supplied. Yet Jackson did not give any attribution for these reports. Only after the event would affidavits attest to the presence of some Indians and Pensacola's relationship to them.[55]

No matter their origin, no credible reports could place hostiles around Pensacola. At the most, frontier Alabama had raised a roaring complaint over its vulnerability—a continuation of those same protests when Jackson pulled away troops for the Florida invasion. Governor Bibb and fellow Alabamians feared that Jackson would merely beat the Florida bush to drive Seminoles and Red Sticks into their backyards. And, indeed, when Jackson had removed most of the regulars from south Alabama, Bibb's prediction for mayhem seemed well founded. Raids increased against isolated farms, some leaving whites dead and Bibb begging for help. He especially wanted to know how to prevent a general Indian war. One was sure to erupt, he thought, when settlers retaliated by killing any Indians they could find, including Allied Creeks.[56]

Yet the Alabama governor did not ask for Jackson's help. Instead, Bibb himself wanted the authority and the means to pursue raiding Indians into Florida. The War Department gave him both, providing federal funds to finance the Alabama militia's pursuit of those Indians thought responsible for the attacks. Bibb ordered his militia to find the Indians in Florida and attack them—unless they took refuge in a Spanish town. In a precise iteration of Calhoun's instructions to Gaines (and what Calhoun assumed to be Jackson's operating orders), Bibb told his militia to contact him if Indians did seek sanctuary with Spaniards. The governor, however, did not think that significant numbers of Indians would do so.[57]

Cooperating with Major W. Young, who commanded the few regulars remaining in the territory, at the end of April the Alabama militia found a small group of Indians north of Pensacola and fell upon them, killing and wounding about thirty. Governor Masot immediately responded to this American campaign in Spanish territory by informing Major Young that he had assailed peaceful Indians. In fact, said Masot, the Indians around Pensacola were not only all peaceful, but paltry in numbers too, totaling no more than eighty-seven, and mostly women and children at that. Masot said they wanted to go home to Alabama, and indeed they did. Just as easy as that, their repatriation into the Creek nation was arranged under the supervision of Big Warrior. Before Jackson began his march on Pensacola, most of the Indians around that town had peacefully departed for Alabama. Perhaps the vagaries of communication prevented Jackson from knowing about the pacification of the Alabama frontier before he marched on Pensacola. There is no reason to believe, however, that he would have remained ignorant of this situation until after he had taken the city.[58]

At Prospect Bluff, Jackson swiftly completed preparations for his march west of the Apalachicola. He issued the necessary orders to his staff designating 7 May as the day they would begin. The day before, as the army buttoned its gear for the one hundred-mile trek to the west, a messenger came rushing into camp. He carried an express letter for Jackson from Thomas Glascock. It contained terrible news.[59]

7

"Unbecoming a Gentleman and a Soldier"

As they returned from Florida, a party of Glascock's Georgia militia-men moved warily in the darkness, feeling their way through the scrub and pines in the April night. They were approaching Jimmy's Town, environs of the larger Chehaw village, the Lower Creek Indian town that just weeks before had contributed men as well as food to Jackson and the Georgia militia on their way to Fort Scott. Now the militiamen were nervous and hungry, the one because they had heard about uniden-tified Indians shooting at some of their number, the other because they had completely run through their supplies after boasting to Jackson about having plenty of food for their trip home. So they were hungry, not yet home, and a little scared. They felt something in the air of this place—something wrong.

A mounted party of Indian warriors saw them, only to flee into a nearby swamp, deaf to reassuring calls of friendship. Not until coming on another group of Indians, huddling at a landing on the Flint River, did the militiamen discover the trouble. These Indians were frightened as well, but they were hungrier than scared, so they listened to pledges that Brigadier General Glascock would protect them. What the fright-ened Chehaws needed to be protected from was not immediately clear, but it would be soon enough.[1]

Their village had been destroyed, the Chehaws said. Their village was the place the Indians variously called Che-au-haw, Cheraw, or

Au-muc-cul-le, literally "pour upon me." Creeks had long regarded it as an important place because of its large oak with a nine-foot diameter trunk. Under this tree's tenting branches Creeks had held momentous councils.[2] Now the village's inhabitants said they did not know why other white soldiers had entered under a white flag only to open fire, kill their people, plunder their town, and hastily leave.[3]

Glascock could not understand it either. After all, he and his militia had entered the town with Jackson only two months before. The Chehaws had supplied the army with forty warriors and had given generously of their food. Now the young brigadier tried to piece together what had happened to them. By the time he had done so, he was horrified. That night he sent the express letter to Andrew Jackson.[4]

What happened to the Chehaw village in April 1818 was in one sense merely another lamentable episode in the long history of mistakes and misjudgments marking Indian-white relations on the American frontier. Those mistakes too often saw overzealous whites, frequently organized as state militia, blurring or even disregarding distinctions between friendly and hostile Indians. At base, that is precisely what happened at Chehaw. Yet the context of the First Seminole War made it even more poignant, and the principal characters in the controversy that followed made the incident more profoundly significant than an ugly event on the frontier.

Whites had attacked Allied Creeks before. Outlaws had preyed upon Indians from towns like Chehaw, particularly when small groups ventured forth in hunting parties. Some Georgia officials sympathized with Indian appeals for redress, but punishing whites for attacking Indians invited political retribution of the first order. Few politicians wanted that kind of trouble; most looked the other way.[5]

In 1817, Governor William Rabun had come to the governor's chair as part of that deal engineered by Crawford to place David Mitchell in the Creek Agency while still perpetuating the governorship as a Crawfordite preserve. During his first eight months in office, Rabun's claim to the job derived solely on Mitchell's resignation and the fact that Rabun, as president of the Georgia Senate, was next in line to fill the vacancy. During the crucial spring and summer of 1817, Rabun fought a determined push by members of the John Clark faction to replace him with their leader. Almost everything the acting governor did was a reflexive response to this situation. The legislature elected him in his own right in November 1817, but the margin of sixty-two to fifty-seven was sufficiently narrow to make the triumph less an endorsement of Rabun than it was a nod to his incumbency.[6]

He openly courted political favor in the backwoods strongholds of the Clark faction. Rabun had done little to stop the whites' predatory behavior on the south Georgia frontier. Because of such indifference to attacks on Indians there, Chehaw was not an isolated incident. It was a pattern, part of a larger cycle of plunder and retaliation endemic to frontier life in early nineteenth century America. The Chehaws knew the potential for unprovoked brutality because whites had pillaged their people in late 1816. A band of thieving murderers operating from the banks of the St. Mary's River had stolen horses and deerskins from a Chehaw hunting party that barely escaped alive. Chehaw elders had restrained their young warriors from revenge, choosing to rely on white authorities to bring the miscreants to justice. It was not the last time they would be disappointed.[7]

No one will probably ever know why on 23 April the Chehaw village was singled out for assault. The departure of the Georgia militia with Jackson's army had left the frontier unsettled and subject to raids by Indians out of Florida, especially in the area of the Ocmulgee River. By mid to late March, the white frontier edged toward panic, and Rabun began to feel the political heat from the wilderness. Reports of Indian attacks in Telfair County prompted a makeshift assemblage of thirty-four men to ramble toward the Flint River by way of Big House Creek. Led into a reckless skirmish at Breakfast Branch by Major Josiah Cawthon, they retreated from the field with seven killed and three wounded.[8]

Between Trader's Hill and Hartford, terrified people clustered together for safety. Ever more vehement calls to the governor for protection agitated Milledgeville. Rabun criticized Jackson for using Georgia militia in an activity—the Florida invasion—that the Georgia government had not authorized. He had insisted, he explained, that Jackson provide for the security of the frontier before traipsing off to Florida.[9]

Yet a standing message from the War Department diminished the weight of Rabun's complaints about Jackson's dereliction and the unauthorized use of Georgia militia. In June 1815, then Secretary of War Alexander Dallas had told the governors of Pennsylvania, Kentucky,

Georgia, Indiana Territory, and Mississippi Territory that because Indians remained restless after the war with Britain, military commanders might have to call on militia to maintain the peace. These commanders perhaps would not have time to go through channels at the War Department, so Dallas asked that the governors cooperate with the military as emergency circumstances would dictate.[10]

Hence, as far as the War Department was concerned, Jackson could exercise authority over the militia in an emergency. Calhoun later set straight any doubt about the exigencies of the First Seminole War and Jackson's method of meeting them. He explained that Jackson had "powers to conduct the war in the manner which he may judge best."[11] The national government was not likely to support Rabun's claim that he was forced to his actions by Jackson's derelict or illegal activity.

In March, Rabun asked that Jackson detach forces from his expedition to protect Georgians in threatened areas. The request, made at that late hour and to a commander whose campaign held unknown predicaments and many potential perils, appears, even at this distance, as unreasonable. Jackson ignored the request, so Rabun activated what militia he could find to proceed to west Georgia to reduce the Indian towns of headmen Hopaunee and Felemma, alleged to be the most hostile east of the Flint River.[12]

Where Rabun scrounged up these Georgia militia contributed to the evolving steps that culminated at Chehaw. In March 1818, the best of the militia was with Jackson crossing into Florida. Rabun had to catch-as-catch-could with those forces he sent to west Georgia. They were a motley patchwork of Chatham County men who had been raised to help reduce Amelia Island, only to miss that venture and later prove tardy in traversing the state to Hartford for the Florida invasion. At Hartford, they were now joined by two companies of cavalry from adjacent counties, two infantry companies mustered from the frontier, and sundry smaller groups to total about 270 men.[13]

To command this police force, Rabun had to resort to Captain Obed Wright of Chatham County, a thirty-year-old man of slender build, five feet eleven inches tall with light blue eyes and light brown hair, who would end his part in this affair as an exile and outlaw.[14] Wright's militia regiment formed part of the Chatham County contingent, but he had not traveled to Hartford with it because illness had delayed his journey. Because Wright had never been mustered into the United States service,

Rabun would later claim that the militia captain's actions fell under the governor's sole authority.[15]

In any event, Rabun now turned Wright loose on the frontier with 270 armed men of dubious training and limited judgment. Wright had instructions to call on the nationalized Georgia militia at Fort Early for assistance, if he thought it necessary.[16]

Wright set out from Hartford heading west on 21 April, under orders to reduce Hopaunee and Felemma's towns. He spent the night at Fort Early. The commander there was Captain Ebeneezer Bothwell, a Georgia militia officer who had been mustered into United States service. Bothwell told Wright that Hopaunee was not hostile; in fact, the Indian had recently found and returned a stolen horse for whites. Bothwell so insisted that Wright's impression of Indian hostility was inaccurate that he refused to accompany the Georgia militia on its expedition. He did, however, accede to Rabun's orders to provide Wright with men from Fort Early's garrison. Wright departed Fort Early on 22 April, moving west toward the Flint River.[17]

Why Wright attacked Chehaw instead of the towns of Hopaunee and Felemma remains a mystery. While still at Hartford, he told Jacob Robinson, who commanded the Laurens County troop, that he had proof that nearby Indian towns "were deceitfully hostile."[18] Wright also reportedly came by information that Hopaunee had relocated to Chehaw, and so he ignored Felemma's town and stopped ten miles short of Hopaunee's. Although the Laurens County troop was not in the governor's orders, Wright while en route sent word to Robinson to bring up his men anyway. Some of Robinson's men refused to leave Hartford without written orders from the governor, but Robinson assured them that Wright had the actual orders in his possession. Robinson nevertheless gave his men the option of accompanying him or remaining at Hartford, but most went with him. When they reached Wright's position, no orders were produced, but instead Wright issued a verbal command that the Laurens men were to participate in the attack.[19]

After crossing the Flint River on the night of 22 April, Wright's men on the next day came upon an Indian youth with two dogs grazing cattle about a half mile outside of Chehaw village. One of the militia claimed that some of the cattle had been stolen from him.[20] The boy offered to go with an interpreter to bring back chiefs to confer, but Wright refused. Instead, he commanded the boy to lead them into the town.[21] As soon as the young Indian had led them to the outskirts of Chehaw, the Georgians killed him and his two dogs. They also shot a Chehaw man who had come out to meet them, scalping him for good measure. Most of the helpless Chehaws ran into their houses, trying to escape the nightmare slowly unfolding in broad April daylight on the streets of their town. Wright's men set the houses on fire. In one house, an old woman and a child screamed as they burned to death. Moving up the street, the militia marked a random path of murder and injury. A badly aimed rifle shattered a confused woman's knee as she stood frozen in her yard. The Tiger King, an elderly chief known to whites as Major Howard, appeared from his house, holding a white flag. Obviously baffled by the mayhem—after all, he had only weeks before furnished Jackson with corn—the old chief confronted the militia. His son meanwhile had taken up a gun, but the Tiger King sternly told him to put it down. As soon as the young man obeyed, the militia shot him dead. His mother, the Tiger King's wife, ran to cover her slain boy's body with her own while the Georgians fired on her husband. He fell to his knees to die under stabbing bayonets and slashing swords. Militiamen then wrenched the Tiger King's earrings from his corpse for grisly souvenirs.[22]

It all took about two hours, marking a leisurely job of butchery and plunder for the marauding Georgians. The Tiger King's son-in-law tried to run away from the village but was caught and hacked to death with swords. A young woman trying to run with her children was killed.[23] No whites suffered wounds, although Wright justified firing the houses with claims that Chehaws were shooting at his men from them.[24] As for Indian casualties, no one would later agree on the human toll of 23 April 1818. Agent David B. Mitchell reported that "many of the inhabitants" died. Little Prince told Mitchell that seven died in the attack. Indian Trader Timothy Barnard said ten. And Wright himself, before he realized that others would view his actions as appalling, claimed that as many as fifty Chehaws perished in the burning houses, although this last figure was undoubtedly an exaggeration.[25] The loss seems to have been at least ten: seven males, an old woman, a young woman, and a female child.[26]

The attack threatened to rouse Indians throughout the countryside, for it was widely known that these Allied Creeks had helped Jackson on his march south. Furthermore, the Tiger King was William McIntosh's uncle. The Allied Creek brigadier heard about the attack when he and his warriors reached Fort Scott to be mustered out of service. McIntosh wrote to Andrew Jackson personally to protest the attack.[27]

Before Jackson could enter the picture, however, Rabun acted to control the situation. His first concern was what the attack would do to the frontier in Twiggs and Pulaski Counties. He ordered a troop of cavalry "to scour the frontier" in that area and to obtain informants (for as much as $3 per day) west of the Ocmulgee to report twice a week.[28] Mitchell warned him that when the Chehaw warriors returned from Florida, there would be trouble, and Timothy Barnard expected unrest unless whites offered some form of reparation. Mitchell promised monetary compensation; both he and Barnard believed that at least Wright should be punished.[29]

Agent Mitchell also tried to calm the situation before Creeks sought revenge for the attack. He sent a message to the Chehaws saying the attack had been a mistake and that those responsible would be punished. He reminded them of the law passed the previous summer by the Creek National Council prohibiting Creeks from practicing indiscriminate revenge. While he reassured the Chehaws that justice would be served, he also arranged to send food to the village. The Chehaws were starving because Wright's men had destroyed their stores of food already depleted by way of provisioning Jackson.[30]

Mitchell had gone to Milledgeville to confront a visibly shaken Rabun. When asked by Mitchell who had ordered the attack, Rabun answered that he had issued some orders, but Wright had deviated from them. Mitchell then said Wright should be punished, but Rabun "evaded" the issue by saying he did not know where Wright was. Rabun left town the next day before Mitchell could continue his inquiries.[31]

Rabun's ambivalence about and ultimate resistance to the punishment of Wright sparked one of the many civil-military controversies that would arise from Jackson's invasion of Florida. The governor answered Mitchell's suggestion of pecuniary compensation with a tortured and halting letter. Wright's men only had orders to chastise hostiles, he explained, thus absolving his office (as eventually would Mitchell) of any blame; yet, moreover, Rabun insisted that Mitchell had heard only the Indian side from Little Prince and Timothy Barnard. The governor now provided the Georgia side of the story, as best he could.

The militia had credible reports, he said, that the belligerent Hopaunee had taken up residence in Chehaw and had become the town's headman. The militia had thus destroyed the town.[32]

Rabun did not give the source for the militia's credible information, nor did he provide any other explanation for the Georgia militia's actions than to dismiss them as an unfortunate turn in the fortunes of war. He then ceased explaining (or trying to) and attacked, objecting to how the incident had been "shamefully represented" by people too quick to forget about Indian depredations. Rabun concluded that nobody should blame these boys for getting carried away.[33]

All the correspondence about the affair was being published in the newspapers, so Rabun undoubtedly wrote for Georgians as much as to Mitchell. In fact, he had read precisely the mood of frontier Georgia, and his words reflected widely held sentiments.[34]

✌

Andrew Jackson's aggressive involvement in the aftermath of the Chehaw massacre would transform a local tragedy into a national controversy. First of all, when he received Glascock's letter the day before departing for Pensacola, he flew into one of his legendary rages and began firing letters in all directions. One message comprised his talk to the Chehaw warriors, uncharacteristically apologizing for the incident while promising just compensation and swift justice. Jackson even suggested that some Chehaws accompany the expedition he was dispatching to arrest Obed Wright, but he also told them not to seek vengeance themselves, warning that such deeds would "bring down on you destruction."[35]

Jackson sent his talk by way of Major John M. Davis, his assistant adjutant general, who was to lead the expedition to apprehend Wright. Jackson told Davis to find Wright at Hartford or, barring that, to get help from Rabun to locate him, arrest him, and take him to Fort Hawkins. There Wright was to stay in "close confinement" until the president could decide what to do with him. Davis was to use an entire company of Tennessee militia and any Georgia militia he could find to make the arrest.[36]

Jackson also wrote to William Rabun that day to describe the attack as unwarranted and wanton. Venting indignation with special ferocity,

Jackson railed at Wright for purposely avoiding any villages that might have contained warriors and then striking down the elderly Chief Howard, who held a flag of truce. More to the point, Jackson charged Rabun with exceeding his prerogative by presuming to give orders where only United States authority could apply. Specifically, Jackson claimed that a state governor does not have the right to issue orders to a military division when the national commander is in the field. He posited that the least Rabun could now do was to help apprehend Wright. Jackson bluntly declared that Wright would stand trial for murder for "this act [that] will to the last age fix a stain upon the character of Georgia."[37]

Jackson embarked upon this serious confrontation for an obvious reason. One biographer has concluded that because Jackson believed the Chehaws to be under his personal protection, he was personally affronted by Wright's attack on them, so he characteristically entered the controversy impetuously and without regard to the deeper consequences.[38] And certainly Jackson's outrage was as justifiable as it is understandable. Yet, any expansive explanation for Jackson's anger as moved by altruism should be tempered by knowledge of his behavior in a similar previous incident. Four years before, when the Tennessee militia attacked allied Cherokees, Jackson defended his men and opposed compensating the victims.[39] The only differences between the Cherokee and Chehaw incidents were the perpetrators and victims, but for Jackson that made all the difference. He defended Tennesseans but assailed Georgians for doing virtually the same thing. In the latter instance, the dispute with William Rabun became personal, a typical circumstance for Jackson that for him overshadowed all other considerations, even constitutional ones. Also, Rabun's connection to the Crawford-Troup political faction possibly exacerbated Jackson's contempt for the state and its citizens.

For his part, Rabun would stand on the high ground of constitutional punctilio. Jackson's assertion that the Georgia governor had no right to issue orders to the Georgia militia while Jackson was in the field struck Rabun as indefensible. "Wretched and contemptible indeed must be our situation if this be the fact," he wrote to Jackson. He pointed out that Wright had never been under Jackson's command because of his tardiness in reaching Hartford. Rabun conveniently ignored the fact that most of the men he instructed to accompany Wright had been mustered into United States service, including Captain Ebeneezer Bothwell, whom he had instructed to all but abandon Fort Early.⁴⁰

So while Jackson made the issue a personal quarrel, Rabun obliged him by doing the same. The governor wrote Calhoun, calling Jackson's letter "a production as inflammitory [*sic*] and indecorus [*sic*], as it is unbecoming a Gentleman and a Soldier."⁴¹ Jackson had also written to Calhoun, including the secretary in his 7 May barrage of Chehaw-related correspondence to tell him about his arrest orders for Wright.⁴² Calhoun and the administration would learn of this dispute just before they heard about the full magnitude of Jackson's activities in Florida. Because of the multiplying controversies the administration would face, it had ample reason to avoid involvement in the personal quarrel between Jackson and Rabun. For the time being, however, Calhoun and Monroe remained blissfully ignorant not only about Jackson's plan to seize Pensacola, but about Chehaw as well. Meanwhile, Jackson and Rabun fought it out over how to atone for the atrocity at Chehaw and whether that atonement would include the punishment of Obed Wright and possibly others. As the altercation expanded, Jackson came to count the governor of Georgia as much an enemy as he did the governor of Pensacola.

The whole controversy hinged on who was to mete out the punishment. Rabun agreed that some kind of investigation should be conducted, and he said he planned to convene a Georgia military court to do so. But first he would have to find Wright, who had been discharged from the militia. Before Rabun could do that, Major Davis arrested Wright in Dublin, Georgia, on 24 May. Yet as Major Davis, per Jackson's orders and authority, transported Wright to Fort Hawkins, Georgia authorities intervened. In Milledgeville, Rabun's nemesis, John Clark, accosted Davis as he transported his prisoner through town. Clark proclaimed that he would protect Georgians' rights if no one else would. Within hours, the Baldwin County Court plucked Wright from Jackson's clutches with a writ of habeas corpus that described Old Hickory's arrest orders as informal because they contained no specific charges. Davis made one last attempt to reclaim his prisoner by requesting that the governor turn Wright over to the army, but Rabun then had Wright arrested and referred the whole matter to James Monroe.⁴³

Rabun wrote to Jackson explaining that the state of Georgia now had custody of Wright, who was being, the governor lied, held in confinement. Technically, Georgia had Wright in custody, but actually Rabun paroled the erstwhile Indian fighter soon after his apprehension.[44] The political situation in Georgia and John Clark's flamboyantly conspicuous efforts to protect Georgians' rights made it impossible for Rabun to do otherwise. Clark, like Jackson, was an unforgiving and indefatigable foe.[45]

∝≥

Before he knew about Chehaw, Jackson had written his 5 May letter to Calhoun explaining why in one week's time he had changed his plans to include the seizure of Pensacola. Rather than sending a small force to scour for Indians west of the Apalachicola and heading back to Nashville and returning most of his regulars to their posts and the Kentucky and Tennessee militia to their homes, he would station garrisons at St. Marks and Fort Gadsden while he marched the remaining 1,092 men toward Spanish Pensacola. He explained the need for such a large force by citing reports that 400 to 500 Indian warriors roamed from that area to assail south Alabama. Jackson also described Masot's reluctance to open the Escambia River for the supply of Fort Crawford as a hostile act. Yet in providing this much information to the secretary of war, Jackson did not say much more. He did not, for example, expressly say that he planned to take Pensacola by force.[46]

In some ways, Jackson was no less cryptic in his orders to his second-in-command, Edmund Pendleton Gaines, but his intentions were far more evident. The same day he wrote to Calhoun, Jackson instructed Gaines to see to the security of the area east of the Apalachicola. That done, Gaines was to appoint a *"confidential"* officer to command every available man, this force to stand ready with two days' rations to march at a moment's notice. Jackson told Gaines that the army would cross the Apalachicola at Ochechee Bluff. "In the event of our enemy fleeing to a Spanish garrison, or receiving succor from thence," he ordered, "you are to view them as enemies and treat them accordingly."[47]

At last he had said it. In an absolute and complete disregard for orders, Jackson told his principal subordinate to attack Spaniards in Florida. Though Jackson would have fought any Indians he encountered, his abrupt decision to move toward Pensacola stemmed from reasons other than an alleged Indian presence in West Florida. The

Innerarity brothers had fed him provocative stories about nefarious Spanish activities to block the Escambia supply route and Spanish encouragement of Indian raids in south Alabama, and Jackson swallowed them whole. When he first invaded Florida in March, he had destroyed a few Indian towns, but it was an activity incidental to his real purpose, which was capturing the Spanish post at St. Marks. Now in May, before he even departed from Fort Gadsden, he knew precisely what he was going to do about Pensacola.[48]

In addition to securing the parts of Florida already in his possession, Jackson had his topographical engineer, Captain Hugh Young, prepare a report outlining the best approaches to the Spanish fortifications at Pensacola. Later, Jackson had this report altered to make it appear as though it were a larger topographical survey depicting all of West Florida rather than what it was, a detailed action map of a predetermined military target. Calhoun had apologized about the lack of maps for the campaign against the Seminoles; he would have been astonished to know that when Jackson rode out of Fort Gadsden on 7 May 1818, the general had in his hand a map for a campaign against Spain.[49]

The cartographic information Young would later add to his doctored report would have come in handy on this march. Given the way the American army approached Pensacola, it is impossible to believe that on this march Jackson possessed detailed information about the land west of Apalachicola. After crossing the river at Ochechee Bluff on 10 May, the army promptly got lost. For twelve days, Jackson thrashed around in the wilderness because his guides did not know the way to Pensacola. Finally stumbling onto a river everyone guessed was the Escambia, the army crossed it and traced its wandering course down toward the Spanish capital.[50]

Governor José Masot did not need this blundering march to alert him to the American army's approach. He had known all along that Jackson was going to come to his city. Indeed, Spanish officials everywhere who knew about Jackson's invasion had feared in March that he would proceed directly to Pensacola. Now Masot tried a tactic that already had failed two of his countrymen; he tried to divert the Americans with a letter. On 18 May, he wrote to Jackson with assurances that any evidence proving that Luengo had supplied hostile Indians would result in that officer's punishment. He insisted also that he had never hindered the movement of supplies up the Escambia. On the contrary, he had run the risk of his government's censure by allowing on his own initiative the Americans to use the Escambia. Masot cheerfully reported, though, that he had lately received authorization from Madrid, so the supplies to Fort Crawford would continue to pass freely.

Finally, he denied Jackson's claim that Pensacola harbored hostile Indians. There were a few Indians living around the town, the governor said, but they were mostly women and children. He mentioned the eighty-seven the Alabama militia had accosted while they were trying to reach Fort Crawford to surrender, but he insisted that Spain had not helped any Indians hostile to the United States. Though he did not mention it, Masot must have marveled at Jackson's estimate that four hundred to five hundred Indian warriors had sought refuge in Pensacola. The town had only four hundred regular inhabitants.[51]

Luengo could have told Masot to save his paper and ink. Jackson kept coming. Once he was over the Escambia, the only thing diverting him from a beeline toward Pensacola was the meandering course of the river. As this army reached the outskirts of the town, Masot sat down at his writing desk again, this time with his jaw set. The governor sternly denounced Jackson's invasion of West Florida and threatened to expel Jackson's army with force if it did not peaceably withdraw. Old Hickory must have smiled at that—expel with force, indeed. Finally, a Spaniard had handed him something resembling a hostile act. True enough, they were only words, but they were inhospitable ones. These words would do to cost His Most Catholic Majesty the capital of West Florida.[52]

⤞⤝

On 23 May, the same day he received Masot's last letter, Jackson took Pensacola without firing a shot. Masot and the town's garrison retreated to Fort Barrancas as Jackson approached. The governor had grimly read the general's reply to his letter, a reiteration of charges about Pensacola helping hostile Indians. Jackson reminded Masot that this would not be the first time the United States had felt it necessary to occupy Pensacola because of Spanish aid to America's enemies. On that previous occasion, Jackson said, the United States had returned the town to Spain, but this time the United States would keep it—at least until Spain could protect the frontier.[53]

Yet Barrancas was not St. Marks, and Masot was not Luengo. Even though he had a garrison of only 175 men in the fort (more than twice as many as Luengo had commanded at St. Marks), Masot did have some formidable artillery. Also unlike at St. Marks, the governor closed the gates of his post so that American officers were not casually visiting and American sick and wounded were not resting in the fort's hospital. Taking Barrancas would require that Jackson do more than bluster outside and stride purposefully in; he would likely have to resort to force.[54]

Force would require a formal siege and considerable time, so Jackson first tried bluster, tingeing it with his usual accusations and naked threats. He assured Masot that the United States Army would protect all private and public property in its capacity as the civil government of Pensacola. He promised Masot and all of his men transportation to Cuba if the governor surrendered the garrison. But any show of resistance, Jackson cautioned, would end with all Spanish soldiers becoming American "prisoners of war."[55]

Gadsden, already reaping the benefits of the campaign with a field promotion to captain, carried Jackson's message with authority to negotiate Masot's surrender. Inside the walls of Barrancas, however, the governor proved implacable, his jaw still set and his resolve to resist unshaken. Not only did he refuse to submit, he again opened the initial argument, denying Jackson's accusations about his city aiding hostile Indians. As evidence, he reminded Jackson about the eighty-seven Creeks sent to surrender to Major Young at Fort Crawford. Then the governor of West Florida gave the American general a civics lesson. Masot cited James Monroe's 25 March message to Congress in which the president described Jackson's only purpose in Florida as chastising hostile Indians. Monroe told Congress that the government had instructed Jackson not to molest Spaniards.[56]

Jackson probably did not know about Monroe's specific message to Congress, but he certainly did know, from Calhoun's orders to Gaines, that the civil officers of his government did not want to attack Spain in Florida. Having Masot point out the United States government's recent iteration of such restrictions was an inconvenient piece of temerity, so Jackson chose simply to ignore it. Instead, he focused exclusively on Masot's declarations of Spanish innocence and snarled over Masot's statement that he would hold Barrancas to the last extremity.[57]

Jackson accused the governor of lying about not helping hostile Indians; the general had an affidavit from witnesses who had seen Spanish officers outside the town on 23 May with seventeen Indians. Of course, Masot had never denied the presence of Indians around Pensacola. He had insisted that his government had never supplied Indians who were fighting Americans. In any event, Jackson's previous count of between four hundred and five hundred warriors had suddenly been reduced in hard documentation to seventeen Indians. On this basis, the general repeated his demand for the surrender of Fort Barrancas. He put Masot on notice: any blood spilled at Pensacola would now be on the governor's hands.[58]

Having thus huffed and puffed his threats to blow the Spanish house down, Jackson began preparing a siege. His staff took stock of the army's fitness for an attack. Subtracting the 100 men occupying Pensacola and 36 on the sick list, Jackson had 956 men for the assault on Barrancas, and facing those numbers the fort looked fairly imposing. On 26 May, he ordered his engineers, led by the indispensable Gadsden, to begin placing artillery. The young captain took a range of about 385 yards from the fort and wheeled a nine-pounder into position; nearly twice that distance away, in a hilltop cemetery, Gadsden had his men sweating and tugging several howitzers into place amid the tombstones. The Spaniards watched from behind their guns at Barrancas until they could not bear it anymore. At first light on 27 May, they opened fire on the American batteries. It was not the Seminole War any longer.[59]

∽∝

American gunners returned fire, but Gadsden had placed the cannon too far away from Barrancas, so the batteries kept up a desultory fire while their officers tugged their chins over their next move. The guns had not rattled Barrancas so much as they had Masot, however, and he sent word that he wanted to reopen talks. When Jackson offered only the same terms as before the siege, Masot refused, and firing recommenced. That night, American engineers and gunners hefted their artillery closer to the fort.[60]

Now within effective range, American cannon the next day did more than jangle the governor's nerves. By afternoon, he again proposed terms, but this time he scribbled them at a trembling table in a cracked room covered with plaster dust. So this time Masot's terms were essentially Jackson's: the governor would surrender the fort if his garrison could go to Havana and Jackson would assume responsibility for Spanish sick and wounded as well as Spanish property in Pensacola. Then Masot added one last item. Apparently mindful of what had happened at St. Marks, he asked to take the Creek chief Opayhola and his family to Havana. Jackson agreed to everything, congratulating himself as he did so on his charity for a defeated foe.[61]

Yet there were limits to his benevolence. Jackson claimed that Masot's surrender gave the United States control over all territory in the governor's jurisdiction. To determine precisely what that entailed, Jackson first ordered a survey and description of all public buildings in Pensacola. The city had thirty-eight government buildings, including blockhouses, barracks, the governor's residence, hospitals, and sentry boxes. Jackson had taken Pensacola again, but this time no one had destroyed its fortifications and diminished its value before leaving.[62]

Old Hickory soon left also. On 29 May, he issued a proclamation that the United States would retain Pensacola until Spain demonstrated it could protect West Florida. Jackson promised the continued enforcement of Spanish civil law, but lest that be confused as maintaining Spanish sovereignty, he also established a United States Customs House and appointed Gadsden as Pensacola's port collector. He also made Colonel William King the military governor of West Florida. Jackson's terms for the return of the province to Spain and his establishment of conspicuous manifestations of American authority meant that the United States now indefinitely owned West Florida, courtesy of the United States Army.[63]

Leaving Colonel King to supervise the discharge of the Tennessee and Kentucky militia, Jackson left Pensacola. He stopped briefly at Fort Montgomery to write his reports and finally close out the entire campaign. He called for two companies of mounted volunteers (presumably from the Alabama Territory) to patrol between the Mobile and Apalachicola Rivers. They were to kill any Indians who refused to leave the area. The sweep would serve a temporary purpose, he thought, because posts along the thirty-first parallel would never be effective. Jackson wrote to Calhoun that only United States forts along the Gulf of Mexico could prevent Indian attacks.[64]

He had taken the fort at St. Marks and had "planted the Star Spangled Banner on the ramparts of Fort Carlos de Barrancas."[65] These were the first steps in establishing that defensive line, and he had told Gadsden to prepare a report on the others that would be needed.[66] So even as

Jackson made the obligatory statements about Spain's continued ownership of West Florida, he built a case for America to keep it. With his
report to Calhoun, he sent witnesses like William Hambly, who could
attest to persistent Seminole hostility and continued Spanish collusion.
Indeed, the former Forbes man who had helped Jackson hang Arbuthnot
was proving increasingly useful. Before leaving for Washington, he
signed an affidavit that he had heard from reliable sources that five hundred Indians at Pensacola had fled upon the United States Army's
approach.[67]

With such dubious testimony, Hambly and other witnesses would
explain why Jackson, ostensibly in Florida to fight Indians, had seized
Spanish Pensacola without an Indian in sight. Eventually, Jackson himself labored to prove that large numbers of Indians had prompted his
march on Pensacola. In September 1818, he sent Captain Hugh Young
to gather affidavits from inhabitants of the area swearing that Indians
had been in the vicinity of Pensacola before the American army arrived.
These affidavits would also claim that the Spanish government had supplied these Indians and had bought stolen American property from
them.[68]

Yet Jackson himself could not have believed much, if any of this
information. If he did, his behavior during May 1818 in West Florida
becomes nonsensical. If he really believed that five hundred hostile
warriors had just been at Pensacola, why did he not pursue them rather
than taking the town and reducing its Spanish fort? If he really believed
that five hundred warriors still roamed the Florida wilderness, why
did he only place small garrisons at Barrancas, St. Marks, and Fort
Gadsden? Why did he send home his Allied Creeks and the Georgia
militia so early? Why did he send home most of his regulars and discharge the Tennessee and Kentucky militia? Why did he leave such a
diminished military presence in the same area that he insisted Luengo
and Masot could no longer control because of their diminished military
capabilities?[69]

It would take a few months, but some people would begin asking
these and other nettlesome questions about what Jackson had done in
Florida. In the meantime, though, Monroe and his cabinet remained
ignorant that any questions would have to be answered, let alone that
they would be such serious ones about why an American army had executed two British subjects on Spanish soil and had forcefully seized

Spanish territory, thereby to make war on Spain without congressional authorization. And with those questions would come another chance for Andrew Jackson to huff and puff, perhaps to blow down another house, this time much closer to home.

8

"There Are Serious Difficulties in This Business"

In Washington, as the various controversies surrounding the Florida invasion came to light, Monroe and his cabinet must have wondered how bad it could get. The attack on St. Marks, the execution of Arbuthnot and Ambrister, the massacre at Chehaw, and finally the unauthorized seizure of Pensacola each unfolded as in a bad dream. The first news arrived at the War Department on 4 May with the delivery of Jackson's initial dispatches announcing the capture of St. Marks. Calhoun immediately informed Monroe and the rest of the cabinet, and with typical resolve the administration elected to do nothing for the moment. Nobody in Washington yet knew about Arbuthnot and Ambrister—their executions had occurred only five days before—but some people had an inkling about Jackson's plans for the rest of Florida.[1]

From its outset the campaign had become part of the Washington gossip machine, complete with widespread speculation about its real intentions. As early as January, Congressman John Tyler of Virginia had said he would "not be at all surprised, if the government went on to take possession of the Floridas."[2] A month later North Carolina's Nathaniel Macon echoed the sentiment. As was his careful habit, he disclaimed any knowledge of Monroe's intentions, but Macon believed that with Jackson's foray into Spanish territory "it seems probable that we may find ourselves in possession of all or nearly all Florida."[3]

Georgia's John Forsyth, chairman of the House Foreign Relations Committee, finally asked Calhoun if Gaines and Jackson had the administration's blessing to invade Florida. Calhoun cagily replied that Monroe's 25 March message to Congress would answer this and other questions about the campaign. It was this message that Masot had so pathetically brandished before Jackson's threats at Pensacola. In short, the president attempted to explain the situation to Congress at roughly the same time Jackson was making a liar out of him.[4]

Actually, the taking of Pensacola was a critically serious affair. Jackson investing an isolated Spanish fort to prevent its falling to Indians (or prevent its assisting hostile Indians) was one thing; taking a Spanish town was another, even if it had not been the capital of West Florida. The Monroe administration does not seem to have imagined the worst. At the end of March, Calhoun remarked that "Spanish affairs at present produce most excitement," but the secretary did not appear overly concerned about what might be happening in Florida.[5] He knew what Jackson's orders said. He seems to have believed that Jackson would obey them.

Also, Calhoun had other military matters on his mind. He had spent most of late winter and spring shepherding through Congress an army organization bill that would create the positions of surgeon general, quartermaster general, judge advocate general, and commissary general. When Congress passed the bill just before adjourning on 20 April, Calhoun could count a great triumph with this first, major step toward bringing efficiency to the War Department. The triumphs would tarnish, however, when news of Jackson's behavior reached Washington to overshadow with charges of military Caesarism and administrative ineptitude all the efficiencies and accomplishments the secretary had accomplished.[6]

Rumors always travel faster than facts, and there were precious few of the latter. Calhoun wrote to Governor Lewis Cass of the Michigan Territory to allay his fears that the Seminole conflict would inflame the entire frontier. The secretary assured Cass that Jackson was done in Florida and not to worry about the tranquility of Michigan's marches.[7] At the 13 May cabinet meeting, no one had yet heard anything beyond those dispatches received nine days before. Furthermore, the administration evinced no alarm about what it knew so far. Monroe decided to extend to St. Marks the policy he had adopted in January toward

Amelia Island. The United States would hold it too until Spain provided sufficient forces to control the area.[8] Ten days later, William Crawford wrote that "nothing has occurred of importance in our foreign relations since the adjournment of Congress."[9] Monroe and his ministers enjoyed roughly a month of blissful ignorance before the storm broke.

The first thunderbolt did not come from Florida, however; it came from Georgia with the news of the massacre at Chehaw village. Before any news of Jackson's seizure of Pensacola reached Washington, Jackson's and Rabun's letters presenting their versions of the incident began arriving in the capital. These communications placed Washington squarely in the middle of the dispute, and nobody in the Monroe administration was happy about it. Even if there had been no personal choler in this argument between Jackson and Rabun, the administration had reason to avoid involvement. Obviously, the attack on Chehaw was unpardonable, and after Calhoun had heard from Jackson—but before he had heard from Rabun—he was describing it so, calling it "the recent and horrid attack upon Chehaw."[10] At first, Calhoun feared that Indian retaliation would further unsettle an already turbulent frontier, but after reflection (and the arrival of Rabun's letter) other concerns intruded.

Calhoun could not have known that Rabun's charge that Jackson had placed himself above Georgia's civilian authority foreshadowed imputations about Old Hickory's lack of submission to federal civilian authority. Perhaps with some sense of irony, Calhoun privately would later condemn Jackson's obvious disregard for civilian control of the military. Yet the secretary knew that such charges were a staple of political debate in the young republic, and when someone like Jackson gave them credence with imperious behavior, politicians of all stripes raised their voices in the familiar chorus of alarm. Rabun could accurately portray Jackson, through his 7 May letter, as believing that military authority was superior to civilian control in some instances, which was to say, really in all instances. But Jackson could as accurately accuse Rabun of a reflexive politicizing that invented chimerical threats of military despotism to divert attention from the real issues.[11]

To Jackson, one of the issues was getting his hands on Obed Wright. While he was taking Pensacola, Jackson assumed Davis was arresting Wright to bring him to Fort Hawkins for trial. On his way to Fort Montgomery, Jackson learned of Wright's liberation by the Baldwin County court and his subsequent parole. Jackson exploded at Rabun, raging that such actions were "an unwarrantable interference with my duties." He insisted that Rabun turn Wright over to him.[12]

By June, the Monroe administration had to face its potential responsibilities. The president and Calhoun were absent from Washington on a southern tour as the trouble over Wright's arrest unfolded. On 2 June Calhoun's chief clerk, Christopher Vandeventer, instructed David B. Mitchell to assure the Chehaws that the perpetrators of the unauthorized attack would be punished by a military tribunal already instigated by Jackson.[13] But such an endorsement of Jackson's exclusive authority in the matter could not stand given the constitutional irregularities it raised. In the meantime, Washington persisted in taking no official notice of the Jackson-Rabun quarrel, although Calhoun for one must have realized the political and constitutional mess it portended. Nevertheless, it would have to make way for a constitutional mess of even greater magnitude.

⸏⸏

Monroe and Calhoun were still on their southern tour in mid-June when they at last heard about Pensacola, not from Jackson but from the newspapers. Everyone knew how the press could be, so Monroe hurried to Washington, expecting to find waiting there a logical explanation from the general. Yet when the president arrived in the capital on 19 June, there was no word from Jackson. The administration had received nothing from him since those preliminary dispatches about St. Marks had arrived six weeks before. Furnished with nothing more substantial than newspaper accounts, Monroe simply did not know what to do. Calhoun had not returned with him—he was in South Carolina checking his crops—but had the secretary been in Washington, he could have done little more than watch Monroe wring his hands. Neither he nor anyone else in the government knew exactly what Jackson had done. The Spanish and British embassies, where attachés read newspapers too, had a number of pressing questions about the matter, and even the French minister, Baron Jean Guillaume Hyde de Neuville, displayed a searching curiosity. It all became a little too much for James Monroe, so he left town, much to the chagrin of Secretary of State Adams, who remained in Washington to answer questions best he could from dubious diplomats and increasingly inquisitive congressmen. Safely ensconced at his farm in Loudoun County, Monroe took refuge among the rolling hills of northern Virginia. He would not reappear until he had an entire cabinet to help him make some decisions.[14]

By July, the pesky newspapers were wondering why no one had heard from Jackson. Sensing trouble brewing for Monroe, Henry Clay began stirring up a little himself, writing to fellow congressmen that Jackson had ignored congressional prerogatives regarding the power to make war. Some of those congressman, however, had already begun to wet fingers to test the winds of public opinion: if the country approved of Jackson's behavior, it would be politically foolish to condemn him. As these various players drew the lines to contest this issue, James Monroe's administration remained undecided about what it would do.[15]

Finally the War Department obtained some hard information on 7 July when William Hambly arrived carrying Jackson's letters of 2 June.[16] Adams immediately read these messages and stuffed them in a pouch for delivery to the president in Loudoun County. After Monroe had studied the letters, he recorded directly on Jackson's report his hope "that his [Jackson's] conduct will be approved, which shows, that he had acted on his own responsibility."[17] The president cryptically left unspoken who was to do this approving, thus revealing not only his continued indecisiveness on this issue but also his desire to avoid any blame for it.

Someone—perhaps it was Adams—had Vandeventer include in this pouch copies of the War Department's orders to Gaines and Jackson authorizing the invasion but prohibiting assaults on Spanish forts.[18] If it was Adams, it was the last time he did anything that might call into question Jackson's rectitude in Florida. The secretary of state had grown waspish over his extra duties, and he wanted Monroe to return to Washington. When Jackson's dispatches arrived, Adams was taking a break from his continuing boundary negotiations with Onís, who was at his country home in Pennsylvania. At last these talks had seemed to be making progress. Madrid's precarious hold on her American colonies had persuaded Foreign Minister José García de León y Pizarro to give Onís greater flexibility in settling disputes with the United States. Onís had eagerly used his increased latitude to advance the stalled talks, at least until he officially heard what had happened at St. Marks and Pensacola. Drawing himself up in quiet outrage, the Spanish minister did not so much return to Washington as he descended on it. In the wee hours of 8 July, a stern message from Onís roused

Adams from his bed. The Spanish minister was threatening to break off all negotiations.

Nor was this all. On the same day Adams sent Jackson's dispatches to Monroe, the French minister had called at the State Department with questions about Pensacola. Adams did not know what to tell him, of course, because the administration had no official position yet. Yet the secretary knew better than to reveal to foreigners any trace of American irresolution. With the clipped surety emblematic of all the Adamses, he told both Hyde de Neuville and Onís that he believed the president would have no objections to Jackson's conduct.[19]

Adams knew better—or, at least, he knew enough about Monroe to know that such a resolute position from the administration was at this juncture most unlikely. After all, he just months before had seen how Monroe stumbled to a conclusion on Amelia Island. Monroe probably felt cornered in the summer of 1818, even while relatively removed from the fray by hiding in Loudoun County. The arrival of all that mail from Washington had marked a most disturbing development in his predicament, and rather than clarify things, it had merely muddled them more. He wanted to support Jackson, but he also knew that the case Jackson made in his 2 June communications was unlikely to convince anyone but the general's partisans that his conduct in Florida had been proper. Monroe knew the ruthlessness of those partisans and the vast political power they were beginning to wield. Indeed, it alarmed him to no end. Writing to James Madison, he moaned that "there are serious difficulties in this business, on which ever side we view it."[20]

Surely, he thought, there was a better justification for what Jackson had done. As the cabinet gathered in Washington, Monroe instructed Calhoun, who had returned on the eighth, to request more papers from Jackson. Monroe had seized on one of Jackson's earlier letters in which he mentioned more detailed reports about the Seminole campaign and the existence of letters found aboard Arbuthnot's *Chance* that confirmed the guilt of the Scot and Robert Ambrister. Jackson had said he was sending these to the War Department, but they had never arrived. Surely those documents would better reveal the absolute necessity of killing the Britons and making war on Spain without congressional consent.[21]

The cabinet could not wait for this additional (and Monroe hoped, exculpatory) evidence before acting to contain the political damage.[22] The administration simply had to make a public statement about its

Florida policy and Jackson's deportment within it. That meant the administration first had to formulate a policy, and with that object as its main priority, the cabinet began meeting on 15 July every day for the next week. To Adams, it was the Amelia Island business all over again: free-ranging discussion (Adams would have called it undisciplined) in which everybody expressed his opinion (Adams would have described it as contentious), with the president taking the counsel of everyone (Adams would have characterized it as chronic indecision).[23]

Adams had already made his decision about what should be done when the cabinet met, and he had revealed it to Monroe. The secretary watched the obvious signs in these meetings that his colleagues too had concluded what Jackson's culpability was and what the government's response should be, and some of it worried him. Calhoun made it clear to Adams that he felt Jackson had disobeyed orders, stirring in Adams fears that Calhoun, though "generally of sound, judicious, and comprehensive mind, seems in this case to be personally offended with the idea that Jackson has set nought the instructions of his Department."[24] Jackson's exploits had instead roused in Adams the instincts of the shrewd Yankee trader. Far more important than Jackson's deliberate disregard of his orders was the practical benefit the United States might enjoy because he had done so. Fifteen years earlier, a younger John Quincy Adams had fretted over the constitutional irregularities of Jefferson's purchasing Louisiana until Secretary of State James Madison had told him to be still and reap the occasional fruits of expediency over principle. Now in 1818, Adams was older, wiser, and ready to do some harvesting of his own.[25]

Adams watched Crawford and Wirt behave precisely the way they had in the Amelia Island discussions. Their responses to any question depended on which way they perceived Monroe to be leaning. Crawford hedged even that, Adams thought, with cunning calculations about what position would most benefit him personally.[26] By the summer of 1818, the president's men had become facile at discerning Monroe's opinion, with the possible exception of Calhoun. If what Monroe wanted was clear to Calhoun in these meetings, he evidently did not care. The others knew, perhaps instinctively, that the president wanted to be convinced that Jackson had done the right thing. Nobody could have remained unaware that James Monroe could not bear the prospect of punishing Andrew Jackson.

Adams led the deliberations, advancing the idea that Jackson's aggressive acts were actually defensive, justified by Spanish aid to the Indians. Calhoun bluntly countered that nothing could sanction this man's blatant disregard of his orders. He tersely stated that Jackson should be court-martialed. If the administration did not thus disavow his conduct, it would have to shoulder the blame for it.

Crawford thought both positions too severely drawn. He preferred to interpret Jackson's action as a misunderstanding. He reminded everyone of Jackson's 6 January letter proposing that Monroe send authorization to seize Florida through John Rhea. When Crawford asked Monroe if he had answered the letter, the question flustered Monroe, but Crawford did not dwell on the matter. Instead he merely said that since the letter had not been answered, Jackson must have assumed that he had Monroe's tacit approval.[27] As unsettling as this line of argument must have been for Monroe, it was certainly even more galling for its advocate. Defending Jackson was hard for Crawford, but he was reading the politics of this situation better than Calhoun was. Outside the realm of principle, Adams's arguments made sense: Spain, the secretary of state said, would now have to realize that her tenuous hold on Florida was slipping. He predicted Onís would make noise over Jackson's invasion but then would resume negotiations to submit to American demands. Leaving aside the possibility of his personal involvement, Monroe must have found this last point appealing. He certainly wanted Florida. Could Jackson's rash acts deliver it to him with, as Adams said, so little bother?[28]

Calhoun remained adamant. How was he ever to control and hence reform his department if Jackson were allowed to behave with such impunity? Desperate for anything to discredit the man, Calhoun leveled grave accusations against Jackson's motives in Florida. The previous winter, Calhoun said, speculators had formed a company in Tennessee to purchase land in and around Pensacola. Rachel Jackson's nephew was involved, and Jackson had written letters of introduction for agents sent to buy the land. Rumor had it that Jackson himself was a silent partner in the enterprise. Now, Calhoun mused, if the United States took possession of West Florida, this land could only surge in value. Adams listened, but he quickly dismissed the land company's activities as coincidental and the stories alleging otherwise as unfounded. It was his clipped certainty again, and again it was partly an artful pretense. In his diary, from which Adams kept no secrets, he would record these conjectures about Jackson's integrity and his arguments against them, wondering a little if the stories were indeed true. He finally confided, "I hope not."[29]

✥

After these lengthy discussions, the cabinet adopted the improbable but, as it happened, politically astute position of having it both ways: Jackson was justified in and should be congratulated for his assault on the Spaniards. His actions, however, neither reflected the administration's policy nor would receive the executive's endorsement. Hence Pensacola would be restored to Spain promptly, St. Marks as soon as Spain could find 250 good men and true to keep it out of the hands of the Indians. Adams was to write instructions to George Erving, United States minister in Madrid, rationalizing what had happened, and the executive would inform Congress in the Annual Message.[30]

Officially they presented a united front ready to face all critics, foreign and domestic. Yet privately Monroe and Calhoun worried about the position they had taken, and Crawford sought to turn it to his political advantage. Calhoun still believed that Jackson had misbehaved, but he also thought that the administration's mixed tactic of supporting the general without endorsing him was a mistake. It was the equivalent of drawing the pail of milk to kick it over, and Calhoun feared that Jackson's people were powerful enough to make everyone shed a goodly number of tears over the spill. On the other side, the secretary could see congressional factions that had already been searching for an excuse to slash his military budget using Jackson's imperious behavior to do so. Monroe also worried about Jackson's response to the administration's awkward vote of confidence. The president wrote Jackson a carefully worded letter of reassurance that nonetheless gently nudged him to provide more evidence. More incredible than Monroe's request for more evidence was his suggestion that Jackson invent some. He suggested that it might be wise for the general to alter his earlier reports to indicate Spanish misconduct rather than mere weakness as provoking the military action. Monroe said he was offering the suggestion because he was certain that Jackson, fatigued and ill, had forgotten to include such evidence in his 2 June reports. Tranquilizing Jackson with soothing communications would become a routine duty for both Monroe and Calhoun for the rest of the year, but the general bristled over this suggestion that he had done something wrong and would have to lie to cover it up. He insisted that he had acted within the bounds of his orders.[31]

Others needed soothing too. Just as Calhoun had found Jackson's behavior objectionable, some people down the avenue in the Capitol were likely to raise a howl over it. As a trickling protest began, Monroe plugged as many holes in the dike as he had fingers, privately writing first to Madison and Jefferson to castigate Jackson for taking St. Marks and Pensacola "on his own responsibility,"[32] even as he explained that to court-martial him "would be the triumph of Spain."[33] He liked the sound of this latter explanation so much that he tried it out on congressional leaders, saying again in private correspondence that to punish Jackson might mislead Spain into thinking that it could keep Florida.[34]

Monroe might have cursed the luck that made this business so complicated, for if humbling Spaniards had been the only point of issue, a few such well-placed letters might have diverted all but the most niggling criticism. But there was much more at stake here. Jackson had been nothing if not thorough in whom he had offended, provoked, and trampled. The consequences of his campaign reached far beyond Florida, even beyond Washington. In addition to Spaniards, the British might be expected to take issue over the execution of Arbuthnot and Ambrister, Congress over the military's presumption of war-making powers, the Chehaws over the murder of their people and the destruction of their village, and William Rabun over Jackson's peremptory contempt for the authority of the governor of Georgia.

From the moment Obed Wright destroyed Chehaw, the incident had threatened to become a political firestorm. While Calhoun and Monroe were still away from Washington in June, Adams with Crawford and Wirt decided that Wright could be prosecuted before the Circuit Court of the United States. They did allow that the federal court might disavow jurisdiction, however. If that happened, they wanted Wright tried before a court-martial "under the direction of the executive of the state of Georgia."[35] Obviously eager to keep Wright out of Jackson's hands yet equally distressed by the offense it would give the general, Monroe upon his return to Washington issued instructions to accomplish the judicial inquiry in federal court. He wanted it to take place in the next term, either in November or December, and with considerable trepidation about the matter remaining unresolved until then, Monroe directed that both Rabun and Jackson be advised of these actions.[36]

Monroe need not have worried even a little. The constitutional issues of civil authority and military justice, the spiny ambiguities of states' rights and national dominion, all bore down upon the fate of Obed Wright, who solved everything almost immediately by fleeing the country. As Rabun went through the motions of arranging for Wright's transfer to federal custody—a custody likely to include a jail cell—the Milledgeville press reported that Monroe had ordered Wright's arrest preparatory to a September trial in the United States Circuit Court. Wright would be charged with murder and the destruction of the Chehaw village, a violation of the Trade and Intercourse Act of 1802.[37] When this report reached Wright, Rabun explained to John Quincy Adams, the young man escaped from Georgia's adjutant general on 27 July.[38] Yet Wright's escape could not have been too difficult given the circumstances of his detention by Georgia authorities. The adjutant general probably did not know Wright's whereabouts even before 27 July. The accused had, in fact, sought help from Laurens County's Jacob Robinson, who had participated in the Chehaw attack. Showing up at Robinson's house in Dublin in late July or early August (Robinson was very vague about the details), Wright told Robinson that the governor had freed him. Wright also allegedly promised Robinson that he would return to stand trial, but he could not bear the interim imprisonment. Robinson gave Wright a canoe, and he was not seen again until reports placed him in St. Augustine and, by year's end, in Havana, Cuba.[39]

Rabun put out a reward for Wright's capture and promised Adams that Georgia would keep looking for him, but it is difficult to believe that the governor was serious or that Adams wanted him to be. Indeed, Wright would never stand trial for the attack on Chehaw.[40] While Wright's escape served to resolve, however raggedly, the problem for Rabun and the national government, it did not satisfy Andrew Jackson.

Unable to let it alone, in August he charged at Rabun again and this time got back a little better than he gave. Rabun recommended to Jackson "that before you undertake to prosecute another campaign, you examine the orders of your superiors with more attention than usual." Rabun said he would explain why he had felt authorized to call for reinforcements from Fort Early when Jackson explained under what authority he had tried to obtain Obed Wright. And as for Jackson's declaration that nobody had reason to fear military despotism from him, Rabun suggested that he offer up the "late proceedings at St. Marks and Pensacola as affording conclusive evidence of that point."[41]

The Monroe administration had only grudgingly entered the dispute and then primarily to placate the Chehaws, doing so by disbursing eight thousand dollars in compensation for the destruction of their village and the murder of their people. By autumn, the Quartermaster's Department would provide them with five thousand rations of flour and cornmeal.[42] It was hardly the justice they deserved. It was certainly less than Jackson had promised.

Many throughout the country found Jackson's behavior in Florida laudatory, reflecting the sentiments of a toast at a public dinner in Nashville shortly after his return: "Major General Jackson—His fame is the offspring of his own merit."[43] Nevertheless, many other people were as alarmed by this popular acclaim as they were by the deeds that had animated it. Rabun's rancorous words portended a controversy that was only beginning.

The president had not satisfied the diplomatic corps, either. British minister Charles Bagot regularly prowled the executive mansion when news about the invasion first hit Washington, and he continued to appear with annoying frequency while the cabinet met in July. Unable to pry from the administration a reason for Arbuthnot and Ambrister's fate and without instructions from London, Bagot made himself a persistent presence simply because he could not think of how else to proceed. Monroe and Adams, however, regarded Bagot's tenacity with mild alarm. Was he signaling a British move to take the Spaniards' part in the larger controversy or was he only interested in Arbuthnot and Ambrister? Suspecting the worst, they elected to answer all Bagot's questions with an unqualified defense of everything Jackson had done.[44] Clipped certainty might not placate anyone, but perhaps it would buy some time.

Once the cabinet made its decision, Adams made the most of the time he had left before a potential rupture in British relations. He wrote to Richard Rush, the United States minister in London, but the vagaries of trans-Atlantic communications put the secretary's envelope on Rush's desk about the same time that Castlereagh was reading Bagot's letter requesting instructions. Adams told Rush that Jackson's campaign would "probably occasion some excitement in Europe," but he added that after being apprised of the facts divulged at the trial of Arbuthnot and Ambrister (the proceedings of the court-martial were still lost in the mail), Great Britain would calm down.[45]

Adams exuded much more confidence in his role than Castlereagh did in his. Bagot's letter put the foreign minister in a quandary. In the first place, without an official report of the trial, he did not even know why Arbuthnot and Ambrister had been killed, let alone whether or not he should care. Moreover, Adams probably knew that Castlereagh desired to maintain cordial Anglo-American relations as much as the secretary did. Rush and United States minister to France, Albert Gallatin, acting as a special envoy to Great Britain, were in the middle of broad negotiations with the British to resolve use of the North American fisheries, the return of slaves taken in the last war, the encouragement of trade, and the fixing of Canadian-American borders. Neither side wanted these talks endangered by extraneous distractions, so while Adams told Rush to bluff his way through embarrassing questions in London, Castlereagh told Bagot not to ask any embarrassing ones in Washington. At the most, the British minister was to find out what he could while taking care not to offend anyone.[46]

While waiting on his instructions, Bagot kept up the routine of haunting the executive's offices, anticipating that London would want him to be more polite than petulant, and thus only gently persisting in his requests for the court-martial proceedings. By the time he finally received them in the second week of September, he had spent a good deal of his time assuring the United States of Britain's friendship and its rebuff of America's Indian enemies.[47]

By then, Castlereagh would perhaps have liked to change places with Bagot, for it was all he could do in England to keep the deaths of the old Scot and young soldier from becoming spurs to war. The public, churned by sensational accounts in the press, perceived the executions as an affront of the first rank, and Castlereagh glumly noted in the fall of 1818 that if the government wanted a brawl with the United States, a large number of Britons would eagerly hold the government's coat. But the larger concerns of trade, fish, and boundaries hemmed Britain's course and resulted in the Convention of 1818 by year's end. Individual voices continued to cry out for justice, even adding Josiah Francis to the list of martyrs, but the popular mood soon found other causes. By the time Parliament took up the issue a year had passed since the executions, and the public's anger had melted into indifference. Castlereagh finally told Bagot to drop this issue. Old Arbuthnot and young Ambrister were dead, but no one in England seemed to care anymore.[48]

The president had not satisfied the diplomatic corps, and Jackson's invasion had injured Spain far more than his execution of Arbuthnot and Ambrister had England. Don Luis de Onís had to do something significant in response, even though he knew at least one compelling reason to maintain cordial relations with the United States: Spain did not want the Americans to keep Florida without the confirmation of diplomatic consent. Onís might have suspected that Monroe did not want to keep it without a diplomatic accord verifying American ownership (he would have been right), but dignity required a dire reaction to Jackson's outrages, so the Spanish minister broke off the negotiations with Adams. Thus he ended talks that had consumed the previous seven months with discussions about Florida and the southwestern boundary of the United States.[49]

Onís lodged demands as predictable as they were quixotic. Eventually seconded by Madrid, he wanted an official apology for Jackson's behavior, a disavowal of his actions, and the removal of all United States forces from Spanish soil. Adams, of course, had predicted this Spanish reaction—it was the noise he expected Onís to make—and had said it would be temporary. Onís proved a fairly dogged actor, but nothing could long disguise that he and his superior, Pizarro, were going through some required motions. Adams defended Jackson's aggression as provoked by Spanish behavior in Florida, but the administration's promise to return Pensacola immediately and St. Marks eventually left the door open just enough for Onís to give up the act and bow to reality. The American position on Pensacola and St. Marks magically became the gist of Spanish demands, and by fall, counting his and Spain's faces relatively saved, Onís resumed negotiations with Adams.[50]

Onís, however, had a thankless task. Continuing revolutions in Latin America and the depredations of pirates threatened to collapse Spain's entire American empire. A negotiated settlement of the United States boundary, even if done at gunpoint, was better than a humiliating disintegration at the hands of rebels and buccaneers. Onís had to appear deliberate while moving quickly enough to outrun American impatience that might motivate another invasion. By now, he could have had no illusions about who was making this policy for the United States. The United States Army had seized Florida on its own initiative, and Adams's insistence that it had been right to do it amounted only to support after the fact. The Spanish minister could not be sure that the peppery little man sitting across the table would not one day have another unexpected American military adventure to justify. He knew, however, that if necessary the secretary would be up to the task, having had some practice.[51]

Monroe and Adams might have exploited this Spanish fear of an uncontrollable military had they not been equally afraid. Unsure about how much Spain was willing to negotiate and uncertain still about Britain's level of interest, the administration quailed before the prospect of again turning Jackson loose. Wagering that another, less hazardous threat might produce the desired effect, Adams hinted that if the boundary issue and the Florida dispute remained unresolved, the United States would have no choice but to recognize as independent the revolutionary Latin American republics.[52]

⊱⊰

Either unaware of or unconcerned about the gales brewing over his actions, Jackson spent much of the summer recuperating from the campaign and settling scores. During the campaign in Florida, the controversy over the accusations against David Mitchell lay dormant but simmering. Once the fighting was done, Gaines and Jackson commenced to pursue their vendetta against the agent.[53]

What seemed to anger Jackson and Gaines the most was that Mitchell had withheld the Allied Creeks when their services were first requested; furthermore, both apparently believed that the agent had tried to prevent the Allied Creeks from ever assisting the army. The best way to bring down Mitchell was to accuse him of breaking the law, however, so they concentrated on allegations that Mitchell had been involved in slave smuggling from Florida.[54]

Gaines became the lead dog who simply would not let go of this bone. He worked tirelessly to gather testimony from army officers who had been near the agency when the slaves arrived there. Colonel David Brearley of the Seventh Infantry had the most firsthand knowledge of the events, and he denied knowing anything about smuggled slaves. Shortly after this, Gaines accused Brearley of having failed to provide boats out of Fort Hawkins to transport supplies to the beleaguered Fort Scott. Brearley was formally acquitted of any negligence in this matter, but his refusal to incriminate Mitchell placed him on Gaines's enemies list along with the agent. Although the general never filed formal charges against Brearley, he apparently implied that Brearley was involved in the slave smuggling also. The colonel eventually felt it necessary to protect his reputation by providing written testimony concerning the slave controversy. In his deposition, Brearley said that he had seen the slaves at the Creek Agency. He had no reason to suspect Mitchell was involved in smuggling them, however, because it had been Mitchell who first suggested the slaves were contraband. It was Brearley's understanding that Mitchell suspected the slaves had been sneaked into the United States from Amelia Island. Mitchell told Brearley that he had informed the War Department about them and had insisted that their reputed owner post a security bond before he took them into the Alabama Territory.[55]

Colonel Brearley would not cooperate, and Gaines could find no other witnesses for the time being to incriminate Mitchell. Yet these problems were only temporary obstacles in this quest. A new allegation against the agent conveniently surfaced in June. Jackson received a letter from a Benjamin Smith accusing William McIntosh of selling the cattle captured during the Seminole War to David Mitchell's son at $5 a head. True enough, Jackson had given the cattle to the Allied Creeks, but he had instructed that they distribute them among their clans to replace the cattle lost in the Creek War. Now learning that McIntosh had apparently ignored these instructions, Jackson flew into another of his fabled rages. He wrote blistering letters to McIntosh and Mitchell insisting that the agent's son return the herds for disbursement as he had instructed. He sent a copy of the letters to Calhoun to add to the dossier of evidence accumulating against David Mitchell.[56]

Mitchell's equanimity evaporated in the face of this latest assault. In a letter that matched the anger of Jackson's, he snapped that it would have been helpful for the general to tell someone beside William McIntosh what was supposed to happen to the cattle. As it was, Mitchell, ignorant of Jackson's wishes, had seen no reason to stop McIntosh and his warriors from selling cattle that evidently belonged to them. Mitchell declared that he had not been involved in these transactions, but he did know that the actual number of cattle sold was much lower than what Jackson had alleged. The Allied Creeks had driven over one thousand head into their nation, he said, selling the others because they had tired of managing the large, unwieldy herd and wanted to diminish its size. Mitchell noted that Jackson had copied his letter to Calhoun, so he was doing likewise with this communication. He was certain that Jackson would not mind.[57]

The relentless campaign against Mitchell continued into the fall and beyond, marked by the continuous statement of these charges by these indefatigable accusers. It would take three years, but the stamina and consistency of his assailants finally did Mitchell in when Monroe removed him from office under a vague cloud of scandal and alleged malfeasance. Historians have generally accepted as true the accusations against David Mitchell, even though the charges against Mitchell were never put to the test of a trial. In his report to Monroe preceding Mitchell's discharge, Attorney General Wirt analyzed the evidence and concluded that the evidence presented for and against Mitchell was so contradictory that it made an absolute determination of guilt or innocence impossible. Having said that, however, Wirt nevertheless went on to draw a conclusion: he believed that Mitchell had some level of involvement in smuggling slaves in from Florida. Yet, the fact remains that the charges were never conclusively proved.[58]

Which means, of course, that David Mitchell was never conclusively exonerated. To be sure, Mitchell made money during his career by engaging in some questionable business deals, but that is not what really brought on his ruin. For Jackson, Mitchell's affiliation with William Crawford was his first transgression. Then he had the temerity to oppose, even if temporarily, Jackson's military plans for Florida. Mitchell fell not because he was a thief and a corruptionist. He had committed a far greater crime than that. He had gotten in Andrew Jackson's way.[59]

Gaines remained in frontier Georgia that summer. He regularly sent reports to Jackson about Indian and black activity in Florida, especially dwelling on the suspected location of Peter McQueen and his purported plans for continuing hostilities. Gaines's fixation on McQueen is hard to explain. Did this professional officer really believe that McQueen's scattered and starving Red Stick refugees would be able to do anything beyond surviving? Many of the Red Sticks and Seminoles were wandering into Fort Gadsden, driven to surrender by their perpetual hunger. The army was repatriating them into the Creek Nation, where they gobbled up already strained food supplies. Yet even food shortages and the tensions of resettling Red Sticks among their former enemies did not disturb the peace. Exhaustion had finally taken its toll. As Calhoun hoped, Jackson's campaign and the continued American military presence had persuaded the Florida Indians that only their complete destruction would result from attacking the United States.[60]

Yet by midsummer, both Gaines and Jackson incredibly were insisting that the military's job in Florida remained unfinished. Gaines wrote to Jackson to express "the hope that [he] may be permitted to act against St. Augustine."[61] In early August, Jackson replied that if Gaines had proof that the Spaniards in St. Augustine were supplying Indians, he could take the town. Jackson authorized Gaines to use available naval forces and to draw ordnance from Charleston.[62] Less than two weeks after Monroe's cabinet had completed its tortured deliberations about how to rationalize Jackson's seizure of St. Marks and Pensacola, the general was authorizing an expedition against the capital of East Florida.

Three days after he had formulated yet another Florida policy, Jackson sat down to write to the administration about it. He told Monroe and Calhoun that he hoped Gaines was already crossing the line to destroy any rebuilt Indian towns on the Suwannee and then march on St. Augustine. Once the United States held that city, Jackson explained, all of Florida should be retained, "which the united voice of the west demand."[63] Jackson included the report Gadsden had prepared on the defenses of American-occupied Florida. As he effervesced over the magnificent farmland in north Florida, the young captain argued that American possession of key strategic points in Florida would prevent foreign powers from penetrating into the southern United States. Jackson casually endorsed the report with comments about how the retention of Florida would force Europe finally to respect the United States.[64]

As these communications made their way to Washington, Calhoun had already issued the administration's instructions to restore Pensacola immediately and its conditions for the return of St. Marks. The need for haste caused him to dispatch the orders directly to Gaines with copies to Jackson because the administration could not reopen negotiations with Onís before the resumption of Spanish authority in West Florida. Calhoun, recalling the two-year controversy about the provenance of orders to Jackson's subordinates, provided Old Hickory with a lengthy explanation about why, just this once, he was communicating directly to Gaines.[65]

As soon as a responsible Spanish official arrived, even if it was the disagreeable Masot, Gaines was to pull the army from Pensacola. He was to restore St. Marks to Spain once its garrison held enough Spanish soldiers to protect it from the Indians. In the case of both Pensacola and St. Marks, the administration wanted all accusations about Spanish malfeasance dropped. If Luengo returned with enough men to garrison St. Marks, Gaines was to give the post back to him. To provide for the security of the American frontier, Calhoun ordered it garrisoned as Gaines thought necessary. The secretary wanted the army to use regular troops, citing the expense of funding state militia, but rather than economy, the continuing quarrel between Jackson and Rabun and the Georgia militia's misbehavior at Chehaw probably guided Calhoun's thinking on this point.[66]

Then Jackson's letter about taking St. Augustine arrived in Washington. Calhoun probably did not even finish reading it before grabbing up a pen. Under no circumstances, he wrote to Gaines, was the army to attack St. Augustine. He repeated his instructions of the previous December that if Gaines believed Spaniards in St. Augustine were supplying Seminoles, he should submit the evidence to the War Department and await further instructions. Probably as much to his chagrin as to the administration's relief, Gaines would receive these orders before he commenced his campaign against East Florida.[67]

Possibly Gaines had not started into East Florida because he had already received Calhoun's instructions ordering the restoration of Pensacola and St. Marks. He immediately issued the necessary orders to Colonel King at Pensacola and Brevet Major Alexander C. W. Fanning at St. Marks. Gaines mused that 250 Spanish soldiers constituted a larger garrison than that of the American occupation, but he believed that it would take more Spanish than United States soldiers to resist an Indian attack.[68]

The correspondence in the fall of 1818 between Gaines, Jackson, their subordinates, and Calhoun illustrates again the problems of slow communication on a military frontier. Yet these messages also reveal a deliberate attempt by Gaines and Jackson to mislead the War Department about the Florida Indian menace. When Gaines heard from his officers in Florida that hundreds of Indians were surrendering to American forces there, he nonetheless continued to prepare an assault against East Florida. Meanwhile he reported to Calhoun that only small numbers of Indians were surrendering and that attacks on frontier settlers were still occurring. He relayed unsubstantiated (and probably groundless) rumors that a large number of Seminoles around St. Augustine planned to strike at south Georgia. Yet at the same time he told Jackson that the proposed expedition to the Suwannee was no longer necessary because hundreds of Indians were surrendering.[69]

Even after Calhoun tried to rein him in, Gaines continued to concentrate on capturing St. Augustine. He collected rations and ordered men and boats to assemble at Fort Gadsden. After descending the Apalachicola to the Gulf of Mexico, he planned to have the expedition round the southern tip of Florida to proceed up to Amelia Island. There he would add regulars and naval forces provided by the War Department to strike St. Augustine. The general apparently expected complete support from a Calhoun baffled with misinformation. He certainly expected the War Department to agree regarding the use of regulars instead of militia. This would be a professional job.[70]

From the moment the administration committed to quitting Pensacola and St. Marks, Calhoun expected some resistance from Jackson and Gaines. Writing Jackson in early September to explain the cabinet's decision, he waxed so agreeable that he admitted the United States should possess Florida for national security. Yet, he also raised the specter of a war with Spain expanding to include Great Britain. Calhoun explained that the country needed time to prepare its defenses before embarking on such a conflict. When he heard that Gaines was possibly on his way to St. Augustine, Calhoun was not baffled. He was simply nonplussed.[71]

He never really believed the doctored information he was receiving from Gaines. There were "so many motives for misrepresentation," Calhoun told Monroe, ". . . that I am incredulous as to most of the reports."[72] He suspected that land speculators originated rumors of Indian attacks to scare squatters away from the ceded land. He would not provide Gaines with any additional soldiers until somebody provided reliable information about Indian belligerence. He wanted more details from Gaines. He did not want him to call up the trigger-happy militia, but instead told him to alert the Allied Creeks to stand ready just in case the Florida Indians were rebounding. The secretary dutifully copied everything to Jackson, but he made no secret that he found incredible Gaines's estimate of two thousand to four thousand Seminole warriors on the St. John's River. Calhoun was not baffled.[73]

He was, however, a little worried and very much alone. After making their initial decisions, the president and his cabinet scattered to the winds, deserting Washington and ironically leaving Calhoun alone to answer the multiplying questions.[74] While the rest of the cabinet took an autumn break before the rumbling Fifteenth Congress reassembled for its second session, Calhoun remained in Washington restraining impatient military commanders and directing surveys of the Creek land cession Mitchell had arranged in January. He also had to supervise the repatriation of surrendering Red Sticks and Seminoles, especially to ensure that Allied Creeks did not strip their former enemies of all their possessions, a right of conquest among Creeks. His plate already full, the last thing Calhoun needed while planning a defense of Jackson's spring invasion was to have another one in the fall.[75]

Calhoun explained to Gaines that if absolutely necessary, the War Department could shift some regulars from the Northern Division. Credible intelligence placed only about five hundred potentially hostile warriors in Florida, however, and Calhoun could not believe those Indians planned to attack the United States. He related to Gaines his conviction that people with wicked motives were spreading alarms over dangers that did not exist. He told the general that whatever happened, the army was to sit tight. It was imperative that the rest of the world not perceive Jackson's campaign in Florida as the first phase of an American land grab.[76]

In the fall of 1818, the military's aggressive posturing had nothing to do with Indians. While Gaines cooked his estimates of Indian strength in East Florida, the only documented hostilities in the Southern Division occurred in West Florida and southern Alabama. Apparently forty to fifty Red Sticks were wandering in the area. Perhaps they were the remnants of those who had fled the region around Pensacola upon Jackson's approach in May. Though no reports depicted them as threatening anyone, their presence frightened settlers, so regulars out of Pensacola and Fort Crawford sallied forth to find them. The soldiers out of Pensacola evidently engaged a party of about twenty-five warriors with indecisive results.[77]

And this was all. Several dozen Indians in West Florida represented no significant threat to the United States, but at least their existence was better documented than that of the thousands of hostile warriors Gaines kept insisting were amassing near St. Augustine. Finally, when Calhoun refused to play gullible, Gaines changed his story. In mid-October, he admitted that his sources had miscounted hostile Seminoles in East Florida. Now conceding there were fewer than two thousand to four thousand warriors (but also insisting that Calhoun's total erred on the low side), he suggested he could easily defeat however many Indians were down there with one thousand men. Indeed, with such a modest host, he would march all the way to Tampa Bay.[78]

As oblivious as ever to unwanted instructions from Washington, Gaines continued his preparations as he spun new justifications for the East Florida campaign. To Jackson he conveyed the news that Spaniards were importing black troops in St. Augustine. It was just the kind of rumor that would jab a knife to the brain of every southerner.[79] To challenge Calhoun's count of Seminoles, Gaines planned to visit Amelia Island to do some counting himself. He wrote to the secretary that Seminoles were killing settlers on the St. Mary's River and he intended to determine how many Indians were in the area "by actual inspection, peaceably if practicable, but at the point of the Bayonet if necessary."[80]

While at Amelia Island, Gaines received a blunt letter from Calhoun. He had written it before receiving Gaines's latest—the secretary's letter took a while to catch up to the general—but Calhoun had seen something like Gaines's latest message coming. In no uncertain terms, Calhoun told Gaines that the president did not want him to start a campaign in East Florida. Instead, he should place his forces in a defensive posture and do nothing unless attacked. Orders did not get much more direct than that, and a glum Gaines finally got the message. A military invasion of East Florida was not going to happen. Not only did the army lack a Scott massacre to justify a campaign, it had nothing at all. When Gaines arrived at Fernandina, he learned that Indian depredations on the St. Mary's River had never occurred. Indeed, nothing had happened on this frontier for the last three months. Seminoles moved in and out of St. Augustine, but at their best they were a ragged bunch with nothing warlike about them. Fear that their surrender would see them moved to the Creek nation and put them at the mercy of avaricious Allied Creeks had kept them stubbornly in the wilderness. By the end of November, even that fear wilted with the approach of winter and continued starvation. Many of these diehards then willingly surrendered.[81]

Andrew Jackson, however, would not let it go. At the end of November, he wrote to Calhoun that Florida Indians, interpreting the impending return of Pensacola as a sign of American weakness, planned to renew the war. He wanted to seize St. Augustine with a campaign ostensibly against the St. John's Seminoles, landing for good measure seven hundred men at Tampa Bay to move on the peninsula's interior.[82] Jackson was not Gaines, so Calhoun hid his exasperation and treated the proposal as a suggestion, a contingency plan for various eventualities. Later, when Spain dragged her feet on fixing the boundary and Florida issues, he actually regarded Jackson's proposition an attractive option, but that was later, after the settlement of many problems that were still urgent in the fall of 1818. After months of hammering home instructions to Gaines about how inappropriate another Florida invasion would be, Calhoun must have groaned over Jackson's letter reviving the issue. The timing was especially bad because on 17 November 1818, the second session of the Fifteenth Congress would receive President James Monroe's Annual Message.[83]

Throughout the summer and fall, members of Congress at home in their districts, other politicians, the newspapers, and the general public had discussed Jackson's invasion and what it all meant. Now, as the administration prepared to present its official justification of what many were calling unjustifiable, the president and his cabinet thought it would be helpful if Jackson could refrain from invading Florida again.

9

"A Rattling among the Dry Bones"

On the domestic front, Jackson's exploits in Florida had at first elicited only muted criticism. In fact, Jackson partisans enthusiastically defended Old Hickory even before any signs of serious reproach appeared. Congressional leaders meanwhile quietly corresponded between districts. Some hoped a reasonable explanation of Jackson's behavior would vindicate him. Others caught the scent of political blood and contrived to advance their own fortunes by discrediting Jackson or Monroe or both.

Monroe and his cabinet had been fortunate in one sense, and perhaps it was the all-important one. When news about Pensacola and Arbuthnot and Ambrister reached the capital, Congress had not been in session. Lack of time and information had been one of the greatest problems assailing the State Department as Adams responded to foreign inquiries, but because the Fifteenth Congress would not convene for its second session until fall, the administration had time to take the measure of public opinion and the potential congressional response.

The administration also by fall had more information about the campaign, but that could pose more of a problem. Monroe's explanation to Congress would be largely the same as the one crafted in the frantic July cabinet meetings, but Congress could insist on many more details than foreign diplomats had the right to expect or demand. Congress had every reason to presume that the administration had gathered a large body of facts surrounding this war; Congress had every right to require that information for its investigation.

In another sense then, Monroe's good fortune was finite, and possibly ephemeral. Even the most sagacious politicians were wary about guessing the congressional mood regarding Jackson's adventure. Only Congress itself and in session—not the passage of time or finely nuanced explanations—would create that mood, let alone reveal it. And in many otherwise certain aspects, certainties here could not be counted. The Rabun-Jackson quarrel did not bode well, for instance, because the Georgia delegation that probably would have supported the conquest of Florida would now have reason to oppose Jackson's invasion on grounds of personal and state loyalty. Likewise, some congressmen and senators who were ardent expansionists were also habitually opposed to the Monroe administration. How inchoate this opposition would be in November 1818 was difficult to say, but some of its membership was assured, and that was cause for concern too. Speaker of the House Henry Clay, consistent proponent of expansion, was also a reflexive adversary of the administration. How many colleagues the gregarious Clay could cajole into his camp simply remained to be seen.

The public mood presented a cheerier prospect. By August, various gestures seemed to mark popular support for Jackson's campaign and Monroe's response to it. If the press followed the people, congressional antagonists might fear the consequences of raising too much of a squawk. With that in mind, the administration aspired to turn all its cards to an advantage. Even the larger body of information could become a blessing, if used correctly. Calhoun, perhaps wiser for watching Adams's clipped certainty, especially hoped to cow Congress with ready answers to all questions. The cabinet in July had floundered to a position based on suppositions, but that was beginning to change by fall. There had been, however, a few anxious days before it changed. In August, Jackson's missing dispatches and the proceedings of Arbuthnot and Ambrister's trial had not appeared, and James Gadsden, sent from Nashville with copies, had yet to reach Washington.[1]

Calhoun particularly stewed over the missing dispatches. Probably he hoped they would contain persuasive evidence to justify Jackson and hence the cabinet's decision. Calhoun had reluctantly acquiesced in that decision, but his anxiety about it would remain unabated until he could see some exculpatory evidence. During the late summer and early fall, the secretary ordered southern post offices scoured for the missing communications, but they never did turn up. They never have. Finally at the end of August, Gadsden arrived with the copies, which at least was something.[2] After perusing the information, though, Calhoun did not think something was enough. Publicly the secretary never wavered in his support for the administration's position, but privately to friends he confided his dissent from it. Jackson's popularity, Calhoun muttered, had made it "inexpedient to punish him."[3]

Yet, as always, one man's expediency was another man's poison.[4] By August, even Andrew Jackson came to realize that his campaign might not excite universal approbation. Some newspapers hinted that his actions were inappropriate. Jackson boasted to his friend and subordinate Richard Keith Call that he could "justify the act both before God and America," but for the time being he knew America would do. "In addition to the evidence I have," Jackson said, "[I want] to get all I can."[5] As he slowly realized that some people actually claimed he had disobeyed orders, he insisted that he had never exceeded his orders at either St. Marks or Pensacola.[6]

Jackson's exasperated message must have exasperated the president as well. Although the administration had been deflecting criticism over this issue for more than two months, Jackson apparently never imagined his behavior in Florida would invite anything but acclaim. Now that it seemed to be provoking reprimands, he pretended not to be worried while doing something about the criticism. His actions against Pensacola seemed most vulnerable, so he dispatched his trusted topographical engineer, Hugh Young, to Alabama Territory and Pensacola to solicit testimony that the Indians in the area had posed a clear danger and that the Spanish government in Pensacola had been supplying and encouraging them. In Pensacola, Young gathered depositions from several citizens: all confirmed that Indians had been entering and leaving Pensacola during the year prior to the American invasion and that some Indians had been present in the town immediately before Jackson's arrival. Nobody could agree on the numbers, however, and estimates of Indian strength that ranged from fifty to two hundred fell far short of Jackson's count of four hundred to five hundred. Most of the witnesses said Masot's government had occasionally given the Indians some food, but no one had any knowledge of the Indians receiving military supplies.[7]

As helpful as this was for Jackson—and, in truth, it was not very helpful at all—Monroe could not have cared less. All the testimony in the world could not resolve the central difference between the administration's story that Jackson had exceeded his orders and Jackson's insistence that he had not. Indeed, Jackson now said the restrictive orders sent to Gaines in December 1817 had never applied to him. Monroe in obvious dismay commented to Calhoun that if Gaines's orders had not applied to Jackson, he had lacked any authority to invade Florida in the first place. Moreover, Monroe did not care for Jackson's obvious and presumptuous disregard for Gaines's orders. The president did not think that some people in Congress would care for it either. The administration and the military simply would have to reconcile their stories before Congress bared its teeth.[8]

Some partisans in the wider political community were already growling loudly. While Monroe and Calhoun tried to calm and correct Jackson, Alabama territorial governor William Bibb put into words what many opponents of the invasion were thinking. Bibb's motivation probably derived from his Georgia background and his ties to William Crawford, but that made his statements no less convincing. He applauded Monroe's promise to return West Florida to Spain as the only constitutionally acceptable position. Yet he criticized the president and his cabinet for not punishing Jackson. "They will gain nothing by it with his friends," Bibb predicted, "and lose much with the thinking part of the nation." He believed that citizens given to thought would agree that "no man should be permitted in a free country to usurp the whole powers of the whole government and to treat with contempt all authority except that of his own will."[9] Others also noted from a different perspective Jackson's habit of disregarding everything but his own will. The executions of Arbuthnot and Ambrister seemed key evidence to prove the point. Congressman John Forsyth of Georgia found it inconceivable that Jackson had executed Robert Ambrister "in direction violation of the sentence of the court by which he was tried."[10]

Under the growing weight of such rebukes and with the sense that Monroe was not a resolute defender, Jackson accelerated his efforts for justification. In October, he concocted yet another excuse for his seizure of Pensacola. Masot's threat to block the transport of supplies up the Escambia River, Jackson claimed, would have starved his entire army. That this was a relatively transparent lie reveals Jackson's expanding anger about this controversy. In the first place, the American invasion force was being supplied up the Apalachicola River, not the Escambia. The army did not leave the Apalachicola region until Jackson had already decided to take Pensacola and hence headed west for the city. The American army did not take Pensacola because it needed the Escambia River supply route; if anything, the army needed the Escambia supply route because Jackson had decided to take Pensacola. In the second place, Jackson had so stripped southern Alabama of regular troops that almost nobody remained there to rely on the Escambia for supply. Jackson, however, made up for the lack of logic with a surplus of bluster: he asserted that his only regret from the Florida campaign was that he had not hanged José Masot.[11]

Monroe simply had to make Jackson stop saying such things. He also had to get Jackson to adjust his story to parallel the administration's. The president anticipated a full congressional investigation that would include demands for all correspondence between the executive and the military. Monroe thought it imperative that Jackson put into writing that he had misunderstood his orders and thus had acted from ignorance rather than willful disobedience. Maybe, just maybe, the administration could then parry congressional accusations that either the president or the general had acted illegally, let alone imperiously. But it did not matter what Monroe wanted. Jackson would not consider any such admission: he insisted that he had understood his orders perfectly.[12]

Stories that Jackson might travel to Washington to mount a personal defense of his actions caused a stir in the capital. Monroe could not have been pleased by such reports, and some congressmen, recalling how Jackson was inclined to defend his honor as much with pistols as polemics, regarded the news with either amusement or alarm. Congressman Richard M. Johnson, a Jackson supporter, chuckled to a colleague on the Kentucky delegation that "there will be a rattling among the dry Bones when he does come."[13]

❧

On 17 November 1818, Monroe's second Annual Message to the second session of the Fifteenth Congress tried to defuse what had the potential to become the most disturbing constitutional controversy to assail a presidency since John Adams had enforced the Alien and Sedition Acts. The First Seminole War would open new vistas for constitutional debate and would reveal the truth about the so-called Era of Good

Feelings. When the dispute came to its withered little conclusion, Congress had conducted the longest debate in its history up to that time. During that debate it wandered into the sensitive areas of congressional authority over war powers, the independence of the executive, the diplomatic delicacy of maintaining relations with a querulous neighbor, the role of the military in a republic, and the political perils of assailing an immensely popular war hero. The discussion also revealed several realities about party unity, sectionalism, and expansionism.

The salient part of Monroe's message was coyly placed in the middle of an otherwise unremarkable relating of ordinary information. In the manner of a timid child caught in mischief, the administration betrayed worry with nonchalance. After the chants standard to such political rituals—Monroe noted that "peace and amity are preserved with foreign nations on conditions just and honorable to our country"—there followed a reference to the talks in London on trade, boundaries, and fisheries. Then it began: "Our relations with Spain remain nearly in the state in which they were at the last session." [14]

What Monroe was saying in a most indirect manner was that relations with Spain were not good, perhaps even bad, perhaps potentially belligerent. The message pointed out that Spain's authority in Florida consisted of a few frontier posts with weak garrisons. Florida had become a haven for predatory adventurers, runaway slaves, and hostile Indians. It was in short a "theater of every species of lawless adventure." Worse, these malevolent elements regularly sallied forth to harass and brutalize the American frontier, aware that they were "protected . . . by an imaginary line which separates Florida from the United States." [15]

Regardless of how imaginary Spain considered this line to be, the United States had destroyed a settlement of brigands on Amelia Island and then sent Andrew Jackson into Florida to pursue hostile Seminoles. Jackson had discovered local Spanish officials cooperating with the Seminoles, so he had occupied Spanish posts at St. Marks and Pensacola. The message assured Congress, "By ordering the restitution of the posts [amiable relations between the United States and Spain] were preserved. To a change of them the power of the Executive is deemed incompetent; it is vested in Congress only." [16]

The promise to lay pertinent documents before Congress did little to answer important issues raised by the message's bland rationalization of a significant military campaign on foreign soil against a power with which the United States was at peace. While some members of Congress might have been ignorant about the particulars of the Florida campaign, many knew more about it than Monroe's message told them. In addition, everyone knew about Secretary of State John Quincy Adams's negotiations with Onís for the acquisition of Florida. The Annual Message had avoided that subject.[17]

Congress would not blithely swallow the terse explanations of Monroe's message. Instead, his version of events formally triggered a full-scale investigation of the First Seminole War.[18] On the day after its presentation, John W. Taylor of New York proposed that various committees of the House take parts of the president's message for inquiry. The routine procedure had been in practice for over twenty years. Two of the committees to be directly involved in the Seminole War investigation—Military Affairs and Foreign Relations—were not technically standing committees, but instead were select committees. Their origin lay in the practice, first implemented in 1797, of referring the President's Annual Message to appropriate committees for their responses. The select committee thus became a de facto fixture in the House even though John Randolph had objected in 1811 to their use in dividing up the Annual Message; at the time Randolph had wanted the Committee of the Whole to discuss the entire message. His objections revealed more than a fastidious desire to maintain protocol. He and others tried to resist the changing structure of the House of Representatives and the way it conducted business. In 1819 this process could have affected the Seminole War debate significantly. Under the select committee structure, committees no longer merely did mere drudgery so that the Committee of the Whole could get to cases more quickly. Committees had grown in influence to write meaningful reports that controlled debate. In short, as a matter of routine, committees could decide what an indolent and perhaps ignorant House would do.[19]

Monroe's message was anything but ordinary and apparently would not allow for any lethargy in the legislature. Attempts by both administration advocates and anti-Jackson partisans to control the committee process devolved into a stalemate that saw the House resorting to the tried, but risky, tradition of debating in the Committee of the Whole. On 3 December, the first of a voluminous set of documents on the Seminole affair arrived from the executive. Just five days after that an elaborate parliamentary ballet was performed in the House of Representatives with the object of controlling the committee process for the administration. It concerned a procedural difficulty about which Massachusetts Representative John Holmes, chairman of the House Foreign Relations Committee, expressed some embarrassment. Holmes said he knew that the Arbuthnot and Ambrister execution had been referred to the Committee on Military Affairs. The war's repercussions on American diplomacy had been sent to Holmes's committee, Foreign Relations. He wanted to know how to proceed without duplicating efforts, without each committee invading the other's areas of responsibility. He then presented a motion to remove the Committee on Military Affairs from any role, leaving the sole investigative responsibility to Foreign Relations.[20]

The debate that followed, consuming the House's attention for two days, saw the great gun carriages of the partisans rolled into place, lines of sight drawn, and a few test rounds fired for preliminary effect. Several realities emerged in the clearing smoke. Holmes, a Jackson supporter, wanted the matter out of the hands of the Committee on Military Affairs. The chairman of that committee was Kentuckian Richard M. Johnson, also a Jackson supporter. He agreed with Holmes, probably because he knew that most of the members on Military Affairs wanted to condemn Jackson's actions, while Foreign Relations would be a much friendlier committee to Jackson.[21]

The Jacksonians tried to find the range to smash the issue. George Poindexter of Mississippi, Henry Baldwin of Pennsylvania, Eldred Simkins of South Carolina, and Joseph Desha of Kentucky were among those who manned the congressional batteries for Old Hickory during this opening engagement. They were only partially successful.

Fortunately for them the most vehement anti-Jackson voice in the House was absent. John Forsyth of Georgia had been the chairman of the House Committee on Foreign Relations before Holmes. In March 1818, while the Seminole campaign was fully underway, Forsyth sponsored a motion to give Monroe congressional authority to take East Florida by force. His motives in this strange incident are cloudy. Adams thought Forsyth was succumbing to the goading of Henry Clay, who had sworn to embarrass the Monroe administration at every turn. Monroe thought Forsyth's gesture most mischievous and was considerably relieved when James Barbour assured him that the committee would not do its chairman's bidding. Forsyth's behavior, however, was most odd.

Earlier he had opposed Clay's demands for American recognition of Latin American independence because it might provoke Spain. Then, inexplicably, he tried to authorize an invasion that was sure to provoke Spain. And failing to secure the authorization, he became a fervent critic of the Florida invasion that took place anyway.[22]

The trust that the administration had put in Forsyth must have been damaged by his actions. Like most presidents and secretaries of state, Monroe and Adams were accustomed to having a friendly chairman on the House Foreign Relations Committee. It got one in Forsyth's replacement, John Holmes. Forsyth left the chairmanship of the House Foreign Relations Committee when George M. Troup resigned his Senate seat in late September 1818. Forsyth was appointed to fill the term to its expiration. Monroe and Adams must have been relieved to have such a fierce opponent of the Florida campaign out of this sensitive position in the House at this critical time. Yet in the Senate, Forsyth proved equally vociferous in his criticisms of Jackson. He wanted the Seminole issue joined in the House, because the House could impeach.[23] Appointed to the Senate select committee charged to investigate the Seminole War, he is given credit for helping to make the committee's report so critical of Jackson. By the time the report was issued, however, Forsyth was gone from the Senate as well. Monroe nominated Forsyth to be the United States minister to Spain to replace George Erving, who was resigning. Monroe did this against Adams's wishes, and Forsyth proved a dreadful diplomat. Whether or not Forsyth was the beneficiary of an administration plan to remove him from both houses of the national legislature cannot be proved. What is certain, however, is that at the height of the controversy over Jackson's actions, one of Jackson's severest critics was busily learning Spanish and packing to leave the country.[24]

Forsyth's motives in opposing Jackson and the Seminole War have been attributed to his allegiance to fellow Georgian William H. Crawford, and Forsyth's departure from the House saw another Crawfordite rushing into the breach. Georgian Thomas W. Cobb used the December procedural debate to make near the end of the second day a series of observations that had nothing to do with the Holmes motion but had everything to do with the constitutional scruples Jackson had violated.[25]

Cobb asserted that the war had been unconstitutional. Could the president, he asked, without the consent of Congress wage war outside the United States? Could an officer of the United States Army, upon his own initiative, decide to make war on a foreign power? If Spain had misbehaved, was it not the duty of the nation, rather than the privilege of an individual, to determine what to do? Finally, Cobb declared that the issue was at its base whether or not the nation could be involved in a war without its consent.[26]

The House, unsettled by the bluntness of Cobb's remarks, voted by large margin to postpone indefinitely action on Holmes's motion. At this point, it was safer to do nothing. Yet, Congress could not postpone indefinitely facing the issues Cobb had raised. The controversy kept the capital humming during the Christmas season. Renewed expectations that Old Hickory himself would put in an appearance soon enough enlivened the talk.[27]

Jackson's friends in Washington kept him apprised of developments there, but nobody could make him tone down his intemperate remarks. If anything, his statements became less politic. He now insisted that holding on to Pensacola was the only way to prevent future problems with Spain. Monroe persisted in his efforts to calm Jackson down, yet he also realized that the return of Pensacola was the one thing that might avert Congress's full fury over the usurpation of its war powers. Jackson simmered so volubly in Nashville that friend John Eaton finally wrote from Washington with some advice. It would be better, he counseled, for Jackson to stay away from the capital. Eaton believed Jackson's legendary temper would at least make matters worse, and possibly it would make Old Hickory indefensible in Congress.[28]

❦

Jackson would not listen, and Monroe surely winced over the impending arrival of this bull in the national china shop. The effect on the congressional investigation was enough of a problem, but Adams's negotiations with Onís also loomed as another serious difficulty. Talks with the Spanish minister were simply not going well. Onís, sensing strength in the administration's embarrassment, had begun lodging extravagant Spanish claims about the border between the United States and Mexico. Adams countered the minister's proposal that the United States abandon all claims to territory west of the Mississippi with a suggestion that the Sabine River form the boundary between the two countries. In response, Onís would only bluster again that Jackson's invasion had been an outrage and Adams's defense of it an affront.[29] It was all most trying for the secretary of state.

Yet he was up to it. By this time, Onís had certainly seen Adams's lengthy instructions to George Erving in Madrid—instructions that contained the bluff justifications for Jackson's exploits. In spite of Onís's scoffing dismissal of the performance, he must have known it was a masterful exhibition of sheer audacity that ultimately would prove difficult to withstand. In short, the continued hard line with Spain would likely convince Madrid that resistance to United States designs on Florida was futile. In his letter to Erving, which was given wide public dissemination, Adams portrayed the United States rather than Spain as the victim. Indeed, he asserted that Spain should compensate the United States for Jackson's invasion rather than the other way around, because the United States had only done what Spain should have. Nor had the secretary let it go at that: a few days later, Adams had instructed Erving to demand the trial of Luengo for helping the enemies of the United States. It was all most trying for the minister from Spain. Yet, he in his own way was up to it too. Until he heard from Madrid, Onís also took a hard line, substituting mulish obstinacy for national resolve. But he was worried; the failure of either the British or the French to come to Spain's defense convinced Onís that if he did not make some kind of deal, Spain would lose Florida and Texas, with no compensation for either.[30]

So nothing was easy. In addition to its diplomatic and domestic problems, the Monroe administration also had to address the military concerns of the perpetually nervous frontier. The government tried to solve some of these problems by persuading Seminoles to migrate to the Creek Nation. Partly to convince Creeks not to loot these new Seminole neighbors of all their possessions, the government held a major conference with the Creeks at the end of November to grant the long-awaited annuity. Nearly four thousand Creeks gathered at Fort Hawkins, where solemn ceremonies alternated with raucous celebrations. It was all satisfying up to a point, but many questions remained unanswered. Some Seminoles rejected the repatriation scheme—how many was hard to say—so the uncertain military situation in Florida continued. And in the wake of the Fort Hawkins conference, David Mitchell announced he would come to Washington at the head of a Creek delegation to address Creek grievances and defend himself against Jackson's charges. The prospect of an inquisitive Congress, an angry Jackson, a defamed Mitchell, and a brooding deputation of Creeks all in town at the same time could not have gladdened anyone in the administration.[31]

Meanwhile, the War Department still occasionally felt the military tugging its leash. American soldiers remained at St. Marks and Pensacola while their general officers suspiciously scrutinized St. Augustine. Jackson in Nashville and Gaines in Fernandina continued to insist that Governor José Coppinger was supplying Seminoles in East Florida with ammunition. Calhoun continued to urge patience with a droning repetition of phrases that by the end of the year practically composed themselves: yes, Jackson's plan for a campaign was sound; yes, the general possibly had cause for suspicion; no, the general could not invade East Florida to seize St. Augustine because the Constitution gave only Congress the privilege of authorizing such a move.[32]

At the end of December, Spanish soldiers outside of St. Augustine arrested United States Army Sergeant Augustus Santee and two American citizens. What Santee and his companions were doing meandering the environs of the capital of East Florida got lost in the lengthy correspondence between Gaines and Coppinger. Gaines, in fact, simply used the incident to renew his calls for an attack on St. Augustine. The Spaniards returned Sergeant Santee and the two civilians, and Calhoun, more blunt than in any of his communications to Jackson, impatiently told Gaines again that he was to do nothing without explicit presidential authorization.[33] The War Department was due some luck, but the Santee incident, coming on the eve of the congressional debates about the Seminole War, was certainly not it.

∝

In Calhoun's view, the administration could not have enough information with which to meet the congressional probe. He continued his efforts to gather as much evidence as he could to justify Jackson's campaign.[34] Adams, for his part, regarded the upcoming congressional investigation with high trepidation. He noted Jackson's "inconsiderate letter to the Governor of Georgia" that along with "other imprudences turned the whole of that State against him." Such high-handed arrogance struck Adams as foolishly borrowing trouble because with it

Jackson had "also turned against him all the Governors of the States and the high sticklers for State rights. All Virginia is against him, for this and other causes."[35] Others noted that most of the newspapers were against the general as well, condemning his actions as unauthorized; congressmen, of course, read these papers.[36] The question of whether they would be significantly influenced by them added another worry to the administration's troubles.

As usual, Adams's observations proved prescient. Jackson's conduct over Obed Wright's arrest and his disdainful attitude toward Governor Rabun invigorated much congressional criticism. The attempt to arrest Wright actually had been one of Jackson's more legally defensible actions, but it was also one of the most flamboyantly imperious. As part of their original requests for papers, both houses of Congress wanted the documents pertaining to this controversy. In the Senate, Abner Lacock sponsored the resolution to obtain these papers, and that in itself was not a good sign for either Jackson or the administration: Lacock would also chair the Senate select committee charged with investigating all of Jackson's actions. Congress was just getting started.[37]

In the House, the one committee that might deliver a negative report on Jackson's performance deliberated through December into January. When the Committee on Military Affairs reported on 12 January 1819, the House plunged into the heart of the controversy. Per its instructions, the committee had limited itself to examining the trials of Arbuthnot and Ambrister. In a brief exposition, the majority report, presented by Thomas M. Nelson, disapproved the proceedings in both the trial and execution of Arbuthnot and Ambrister. The report, both by implication and expression, severely criticized Jackson's actions.[38]

In a much more extensive account of the events surrounding the executions, Richard M. Johnson, chairman of the committee and in this instance representing a minority of three, traced the course of the Seminole War from its origins to its conclusion. Johnson also broadened the scope of his report, technically against the House's instructions, to address two questions. Was Jackson justified in taking St. Marks and Pensacola? And was he justified in punishing Arbuthnot and Ambrister? Answering both questions in the affirmative, Johnson took the opportunity to heap heavy praise on Jackson for this and past services to the country.[39]

Johnson's motives in supporting Jackson could have stemmed from the Kentuckian's experiences as an Indian fighter. He claimed to be the man who killed Tecumseh at the Battle of the Thames. Yet Johnson was what today we would call an operator. Associated with the congressional "salary grab" of 1816, he took the measure of public anger and switched sides to secure its repeal. He and fellow Kentuckian Henry Clay were allies, and he would support Clay in 1824 until Clay drifted into the Adams camp. That he opposed Clay in 1819 on the Seminole controversy was so remarkable that observers did remark on it. Johnson had a sizable interest in remaining in good standing with the War Department. He was in the process of securing lucrative contracts for his brother James to supply steamboats for the upcoming Yellowstone expedition of spring 1819.[40]

Cobb took the cue from the scope of Johnson's minority report to say that the majority report had not gone far enough in its condemnation. The House, now having reached an impasse within the committee report process, constituted itself as the Committee of the Whole. In this forum Cobb excoriated Jackson's actions as unconstitutional and dishonorable. He proposed three resolutions that opened the "door for a discussion, as wide as could be." The first resolution called for legislation to prohibit the execution of army captives without the approval of the president. The second called for a formal disapproval of the seizure of St. Marks and Pensacola as unconstitutional. And the third called for legislation to prohibit the dispatch of troops to foreign soil without the authorization of Congress.[41]

Congress then proceeded to do what it does best: talk to itself. For the next twenty-six days, thirty-two speakers addressed virtually every aspect of the Florida invasion and its implications for the Constitution and political liberties of the republic.[42] Of those thirty-two, Southerners made up the overwhelming majority, mostly from Virginia. Yet support for or opposition to Jackson's actions cut across regional lines and even mottled the complexion of state politics. Five of the ten Virginians were anti-Jackson, and the two Pennsylvanians who spoke fell on either side of the issue. These debates, however, tell us little beyond the fact that the issue was divisive and, for some, confusing. Virginian John Floyd admonished that "if there is censure anywhere, it is due to Congress for not having performed their duty." There was little agreement, even among those on the same side. Richard Johnson insisted that "this was no mere party squabble," but the pro-Jackson George Strother of Virginia (a relative of Edmund Pendleton Gaines) said that the debate was clearly a manifestation of party spirit.[43]

Whatever the case, many at the time thought the aspirations of ambitious men compelled them to their actions during the debates, and historians have endorsed the judgment. Crawford was the most brazen political climber in the cabinet, and being more brazen than his colleagues was no mean achievement. Henry Clay was his counterpart in the legislature. The variety of maneuvers from these and other ambitious men manifested the political instability of the times.[44] The aged Nathaniel Macon was only half right when he called the post–War of 1812 years "a period of calm with all looking beyond [Monroe]."[45] All were looking beyond Monroe, but as the Seminole War debates show, not calmly. The disintegration of the congressional caucus—the body that had been choosing Republican presidential nominees since Jefferson's time—was not yet completely apparent, but its waning influence offered new opportunities to the sagacious and made for an exciting uncertainty about what lay over the political horizon.[46]

Such observations, however, would have offered the administration little consolation. Instead, Monroe had to watch the congressional investigation fan itself to a potential flashpoint. It was most disturbing to see the debate broaden, with the House calling for more and more documents. Members wanted information about everything from the current status of American-occupied Florida to the destruction of Negro Fort in 1816. As the administration's Florida policy came to resemble a bottomless Pandora's box, some congressmen began to consider the unthinkable: all this fuss was not just politics; Andrew Jackson had violated the United States Constitution.[47]

And yet, to just as many, if not more, it all seemed purely political. Concerns about constitutionality would be overshadowed by obviously partisan behavior. Everyone knew, for instance, that Monroe's failure to offer Henry Clay the State Department had disappointed him greatly. Thereafter, the Kentuckian had used every opportunity to pester the administration from the speaker's chair and the floor of the House of Representatives. His transparent motives have made his the most famous speech of the Seminole War debates in the House. Clay's obvious wish to embarrass the administration had some members of the House reminding him that he had earlier called for the occupation of West Florida. Yet his motives were not entirely self-interested, and his actions were potentially damaging to his own political fortunes. Just two weeks before his speech, even Clay, the master head-counter, could not measure the mood in Congress. Unsure that there would be any tangible action against Jackson, Henry Clay nevertheless took a stand.[48]

The House exhibited a festive atmosphere on 20 January, the day Clay rose to speak. Excited ladies packed the galleries, from where they reached over the rails to receive treats of oranges and cakes hoisted aloft on long poles by congressmen.[49] What Congress and this crowd heard that day was a speech by Henry Clay that despite its self-interested purpose, spoke the truth more often than not. Amidst much hyperbole and obviously overstated sympathy with the Indians, Clay hit the core of the major points. Jackson had violated the Constitution. He had acted with autocratic abandon, breaking the laws of his country as well as of nations. Too much ad hominem attack on Clay has obscured the truth of his statements and has deliberately or inadvertently shielded Jackson from charges that would have made a Caesar blush. Clay undeniably desired to damage Jackson's popularity. Yet that does not cancel the validity of Clay's question: "Are former services, however eminent, to protect from even inquiring into recent misconduct?" Jackson partisans John Holmes and Alexander Smyth possibly squirmed under Clay's biting sarcasm that brought laughter from the galleries, but more than likely the unpleasant truth of Clay's remarks discomfited them even more.[50]

Clay's speech, while the most famous, was not the best one delivered against Jackson's actions. Joseph Hopkinson of Pennsylvania, son of a signer of the Declaration of Independence and himself a defender of Associate Justice Samuel Chase at his impeachment trial in 1804, provided the most measured evaluation of the entire debate. He sympathized with the Seminoles without indulging in Clay's histrionics. He justified the crossing of the Florida line and the capture of St. Marks, but he condemned the occupation of Pensacola and the execution of Arbuthnot and Ambrister. With lawyerly calm and detached deliberateness, Hopkinson made Clay's case without the taint of Clay's ambition.[51]

None of this apparently mattered, though. The anti-Jackson speakers arraigned the general on constitutional and legal grounds, a light burden for a popular target and a dry charge for a capricious public. Jackson's friends defended him by referring to the practical necessity required by frontier realities. They painted lurid word portraits of Indian atrocities on the frontier and Spanish perfidy in abetting them. Defenders included descriptions of Jackson's gallant conduct at New Orleans, clothing him in the garments of the hero while chiding the nation for its potential ingratitude. In all, Jackson's partisans mounted an impressive defense.[52]

James Monroe and his War Department emerged from the congressional controversy virtually untouched by criticism. Of those eleven Congressmen opposing Jackson's actions, only two (Cobb and Hopkinson) came close to criticizing the executive for issuing unclear orders or allowing Jackson too much latitude.[53] Watching the debate from the Senate, New York's Rufus King made an oblique reference to the administration when he mused that "as other persons besides Jackson are affected, the presumption is that no censure will be voted."[54] One observer of Henry Clay's 20 January speech noted that "every person had expected him to be very severe on the President and seemed rather disappointed by his moderation."[55] Clay nevertheless thought he had cleverly found the central problem of Jackson's supporters. If Jackson had been right in seizing the Spanish posts, Monroe had been wrong in ordering their return.[56]

The ploy left Jackson's supporters unfazed. In fact, they knew that their foes desired to leave Monroe out of the question, and so they sought to tie the Tennessean to the Virginian at every turn. George Poindexter of Mississippi told the House that Jackson and Monroe "must stand or fall together." Others in Jackson's camp adopted the tactic, insisting that Congress could not move against Jackson without also moving against Monroe. Nobody wanted to do that. Alexander Smyth of Virginia gave an ominous warning that the independence of the executive and hence the very principle of separation of powers was at stake.[57]

While these speeches droned on in the House, Abner Lacock's Senate select committee quietly collected depositions and sifted through official documents. On 23 January, Jackson arrived in Washington, and on the advice of friends, adopted an uncharacteristically sedate attitude about the House investigation. Clay's speech made him angry, of course, and moreover it made the Kentuckian an enemy for life, but for the time being Jackson did little more than scowl over the verbal assaults of his enemies. Perhaps realizing that his friends had control of the affair in the lower chamber, Jackson thus granted his supporters a large boon. As one historian has asserted, a calm Jackson belied charges that he was an uncontrollable threat to the republic.[58]

Yet, it was all an act, and in private he was far from composed. He directed friends to engineer a newspaper campaign against Clay. He swore that he would personally challenge Clay to a duel after Congress adjourned. Friends who watched these fulminations must have counted themselves lucky that at least the general was willing to wait that long before killing the Speaker of the House. But that luck had its limits, too; Jackson could not control his anger over the Senate investigation. The select committee, appointed on 18 December 1818 to investigate the war, especially Jackson's taking of the Spanish posts, carried on its work deliberatively while the House conducted its flamboyant debates, and the careful and thorough collection of evidence enraged Jackson.[59] Soon, he embarked upon a series of shameful attempts at intimidation, and his behavior and voiced threats were disturbing enough to have members of the committee carrying firearms.[60] At one point, Jackson blustered that he would cut off a Senator's ears. Committee chairman Lacock was a farmer of the Pennsylvania frontier and did not scare easily. "I have passed [Jackson's] lodging every day," he laconically announced, "and still have my ears."[61]

⁂

Jackson would have cut up a good deal more of William H. Crawford if he had gotten the chance. Old Hickory believed the treasury secretary was the mastermind behind the congressional probe. In fact, Crawford's presumed role in the affair became an idée fixe for the general. He ranted to anyone who would listen that Clay had merely been doing Crawford's bidding. Every other effort to sully his reputation, Jackson roared, also originated in the bosom of the Georgia viper. Such vehemence and vitriol surprised John Quincy Adams. He first met Jackson when the general arrived in the capital, and only a week after their introduction, the secretary saw the fabled Jacksonian fury. At Adams's lodgings as the two studied a map, Jackson erupted into a violent denunciation of Crawford. Adams, somewhat shaken, tried to reassure Jackson that cabinet proceedings had revealed no evidence of Crawford's bad faith, but Jackson would not hear it. He insisted that Crawford was capable of anything; the reptile even intended, Jackson blared, to work with that other reptile Clay to unseat Monroe in 1820.[62] In Jackson's political imagination, no hydra-headed monster could assume more treacherous proportions than that.

Yet, it was all a fantasy born out of Jackson's fevered anxieties. Projecting to others his own habits of personally motivated animosity, he could not understand a factional world where enemies abided rather than annihilated each other, where the besting of an opponent did not have to include his obliteration. He could not absorb and hence would never adopt the icy cordiality that expressed rank disagreement in showy rhetoric. Such displays for others seldom signified personal enmity. In politics, however, just as in war and in love, the rules were always different for Andrew Jackson. He could defame with the goal of destroying the characters of his adversaries, but he would threaten to carve anyone up who repaid him for the job with the same rhetorical coin. It was a startling revelation for someone like Adams or Clay, because as different as these two were, they understood that political discourse required the giver of insults to do some taking of them as well. It was also troubling to encounter this astoundingly popular man who played the game nastier than most while insisting he alone remained above it. Watching him quiver in rages against real and imagined antagonists was unsettling, because one had to ponder that Jackson was either crazy or calculating.

In 1819, Congress said he was neither. On 8 February, coincidentally the same day that the United States Army returned Pensacola to Spain, the House of Representatives concluded its investigation of the Seminole War. First as the Committee of the Whole then formally as the House, the Fifteenth Congress voted down all resolutions that even hinted at a condemnation of Jackson and his exploits in Florida. Some writers have suggested that had anybody really taken Jackson to task rather than indulging in polemics and partisanship, he might have lost these crucial votes.[63] Yet neither Jackson nor the administration was in much danger from the House of Representatives.

In the Senate, Abner Lacock kept his ears but lost the day. The certainty that by early 1819 the Adams-Onís negotiations were advancing to a favorable conclusion thanks to the Florida invasion deflated the chances of those arguing for constitutional principles. Before Lacock brought in the select committee's report, the signed Adams-Onís Treaty arrived in the Senate. When Lacock presented his committee's highly critical report on 24 February 1819, it was already a dead letter. That body ratified the Adams-Onís Treaty the same day. The Senate never voted on Lacock's report, but it was published. Jackson enlisted John Overton to draft a vindication, and Senator Rufus King, who had just met Jackson at the outset of the controversy in 1819, presented it as a Memorial to the Senate in February 1820. Thus Jackson and his friends denounced the Lacock report even though it was never to be debated, let alone voted on in the Senate. It chose silence, and Jackson had the last word.[64]

∽✥∽

The negotiations between Adams and Don Luis de Onís had finally produced a treaty ceding Florida to the United States. The news all but shut down criticism of Jackson's campaign. The major impediments to a settlement in the last weeks of the negotiations had been the boundary issue and the diplomatic status of the Latin American revolutionary republics. As a bargaining ploy, Adams had pressed for the Rio Grande as the Mexican-American boundary, thereby to acquire Texas as well as the Floridas, but Onís had countered with what he perceived as an equally outrageous proposal: the United States, he said, should forfeit the bulk of the Louisiana Purchase and accept the Mississippi River as its boundary with Spanish territory. At that point, Jackson's military aggression and even more importantly the administration's unwillingness to disavow it shook Onís's resolve. When it became clear that Congress would acquiesce in the president's position, the minister settled on the compromise boundary at the Sabine River and was happy to get that much. The resolved boundary and a Spanish promise to disavow any Florida land grants made after January 1818 cleared the way for Adams and Onís to sign a treaty on 22 February 1819.[65]

In spite of this tidy resolution of the Florida controversy and Jackson's actions, more than a few people were troubled. Many questions remained unanswered. Two days after the House voted down the anti-Jackson resolutions, Clay renewed his calls for United States recognition of Latin American independence.[66] Clay undoubtedly did this to embarrass Monroe and Adams, but it made the issue no less compelling. Indeed, the position of the United States on the recognition question would burden ratification efforts in Madrid with uncertainties for two more years. And in the United States, the entire Florida business hung like a specter over the political establishment. The nagging feeling persisted that perhaps neither the president nor Congress had done the right thing about Jackson's conduct. In his private letters, Monroe returned to the issue repeatedly, protesting too much that he had acted in the best interests of the country.[67] Yet even for those who applauded the acquisition of Florida, there lingered an irksome sense that iniquity bounded the whole matter.[68] The names Arbuthnot, Ambrister, and Pensacola occasionally occurred in pausing conversations that caused some men to furrow their brows and gaze absently at the floor.

The enormous popularity of Jackson overshadowed everything. His ambitions, matched only by his reputation, so alarmed virtually everyone in Washington that men began behaving most oddly indeed. Thoroughgoing expansionists such as Clay, Cobb, and Forsyth, who had been demanding that the government pacify the Georgia frontier by annexing Florida, suddenly swore off expansionism to oppose Jackson. Clay wanted to be president, and Cobb and Forsyth's man, Crawford, longed to replace Monroe. The shallow motives of many who claimed they acted to protect the Constitution were easily perceived by Jackson partisans, who gleefully exposed inconsistencies and self-interest in their opponents' arguments.

Thus, on the surface an arrogant and aggressive military chieftain turned the Constitution on its head while civilian authorities danced at his feet. Andrew Jackson made war on Spain without authorization from Congress. Perhaps he had the tacit prior approval of the president. Certainly he had Monroe's consent after the fact. Yet the former would not have made Jackson's behavior legal, and the latter did not. Jackson's brazen adventure nevertheless had worked: the Florida plum dropped into the administration's lap. Monroe had admitted that it would be foolish to put Jackson on trial because, among other things, it might mislead Spain into thinking she could keep Florida.[69] So in 1819, George Washington's cherished principle of an army controlled by civilians was sacrificed by both executive and legislature to the expedient rewards of military success.

The business was not quite finished, however. Congress has always been composed of politicians, a species that habitually carries out its most direct actions indirectly. Some men, for the moment timid or abashed, for the moment with their eyes lowered, would in time raise them. They would swallow. They would have the last word.

Epilogue

If measured as merely Jackson's invasion, the First Seminole War was a brief little conflict, scarcely more than two months long. Yet the causes for the war stretched back years to the Creek War of 1813–14 and the Patriot War of 1812–13. The effects of the war also would be gauged in years, especially for the Indian participants on both sides.

Jackson's invasion altered forever the Seminole way of life. In the immediate sense, it had destroyed their dwellings and scattered them to the south; in the long term, his campaign had resulted in the American acquisition of Florida, thus placing the Seminoles in United States territory. In almost no time, Americans viewed the continued presence of these Indians and their black vassals as an obstacle to settlement and an internal threat to the peninsula's security.

The initial solution for these problems was the relocation of Seminoles to the Creek Nation. The army had presented the Seminoles with this plan prior to the Adams-Onís Treaty, and they had never exhibited much enthusiasm for it. Creeks did not like the idea either, a fact made plain by the Creek delegation Mitchell and McIntosh led to Washington in February 1819. Introducing to Monroe "these strate [sic] men of my nation," Big Warrior, elderly and ailing, hoped that the president would heed their requests.[1] They wanted a larger indemnity for the Chehaw massacre. They wanted the boundary fixed between their land and Florida so everyone would know what belonged to the United States and what belonged to Creeks. They wanted the controversy resolved over the confiscated Seminole cattle. And they wanted an equitable adjustment in the pay to Allied Creek warriors, thus to redress the difference between their $5 per month and the militia's $8 per month.[2]

After hearing about the Seminole repatriation scheme, the delegation added another compensatory demand to its list: if the American plan rested on the claim that Seminoles were Creeks, the United States should pay the Creek Nation for another land cession—specifically the one created by the Seminole evacuation. Calhoun countered that the Creeks had no rights to Florida land. The secretary then lectured the delegation that the only hope for Creek survival lay in the adoption of white culture. They should, he counseled, use American annuities to educate their people toward that goal. The secretary's advice, however, was as empty of benevolence as it was condescending. He had barely finished uttering it to the Creeks when he pulled Mitchell aside to give him instructions to negotiate yet another land cession from these people, this time near Fort Hawkins.[3]

So the "strate" men of Big Warrior's nation who moved amid the clamoring bustle of Washington felt the steady thrum of the new American engine that would drive the destinies of their people and their places. Gaines continued to train Allied Creek warriors in case the army needed them again. Mitchell rubbed his finger over another section of the map that displayed an ever-shrinking Creek domain. And the government prepared to move into the contracting Creek Nation even more people, some of them mortal enemies.[4] William McIntosh felt the mighty pounding of that engine and made his choice. The acquisition of Florida would put the Seminoles at the mercy of the United States; the Creeks already were. McIntosh had never hesitated to make money any way he could and had never let loyalty to his people stand in the way of his financial gain. Now he saw the future, and it was not Indian. His only hope of maintaining a particle of independence, he thought, was with personal wealth. Embracing the dictum that the rich are never wrong, he climbed over the next few years to fabulous affluence, primarily by helping the United States acquire larger and larger expanses of Creek acreage. McIntosh's greatest asset for his American friends was his influence within the nation. An 1817 Creek law made it a capital offense to alienate additional soil, but McIntosh persuaded other Creek leaders to make exceptions. It worked at first, but when headmen grew increasingly reluctant to skirt the law, McIntosh flouted it. Fraud and deception increasingly marked his dealings. In 1825, he was the moving force behind the Treaty of Indian Springs, which was nothing more than a prelude to Indian removal. It transferred Creek land to the United States for an equal amount in Arkansas. It also vindicated the old Red Stick prophets, for it at last revealed what Benjamin Hawkins's acculturation efforts had in their failure made inevitable. When Thomas Jefferson purchased Louisiana, the benevolent republican impulse proposed Indian removal to lands there as a way to protect the Indian from extinction while giving enlightened civilization time to correct his barbarities. Twenty years later, the impulses were no longer as benevolent, but the impetus for removal took on new vigor as the newest old idea in American Indian policy. The Red Stick prophets had seen the future, too, and had died trying to change it.[5]

So did McIntosh. In the wake of the Treaty of Indian Springs, Creek anger at his treachery forced an ugly decision. Once the principal law mender for the nation, William McIntosh himself was now judged a capital transgressor. Little Prince sent the warriors, and they arrived at one of McIntosh's inns on the morning of 30 April 1825. They called out the guests and then set the building on fire. From inside, McIntosh gamely traded potshots with his attackers until the blaze flushed him from the house. Knocked down by a bullet, he was still conscious when the warriors dragged him clear of the fire. One then clutched a knife and thrust it into McIntosh's chest. A blade through his heart, the child of the Wind Clan was dead.[6]

❧

When the Seminole War debates ended in Congress in early 1819, Andrew Jackson swung between a gloating celebration of what he called the "triumph over my enemies" and the desire to shoot them all with dueling pistols.[7] He basked in the accolades from Tennesseans and watched with undisguised pleasure the surge of his popularity nationwide. His friends watched all this too, grateful for both the acclaim and its soothing effect on the general. At the end, he chose to put away his promise to kill his congressional critics.[8]

The forbearance did not, however, signal a mellowing temperament. His misadventure taught him nothing about discretion, and throughout the spring and summer of 1819 he continued to warn the administration that the war in Florida was not over. British traders would return, he insisted, to renew their nefarious activities among the Indians. The Spaniards would again abet the enterprise. Jackson said the only way to settle the matter was to execute such people. Undoubtedly interpreting it as a commentary on his behavior at St. Marks, he shook his gnarled finger at recent War Department orders that prohibited drumhead courts-martial of white provocateurs; instead these suspected malefactors would now be remanded to the executive.[9]

On the whole, however, Jackson's domestic enemies kept him preoccupied. In the midst of the chorus of praise, a number of dissonant voices persisted after the congressional investigation, and Jackson did more than mutter that they should be taught to change their tune. He declared that Senator John Williams, a Tennessee political rival and a persistent critic of Jackson's conduct in Florida, should be removed from office for exhibiting such temerity. David Mitchell had not only initially opposed the Florida invasion, he was tied to the dreaded monster Crawford. Jackson worked for the next several years with Crawford's Georgia rivals, especially John Clark, to demolish the reputations of the treasury secretary and his friends both as public servants and honorable people.[10]

In the meantime, Spain's behavior over the Adams-Onís Treaty proved to many that Madrid found honesty a naive abstraction at best. John Forsyth carried the treaty with him to Spain, and when he arrived there in May 1819, he instructed the U.S.S. *Hornet* to stand ready at Cadiz to return the ratified agreement to the States. Forsyth rightly believed haste a priority because the treaty required its own ratification by 22 August. Ferdinand VII, however, stalled with a series of delays so persistently obtuse that the *Hornet* finally sailed sans treaty. The ship's reappearance in the United States without a validated accord occasioned in the government first bewildered dismay and then smoldering anger. Onís had adhered to Madrid's instructions, and now the Spanish government's refusal to confirm its own arrangements struck the administration as extreme bad faith.[11]

The development caused even more consternation because of its timing. Some parts of the country had bubbled with excitement over the flush economic benefits Florida promised. The exhilaration went off the boil as August came and went with the chances for Spain's concurrence in the cession apparently growing more remote. In the fall, the administration coped with the first concussions of a major economic panic brought on by the tightening of the Bank of the United States's irresponsible credit practices. Forsyth's speculation that the British might be coaching the Spanish could only have alarmed the president.[12]

Jackson needed no such complex explanations. He knew that "the treachery and perfidy of the Spanish character" was responsible for all postponements.[13] In the fall, he wanted to invade Florida again, and John Quincy Adams himself joined a growing list of people who wanted the same thing. Everyone except Jackson believed Congress would have to give the nod to this next affair. Attorney General William Wirt chuckled over the spectacle of another invasion, this one unencumbered by the taint of domestic illegality. He privately remarked that no one would "enjoy the luxuriant frolic more than Jackson would," which was a tolerably safe guess. "Stand clear all you Arbuthnots and Ambristers," he loudly trumpeted in a letter that only a friend would see.[14]

By December, though, such talk had moved beyond amused conjecture. Calhoun ordered Jackson to post the bulk of his Southern Division on the Florida line. Old Hickory sent spies to scout the strength of St. Augustine, and Adams joined the War Department's efforts to gauge congressional support for another invasion. There was little time for such assessments, though. Monroe asked for Congress to authorize a campaign in his Annual Message, undoubtedly hoping he would have congressional consent before the coiled Jacksonian spring vaulted toward the Castillo de San Marcos.[15]

Nobody really knew why Spain refused to act. The only source of information the administration had was John Forsyth because Onís as amicably as possible had asked to return to Spain in April 1819. His replacement, Don Francisco Dionsio Vives, would not arrive for a year, and Madrid meanwhile reeled under the combined blows of the colonial revolts and a domestic revolution against Ferdinand VII.[16] When Vives finally arrived in April 1820, he relayed Madrid's nagging concern that the United States still aided Latin American rebels as a prelude to recognizing their sovereignty. The State Department might have cursed Henry Clay for playing politics with this issue and thereby creating this impression. Whether Spain really delayed ratification because of these particular fears, the Kentuckian's incessant clamoring for American recognition of Latin American independence nonetheless had handed Spain an excuse for its behavior.[17]

Congress would not be rushed on either Monroe's military matter or Clay's diplomatic initiative. In the first place, it was embroiled in divisive debates over the Missouri Territory's admission to the Union as a slave state. After resolving this thorny slavery dispute, few congressmen wanted to help Clay embarrass Monroe by tweaking Ferdinand VII's colonial nose; thinking Jackson had killed enough people for the moment, even fewer congressmen wanted to turn him loose in Florida again. The president could sniff political defeat better than a hound a rabbit, so he abruptly withdrew his military authorization request.[18]

Spain finally acted in the fall of 1820. Moving with torpid deliberation, the Cortes and then the king ratified the Adams-Onís Treaty. The United States followed suit to exchange confirmations in February 1821. It had taken a military invasion, months of sweated negotiations, and two years of trifling delays, but on 10 July 1821, the Spanish flag dropped down the staff at the Castillo de San Marcos. It had flown there with only a two-decade interruption for nearly two and a half centuries.[19] Governor José Coppinger, in just that many minutes, became the former governor of East Florida, not only because of the Spanish cession but also because the United States had eliminated East and West Florida to unite the peninsula under a single territorial administration.

The lowering of His Most Catholic Majesty's standard and the hoisting of the Stars and Stripes was more than profoundly symbolic: it signaled a new reality to which Coppinger, the last imperial governor in Spanish East Florida, could not have been blind. That new flag snapped with the same resonant rhythms McIntosh and the Creek delegation had felt from the thrumming machine in Washington months before and nearly a thousand miles away. Now Coppinger doubtless felt the pounding of that machine trembling his earth, too. Gazing above the ramparts of the Castillo, he could see fluttering in the breeze the future, and it was not Spanish.

∾

The new governor of American Florida, appointed the previous April, did not attend the ceremony in St. Augustine. Andrew Jackson preferred Pensacola. He was more familiar with it.

Jackson was also no longer a major general in the United States

Army. Perhaps the final act of the congressional response to the First Seminole War had not been performed in February 1819, but rather was staged on 23 January 1821. Numerous charges of Caesarism in the republic permeated the debates in Congress during January 1819. Calhoun worried that Jackson's actions would portray the army (and the War Department) as a threat to the republic and hence invite as well as justify budget cutting by Congress.[20] In the House in January 1819, some members put the threat succinctly: if Cobb's resolutions failed, the army should be reduced. Richard Anderson of Kentucky objected violently to this scheme "to reach an obnoxious officer." [21]

But reach him they did. Nervous congressmen, worried about what Jackson's behavior possibly presaged, provided fertile ground for those planting the seeds for Jackson's removal. And when the financial Panic of 1819 furnished an impetus for federal budget cuts, Crawford saw his salient. It was almost too delicious, because Crawford had already predicted that Jackson's conduct would spur the forces of military reduction. Now armed with a genuine financial crisis, the treasury secretary began quietly suggesting that the best way to keep the government within its budget was to cut military spending.[22]

Major General Jacob Brown, Jackson's counterpart in the Northern Division, wrote in early 1820 that "there is, I fear, a fixed determination at all hazards to legislate Genl Jackson out of the service." [23] Yet Congress was busy, first debating the Missouri question and then mulling over the uncertainties regarding the Spanish treaty. After Congress adjourned in the spring of 1820, Crawford spent the remainder of the year exhausting all his ingenuity to prepare the government's budget for 1821. When he had finished cooking his books, the treasury secretary had a strong case for imposing drastic economies in federal spending, especially at the expense of the military.[24]

Calhoun had seen it coming, but Crawford's young colleague possibly never really understood that the move against the military was as much political as it was budgetary. Thinking his department's economies would deflect economizers, he resurrected a plan for an Expansible Army. Others had proposed similar ideas in the earliest days of the republic, and Calhoun now seized upon the concept as a way to prevent the total evisceration of his military. The plan called for the reduction in the size of units with the retention of all officers. In the event of war, the plan's proponents argued, a corps of experienced soldiers commanded by a cadre of skilled officers would be in place to train new recruits for action.[25]

Crawford found little to recommend the plan because, for him, it circumvented the whole point of his drive for thrift. Naturally he did not openly declare his greatest objection—that the plan would make Calhoun look innovative and competent. The young secretary with all those new, glittering ideas at the War Department was becoming quite a nuisance for Crawford, and cutting the military was a sure way to cut this Carolina pup's tail down to size. Calhoun's plan also would leave Andrew Jackson in place, a position sure to garner him more glory, renown, and popularity. So Crawford sicced his congressional dogs. Leading the attack in the House, Thomas W. Cobb declared that he could "see no utility in an army of officers" and introduced measures to reduce the military in January 1821.[26]

Calhoun's plan never stood a chance. Amid renewed charges that Caesarism permeated the military, congressmen shook their heads over the Expansible Army's diminished reliance on militia. Jackson's role in the Chehaw affair and his behavior toward Governor William Rabun had made this already sensitive issue freshly topical, and states' rights champions clearly would not sanction a reduction of the militia's part in protecting the republic. The militia, after all, was the first line of defense against, for one thing, internal military despotism.[27]

So in January 1821, long after the threats to cut off senators' ears had been consigned to the inventory of Washington anecdotes, six years after the Battle of New Orleans, and nearly three years after the First Seminole War, Congress reduced the army to six thousand men and dropped one of the two major generals then in service. Because he was junior in his appointment to Jacob Brown, Jackson was legislated out of the army when Congress cut the number of military divisions from two to one. Ostensibly in the interest of the budget, Congress removed Andrew Jackson from the military establishment of the United States of America. Perhaps not everyone who cut the military budget in 1821 did so to eliminate Jackson, but certainly many men in and out of Congress saw Old Hickory as less a threat out of the army than in it. Now Jackson was James Monroe's problem.[28]

With the exchange of ratification of the Adams-Onís Treaty quickly following the military reduction, a logical solution to the Jackson problem presented itself to Monroe. In 1818, the president had asked

Thomas Jefferson his opinion about making Jackson minister to the Russian czar's court in St. Petersburg. Jefferson thought the idea absurd; Jackson's temper would provoke a Russian-American crisis within weeks of his arrival. Monroe agreed and dropped it. Yet what trouble could Jackson cause in American Florida? So as a consolation, Jackson was made Florida's first territorial governor. His acceptance of the post greatly relieved the administration. "It has afforded," Calhoun said, "almost universal satisfaction."[29]

Nevertheless, Jackson's tenure as governor would be brief, and his residence in Florida even briefer. It would be lively, though. He traveled to Pensacola in June 1821 to receive the territory from the last Spanish governor of West Florida, José Callava. From the outset, the two argued, first over the schedule for the official exchange of jurisdiction. Callava finally ceded his authority to Jackson on 17 July 1821, but their relationship, initially caustic, soon turned worse. Callava remained in West Florida for several weeks after the formal cession to resolve some business concerning Spanish property in Pensacola. Meanwhile, Jackson took a personal interest in the claims of a woman who alleged that Forbes and Company had defrauded her late father's estate. Papers in the Spanish archives presumably held proof of the malfeasance. Callava had naturally taken possession of these archives upon leaving office, and while he might have had to give up West Florida, he refused to surrender official documents. Forcibly abducted from his bed, the former governor of West Florida found himself before the new American governor of Florida. Jackson gave Callava a tongue lashing, and Callava soon was matching him curse for curse. Callava again refused to surrender the papers, so Jackson threw him in jail. He was released the following day, but his detention complicated Spanish-American diplomacy even as it provided Jackson watchers with one more example of Old Hickory's temper and indecorous, unseemly deportment. At least he had not hanged anybody—this time.[30]

∞

With the growing inclination for removal, American officials saw Seminole repatriation in the Creek Nation as the first step toward placing them in the West. Still, the Seminoles who did not want to join the Creeks in Alabama certainly did not want to go with them to Arkansas.

Seminole opposition forced the United States to seek an alternative as another line of even less resistance. These Indians would be sequestered in areas of Florida removed from the coast. United States treaty commissioners implemented this new policy in 1823 with the Treaty of Moultrie Creek.[31] Still, white Floridians and the federal government regarded the arrangement as temporary, and when these groups in time again tried to set in motion a removal policy they would provoke the Second Seminole War. Lasting from 1835 through 1842, it would be the most protracted Indian war ever waged by the United States. Ironically, it began during the presidency of Andrew Jackson.

Those Seminoles formed a resistance to American authority that was as unyielding as it was persistent. Many Indians in Florida, however, confronting the stark alternatives of starvation or submission, had chosen capitulation and removal as their only option long before. One of those who migrated west shortly after the First Seminole War was Milly Francis. In 1842, Major Ethan Allen Hitchcock found her in Arkansas, impoverished and wearing little of the great beauty of her youth. Her forty-some-odd years had relentlessly eroded it. Her husband was dead, as were five of their eight children. Hitchcock listened to her story about saving Duncan McKrimmon during the First Seminole War, yet he knew about it anyway; indeed, he had searched out the famous Red Stick "Pocahontas" to hear firsthand about her consummate act of kindness. No, she had not married McKrimmon. This woman old before her time said that Robert Ambrister also had proposed to her. Hitchcock believed the embellishment, though it was likely nothing more than Milly adorning with a little fib the memories of when she had been comely and courted. Now, listening to the story made Hitchcock sad.

He had his own memories of the war, primarily because he had missed it. Newly appointed a second lieutenant, fresh-faced Ethan Allen Hitchcock was at Fort Bowyer when a ship en route to Jackson's campaign anchored off Mobile to ride out gusting headwinds. Hitchcock had watched the ship buck at its rode for two weeks, envious of the men on it for the adventures they would face. One of them was his brother-in-law, Major George P. Peters, West Point class of 1807, a distinguished veteran who bore a wound from the Battle at Tippecanoe. In 1818, Peters was an assistant adjutant general with the Third Artillery and bound for more glory in Florida. Hitchcock wanted to go too, but the War Department needed him at Fort Bowyer, so he watched his brother-in-law depart for the peninsula. Peters had died at Fort Gadsden in 1819. He was thirty years old.[32]

So the army major and the Creek woman had something in common—both had lost family in Florida. Hitchcock's meeting with Milly Francis left him deeply affected. He began entreating Congress to grant her a pension, and a two-year effort finally produced an act appropriating for her a $96 annuity and calling for the striking of a medal to commemorate her rescue of Duncan McKrimmon. The United States government took another four years to send the first installment of the pension. By then, Milly Francis was dying.[33]

Yet it did not matter that the money was late. The war, for her, was becoming an ever dimmer memory, its victims fading martyrs, its victors fading foes. Her father had been in his grave thirty years, Andrew Jackson in his three, and Milly was slipping away to hers. Her father had always claimed he could fly, and Milly in the darkling light probably knew that she would not need money or medals to do so herself. She would just close her eyes. The war was over.

Notes

The following abbreviations are used throughout this section:

ASPFR—American State Papers: Foreign Relations
ASPIA—American State Papers: Indian Affairs
ASPMA—American State Papers: Military Affairs
GLB—Governors Letterbook
LRAGO—Letters Received by the Adjutant General's Office
LRSWR—Letters Received by the Office of the Secretary of War
LSSIT—Letters Sent by the Superintendent of Indian Trade
LSSWIA—Letters Sent by the Secretary of War Relating to Indian Affairs
WDLR—Records of the Office of the Secretary of War, Letters Received
WDLSMA—Secretary of War, Letters Sent, Military Affairs

Prologue

1. For Jackson's involvement in the Burr Conspiracy, see Robert V. Remini, *Andrew Jackson and the Course of American Empire, 1767–1821* (New York: Harper and Row Publishers, 1977), 145–59; Milton Lomask, *Aaron Burr: The Conspiracy and Years of Exile, 1805–1836* (New York: Farrar, Straus, Girous, 1982), 68–69, 134, 136, 195; and Thomas Perkins Abernethy, *The Burr Conspiracy* (New York: Oxford University Press, 1954), 8, 28, 71, 111, 235, 240.

CHAPTER 1
"The Cream of Creek Country"

1. James W. Holland, "Andrew Jackson and the Creek War: Victory at the Horseshoe," *Alabama Review* 21 (October 1968): 243–75.

2. Jackson to Hawkins, August 1814, Andrew Jackson Papers, Library of Congress, Washington, D.C. Hereafter cited as Jackson Papers, LC.

3. Jackson to Willie Blount, 9 August 1814, Jackson Papers, LC.

4. See Kathryn E. Holland Braund, *Deerskins & Duffels: The Creek Indian Trade with Anglo-America, 1685–1815* (Lincoln and London: University of Nebraska Press, 1993), 3–4, and Michael D. Green, *The Politics of Indian Removal: Creek Government and Society in Crisis* (Lincoln: University of Nebraska Press, 1982), 2, for the probable origin of the name "Creek" as applied to the Muskogee Indians.

5. Green, *Politics of Indian Removal,* 36–37; Braund, *Deerskins & Duffels,* 184.

6. C. L. Grant and Gerald H. Davis, "The Wedding of Col. Benjamin Hawkins," *North Carolina Historical Review* 54 (July 1977): 308.

7. Braund, *Deerskins and Duffels,* 184. According to Joel W. Martin, *Sacred Revolt: The Muskogees' Struggle for a New World* (Boston: Beacon Press, 1991), 79–81, Creeks with white fathers brought more white culture into Creek society and after 1783 "dominated Muskogee politics." Martin asserts that mixed-blood domination was one of the things that Red Stick nativists objected to. Nevertheless, the most prominent Red Stick chiefs—Peter McQueen and William Weatherford—were mixed-bloods.

8. Braund, *Deerskins and Duffels,* 183–84.

9. Ibid., 4–5, 184–85; Green, *Politics of Indian Removal,* 36–37.

10. Kathryn E. Holland Braund, "The Creek Indians, Blacks, and Slavery," *Journal of Southern History* 57 (November 1991): 622; Green, *Politics of Indian Removal,* 11–12, 39–41; William C. Sturtevant, "Creek and Seminole," in *North American Indians in Historical Perspective,* ed. Eleanor B. Leacock and Nancy Lurie (New York: Random House, 1971), 105–6. Joel W. Martin believes that the Creek War emerged primarily from religious motives because Creeks believed that contact with their spiritual world would empower them to expel colonizers from their lands. See Martin, *Sacred Revolt,* x.

11. Merritt B. Pound, *Benjamin Hawkins, Indian Agent* (Athens: University of Georgia Press, 1951), 209–10; also see Henry DeLeon Southerland, Jr., and Jerry Elizah Brown, *The Federal Road through Georgia, the Creek Nation, and Alabama, 1806–1836* (Tuscaloosa: The University of Alabama Press, 1989), 2, 20, 58. Price gouging became so rampant on the Federal Road that eventually the War Department would tell the Creek Agency to regulate the prices. Also, travelers on the Federal Road offered easy prey for highwaymen who roamed it blithely from 1811 to 1818, the most infamous of whom was Joseph Thompson. See Southerland and Brown, *Federal Road,* 59, 98–99.

12. Benjamin W. Griffith, Jr., *McIntosh and Weatherford: Creek Indian*

Leaders (Tuscaloosa: University of Alabama Press, 1988), 73, 77; also see Woodward to F. A. Rutherford, 2 April 1858, in Thomas S. Woodward, *Woodward's Reminiscences of the Creek or Muscogee Indians, Contained in Letters to Friends in Georgia and Alabama* (Montgomery, Alabama: Barrett & Wimbish, 1859; reprint edition, Tuscaloosa: Alabama Book Store, 1939), 37. A recent biography of Hawkins claims erroneously that the agent and the headman were good friends. See Florette Henri, *The Southern Indians and Benjamin Hawkins, 1796–1816* (Norman: University of Oklahoma Press, 1986), 269. For a contrary view, based upon documentary evidence, see Green, *Politics of Indian Removal*, 38–40. Also see Gregory Evans Dowd, *A Spirited Resistance* (Baltimore: Johns Hopkins Press, 1992), 156.

13. Kathryn E. Holland Braund's *Deerskins & Duffels* provides the most detailed account of how the deerskin trade impinged upon Creek traditions and values. See also Gregory A. Waselkov and Brian M. Wood, "The Creek War of 1813–1814: Effects on Creek Society and Settlement Pattern," *Journal of Alabama Archaeology* 32, no. 1 (1986): 2–3, 6. Even before Tecumseh's visit, many Creeks believed that only through cooperation could Indians resist white encroachment. See Martin, *Sacred Revolt*, 118.

14. Braund, *Deerskins and Duffels*, 7–8; Green, *Politics of Indian Removal*, 7; James W. Covington, *The Seminoles of Florida* (Gainesville: University Press of Florida, 1993), 7; J. Leitch Wright, Jr., *Creeks and Seminoles: The Destruction and Regeneration of the Muscogulge People* (Lincoln: University of Nebraska Press, 1986), 171.

15. Ross Hassig, "Internal Conflict in the Creek War of 1813–1814," *Ethnohistory* 21 (1974): 261, 264. Another characteristic of nativists seems economic. Those not tied to the Miccos (the civil headmen of towns) and hence not financially benefitting from Hawkins's civilization program tended to join the nativist movement. See Waselkov and Wood, "Creek Settlement Pattern," 7–8. Martin, *Sacred Revolt*, x, believes that the Creeks who took up arms felt that contact with their spiritual world would allow them to expel colonizers from their lands, hence the Creek Civil War was a religious movement.

16. Frank Lawrence Owsley, Jr., *Struggle for the Gulf Borderlands: The Creek War and the Battle of New Orleans* (Gainesville: University Presses of Florida, 1981), 11.

17. Owsley, *Borderlands*, 16; also see Green, *Politics of Indian Removal*, 41–42.

18. J. D. Rouseaux to William McIntosh, 14 July 1813, Telamon Cuyler Collection, University of Georgia Libraries, Athens, Georgia.

19. Owsley, *Borderlands*, 9–10.

20. Frank L. Owsley, Jr., "British and Indian Activities in Spanish West Florida during the War of 1812," *Florida Historical Quarterly* 46 (1967): 114–15.

21. Congratulatory letters to Creeks from Spanish officials that promised the Indians supplies fell into American hands after the Fort Mims Massacre. See Owsley, *Borderlands*, 40; Wright, *Creeks and Seminoles*, 165, 170–72; Ferdinand Claiborne to Peter Early, 14 August 1813, Indian Files, Record Group

4–2–46, File 2, Box 76, Georgia Department of Archives and History, Atlanta, Georgia.

22. Big Warrior to Hawkins, 26 July 1813, Hawkins to Big Warrior, 27 July 1813, Big Warrior File, Georgia Department of Archives and History, Atlanta, Georgia.

23. Big Warrior to Hawkins, 4 August 1813, Big Warrior File; also see William S. Coker and Thomas D. Watson, *Indian Traders of the Southeastern Borderlands: Panton, Leslie and Company and John Forbes and Company, 1783–1847* (Gainesville: University Presses of Florida, 1986), 279–80.

24. Marquis James's account of the Fort Mims massacre is typical of the prejudices that for years bound the study of Native American culture: "On August 30, 1813, the seven-eighths white leader of the Creeks [Weatherford] surprised his half-white adversary [Major Daniel Beasley]." See Marquis James, *The Life of Andrew Jackson Complete in One Volume* (New York: The Bobbs-Merrill Company, 1938), 157. Also see, Frank L. Owsley, Jr., "The Fort Mims Massacre," *Alabama Review* 24 (July 1971): 192–204.

25. Big Warrior to Governor David B. Mitchell, 2 August 1813, Big Warrior to Little Prince, 4 August 1813, Big Warrior File.

26. Big Warrior to Hawkins, 24 August 1813, Big Warrior and Little Prince to Hawkins, 7 October 1813, Big Warrior File.

27. James C. Bonner, "William McIntosh," in *Georgians in Profile: Historical Essays in Honor of Ellis Merton Coulter,* ed. Horace Montgomery (Athens: University of Georgia, 1958), 121–22; Thurman Wilkins, *Cherokee Tragedy: The Story of the Ridge Family and the Decimation of a People* (New York: Macmillan, 1970), 65.

28. Bonner, "McIntosh," 65; Wright, *Creeks and Seminoles,* 186; Green, *Politics of Indian Removal,* 54–56, 59, 72; Griffith, *McIntosh and Weatherford,* 65; Martin, *Sacred Revolt,* 125.

29. Wilkins, *Cherokee Tragedy,* 62–63; Green, *Politics of Indian Removal,* 38–39.

30. Francis Paul Prucha, *The Sword of the Republic: The United States Army on the Frontier, 1783–1846* (London: The Macmillan Company, 1969; reprint ed., Lincoln: University of Nebraska Press, 1986), 115.

31. See for example Francis Paul Prucha, "Andrew Jackson's Indian Policy: A Reassessment," *Journal of American History* 56 (December 1969): 527–30.

32. Jackson to John McKee, 30 January 1793, quoted in Remini, *Jackson and the Course of American Empire,* 71. Remini believes that frontier conditions created the fiery Indian-fighter that Jackson became. See pages 70–71, 84.

33. James, *Jackson,* 91–94; Remini, *Jackson and the Course of American Empire,* 136–143.

34. The most charitable interpretation of Jackson's involvement in the Burr conspiracy is in Remini, *Jackson and the Course of American Empire,* 147–48. During Burr's grand jury trial in Richmond, Jackson publicly defended him while condemning James Wilkinson and Thomas Jefferson. See Lomask, *Aaron Burr,* 250; Abernethy, *Burr Conspiracy,* 235.

35. Abernethy, *Burr Conspiracy,* 8.

36. Jackson to Pinckney, 28 March 1814, *American State Papers: Indian Affairs*, 2 vols. (Washington, D.C.: Gales and Seaton, 1832), 1:448. Hereafter cited as *ASPIA*.

37. Jackson to Willie Blount, 31 March 1814, *ASPIA*, 1:491.

38. Ibid., 1:492. William G. McLoughlin, *Cherokee Renascence in the New Republic* (Princeton, New Jersey: Princeton University Press, 1986), 194, says that five Allied Creeks were killed at Horseshoe Bend and fourteen were wounded. As for the prisoners taken there, the Cherokees took some of them, others were turned over to McIntosh's Allied Creeks, and the balance were transported to Huntsville. See Holland, "Jackson and the Creek War," 265.

39. Jackson to Pinckney, 5 April 1814, in John Spencer Bassett, ed., *Correspondence of Andrew Jackson*, 7 vols. (Washington, D.C.: Carnegie Institute of Washington, 1926–1935), 1:495. Hereafter cited as Jackson, *Correspondence*. Also see Holland, "Jackson and the Creek War," 267.

40. Some historians believe that Horseshoe Bend completely broke the Red Sticks' fighting spirit as well as their material ability to continue fighting. According to this interpretation, the nativists' flight to Pensacola reflected their desire merely to escape, never to fight again, and to swear off revenge. See, for example, Bernard W. Sheehan, *Seeds of Extinction: Jeffersonian Philanthropy and the American Indian* (Chapel Hill: University of North Carolina Press, 1973), 216. The activities of Peter McQueen and Josiah Francis belied such peaceful intentions, as will be seen in chapter two.

41. Hawkins to Thomas Pinckney, 24 April 1814, in Benjamin Hawkins, *Letters, Journals, and Writings of Benjamin Hawkins*, 2 vols., ed. C. L. Grant, (Savannah: The Beehive Press, 1980), 2:679. As late as May rumors circulated that Peter McQueen and his followers were in Florida trying to ally with Seminoles. Hawkins nervously reported that the Coweta (Allied) Creeks had expressed a determination to go after these remnants to "destroy them." See Hawkins to Pinckney, 17 May 1814, in Hawkins, *Writings*, 2:681.

42. Jackson to Pinckney, 14 April 1814, in Jackson, *Correspondence*, 1:500. Joel Martin estimates that as many as two thousand Red Stick nativists along with some blacks went to Florida after Horseshoe Bend. See Martin, *Sacred Revolt*, 163.

43. Pinckney to Jackson, 7 April 1814, Jackson to Pinckney, 17 April 1814, Jackson, *Correspondence*, 1:496, 502.

44. Owsley, "British and Indian Activities," 115–16. James Wilkinson had taken Mobile, part of the disputed Louisiana Purchase, into American possession in April 1813. See Julius Pratt, *Expansionists of 1812* (New York: Macmillan Company, 1925; reprint edition, Gloucester, Massachusetts: Peter Smith, 1957), 237.

45. Owsley, "British and Indian Activities," 117–18. As students of the War of 1812 know, Lafitte rebuffed British overtures and instead provided Andrew Jackson with vital powder and ordnance at the Battle of New Orleans.

46. Holland, "Jackson and the Creek War," 268; also see Jackson to Pinckney, 17 April 1814, Jackson, *Correspondence*, 1:502.

47. Remini, *Jackson and the Course of American Empire*, 218–19. Jackson

had one of his militiamen, seventeen-year-old John Woods, shot on the march south for insubordination. See Michael Paul Rogin, *Fathers and Children: Andrew Jackson and the Subjugation of the American Indian* (New York: Vintage Books, 1975), 154–55.

48. Secretary of War John Armstrong to General Pinckney, 17 March 1814, *ASPIA,* 1:836.

49. Armstrong to Pinckney, 20 March 1814, *ASPIA,* 1:837.

50. James Doster, *The Creek Indians and Their Florida Lands, 1740–1823,* 2 vols. (New York: Garland Publishing, 1974), 2:102–3. Also see Owsley, *Borderlands,* 86; Pound, *Hawkins,* 234–35.

51. Pinckney to Jackson, 18 May 1814, Jackson, *Correspondence,* 2:2–3. Hawkins had told his son at the end of April that under Pinckney's new terms for the treaty the Creeks would lose the amount of land deemed suitable by the government. Yet the agent remained under the impression that the Allied Creeks would retain the bulk of their land, and only construction and transportation privileges would be conceded to the United States. See Hawkins to William Hawkins, 26 April 1814, Hawkins, *Writings,* 2:680.

52. Pinckney to Jackson, 22 April 1814, Jackson, *Correspondence,* 1:506.

53. Harry Toulmin to Jackson, 22 June 1814, Jackson, *Correspondence,* 2:9–11.

54. Armstrong to Jackson, 22 May 1814, Jackson, *Correspondence,* 2:4; Armstrong to Jackson 28 May 1814, Jackson Papers, LC; Holland, "Jackson and the Creek War," 271.

55. Armstrong to Jackson, 24 May 14, Jackson, *Correspondence,* 2:4.

56. Hawkins to Armstrong, 7 June 1814, *ASPIA,* 1:858.

57. Ibid.

58. Jackson to David Holmes, 18 April 1814, Jackson, *Correspondence,* 1:505.

59. Rogin, *Fathers and Children,* 157.

60. Daniel Usner, Jr., "American Indians on the Cotton Frontier: Changing Economic Relations with Citizens and Slaves in the Mississippi Territory," *Journal of American History* 72 (1985): 315, implies that Jackson had just such ulterior motives for making the Fort Jackson cession as large as it was.

61. Jackson to Overton, 10 August 1814, Jackson Papers, LC; also see Holland, "Jackson and the Creek War," 272. Jackson justified the size of the cession to Armstrong with just such an argument.

62. Jackson to Hawkins, 11 July 1814, Jackson Papers, LC.

63. Owsley, *Borderlands,* 88.

64. Rogin, *Fathers and Children,* 158.

65. Pound, *Hawkins,* 237.

66. Jackson's friend John Eaton noted the general's low opinion of the Allied Creeks. See Owsley, *Borderlands,* 89.

67. Meeting of the Creeks with Jackson and Hawkins, 8 August 1814, *ASPIA,* 1:837. Jackson and Hawkins were given three-mile tracts of land as part of an Allied Creek package that included smaller sections presented to Alexander Cornells and George Mayfield. Owsley believes that the Jackson grant was

the Allied Creeks' way of shaming him. See Owsley, *Borderlands,* 90. Congress disallowed the land grant, in spite of Madison's endorsement and Jackson's unflagging efforts. See Madison to House of Representatives, 18 January 1815, *ASPIA,* 2:26; Colonel Arthur P. Hayne to Jackson, 27 March 1816, Jackson, *Correspondence,* 2: 237; Rogin, *Fathers and Children,* 158.

68. Treaty of Fort Jackson, made on 9 August 1814, *ASPIA,* 1:826; Jackson to Blount, 9 August 1814, Jackson Papers, LC.

69. John Sugden, "The Southern Indians in the War of 1812: The Closing Phase," *Florida Historical Quarterly* 60 (January 1982): 277.

70. Jackson to Overton, 10 August 1814, Jackson Papers, LC; Jackson to Armstrong, 10 August 1814, *ASPIA,* 1:838.

71. Benjamin Hawkins to Armstrong, 10 August 1814, Records of the Office of the Secretary of War, Letters Received, National Archives, Washington, D.C. Hereafter cited as WDLR.

72. Owsley, *Borderlands,* 91; Doster, *Creek Indians,* 2:122–25.

73. Pound, *Hawkins,* 237. For the conspicuous absence of Hawkins's correspondence, see Owsley, *Borderlands,* 90–91. The register and summary of Hawkins's letters, however, remained. In a 16 August 1814 letter, the Indian agent requested that Jackson be replaced as a negotiator.

74. Doster, *Creek Indians,* 2:122–25; Sugden, "Southern Indians," 290.

75. This view of the treaty's consequences is the consensus among students of the period. See, for example, Edgar B. Wesley, *Guarding the Old Frontier: A Study of Frontier Defense from 1815 to 1825* (Minneapolis: University of Minnesota Press, 1935), 15; Owsley, *Borderlands,* 95; Sugden, "Southern Indians," 273–74; Southerland and Brown, *Federal Road,* 50.

76. Sugden, "Southern Indians," 278; Owsley, *Borderlands,* 90; Charles C. Jones, Jr., *The Dead Towns of Georgia* (Savannah, Georgia: Morning News Steam Printing House, 1978), 240.

77. Senator Jesse Wharton to Jackson, 16 February 1815, Jackson, *Correspondence,* 2:171.

78. Owsley, *Borderlands,* 89.

CHAPTER 2
"Children of Nature"

1. Jackson to Armstrong, 10 August 1814, Jackson Papers, LC; also see Jackson to Armstrong, 31 July 1814, Jackson, *Correspondence,* 2:23. Fort Bainbridge was about twenty-five miles west of Fort Mitchell in Alabama Territory, Fort Hull lay a little south of present-day Tuskegee, and Fort Decatur was on the east bank of the Tallapoosa, just opposite of Tuckabatchee.

2. Jackson to Armstrong, 13 June 1814, Armstrong to Jackson, 25 June 1814, Jackson to Armstrong, 27 June 1814, Jackson to Holmes, 19 June 1814, Jackson, *Correspondence,* 2:7–8, 11–12.

3. Armstrong to Jackson, 18 July 1814, Jackson, *Correspondence,* 2:13;

Wilburt S. Brown, *The Amphibious Campaign for West Florida and Louisiana, 1814–1815* (University, Alabama: University of Alabama Press, 1969), 23, 28.

4. Owsley, *Borderlands,* 93.

5. Sugden, "Southern Indians," 275, 279.

6. Wright, *Creeks and Seminoles,* 186; Hawkins to Peter Early, 25 May 1814, Hawkins, *Writings,* 2:681; Blount to Secretary of War, 13 June 1814, WDLR; Harry Toulmin to Jackson, 22 June 1814, Jackson to Armstrong, 30 July 1814, Jackson, *Correspondence,* 2:9–11, 22.

7. Jackson to Armstrong, 19 August 1814, Jackson Papers, LC; Jackson to Coffee, 17 July 1814, Jackson to Armstrong, 24 July 1814, 5 August 1814, Jackson to Blount, 27 August 1814, Jackson to Monroe, 5 September 1814, Jackson, *Correspondence,* 2:16, 19–20, 30, 34, 42. Also see Sugden, "Southern Indians," 289. Monroe too believed that the Spanish might sell the Floridas to the British to keep them out of American hands. He believed that if America possessed the peninsula, the government could use it as a bargaining chip with the British to secure concessions on the impressment issue. See Monroe to Gallatin, 6 May 1813, Stanislas Murray Hamilton, ed., *The Writings of James Monroe,* 7 vols. (New York: G. P. Putnam's Sons, 1898–1903), 5:259.

Many historians have discounted the American claim that Britain wanted to do more in Florida than harry the American war effort. Americans, it would seem, described British aims as acquisitive to justify their desires to annex Florida. Kinley Brauer, however, believes that the British habit of economic imperialism could only have encouraged designs on Florida. See Kinley J. Brauer, "The United States and British Imperial Expansion, 1815–1860," *Diplomatic History* 12 (Winter 1988): 20–22.

8. Reginald Horsman, "The Dimension of an 'Empire for Liberty': Expansionism and Republicanism, 1775–1825," *Journal of the Early Republic* 9 (Spring 1989): 6.

9. Ibid., 12; David J. Weber, *The Spanish Frontier in North America* (New Haven, Connecticut: Yale University Press, 1992), 297; Thomas P. Abernethy, *The Formative Period in Alabama, 1815–1828,* 2nd ed. (University, Alabama: University of Alabama Press, 1965), 22–23. In 1810, William Crawford expressed the belief that the Floridas would have to become part of the United States to prevent their being taken by a stronger nation, yet he also said that an American seizure would be immoral. See Crawford to David B. Mitchell, 7 January 1810, David B. Mitchell Papers, Ayer Collection, Newberry Library, Chicago, Illinois.

10. Chase C. Mooney, *William H. Crawford, 1772–1834* (Lexington: University Press of Kentucky, 1974), 44.

11. Lyle N. McAllister, "Pensacola During the Second Spanish Period," *Florida Historical Quarterly* 37 (January–April 1959): 312–15; Mooney, *William H. Crawford,* 314; Sugden, "Southern Indians," 279; Rembert W. Patrick, *Florida Fiasco: Rampant Rebels on the Georgia-Florida Border, 1810–1815* (Athens: University of Georgia Press, 1954), 30, 49. Also see Frederick C. Ogg, "The American Intervention in West Florida," *Mississippi Valley Historical Association, Proceedings* 4 (1912): 49–50; Remini, *Jackson and the Course of American Empire,* 191; Pratt, *Expansionists of 1812,* 12, 13.

12. Owsley, *Borderlands,* 90, 178; Martin, *Revolt;* Wright, *Creeks and Seminoles,* 180; Sugden, "Southern Indians," 273.

13. John K. Mahon, "British Strategy and Southern Indians: War of 1812," *Florida Historical Quarterly* 44 (1966): 287; James W. Covington, "Migration of the Seminoles into Florida: 1700–1820," *Florida Historical Quarterly* 46 (1968): 354; Howard F. Cline, *Notes on the Colonial Indians and Communities in Florida, 1700–1821; Notes on the Treaty of Coweta* (New York: Garland Publishing Co., 1974), 51, 229–31.

14. Patrick, *Florida Fiasco,* 176, 182–83; Benjamin Hawkins to David B. Mitchell, 13 September 1812, Hawkins, *Writings,* 2:618.

15. Covington, *Seminoles,* 5, 6, 12.

16. Kenneth W. Porter, "Billy Bowlegs (Holata Micco) in the Seminole Wars," *Florida Historical Quarterly* 45 (1967): 221.

17. One of the most objectionable parts of Hawkins's acculturation plans was the elimination of the clan as a dispenser of justice, for the Seminoles never relinquished the custom of blood justice. The closest relative of a victim had to retaliate. See John W. Griffin, ed., "Some Comments on the Seminoles in 1818," *Florida Anthropologist* 10 (1957): 45.

18. Wilton M. Krogman, "The Racial Composition of the Seminole Indians of Florida and Oklahoma," *Journal of Negro History* 19 (October 1934): 419. Covington maintains that both Muskogee and Miccosukee (Hitchiti) speakers migrated into Florida and that some were perhaps bilingual. See Covington, "Migration of the Seminoles," 351. The Alachua (eastern) and Miccosukee or Apalachee (western) bands of the Seminoles both spoke Hitchiti as their main tongue. The Alachua band, descendants of the venerated Payne and the younger Bowlegs, were perhaps the original Seminoles. See Kenneth W. Porter, "Origins of the St. John's River Seminole: Were They Mikasuki?" *Florida Anthropologist* 4 (1951): 39–40.

19. Journal of Alexander Arbuthnot, *American State Papers: Foreign Relations,* 6 vols. (Washington: Gales & Seaton, 1834), 4:609. Hereafter cited as *ASPFR.*

20. Alan K. Craig and Christopher Peebles, "Ethnohistorical Change among the Seminoles, 1740–1840," *Geoscience and Man* 5 (June 10, 1974): 91–92.

21. Some hold that "Seminole" derives from the Spanish *cimarron,* meaning "wild" or "runaway." See Charles H. Fairbanks, *Ethnohistorical Report on the Florida Indians* (New York: Garland Publishing Company, 1974), 4. Generally everyone believes that translation is too pejorative. John R. Swanton is probably most accurate in his assessment of the name as denoting, in the Indian tradition of literalism, those who had physically separated themselves from others. See John R. Swanton, *The Indian Tribes of North America,* Smithsonian Institution Bureau of American Ethnology, Bulletin 145 (Washington, D.C.: Smithsonian Institution Press, 1952), 139.

22. Craig and Peebles, "Ethnohistorical Change," 92; see also Cline, *Notes on the Colonial Indians,* 50, for the role of blacks in Seminole farming. Kevin Mulroy, "Ethnogenesis and Ethnohistory of the Seminole Maroons," *Journal of World History* 4 (Fall 1993): 292, 295; Kenneth W. Porter, "Negroes and the Seminole War," *Journal of Negro History* 30 (1945): 252.

23. Porter, "Seminole War," 253; John D. Milligan, "Slave Rebelliousness and the Florida Maroon," *Prologue* 6 (Spring 1974): 6–7.

24. Abel Poitreneau, "Demography and the Political Destiny of Florida during the Second Spanish Period," *Florida Historical Quarterly* 66 (April 1988): 438–39, 441–42.

25. John Anderson to Secretary of War, 20 June 1814, WDLR; Pratt, *Expansionists of 1812,* 120–22.

26. Patrick, *Florida Fiasco,* 49–50, 93, 100.

27. Pratt, *Expansionists of 1812,* 104, 201; Patrick, *Florida Fiasco,* 113, 180–83.

28. Thomas P. Abernethy, "Florida and the Spanish Frontier, 1811–1819," in Lucius F. Ellsworth, ed., *The Americanization of the Gulf Coast, 1803–1850* (Pensacola: Historic Pensacola Preservation Board, 1972), 97. The vote in the House was seventy to forty-eight for annexation.

29. Pratt, *Expansionists of 1812,* 118–19; Patrick, *Florida Fiasco,* 143; Crawford to Mitchell, 11 April 1812, Mitchell Papers, Newberry Library.

30. John McIntosh to Mitchell, 28 June 1812, David Bridie Mitchell Personal Miscellaneous Papers, New York Public Library, New York, New York.

31. Patrick, *Florida Fiasco,* 176. As noted in chapter 1, the achievement of status and influence in Creek (and because of common origins, Seminole) culture frequently saw young men itching for war while the older men opposed it. Some historians see the blacks and the Seminoles as nothing more than Spanish pawns in the Patriot War, doing the bidding of St. Augustine's Governor Kindelan. Hawkins, however, believed that the Seminoles were being led by prophets in the same way that Red Stick nativists were. See Hawkins to Mitchell, 13 September 1812, Hawkins, *Writings,* 2:618. Also see Hawkins to William Eustis, 3 August 1812, 2:613; Pound, *Hawkins,* 217–18, 220.

32. Pratt, *Expansionists of 1812,* 202; Patrick, *Florida Fiasco,* 185–86.

33. Pratt, *Expansionists of 1812,* 210, 215; Patrick, *Florida Fiasco,* 214–15. The Georgia legislature would not authorize Mitchell to take independent action against the Seminoles. See page 216. In August 1812, Lieutenant Colonel Smith of the St. Mary's garrison wanted reinforcements to destroy Seminole villages, and Monroe began making preparations to do so. See Wanjohi Waciuma, *Intervention in the Spanish Floridas, 1801–1818: A Study of Jeffersonian Foreign Policy* (Boston: Branden Press, 1976), 325, 346–47.

34. Pound, *Hawkins,* 221.

35. Patrick, *Florida Fiasco,* 226–27; Pratt, *Expansionists of 1812,* 220–21.

36. Abernethy, "Spanish Frontier," 100; Patrick, *Florida Fiasco,* 229.

37. Pratt, *Expansionists of 1812,* 223, 231; Kenneth W. Porter, "Negroes and the East Florida Annexation Plot," *Journal of Negro History* 30 (1945): 25; Abernethy, "Spanish Frontier," 100; Covington, "Migration of the Seminoles," 354.

38. Porter, "Annexation Plot," 26–27; Porter, "Seminole Wars," 256; Covington, "Migration of the Seminoles," 355. In 1818, it would be estimated that Bowlegs had about seventy warriors and two hundred blacks living in separate villages on the river. See Craig and Peebles, "Ethnohistorical Change," 88.

39. Pratt, *Expansionists of 1812,* 242–46; Patrick, *Florida Fiasco,* 149, 239, 245; Abernethy, "Spanish Frontier," 104–5; Waciuma, *Jeffersonian Foreign Policy,* 355. The Senate voted sixteen to fourteen against annexation. The administration's caution in bringing this matter before the Senate, even though it would have been originally discussed in a friendly committee, bewildered Crawford, who worried about how much longer Georgia militia could be kept in the field. See Crawford to Mitchell, 14 November 1812, 26 December 1812; 9 January 1813, Mitchell Papers, Newberry Library.

40. As late as January 1815, the governor of East Florida complained about Georgians committing violence from across the border. See Governor Peter Early to Lieutenant Colonel William Scott, 11 January 1815, Governors' Letterbook, May 18, 1814 to October 30, 1827, Georgia Department of Archives and History, Atlanta, Georgia, hereafter cited as GLB; also see Patrick, *Florida Fiasco,* 275.

James Monroe, for one, did not believe the abandonment of East Florida had anything to do with American designs on West Florida. As late as May 1813, he insisted that the possession of West Florida was "a question settled." See Monroe to Gallatin, 5 May 1813, Hamilton, *Writings of Monroe,* 5:253.

41. Sugden, "Southern Indians," 274, 279–81. The British felt that the Red Stick attack on Fort Mims had been premature because it brought American forces into the Gulf region before British forces could arrive in any strength. See Owsley, *Borderlands,* 96.

42. William H. Robertson to Brigadier General Thomas Flournoy, 17 June 1814, Flournoy to Hawkins, 19 June 1814, Hawkins to Armstrong, 15 June 1814, and 13 July 1814, *ASPIA,* 1:859–60; Jackson to Governor Holmes, 21 July 1814, Jackson, *Correspondence,* 2:19; Proclamation of Admiral Cochrane, 2 April 1814, Vincente Sebastian Pintado Papers, Library of Congress, Washington, D.C.; Owsley, *Borderlands,* 4. The British also planned to use black Jamaican soldiers, something that angered Americans more than anything else. See Owsley, *Borderlands,* 94.

43. Owsley, *Borderlands,* 101–3; Mahon, "British Strategy," 290–91.

44. Hawkins to Peter Early, 15 June 1814; Hawkins to Armstrong, 21 June 1814, Hawkins, *Writings,* 2:683–85. Hawkins told Armstrong that the British had left behind fifty men with arms and ammunition to train the Indians.

45. Mark F. Boyd, "Events at Prospect Bluff on the Apalachicola River, 1808–1818: An Introduction to Twelve Letters of Edmund Doyle, Trader," *Florida Historical Quarterly* 16 (October 1937): 74–75; Coker and Watson, *Indian Traders,* 281; Sugden, "Southern Indians," 281.

46. Mahon, "British Strategy," 289; for Perryman as Kinache and Capachamico, see Wright, *Creeks and Seminoles,* 126.

47. Sugden, "Southern Indians," 280–82, 284–86.

48. Hawkins to Armstrong, 16 August 1814, *ASPIA,* 1:860; Willie Blount to Armstrong, 20 June 1814, Joseph Anderson to Armstrong, 20 June 1814, WDLR; Owsley, "Pensacola," 178–79.

49. Sugden, "Southern Indians," 282–83.

50. Mahon, "British Strategy," 292; Sugden, "Southern Indians," 290.

51. Claiborne to Jackson, 29 August 1814, Jackson, *Correspondence,* 2:36.

52. Big Warrior to Hawkins, 25 August 1814, Jackson, *Correspondence,* 2:36.

53. There is some evidence to suggest that the British consciously used black West Indian soldiers and recruited slaves to frighten American southerners into submission. See Owsley, *Borderlands,* 98; also see Sugden, "Southern Indians," 288.

54. Sugden, "Southern Indians," 284–86; Brown, *Amphibious Campaign,* 27.

55. Owsley, *Borderlands,* 105. Also see Sugden, "Southern Indians," 287.

56. Sugden, "Southern Indians," 274, 277, 300; Hawkins to Armstrong, 16 August 1814, *ASPIA,* 1:860; Wright, *Creeks and Seminoles,* 189.

57. Owsley, *Borderlands,* 104–5.

58. Sugden, "Southern Indians," 287.

59. Anonymous to Manrique, 8 August 1814, in Arséne Lacarrière Latour, *Historical Memoir of the War in West Florida and Louisiana in 1814–15,* a facsimile reproduction of the 1816 edition (Gainesville: University of Florida Press, 1964), vii; Owsley, *Borderlands,* 105; Boyd, "Prospect Bluff," 70.

60. Proclamation of Edward Nicholls, 29 August 1814, Latour, *Historical Memoir,* vii–viii.

61. Coker and Watson, *Indian Traders,* 284–85; Thomas C. Kennedy, "Sibling Stewards of a Commercial Empire: The Innerarity Brothers in the Floridas," *Florida Historical Quarterly* 67 (January 1989): 277. Innerarity had been in contact with Americans at least since August 1813, when he reported that the Spaniards in Pensacola were too weak to resist Creek demands for arms and ammunition. See Ferdinand Claiborne to Governor of Georgia, 14 August 1813, Indian Files, File 2, Box 76, Georgia Department of Archives and History, Atlanta, Georgia.

62. Order of the Day for the First Colonial Battalion of the Royal Corps of Marines, 26 August 1814, Latour, *Historical Memoir,* xxv, 35–40; Sugden, "Southern Indians," 291–92; General Orders, Mobile, 17 September 1814, *ASPIA,* 1:860–61; Jackson to Monroe, 17 September 1814, Jackson, *Correspondence,* 2:50; Owsley, "Pensacola," 178. Latour numbered the Indian contingent at six hundred. See *Historical Memoir,* 34.

63. Coker and Watson, *Indian Traders,* 285.

64. Hawkins to Pinckney, 25 April 1814, 17 May 1814, Hawkins, *Writings,* 2:679, 681; Big Warrior to Hawkins, 25 August 1814, Jackson, *Correspondence,* 2:36.

65. Jackson to Colonel Robert Butler, 27 August 1814, Jackson, *Correspondence,* 2:32. Jackson said he expected the British to land ten thousand more soldiers at Pensacola any day.

66. Hawkins to Jackson, 30 August 1814, Hawkins, *Writings,* 694–95; Jackson to Hawkins, 19 September 1814, *ASPIA,* 1:861; Jackson to Monroe, 14 October 1814, Jackson, *Correspondence,* 2:73; John K. Mahon, "British Strategy," 289, 292; Sugden, "Southern Indians," 283, 289.

67. Jackson to Monroe, 14 October 1814, Jackson, *Correspondence,* 2:73; Hawkins to Monroe, 5 October 1814, 12 October 1814, Hawkins, *Writings,* 2:696. Bonner says that McIntosh went to Pensacola to spy on the British, but

this seems unlikely. Probably Bonner has mistaken the intelligence that Mc-Intosh received from the Seminoles with an actual reconnoiter by the Allied Creek. See Bonner, "McIntosh," 123.

68. Hawkins to James Monroe, 5 October 1814, Hawkins to Peter Early, 26 October 1814, Hawkins to Little Prince and Big Warrior, 3 November 1814, Hawkins to Jackson, 11 November 1814, Hawkins, *Writings,* 2:696, 698, 700, 704; Major Philip Cook to Early, 7 November 1814, same to same, 16 November 1814, in "Creek Letters, Talks, and Treaties, 1705–1839," 4 vols., Georgia Department of Archives, Atlanta, Georgia, 3:862, 864; Timothy Barnard to Hawkins, 3 November 1814, Telamon Cuyler Collection; Dowd, *Spirited Resistance,* 172.

69. Hawkins to Jackson, 30 August 1814, Hawkins to Monroe, 5 October 1814, same to same, 12 October 1814, Hawkins, *Writings,* 2:694–96; Jackson to Hawkins, 19 September 1814, General Orders, 17 September 1814, *ASPIA,* 1:860–61; William F. Bowen to Major J. C. Warren, 8 October 1814, Hawkins, *Writings,* 2:78; Monroe to Jackson, 10 October 1814, Jackson, *Correspondence,* 2:71; Sugden, "Southern Indians," 291–92; Boyd, "Prospect Bluff," 70; Doster, *Creek Indians,* 2:107. The promised blankets and other goods did not arrive until the summer of 1815.

70. William Robinson and Charles Muir to Jackson, 28 July 1814, Jackson to Monroe, 31 October 1814, Jackson, *Correspondence,* 2:21–22, 85.

71. Owsley, *Borderlands,* 112–13; Covington, "Migration of the Seminoles," 286–87, 292, 295; Remini, *Jackson and the Course of American Empire,* 241; Report of John Gordon, 20 July 1814, Jackson to Manrique, 12 July 1814, Manrique to Jackson, 26 July 1814, Jackson to Manrique, 24 August 1814, Manrique to Jackson, 30 August 1814, Jackson to Manrique, 9 September 1814, Monroe to Jackson, 21 October 1814, Jackson to Monroe, 26 October 1814, Jackson, *Correspondence,* 2:15–17, 20, 28–29, 37–40, 44–45, 79, 82–83; Sugden, "Southern Indians," 292. In early December Monroe wrote to Jackson, "I hope that my letter to you of the 21st of October had reached you in time to prevent the attack which you then contemplated making on the British at Pensacola. As the conduct of the Spanish authorities there may justify the measure, the President desires that it may be avoided, in the hope that the new efforts which he is now making to obtain justice and preserve amity with that power, may be successful[.]" See Monroe to Jackson, 7 December 1814, Hamilton, *Writings of Monroe,* 5:301.

72. See Pemberton to Allen, 17 October 1814, WDLR.

73. Sugden, "Southern Indians," 293, 295; Owsley, "Pensacola," 177; John Innerarity to James Innerarity, 10 November 1814, in John Innerarity, "Letters of John Innerarity: The Seizure of Pensacola by Andrew Jackson, November 7, 1814," ed. Julian C. Yonge, *Florida Historical Quarterly* 9 (1931): 127; Coker and Watson, *Indian Traders,* 286.

74. Hawkins to Armstrong, 16 August 1814, *ASPIA;* Brown, *Amphibious Campaign,* 23. Hawkins says Jackson pulled out of Fort Jackson on 11 August, but Latour, *Historical Memoir,* 26, says Jackson was at Fort Jackson as late as 15 August.

75. Major Jasper Smith to Colonel Philip Pipkin, 20 September 1814, Major

Alexander Ralston to Jackson, 10 October 1814, Jackson, *Correspondence,* 2:60, 71.

76. Jackson to "The Free Coloured Inhabitants of Louisiana," 21 September 1814, Latour, *Historical Memoir,* xxxi; Mahon, "British Strategy," 293; Ruth A. Fisher, ed. "The Surrender of Pensacola as Told by the British," *American Historical Review* 54 (January 1949): 327–28. General Orders, T. T. Hayne, Acting Adjutant General, to Jackson, 15 September 1814, Mississippi Territory, Military Correspondence, Alabama Department of Archives and History, Montgomery, Alabama; Owsley, "Pensacola," 178–79; Brown, *Amphibious Campaign,* 49–50.

77. Jackson to Manrique, 6 November 1814, same to same, 6 November 1814, Manrique to Jackson, 6 November 1814, Jackson, *Correspondence,* 2:92–93; Latour, *Historical Memoir,* 45–46.

78. Manrique to Jackson, 7 November 1814, Jackson, *Correspondence,* 2:94.

79. John Innerarity to James Innerarity, 10 November 1814, Innerarity, "Letters," 128–29; Sugden, "Southern Indians," 296; Stanley Faye, "British and Spanish Fortifications of Pensacola, 1781–1821," *Florida Historical Quarterly* 20 (January 1942): 288; Latour, *Historical Memoir,* 47–50.

80. Jackson to Monroe, 20 November 1814, Jackson, *Correspondence,* 2:101; also see Owsley, *Borderlands,* 112.

81. Monroe to Jackson, 7 December 1814, Hamilton, *Writings of Monroe,* 5:301.

82. Jackson to Manrique, 11 November 1814, Jackson to Monroe, 14 November 1814, Jackson, *Correspondence,* 2:95–99; Sugden, "Southern Indians," 292, 296–97; Owsley, "Pensacola," 175, 182–84. Weber mistakenly has Jackson destroying the fortifications in Pensacola and then abandoning the town. See Weber, *Spanish Frontier,* 298.

83. John Innerarity to James Innerarity, 10 November 1814, "Letters," 128–30; ? to Sebastian Kindelan, 4 January 1815, East Florida Papers, Library of Congress, Washington, D.C., vol. 42; Coker and Watson, *Indian Traders,* 301–2; Owsley, *Borderlands,* 176.

84. Owsley speculates as much. See Owsley, "British and Indian Activities," 120.

85. Faye, "British and Spanish Fortifications," 288–90; Owsley, "British and Indian Activities," 119.

86. Forbes apparently hoped for American success because of British disregard for Forbes's property rights. See Sugden, "Southern Indians," 294.

87. Philip Cook to Peter Early, 16 November 1814, Louise Frederick Hays, ed. and comp., "Unpublished Letters of Timothy Barnard," Typescript (Atlanta: Georgia Department of Archives and History, 1939), 306.

88. Major Philip Cook to Governor Early, 7 November 1814, "Creek Letters," 3:862; Hawkins to Early, 26 October 1814, 30 October 1814, Hawkins to commanders of Forts Lawrence, Perry, and Mitchell, 3 November 1814, Hawkins to Little Prince and Big Warrior, 4 November 1814, Hawkins to Jackson, 4 November 1814, 11 November 1814, Hawkins, *Writings,* 2:698–701, 704.

89. Hawkins to Peter Early, 3 November 1814, Hays, "Letters of Timothy Barnard," 305–6. Also see John Floyd to Peter Early, 1 September 1814, *Georgia Military Affairs,* 9 vols., Georgia Department of Archives, Atlanta, Georgia, 1940, 4:5.

90. General Order, 16 November 1814, Jackson, *Correspondence,* 2:100.

91. *Augusta Chronicle,* 13 January 1815; Owsley, *Borderlands,* 174–75; Sugden, "Southern Indians," 297; Brown, *Amphibious Campaign,* 56; Jackson to Brigadier General James Winchester, 22 November 1814, Jackson, *Correspondence,* 2:105; John Floyd to Mary Floyd, 13 December, 28 December 1814, John Floyd, "Letters of John Floyd, 1813–1838," *Georgia Historical Quarterly* 33 (1949): 244–45; Ventura Morales to Ramirez, 3 November 1817, Juan Ventura Morales, "Juan Ventura Morales to Alexandro Ramirez, November 3, 1817," *Boletín del Archivo Nacional* 13 (January–February 1914): 16.

92. Owsley, *Borderlands,* 135; Owsley, "British and Indian Activities," 120; Sugden, "Southern Indians," 300–301.

93. Hawkins to Monroe, 1 January 1815, same to same, 7 January 1815, same to same, 23 January 1815. Hawkins to Early, 15 February 1815, same to same, 20 February 1815, same to same, 24 February 1815, Hawkins, *Writings,* 2:712–13, 715, 717–19; Owsley, *Borderlands,* 176.

94. Hawkins to Monroe, 7 January 1815, Hawkins to Early, 24 February 1815, Hawkins, *Writings,* 2:713, 719; Coker and Watson, *Indian Traders,* 292–93; Mahon, "British Strategy," 298–99.

95. Jackson to Brigadier General James Winchester, 30 January 1815, Jackson, *Correspondence,* 2:154; Hawkins to Early, 20 February 1815, Hawkins, *Writings,* 2:718; Owsley, *Borderlands,* 170.

96. Jackson to Winchester, 30 January 1815, Jackson, *Correspondence,* 2:154; Latour, *Historical Memoir,* 207–13; Coker and Watson, *Indian Traders,* 298–99; Owsley, *Borderlands,* 174.

97. Article Nine read, in part: "The United States of America engage to put an end, immediately after the ratification of the present treaty, to hostilities with all the tribes or nations of Indians, with whom they may be at war at the time of such ratification; and forthwith to restore to such tribes or nations, respectively, all the possessions, rights, and privileges, which they may have enjoyed or been entitled to in one thousand eight hundred and eleven, previous to such hostilities." See Latour, *Historical Memoir,* cxiii.

98. Bradford Perkins, *Castlereagh and Adams: England and the United States, 1812–1823* (Berkeley and Los Angeles: University of California Press, 1964), 36, 78, 88–89, 101.

99. J. Leitch Wright, Jr., "A Note on the Seminole War as Seen by the Indians, Negroes, and Their British Advisors," *Journal of Southern History* 34 (1968): 570–71.

100. Sugden, "Southern Indians," 304–5; Proceedings of 2 February 1819, Deposition of Sergeant Samuel Jervais, 9 May 1815, *Annals of the Congress of the United States,* 42 vols. (Gales and Seaton, 1834–1856), 15th Cong., 2nd sess., 958.

101. Hawkins to Early, 26 February 1815; Hawkins to Jackson, 27 February

1815, Hawkins, *Writings,* 2:720–21; Secretary of War to Jackson, 3 March 1815, Letters Sent by the Secretary of War Relating to Indian Affairs, 1800–1824, National Archives, Washington, D.C. Hereafter cited as LSSWIA; ? to Sebastian Kindelan, 4 January 1815, East Florida Papers.

102. Hawkins to Monroe, 6 March 1815, Hawkins to Early, 21 April 1815, Hawkins, *Writings,* 2: 722–24; Hugh M. Thomason, "Governor Peter Early and the Creek Indian Frontier, 1813–1815," *Georgia Historical Quarterly* 45 (1961): 235.

103. Hawkins to Nicholls, 19 March 1815, Hawkins to Jackson, 24 March 1815, Nicholls to Hawkins, 28 April 1815, Hawkins, *Writings,* 2: 723–24, 729–30; Nicholls to Hawkins, 2 April 1815, Jackson, *Correspondence,* 2: 208–9. Article One of Ghent did call for the reimbursement of American slave-owners for the runaways lured by the British, and London complied in a number of cases. It could not have been happy that Nicholls's slave smuggling compounded its pecuniary obligation in this matter. See Coker and Watson, *Indian Traders,* 298. Spaniards also wanted to reclaim the slave property that the British had taken to Prospect Bluff. See Robert Spencer to Vincente Pintado, 31 March, 4 April 1815, Pintado Papers. Surprisingly, they did not find Nicholls completely uncooperative, and they tended to blame George Woodbine more than his superior for their runaway problem. See Pintado to Josef de Soto, 29 April 1815, Pintado Papers.

104. Nicholls to Hawkins, 12 May 1815, *ASPFR,* 4:549; Sugden, "Southern Indians," 370.

105. Gaines to Acting Secretary of War Alexander Dallas, 14 May 1815, 22 May 1815, *ASPFR,* 4:551–52.

106. Hawkins to Nicholls, 24 May 1815, 28 May 1815, Hawkins, *Writings,* 2:728, 732–33; Doster, *Creek Indians,* 2:143–44.

107. Hawkins to Jackson, 26 May 1815, Jackson, *Correspondence,* 2:208.

108. Hawkins to Gaines, 14 June 1815, Hawkins, *Writings,* 2:736; Dallas to Hawkins, 6 June 1815, LSSWIA.

109. Wright, *Creeks and Seminoles,* 188.

110. Ibid., 190; Covington, "Migration of the Seminoles," 355.

CHAPTER 3
"A Blow in Another Quarter"

1. Owsley, *Borderlands,* 181–82; Secretary of State to Mr. Baker, 10 July 1815, Adams to Secretary of State, 19 September 1815, Adams to Castlereagh, 21 March 1816, *ASPFR,* 4: 553–54, 555; Perkins, *Castlereagh and Adams,* 285; Bimbury to Nicholls, 7 September 1815, Public Records Office, Foreign Office File 115, vol. 32, Library of Congress, Washington, D.C.; William Earl Weeks, *John Quincy Adams and American Global Empire* (Lexington: University Press of Kentucky, 1992), 107; Frank L. Owsley, "Prophet of War: Josiah Francis and the Creek War," *American Indian Quarterly,* 9 (1985): 286.

2. Hawkins to Dallas, 5 May 1815, Hawkins to Pinckney, 12 May 1815, Hawkins, *Writings,* 2:725–26; Doster, *Creek Indians,* 2:146–47, 186.

3. Hawkins to Dallas, 19 May 1815, Hawkins to Early, 20 May 1815, Hawkins, *Writings,* 2:727, 734–35.

4. James W. Silver, *Edmund Pendleton Gaines: Frontier General* (Baton Rouge: Louisiana State University Press, 1949), 54, 56; Peter Early to Sebastian Kindelan, 24 May 1815, 1 June 1815, GLB; Rogin, *Fathers and Children,* 175; Anthony F. C. Wallace, *The Long, Bitter Trail: Andrew Jackson and the Indians* (New York: Hill and Wang, 1993), 5.

5. Silver, *Gaines,* 56–7; R.S. Cotterill, *The Southern Indians: The Story of the Civilized Tribes before Removal* (Norman: University of Oklahoma Press, 1954), 194; Hawkins to Dallas, 8 July 1815, Hawkins to Jackson, 17 July 1815, Hawkins, *Writings,* 2:739, 742; Dowd, *Spirited Resistance,* 191; Dallas to Gaines, 5 July 1815, Secretary of War, Letters Sent, Military Affairs, National Archives, Washington, D.C., hereafter cited as WDLSMA; Jackson to Dallas, 20 June 1815, Jackson, *Correspondence,* 2:210; Statement of Annuities, 22 February 1816, *ASPIA,* 2:29.

6. Jackson's Talk to Creeks, 4 September 1815, Jackson, *Correspondence,* 2:216; Speech of Tustennuggee Thlucco (Big Warrior), 18 September 1815, Hawkins, *Writings,* 2:754–55.

7. Hawkins to Gaines, 17 October 1815, Hawkins to Jackson, 1 December 1815, Hawkins, *Writings,* 2:753, 765; Graham to Gaines, 24 October 1815, LSSWIA; *Niles Weekly Register,* 28 October 1815, 9:151.

8. Crawford to Hawkins, 16 October 1815, LSSWIA.

9. Gaines to Jackson, 12 December 1815; Jackson, *Correspondence,* 2:222; Hawkins to Crawford, 8 December 1815, Hawkins, *Writings,* 2:765; Woodward to J. J. Hooper, 20 December 1858, Woodward, *Reminiscences,* 153; Crawford to Barnett, Hawkins, and Gaines, 20 December 1815, LSSWIA; Doster, *Creek Indians,* 2:176.

10. Rembert W. Patrick, *Aristocrat in Uniform: Duncan L. Clinch* (Gainesville: University of Florida Press, 1963), 24–6; E. Cutler to Daniel Parker, 16 January 1816, Letters Received by the Adjutant General's Office, National Archives, Washington, D.C., hereafter cited as LRAGO; Barnett to Crawford, 27 January 1816, WDLR; Crawford to Jackson, 27 January 1816, WDLSMA; Crawford to Gaines, 27 January 1816, *Creek Letters;* Rogin, *Fathers and Children,* 174.

11. Hawkins to Crawford, 6 January 1816, Hawkins to Jackson, 12 August 1815, Hawkins, *Writings,* 2:767; Pintado to Antonio Bocarro, 9 February 1816, Pintado Papers; Boyd, "Prospect Bluff," 71–74; Doster, *Creek Indians,* 2:157; Wright, *Creeks and Seminoles,* 190–91; Ventura Morales to Ramirez, 3 November 1817, Ventura Morales, "Letter," 16; Milligan, "Slave Rebelliousness," 10; Patrick, *Clinch,* 27–28.

12. Mann P. Lomas to Daniel Parker, 2 February 1816, LRAGO.

13. Hawkins to Crawford, 3 February 1816, Hawkins to Crawford, 16 February, Hawkins, *Writings,* 2:771, 773; Doster, *Creek Indians,* 2:169.

14. José L. Franco, *Politica Continental América de España en Cuba, 1812–1830* (Havana: Archivo Nacional de Cuba, 1947), 57.

15. Jackson to Gaines, 12 March 1816, WDLR; Jackson is quoted in Doster, *Creek Indians,* 2:173.

16. Doster, *Creek Indians,* 2:170; Gaines to Crawford, 20 March 1816, Gaines to Jackson, 20 March 1816, United States Congress, House of Representatives, *Serial Set,* 15 Cong., 2nd sess., H. Doc. 122, hereafter cited as H. Doc. 122; Gaines to Jackson, 22 March 1816, WDLR.

17. Crawford to Coffee, 14 March 1816, LSSWIA; Rogin, *Fathers and Children,* 174–76.

18. Crawford to Jackson, 15 March, 1816, WDLSMA.

19. Hawkins to Crawford, 16 February 1816, 2 April 1816, Hawkins, *Writings,* 2:773–74, 780; Hawkins to Jackson, 21 March 1816, Hays, "Letters of Timothy Barnard," 308; Sugden, *Southern Indians,* 310.

20. Big Warrior to Jackson, 16 April 1816, Gaines to Jackson, 18 April 1816, Jackson, *Correspondence,* 2:239–40.

21. Hawkins to Jackson, 21 April 1816, Hawkins to Graham, 23 April 1816; Hawkins to Tustennuggee Hopoi (Little Prince), 30 April 1816, Hawkins, *Writings,* 2:782, 785; Talk of Little Prince, 26 April 1816, Gaines to Secretary of War, 30 April 1816, *ASPFR,* 4:557–58. How strong an effort Little Prince made in his efforts to persuade Seminoles to destroy Negro Fort is difficult to determine; he did, however, provide intelligence about hostile Seminole strength, judging it to be about three hundred warriors. See Patrick, *Clinch,* 26.

22. Jackson to Gaines, 8 April 1816, Jackson, *Correspondence,* 2:238–39.

23. Gaines to Crawford, 6 April 1816; Isaac L. Baker to Amelung, 23 April 1816, H. Doc. 122; Jackson to Zuñiga, 23 April 1816, *ASPFR,* 4:499; Boyd, "Prospect Bluff," 76.

24. Pintado to Josef de Soto, 29 April 1815, Pintado Papers.

25. Baker to Amelung, 23 April 1816, H. Doc. 122; Boyd, "Prospect Bluff," 76; Coker and Watson, *Indian Traders,* 306.

26. Jackson to Crawford, 24 April 1816, WDLR.

27. Gaines to McDonald, 30 April 1816, Clinch to Gaines, 7 May 1816, 9 May 1816, WDLR.

28. Hawkins to Gaines, 3 May 1816, Hawkins to Mitchell, 10 May 1816, Hawkins to Crawford, 10 May 1816, Hawkins, *Writings,* 2:785–86; Clinch to Gaines, 9 May 1816, WDLR.

29. Clinch to Gaines, 9 May 1816, WDLR.

30. Jackson to Crawford, 12 May 1816, WDLR.

31. Crawford to Jackson, 20 May 1816, WDLSMA.

32. Crawford to Jackson, 21 May 1816, LSSWIA.

33. Jackson to Crawford, 2 June 1816, WDLR.

34. Jackson to Crawford, 9 June 1816, WDLR.

35. Gaines to Patterson, 22 May 1816, Letters Received by the Secretary of the Navy from Captains, 1805–61, Naval Records Collection of the Office of Naval Records and Library, National Archives, Washington, D.C., hereafter cited as Captains Letters.

36. Hawkins to Zuñiga, 24 May 1816, Hawkins to McDonald, 22 May 1816, Hawkins, *Writings,* 2:786–87, 789; Freeman to Gaines, 23 May 1816, WDLR.

37. Hawkins to McDonald, 22 May 1816, Hawkins to Crawford, 24 May 1816, Hawkins, *Writings*, 2:786–89; Gaines to Clinch, 23 May 1816, Gaines to Croghan, 23 May 1816, Gaines to Mitchell, 24 May 1816, WDLR; Gaines to Crawford, 24 May 1816, H. Doc. 122; Tooke to Mitchell, 20 June 1816, Georgia Adjutant General, Military Affairs, Georgia Department of Archives, Atlanta, Georgia.

38. Zuñiga to Jackson, 26 May 1816, *ASPFR*, 4:556.

39. Franco, *Politico*, 71–73.

40. Amelung to Jackson, 4 June 1816, in Harold D. Moser, David R. Hoth, and George H. Hoeman, eds., *The Papers of Andrew Jackson*, 4 vols. (Knoxville: University of Tennessee Press, 1980–1994), 4:39–40, hereafter cited as Jackson, *Papers*. Jackson to Crawford, 15 June 1816, WDLR.

41. Gaines to Jackson, 3 June 1816, WDLR; Patrick, *Clinch*, 27; Patterson to Loomis, 19 June 1816, Captains Letters.

42. Henri, *Hawkins*, 317.

43. Patrick, *Clinch*, 27; Pleasonton to Calhoun, 11 April 1818, John C. Calhoun, *The Papers of John C. Calhoun*, edited by William Edwin Hemphill, Robert L. Meriwether, and Clyde N. Wilson, 20 vols. (Columbia: University of South Carolina Press, 1959–1988), 2:241.

44. Patrick, *Clinch*, 29; Coker and Watson, *Indian Traders*, 307; Crawford to Gaines, 1 July 1816, WDLSMA.

45. Loomis to Patterson, 15 August 1816, Patterson to Crowninshield, 15 August 1816, Captains Letters; Milligan, "Slave Rebelliousness," 15.

46. Patrick, *Clinch*, 29–30; Loomis to Patterson, 13 August 1816, Captains Letters; Clinch to Butler, 27 August 1816, *Niles Weekly Register*, 20 November 1819, 186–87.

Edmund Doyle and William Hambly continued to operate the Forbes Store at Prospect Bluff after the British left. But as the deerskin trade declined, they saw more potential profit in trading with the United States fort above the Florida line. They regularly supplied the soldiers there with information about Seminole and black activity in West Florida. See Wright, *Creeks and Seminoles*, 191; Coker and Watson, *Indian Traders*, 307. Also, the Inneraritys were distressed that blacks controled the area around Prospect Bluff after the British left. They accused the fugitive slaves of piracy. See Boyd, "Prospect Bluff," 75.

47. Patrick, *Clinch*, 30; Loomis to Patterson, 13 August 1816, Captains Letters; Milligan, "Slave Rebelliousness," 15.

48. Patrick, *Clinch*, 30–31; Loomis to Patterson, 13 August 1816, Captains Letters; Clinch to Butler, 27 August 1816, *Niles Weekly Register*, 20 November 1819, 187; Milligan, "Slave Rebelliousness," 16. The identity of the leader Garçon has always been a mystery. He was possibly a free black mentioned by Vincente Pintado in the fall of 1815 as traveling from Pensacola to Mobile to discuss something with Forbes agent James Innerarity. Pintado was the surveyor general of Spanish West Florida. See Pintado to John Innerarity, 27 September 1815, Pintado Papers.

49. Loomis to Patterson, 13 August 1816, Captains Letters; Milligan, "Slave Rebelliousness," 15–16.

50. Loomis to Patterson, 13 August 1816, Captains Letters; Patrick, *Clinch,* 31.

51. Loomis to Patterson, 13 August 1816, Captains Letters. Clinch claimed that the weight of the eighteen-pounders made it impossible to move them from the vessels to the site of the battery. See Clinch to Butler, 27 August 1816, *Niles Weekly Register,* 20 November 1819, 187; Spencer Tucker, *The Jeffersonian Gunboat Navy* (Columbia: University of South Carolina Press, 1993), 175.

52. Loomis to Patterson, 13 August 1816, Patterson to Crowninshield, 15 August 1816, Captains Letters; Patrick, *Clinch,* 32.

53. Loomis to Patterson, 13 August 1816; Statement of ?, 30 July 1816, Patterson to Crowninshield, 15 August 1816, Captains Letters; Milligan, "Slave Rebelliousness," 14; Patrick, *Clinch,* 27. Daniel Patterson would later request that Loomis and his men be compensated.

54. Loomis to Patterson, 13 August 1816, Captains Letters; Boyd, "Prospect Bluff," 81.

55. Clinch to Butler, 27 August 1816, *Niles Weekly Register,* 20 November 1819, 17:188; Patrick, *Clinch,* 33; Wright, *Creeks and Seminoles,* 199; Boyd, "Prospect Bluff," 81.

56. Crawford to Mitchell, 24 September 1816, Telamon Cuyler Collection.

57. Benjamin Houmans to Patterson, 5 October 1816, Captains Letters.

58. Patrick, *Clinch,* 35; Boyd, "Prospect Bluff," 82. Clinch's report eventually did appear in *Niles Weekly Register,* 20 November 1819, 186–88.

59. John Lewis to Governor Coppinger, 2 September 1816, East Florida Papers; William Gibson to Governor Mitchell, 31 July 1816, "Creek Letters"; Porter, "Seminole War," 265; Kenneth W. Porter, "The Negro Abraham," *Florida Historical Quarterly* 25 (1946): 7; Kevin Mulroy, *Freedom on the Border: The Seminole Maroons in Florida, the Indian Territory, Coahuila, and Texas* (Lubbock: Texas Tech University Press, 1993), 15.

60. Superintendent to Crawford, 5 September 1816, Letters Sent by the Superintendent of Indian Trade, 1806–1823, National Archives, Washington, D.C., hereafter cited as LSSIT; Deposition of Israel Barber before John Floyd, 7 October 1816, East Florida Papers, vol. 42; William Gibson to Mitchell, 31 July 1816, "Creek Letters;" William Gibson and William Bailey to Mitchell, 5 November 1817, Gibson to Mitchell, 13 December 1816, Telamon Cuyler Collection.

61. Martin Hardin to Mitchell, 2 October 1816, Hardin to Mitchell, 28 December 1816, Telamon Cuyler Collection; *Augusta Chronicle,* 23 August 1816; Crawford to Bolling Hall, 25 September 1816, WDLSMA; Jeffrey Lynn Thomason, "Acquisition by Foray," (master's thesis, Austin Peay State University, Clarksville, Tennessee, 1975), 44.

62. For samples see William Scott to Mitchell, 7 September 1816, Kingsley to Mitchell, 13 September 1816, Telamon Cuyler Collection.

63. Crawford to Mitchell, 24 September 1816, Clinch to Mitchell, 28 October 1816, Telamon Cuyler Collection; Clinch to Gaines, 26 December 1816, LRAGO.

64. Jackson, David Meriwether, and J. Franklin to Crawford, 20 September

1816, *ASPIA,* 2:104; Henri, *Hawkins,* 305; Wallace, *Jackson and the Indians,* 51–2.

65. Big Warrior and Little Prince to Madison, 31 October 1816, WDLR.

66. Patrick, *Clinch,* 34; Henri, *Hawkins,* 317; Green, *Politics of Indian Removal,* 52–53; Crawford to Mitchell, 28 October 1816, Mitchell Papers, Newberry Library. Sketch of David B. Mitchell is in George White, ed., *Historical Collections of Georgia* (New York: Pudney & Russell, Publishers, 1855; reprint ed., Baltimore: Genealogical Publishing Company, 1969), 224–26.

67. Crawford to Mitchell, 20 October 1816, 28 October 1816, 22 November 1816, Graham to Mitchell, 27 January 1817, Mitchell to Graham, 20 February 1817, Mitchell Papers, Newberry Library; Mitchell to Crawford, 10 November 1816, same to same, 30 December 1816, Mitchell to Graham, 20 February 1817, Secretary of War, Letters Received, Registered Series, National Archives, Washington, D.C., hereafter cited as LRSWR.

68. Jackson to Monroe, 12 November 1816, Monroe to Jackson, 14 December 1816, Jackson, *Correspondence,* 2:264, 266; Roger Spiller, "John C. Calhoun as Secretary of War 1817–1825," (PhD. diss., Louisiana State University, 1977), 36.

69. Crawford to Mitchell, 2 October 1816, Mitchell Papers, Newberry Library; Jackson to Coffee, 26 December 1816, John Coffee Papers, Alabama Department of Archives and History, Montgomery, Alabama; Reginald Horsman, *The Origins of Indian Removal, 1815–1824* (East Lansing: Michigan State University Press, 1970), 5–6.

70. Arbuthnot Journal, 23 October, 27 October, *ASPFR,* 4:609; Wright, *Creeks and Seminoles,* 193.

71. Coker and Watson, *Indian Traders,* 310–12; Wright, *Creeks and Seminoles,* 193.

72. Arbuthnot Journal, 8 November, 9 November 1816, Bowlegs to Coppinger, 18 November 1816, Adams to Erving, 2 December 1818, *ASPFR,* 4:608–9, 547; Sugden, "Florida Indians," 310; Porter, "Seminole War," 266–67.

73. Masot to Cienfuegas, 10 January 1817, Papeles Procedentes de Cuba Archivo General de Indias, Legojo 1874, Letter 29, Library of Congress, Washington, D.C., hereafter cited as Archivo General de Indias. King to Gaines, 28 January 1817, Gibson to Mitchell, 4 January 1817, LRSWR; Mitchell to Secretary of War, 6 January 1817, GLB.

74. Floyd to Mitchell, 19 January 1817, "Creek Letters," 3:879; Mitchell to Gaines, 5 February 1817, GLB; Gaines to Mitchell, 5 February 1817, Mitchell to Secretary of War, 6 February 1817, R. Sands to Commander at Fort Hawkins, 2 February 1817, *American State Papers: Military Affairs,* 7 vols. (Washington: Gales and Seaton, 1832–1861), 1:691, hereafter cited as *ASPMA;* Graham to Jackson, 25 January 1817, WDLSMA; Clinch to Gaines, 26 December 1816, LRAGO; Crawford to Mitchell, 27 January 1817, Mitchell Papers, Newberry Library.

75. Onís to Monroe, 2 January 1817, *ASPFR,* 4:184; Masot to Cienfuegas, 10 January 1817, Archivo General de Indias, Legajo 1874, Letter 29.

76. Gaines to Mitchell, 14 February 1817, Gaines to Secretary of War, 14 February 1817, LRSWR.

77. Mitchell to Gaines, 8 February 1817, GLB.

78. William Gibson, Thomas Miller, and William Bailey to Mitchell, 8 February 1817, Telamon Cuyler Collection.

79. Archibald Clark to Mitchell, 26 February 1817, *Creek Letters,* 3:881; Clark to Gaines, 26 February 1817, Letters received by the Office of the Secretary of War Relating to Indian Affairs, National Archives, Washington, D.C., hereafter cited as LRSWIA; Gibson to Mitchell, 26 February 1817, GLB.

Whether Garrett had ever participated in raids into Florida is unknown, although he was later turned down when he made an Indian Depredation claim for the loss of property in the Seminole raid on his house. Such a rejection could have been for other reasons, perhaps because the Indians were not from the United States. See Deposition of Obadiah Garrett, 23 January 1835, Indian Files, Box 74, File 2. See Larry Clifford Skogen, "'To Preserve Peace on the Frontiers': Indian Depredation Claims and Native American Policy, 1796—1920" (Ph.D. diss., Arizona State University, 1993), 39–74, for an explanation of the government's policies on Indian depredation claims.

Ironically, Garrett's employer, Israel Barber, often complained about raids of Georgians into Florida because of the reprisals they invited against citizens of St. Mary's County. See Affidavit of Israel Barber in Gibson, Miller, and Bailey to Mitchell, 8 February 1816, Telamon Cuyler Collection; Affidavit of Israel Barber before John Floyd, 7 October 1816, East Florida Papers, vol. 42.

CHAPTER 4
"Shall We Be Permitted to Visit the Spaniards?"

1. *Augusta Chronicle,* 27 February 1817; McIntosh et al. to Madison, 15 January 1817, McIntosh et al. to Graham, 10 March, 15 March, 17 March 1817, LRSWIA.

2. Graham to McIntosh et al. 3 March 1817, LSSWIA; Southerland and Brown, *Federal Road,* 112; Abernethy, *The Formative Period in Alabama,* 49. Georgians also saw to it that when the prime cotton lands on the Alabama were placed up for auction, the sale was held in Milledgeville. See Southerland and Brown, *Federal Road,* 113.

3. Perryman to Sands, 24 February 1817, Mitchell to Graham, 30 March 1817, *ASPMA,* 1:681–83; *Niles Weekly Register,* 12 April 1817, 112.

4. Bagot to Moodie, 29 January 1817, *ASPFR,* 4:591; James Fred Rippy, *Rivalry of the United States and Britain over Latin America, 1808–1830* (Baltimore: The Johns Hopkins Press, 1929; reprint edition, New York: Octagon Books, 1964), 59–60.

5. Wright, *Creeks and Seminoles,* 203; Samuel Flagg Bemis, *John Quincy Adams and the Foundations of American Foreign Policy* (New York: Alfred A. Knopf, 1949), 305–6; Philip C. Brooks, *Diplomacy and the Borderlands: The*

Adams-Onís Treaty of 1819 (Berkeley: University of California Press, 1939; reprint edition, New York: Octagon Books, 1970), 63; Onís to Secretary of State, 15 March 1817, *ASPFR,* 4:189.

6. Brooks, *Diplomacy and the Borderlands,* 2, 76–77.

7. Harry Ammon, *James Monroe: The Quest for National Identity* (New York: McGraw-Hill, 1971; reprint edition, Charlottesville and London: University of Virginia Press, 1990), 359; Monroe to Shelby, 20 February 1817, Hamilton, *Writings of Monroe,* 6:1–2; Monroe to Jackson, 1 March 1817, Jackson, *Correspondence,* 2:276.

8. Jackson to Graham, 26 February 1817; Jackson to Monroe, 4 March 1817; Division Order, 22 April 1817, James Monroe Papers, Library of Congress, Washington, D.C. Hereafter cited as Monroe Papers, LC.

9. Division Order, 22 April 1817, Monroe Papers, LC.

10. Arbuthnot to Commander of Fort Gaines, 3 March 1817, *ASPMA,* 1:682.

11. Gaines to Graham, 3 April 1817, LRSWIA.

12. Sands to King, 15 March 1817, *ASPMA,* 1:683; *Augusta Chronicle,* 15 March 1817; Rabun to Graham, 18 March 1817, Culloh to Graham, 24 March 1817, LRSWR; Annie C. Waters, "A Documentary History of Fort Crawford (Located in East Brewton, Escambia County [Alabama])," *Escambia County Historical Quarterly* 3 (September 1975): 7; Mitchell to Graham, 30 March 1817, "Letters of Timothy Barnard," 308; Culloh to Gaines, 3 April 1817, in Frank S. Jones, *History of Decatur County Georgia* (Spartanburg, SC: The Reprint Company, 1980), 139.

13. Gaines to Graham, 20 March 1817, LRSWIA; Gaines to Masot, 18 March 1817, Gaines to Gray, 18 March 1817, Waters, "Documentary History of Fort Crawford," 2, 6, 7; Gaines to Graham, 3 April 1817, Gaines to Brearley, 8 April 1817, Gaines to Masot, 8 April 1817, Brearley to Masot, 10 April 1817, Masot to Brearley, 11 April 1817, Masot to Brearley, 16 April 1817, Masot to Brearley, 21 April 1817, Masot to Gaines, 12 April 1817, Brearley to Masot, 18 April 1817, Brearley to Masot, 20 April 1817, Brearley to Masot, 23 April 1817, Gaines to Graham, 30 April 1817, LRSWR.

14. Graham to Rabun, n.d., Floyd to Bailey, 7 April 1817, *Georgia Military Affairs,* 4:313, 324–25; Gaines to Commander, Charleston, 16 April 1817, LRAGO; *Augusta Chronicle,* 3 May 1817; Rabun to Floyd, 29 April 1817, GLB; Davis to Hayne, 30 April 1817, Clarence Edward Carter, ed., *The Territorial Papers of the United States,* 28 vols. (Washington, D.C.: Government Printing Office, 1934–1975), 18:93–94.

15. Crawford to Holmes, 22 April 1817, Mississippi Territory, Governor's Correspondence, Alabama Department of Archives and History, Montgomery, Alabama; Gaines to Graham, 20 March 1817, Glassell to Gaines, 22 April 1817, LRSWIA.

16. Jackson to Graham, 29 April 1817, LRSWR.

17. Floyd to Mitchell, 26 February 1817, Georgia Adjutant General, Military Affairs, Georgia Department of Archives and History, Atlanta, Georgia, hereafter referred to as Georgia Adjutant General File; Floyd, Division Orders, 26 February 1817, Floyd, Division Orders, 7 April 1817, Floyd to Rabun,

9 May 1817, Floyd to Rabun, 5 June 1817, Report of William Bailey, 28 May 1817, Floyd to Bailey, 30 May 1817, *Georgia Military Affairs,* 4:321, 323–24, 337; Rabun to Floyd, 5 June 1817, GLB.

18. Rabun to Floyd, 18 June 1817, GLB.

19. Tattnall to Rabun, 20 March 1817, Telamon Cuyler Collection; Hopkins to Rabun, 24 April 1817, "Creek Letters," 3:891.

20. Montgomery to Rabun, 3 July 1817, Telamon Cuyler Collection; Rabun to Floyd, 8 August 1817, GLB.

21. Floyd to Rabun, 10 July 1817, *Georgia Military Affairs,* 4:343; Hambly to Arbuthnot, 10 May 1817, *ASPFR,* 4:579.

22. Gaines to Masot, 12 May 1817, LRSWR.

23. Graham to Gaines, 6 June 1817, WDLSMA; Gaines to Graham, 28 May 1817, LRSWR; Silver, *Gaines,* 67–68.

24. *Augusta Chronicle,* 14 May 1817; Abernethy, "Spanish Frontier," 111; *Narrative of a Voyage to the Spanish Main in the Ship Two Friends,* Introduction by John W. Griffin (1819; reprint edition, Gainesville: University Presses of Florida, 1978), 185; Franco, *Politica,* 74.

25. United States Congress, *Serial Set,* vol. 14, *Message of the President, 17 November 1818,* 15th Cong., 2nd sess., S. Doc. 1; *Narrative of a Voyage,* 13; Abernethy, "Spanish Frontier," 112–13.

26. Crawford to Tait, 12 July 1817, Tait Family Papers, Alabama Department of Archives and History, Montgomery, Alabama; Floyd to Rabun, 19 August 1817, *Georgia Military Affairs,* 4:35.

27. Crawford to Tait, 31 July 1817, Tait Family Papers.

28. Monroe to Jackson, 4 August 1817, Jackson to Monroe, 12 August 1817, Jackson, *Correspondence,* 2:319–20; Monroe to Jackson, 5 October 1817, Monroe Papers, LC.

29. Graham to Gaines, 8 May 1817, WDLSMA; Gaines to Graham, 4 June 1817, *The New American State Papers, Military Affairs,* 19 vols. (Wilmington, Delaware: Scholarly Resources, 1979), 9:3; Gaines to "Inhabitants of Murder Creek," 12 July 1817, *ASPMA,* 1:684.

30. Gaines to Jackson, 10 July 1817, Jackson, *Correspondence,* 2:305; G. Leftwick to Gaines, 28 July 1817, *ASPMA,* 1:684.

31. Mitchell to Graham, 17 July 1817, LRSWR; Crawford to Mitchell, 24 August 1817, Mitchell Miscellaneous Papers, NYPL; *Niles Weekly Register,* 16 August 1817, 399; *Augusta Chronicle,* 26 July 1817.

32. Gaines to Rabun, 20 July 1817, "Creek Letters," 3:895.

33. Gaines to John Williams, 12 July 1817, LRAGO.

34. Jeanne T. Heidler, "The Military Career of David Emanuel Twiggs" (Ph.D. diss., Auburn University, 1988), 2.

35. Ibid., 7; Boyd, "Prospect Bluff," 84; Twiggs to Mitchell, 4 August 1817, *ASPMA,* 1:750.

36. Graham to Jackson, 14 August 1817, LSSWIA; Gaines to Parker, 20 August 1817, LRAGO; Gaines to Graham, 25 August 1817, *ASPMA,* 1:684; Gaines to Jackson, 25 August 1817, Jackson, *Correspondence,* 2:322; Abernethy, *Alabama,* 66.

37. Porter, "Seminole Wars," 267–68; Gaines to Jackson, 31 August 1817, Jackson, *Correspondence,* 2:323; Arbuthnot to Nicholls, 26 August 1817, *Narrative of a Voyage,* 226; Silver, *Gaines,* 70.

38. Response of Indians to Gaines, 11 September 1817, Twiggs to Gaines, 17 September 1817, *ASPMA,* 1:684–85.

39. Gaines to Jackson, 1 October 1817, Jackson, *Papers,* 4:140–41; Gaines to Graham, 1 October 1817, *ASPMA,* 1:685. Fowltown was located near modern Bainbridge, Georgia. See *Historic Chattahoochee Commission, Chattahoochee Trace Historical Markers in Alabama and Georgia* (Eufaula, Alabama: Historic Chattahoochee Commission, 1983), 56.

40. Waters, "Documentary History of Fort Crawford," 10; Gaines to Muhlenberg, 11 October 1817, Gaines to Ripley, 18 October 1817, LRAGO; Graham to Gaines, 30 October 1817, LSSWIA.

41. Holmes to Gaines, 19 October 1817, Mississippi Territory, Governor's Correspondence; Ventura Morales to Ramirez, 3 November 1817, Ventura Morales, "Ventura Morales," 9, 11, 17, 20.

42. *Narrative of a Voyage,* 14; Abernethy, "Spanish Frontier," 113–14; Adams to Monroe, 30 September 1817, in Worthington Chauncy Ford, ed., *The Writings of John Quincy Adams,* 7 vols. (New York: The MacMillan Company, 1913–17), 6:207; Ventura Morales to Ramirez, 3 November 1817, Ventura Morales, "Ventura Morales," 9, 20; Wayne to Homans, 27 September 1817, *ASPFR,* 4:603; Boyd, "Prospect Bluff," 86.

43. Franco, *Politica,* 76; *Narrative of a Voyage,* 15–19, 113; Abernethy, "Spanish Frontier," 115–16.

44. Gaines to Muhlenberg, 11 October 1817, LRAGO.

45. Gaines's Talk to Chief and Warriors, November 1817, Gaines to Jackson, 9 November 1817, Gaines to Graham, 9 November 1817, *ASPMA,* 1:686, 688; Gaines to Rabun, 9 November 1817, "Creek Letters," 3:900.

46. Crawford to Mitchell, 3 October 1817, Graham to Mitchell, 3 November 1817, Mitchell Miscellaneous Papers, NYPL; Mitchell to Graham, 12 October 1817, LRSWR.

47. Graham to Rabun, 12 November 1817, Graham to Gaines, 12 November 1817, WDLSMA; Fayette Robinson, *An Account of the Organization of the Army of the United States, with Biographies of Distinguished Officers of All Grades,* 2 vols. (Philadelphia: Butler and Company, 1848), 2:119; Glascock to Rabun, 18 November 1817, *Georgia Military Affairs,* 4:368.

48. Robinson, *Organization of the Army,* 2:119; *Augusta Chronicle,* 3 December 1817; Proceedings, 2 February 1819, *Annals of Congress,* 15 Cong., 2nd sess., 989.

49. Boyd, "Prospect Bluff," 41, 85; Gaines to Twiggs, 20 November 1817, Twiggs to Gaines, 21 November 1817, Jackson, *Correspondence,* 2:334; Gaines to Graham, 21 November 1817, LRSWR; Gaines to Rabun, 21 November 1817, "Creek Letters," 3:901; Gaines to Jackson, 21 November 1817, *ASPMA,* 1:686; Heidler, "Twiggs," 9.

50. Captain John McIntosh to Senator Abner Lacock, 5 February 1819, *ASPMA,* 1:747; Gaines to Graham, 26 November 1817, LRSWR.

51. Silver, *Gaines,* 71; Written Testimony of David B. Mitchell to Senate, 23 February 1819, *ASPMA,* 1:749.

52. Rabun to Gaines, 24 November 1817, GLB; Gaines to Graham, 26 November 1817, LRSWR.

53. Boyd, "Prospect Bluff," 87; Wright, *Creeks and Seminoles,* 200; Gaines to Muhlenberg, 18 November 1817, LRAGO; Scott to Gaines, 28 November 1817, *ASPMA,* 1:688; Gaines to Clinch, 30 November 1817, LRSWR.

54. Spiller, "Calhoun as Secretary of War," 40–44; Crawford to Yancey, Bartlett Yancey Papers, Southern Historical Collection, University of North Carolina, Chapel Hill, North Carolina; Adams to John Adams, 24 November 1817, Ford, *Writings of Adams,* 6:268. Clay had originally appointed New York representative Peter B. Porter to head the Foreign Relations Committee, but he resigned from Congress. Clay acceded to the wishes of the members when they elected Calhoun to succeed Porter. See Margaret L. Coit, *John C. Calhoun: An American Portrait* (Boston: Houghton-Mifflin, 1950), 72.

55. Message of the President, 2 December 1817, *U.S. Serial Set,* vol. 15, Senate Journal, 15th Cong., 1st sess., 15; Graham to Gaines, 2 December 1817, LSSWIA.

56. Gaines to Graham, 2 December 1817, *ASPMA,* 1:687.

57. Ibid.

58. Calhoun to Gaines, 9 December 1817; Calhoun to Gaines, 16 December 1817, LSSWIA.

CHAPTER 5
"The Supreme Law of Nature and Nations"

1. Porter, "Seminole Wars," 268–69; Mitchell to Graham, 14 December 1817, *ASPMA,* 1:688; Mitchell to Rabun, 15 December 1817, Telamon Cuyler Collection; Mitchell to Bibb, 15 December 1817, Governor William W. Bibb Papers, Alabama Territory, Alabama Department of Archives and History, Montgomery, Alabama.

2. Gaines to Mitchell, 2 December 1817, Telamon Cuyler Collection; Mitchell to Graham, 14 December 1817, *ASPMA,* 1:688.

3. Mitchell to Graham, 14 December 1817, *ASPMA,* 1:688–89; Little Prince to Mitchell, 30 December 1817, LRSWIA.

4. Mitchell to Graham, 14 December 1817, *ASPMA,* 1:688–89; Little Prince to Mitchell, 30 December 1817, LRSWIA; Hambly and Doyle to Jackson, 2 May 1818, *Annals of Congress,* 15th Cong., 2nd sess., 966; Boyd, "Prospect Bluff," 88–89.

5. Coker and Watson, *Indian Traders,* 315.

6. Boyd, "Prospect Bluff," 83; Coker and Watson, *Indian Traders,* 313; Arbuthnot to Hambly, 3 May 1817, *Narrative of a Voyage,* 229–31.

7. Coker and Watson, *Indian Traders,* 313–15; Boyd, "Prospect Bluff," 83.

8. Power of Attorney, 17 June 1817, Arbuthnot to Cameron, n.d., *Narrative of a Voyage,* 213, 218; Arbuthnot to Nicholls, 26 August 1817, in James Parton, *Life of Andrew Jackson,* 3 vols. (New York: Mason Brothers, 1861), 2:414.

9. Arbuthnot to Nicholls, 26 August 1817, Parton, *Life of Jackson,* 2:415; Dowd, *Spirited Resistance,* 189; Boyd, "Prospect Bluff," 85; Coker and Watson, *Indian Traders,* 316–17. Coker and Watson repeat Peter Cook's assertion that Arbuthnot had personally accused Hambly and Doyle of selling Indian land and sentenced them during their captivity to torture. Cook was Arbuthnot's chief clerk and did not like his employer. He became friends with Hambly and Doyle. There is no evidence other than Cook's hostile testimony to cast Alexander Arbuthnot in such a light. In fact, Hambly and Doyle never were tortured, and they certainly would have been had Arbuthnot countenanced, let alone stipulated it.

10. Glascock to Rabun, 3 December 1817, *Georgia Military Affairs,* 4:371; *Augusta Chronicle,* 6 December, 13 December 1817; Gaines to Rabun, 14 December 1817, "Creek Letters," 3:902.

11. Jackson to Trimble, 2 December 1817, Mississippi Territory, Governor's Correspondence; Gaines to Secretary of War, 2 December 181, same to same, 15 December 1817, Irvin to Arbuckle, 23 December 1817, *ASPMA,* 1:687–89, 692; Arbuckle to Graham, 19 December 1817, Arbuckle to Gaines, 20 December 1817, *U.S. Serial Set,* 15th Cong., 1st Sess., S. Doc. 87, 6.

12. Arbuckle to Graham, 19 December 1817, *U.S. Serial Set,* S. Doc. 87; Arbuckle to Gaines, 20 December 1817, Arbuckle to Gaines, 21 December 1817, Muhlenberg to Arbuckle, 19 December 1817, Irvin to Arbuckle, 23 December 1817, *ASPMA,* 1:690–92.

13. Arbuckle to Gaines, 21 December 1817, Muhlenberg to Arbuckle, 16 December 1817, same to same, 19 December 1817, Irvin to Arbuckle, 23 December 1817, Arbuckle to Gaines, 27 December 1817, *ASPMA,* 1:691–92; Thomas to Rabun, 30 December 1817, Telamon Cuyler Collection.

14. Calhoun to Bankhead, 12 December 1817, Bankhead to Graham, 20 December 1817, Calhoun to Bankhead, 16 December 1817, Calhoun, *Papers,* 2:11, 20, 29; Carlos G. Calkins, "The Repression of Piracy in the West Indies, 1814–1825," *United States Naval Institute Proceedings* 37 (December 1911): 1213; Gaines to Rabun, 27 December 1817, *Georgia Military Affairs,* 4:381.

15. Bankhead to Calhoun, 27 December 1817, Gaines to Calhoun, 30 December 1817, LRSWR; Gaines to Rabun, 27 December 1817, *Georgia Military Affairs,* 4:381.

16. William P. Cresson, *James Monroe* (Chapel Hill: University of North Carolina Press, 1946; reprint edition, Hamden, Connecticut: Archon Books, 1971), 304; Calhoun to Jackson, 26 December 1817, Jackson, *Papers,* 4:163.

17. Calhoun to Jackson, 26 December 1817, Jackson, *Correspondence,* 2:341–42.

18. Spiller, "Calhoun as Secretary of War," 73–74, 79, 85–87.

19. Jackson to Lewis, 8 December 1817, Andrew Jackson–William B. Lewis Letters, 1817–1845, Pierpont Morgan Library, New York, New York; Monroe

to Jefferson, 23 December 1817, Hamilton, *Writings of Monroe,* 6:47; Spiller, "Calhoun as Secretary of War," 110–11; Calhoun to Jackson, 29 December 1817, Jackson, *Correspondence,* 2:343.

20. Calhoun to Jackson, 11 December 1817, same to same, 26 December 1817, Calhoun, *Papers,* 2:10, 24; Jackson to Graham, 16 December 1817, *ASPMA,* 1:689.

21. Calhoun to Jackson, 26 December 1817, Jackson, *Papers,* 4:163.

22. Monroe to Jackson, 14 December 1816, Jackson, *Correspondence,* 2:266. Gaines believed his new orders would allow him to end the Seminole problem once and for all, and yet he found nothing ambiguous about what the military could and could not do in Florida. On 16 January 1818, he wrote to Governor Rabun that the secretary of war had authorized him "to follow the hostile Indians over the Florida line and attack them within its limits, unless they shelter themselves under a Spanish post." See Gaines to Rabun, 16 January 1818, Edmund Pendleton Gaines File, Lyman Draper Manuscript Collection, Wisconsin State Historical Society, Madison, Wisconsin.

23. Luengo to Arbuthnot, 25 December 1817, *ASPFR,* 4:580: Franco, *Politica,* 90–92; Adams to Rodney, 21 November 1817, Caesar Rodney and Caesar A. Rodney Papers, New York Public Library, New York, New York, hereafter referred to as Rodney Papers.

24. Coppinger to Commander of U.S. Forces, 30 December 1817, LRSWR; Allan Nevins, ed., *The Diary of John Quincy Adams, 1794–1845: American Political, Social, and Intellectual Life from Washington to Polk* (New York: Longmans, Green and Co., 1928), 190–91; Spiller, "Calhoun as Secretary of War," 39; Calkins, "Repression of Piracy," 1215; Calhoun to Bankhead, 15 January 1818, WDLSMA; Richard C. Anderson Diary, Entry for February 1818, Library of Congress, Washington, D.C.; Adams to Collins, 31 December 1817, Ford, *Writings of Adams,* 6:284–85; Lester D. Langley, *Struggle for the American Mediterranean: United States–European Rivalry in the Gulf-Caribbean, 1776–1904* (Athens: University of Georgia Press, 1976), 19.

25. Jackson to Monroe, 6 January 1818; Monroe Papers, LC.

26. Monroe Statement, 1831, Monroe Papers, LC; Richard R. Stenberg, "Jackson's 'Rhea Letter' Hoax," *Journal of Southern History* 2 (November 1936): 480–82; Marguerite B. Hamer, "John Rhea of Tennessee," *East Tennessee Historical Society Publications* 4 (January 1932): 42.

27. Remini, *Jackson and the Course of American Empire,* 348–49; Herbert Bruce Fuller, *The Purchase of Florida: Its History and Diplomacy* (1906; reprint edition, Gainesville: University of Florida Press, 1964), 328.

28. Ammon, *Monroe,* 416–17; Cresson, *Monroe,* 305, 495–98.

29. Hamer, "Rhea," 43.

30. Rhea to Jackson, 18 December 1818, Jackson, *Correspondence,* 2:403–4; *Annals of Congress,* 15th Cong., 2nd sess., 855–70, 867.

31. See, for example, Richard Anderson Diary, 13 July 1818, LC.

32. Monroe to Jackson, 5 October 1817, Jackson, *Correspondence,* 2:329. To Crawford, Monroe wrote that the Spaniards were "pushing a quarrel with us, in the hopes of drawing their allies into it on her side." See Monroe to Craw-

ford, 29 January 1818, William H. Crawford Papers, Library of Congress, Washington, D.C.

33. Calhoun to Gaines, 26 December 1817, WDLSMA; Prucha, *Sword of the Republic,* 132.

34. Rabun to Floyd, 16 December 1817, GLB; Calhoun to Blount, 30 December 1817, LSSWIA.

35. Gaines to Calhoun, 3 January 1818, *U. S. Serial Set,* 15 Cong., 2nd sess., S. Doc. 35, 18; Arbuckle to Jackson, 12 January 1818, *ASPMA,* 1:695.

36. Boyd, "Prospect Bluff," 87; Arbuckle to Jackson, 12 January 1818, Gaines to Calhoun, 9 January 1818, *ASPMA,* 1:690, 695.

37. Bertha Sheppard Hart, *The Official History of Laurens County, 1807–1941* (Atlanta: Cherokee Publishing Company, 1972), 120; Floyd to Rabun, 20 November 1817, Georgia Adjutant General; Glascock to Gaines, 11 January 1818, Gaines File, Wisconsin State Historical Society.

38. Glascock to Gaines, 10 January 1818, *ASPMA,* 1:693; Hall to Calhoun, 17 January 1818, Calhoun, *Papers,* 2:79; Frazer to Wallace, 16 June 1818, P.R.O., F.O. 115, vol. 31, LC.

39. Jackson to Calhoun, 12 January 1818, Jackson, *Correspondence,* 2:347; Jackson to Coffee, 14 January 1818; same to same, 27 January 1818, Jackson Papers, LC.

40. Written Testimony of David B. Mitchell to Senate, 23 February 1819, *ASPMA,* 1:749; Mitchell to Gaines, 7 January 1818, Mitchell Papers, Newberry Library; Mitchell to Rabun, 8 January 1818, *Niles Weekly Register,* 7 February 1818, 390; Mitchell to Calhoun, 6 January 1818, LRSWIA; Peter A. Remsen, "Across Georgia and into Alabama, 1817–1818," edited by William B. Hesseltine and Larry Gara, *Georgia Historical Quarterly* 37 (December 1953): 334.

41. Remsen, "Across Georgia," 334; Gaines to Calhoun, 12 January 1818, LRSWIA.

42. Mitchell to Gaines, 30 January 1818, Mitchell Papers, Newberry Library.

43. Mitchell to Calhoun, 3 February 1818, LRSWIA.

44. Mitchell to Jackson, 22 March 1818, Mitchell Papers, Newberry Library.

45. Crawford to Mitchell, 3 April 1818, Mitchell Papers, Newberry Library.

46. Gaines to O. W. Callis, 12 January 1818, Arbuckle to Gaines, 13 January 1818, Gaines to Orr, 19 January 1818, *ASPMA,* 1:694–95; Gaines to Brearley, 21 January 1818, LRAGO; Spiller, "Calhoun as Secretary of War," 89; Calhoun to Monroe, 28 January 1818, Jackson to Calhoun, 11 February 1818, Calhoun to Gaines, 23 February 1818, Calhoun to Monroe, 7 March 1818, Calhoun, *Papers,* 2:100, 131, 155, 178–79. Orr eventually tried to explain his neglect by writing to Calhoun that the reason the rations never reached the army was because Woodbine would not allow the transports to pass up the Apalachicola. Woodbine, of course, was not on the Apalachicola, and there was no attempt by anyone to impede the movement of supply boats up the Apalachicola after Muhlenberg's arrival in mid-January. See Orr to Calhoun, (no day) March 1818, Calhoun, *Papers,* 2:220.

47. Jackson to Calhoun, 13 January 1818, Jackson to Calhoun, 20 January

1818, Gaines to Calhoun, 30 January 1818, *ASPMA,* 1:694, 696, 744; Calhoun to Gaines, 22 January 1818, Calhoun to Jackson, 2 March 1818, Calhoun to Mason, 18 April 1818, Calhoun, *Papers,* 2:86, 189, 251.

48. Arbuckle to Gaines, 13 January 1818, *ASPMA,* 1:695; Arbuckle to Glascock, 18 January 1818, *U.S. Serial Set,* vol. 14, 15 Cong., 2nd sess., S. Doc. 35, 31–32; Gaines to Jackson, 19 February 1818, LRAGO; Arbuckle to Jackson, 12 February 1818, 15 Cong., 2nd sess., S. Doc. 136, 21.

49. Woodward to Hooper, 20 December 1858, Woodward, *Reminiscences,* 136–38; Heard to ?, 22 January 1818, *ASPMA,* 1:693.

50. *Milledgeville Republican and Reflector,* 3 February 1818; Major Clinton Wright to Gaines, 26 January 1818, *ASPMA,* 1:693; John Banks, *A Short Biographical Sketch of the Undersigned by Himself* (Austell, Georgia: Privately Published, 1936), 9. Accusations by Rabun that some of the militiamen from the previous muster had never been paid could have also contributed to slow recruiting. Rabun to Calhoun, 12 February 1818, LRSWR.

51. Jackson to Coffee, 14 January 1818, Jackson Papers, LC; Jackson to Rachel, 10 February 1818, Jackson, *Correspondence,* 2: 353.

52. Gaines to Jackson, 19 January 1818, LRAGO; Gaines to Calhoun, 23 January 1818, Jackson to Calhoun, 20 January 1818, *ASPMA,* 1:692, 696–97; Remini, *Jackson and the Course of American Empire,* 351; Charles Raymond Paine, "The Seminole War of 1817–1819," (Master's thesis, University of Oklahoma, 1938), 70; Gadsden to Calhoun, 21 January 1818, LRSWR; Jackson to Calhoun, 21 January 1818, Calhoun, *Papers,* 2:84; *Niles Weekly Register,* 27 March 1819, 87.

53. James F. Doster, "Land Titles and Public Land Sales in Early Alabama," *Alabama Review* 16 (April 1963): 121; Coffee to Jackson, 12 February 1818, Jackson, *Correspondence,* 2:353.

54. Jackson to Calhoun, 27 January 1818, Jackson, *Papers,* 4:172–73; Calhoun to Jackson, 19 February 1818, Calhoun, *Papers,* 2:148; Calhoun to Jackson, 29 January 1818, LSSWIA; Gaines to Calhoun, 30 January 1818, *ASPMA,* 1:694.

55. Monroe to Calhoun, 30 January 1818, Calhoun, *Papers,* 2:104.

56. Bankhead to Coppinger, 3 January 1818, East Florida Papers; Onís to Adams, 8 January 1818, T. Frederick Davis, "McGregor's Invasion of Florida," *Florida Historical Quarterly* 7 (July 1928): 61; Bemis, *Adams and Foreign Policy,* 305, 308; Glyndon Van Deusen, *The Life of Henry Clay* (Boston: Little, Brown and Company, 1937), 117–23; Speech of 24–25 March 1818, Robert Seager II, Mary W. M. Hargreaves, and James T. Hopkins, eds., *The Papers of Henry Clay,* 11 vols. (Lexington: University of Kentucky Press, 1959–1992), 2:516–17.

57. Monroe to Crawford, 29 January 1817, Crawford Papers, LC; Perkins, *Castlereagh and Adams,* 286–87; Wright, *Creeks and Seminoles,* 197.

58. Jackson to Calhoun, 10 February 1818, Jackson to Calhoun, 14 February 1818, *ASPMA,* 1:697; Brearley to Jackson, 21 February 1818, "Fort Mitchell, Alabama," *Alabama Historical Quarterly* 21 (1959): 10; Early County Historical Society, *Collections of the Early County Historical Society,* vol. 1 (Colquitt, Georgia: Automat Printers, 1971), 31.

59. Jackson to Calhoun, 26 February 1818, *ASPMA,* 1:698; Woodward, *Reminiscences,* 155.

60. *Niles Weekly Register,* 4 April 1818, 104; Woodward to Hooper, 20 December 1858, Woodward, *Reminiscences,* 156; Arbuckle to Jackson, 6 March 1818, Jones, *Decatur County,* 171.

61. Jackson to Calhoun, 26 February 1818, *ASPMA,* 1:698; Banks, *Biographical Sketch,* 10–11; Remini, *Jackson and the Course of American Empire,* 352.

62. Gaines to Rabun, 23 January 1818, *Milledgeville Republican and Reflector,* 27 January 1818; Calhoun to Mitchell, 23 January 1818, Mitchell to Calhoun, 3 February 1818, Calhoun, *Papers,* 2:91, 115–16; Arbuthnot to Mitchell, 19 January 1818, *ASPFR,* 4:591.

63. Graham to Mitchell, 31 October 1817, Treaty with Creeks, 22 January 1818, Mitchell to Calhoun, 28 January 1818, *ASPIA,* 2:151–53; Grace N. Schwartzman and Susan K. Barnard, "A Trail of Broken Promises: Georgians and Muscogee/Creek Treaties, 1796–1826," *Georgia Historical Quarterly* 75 (1991): 705.

64. Mitchell to Rabun, 13 February 1818, *Milledgeville Republican and Reflector,* 24 February 1818; Mitchell to Calhoun, 18 February 1818, Calhoun, *Papers,* 2:146; Mitchell to Gaines, 23 February 1818, Mitchell Papers, Newberry Library; Mitchell to Calhoun, 24 February 1818, LRSWR.

65. Arbuckle to Calhoun, 13 February 1818, Arbuckle to Jackson, 7 March 1818, Jones, *Decatur County,* 156–57, 169; Banks, *Biographical Sketch,* 11; Woodward to Hooper, 20 December 1858, Woodward, *Reminiscences,* 158–59; Jackson to Calhoun, 25 March 1818, *ASPMA,* 1:698.

CHAPTER 6
"The Consciences of Some Men"

1. Wright, *Creeks and Seminoles,* 202–3; Wright, "Note on the Seminole War," 565; Thomason, "Acquisition by Foray," 37; Michael Paul Duffner, "The Seminole-Black Experience in Florida: An Example of Minority Cooperation," (Master's thesis, George Mason University, 1973), 95; William B. Skelton, *An American Profession of Arms: The Army Officer Corps, 1784–1861* (Lawrence: University Press of Kansas, 1992), 333–34; Porter, "Seminole War," 279–80.

2. Strength Report, Southern Division, 1818, *ASPMA,* 1:790; Ethan Allen Hitchcock, *Fifty Years in Camp and Field: Diary of Major-General Ethan Allen Hitchcock, U.S.A.,* ed. W. A. Croffut (New York and London: G. P. Putnam's Sons, 1909), 45.

3. Bibb to Calhoun, 27 March 1818, Bibb to Calhoun, 15 April 1818, *ASPMA,* 1:699; Francis Paul Prucha, *A Guide to Military Posts of the United States, 1789–1895* (Madison: The State Historical Society of Wisconsin, 1964), 68; Trimble to Calhoun, 12 February 1818, Calhoun to Trimble, 4 March 1818, Trimble to Calhoun, 31 March 1818, Calhoun, *Papers,* 1:136, 174, 219; Call to

Masot, 26 February 1818, Legajo 1876, Letter No. 396, Archivo General de Indias; Jackson to Masot, 25 March 1818, Jackson, *Correspondence,* 2:335.

4. Cresson, *Monroe,* 306; Jackson to Calhoun, 25 March 1818, *ASPMA,* 1:698.

5. Jackson to Calhoun, 25 March 1818, *ASPMA,* 1:698.

6. Jackson to Calhoun, 25 March 1818, *ASPMA,* 1:698; Banks, *Biographical Sketch,* 11–12.

7. Banks, *Biographical Sketch,* 12; Jackson to Calhoun, 25 March 1818, *ASPMA,* 1:698; Boyd, "Prospect Bluff," 90.

8. Woodward to Hooper, 20 December 1858, Woodward, *Reminiscences,* 154, 159–60.

9. T. Frederick Davis, "Milly Francis and Duncan McKrimmon: An Authentic Florida Pocahontas," *Florida Historical Quarterly* 21 (January 1943): 255–58; Wright, *Creeks and Seminoles,* 200; *Niles Weekly Register,* 30 January 1819, 432; Hitchcock, *Diary,* 151–53.

10. Jackson to Calhoun, 25 March 1818, *ASPMA,* 1:698; John McIntosh to Jackson, 19 March 1818, Jones, *Decatur County,* 171–72; Edward Brett Randolph Diary, 16–20 March 1818, Southern Historical Collection, University of North Carolina, Chapel Hill, North Carolina.

11. Jackson to Calhoun, 25 March 1818, *ASPMA,* 1:698.

12. Jackson to McKeever, 25 March 1818, *Niles Weekly Register,* 20 March 1818, 80.

13. McIntosh's Brigade, Creek Indian Warriors, Seminole War, 1817–1818, Military Service Records, Box 50822, National Archives, Washington, D.C.; Frye to Lacock, 20 February 1819, Testimony of David B. Mitchell, 23 February 1819, Jackson to Calhoun, 25 March 1818, *ASPMA,* 1:699, 746, 749; Bonner, "McIntosh," 124–25; McIntosh to Jackson, 24 March 1818, Jones, *Decatur County,* 172–73.

14. Randolph Diary, 29, 31 March 1818; Butler to Park, 3 May 1818, *ASPMA,* 1:703.

15. Banks, *Biographical Sketch,* 12; Butler to Parker, 3 May 1818, Frye to Lacock, 23 February 1819, Statement of James Gadsden, 30 June 1819, *ASPMA,* 1:703, 746, 761; Hayne to Calhoun, 28 March 1818, Calhoun, *Papers,* 2:213.

16. Butler to Parker, 3 May 1818; Statement of Gadsden, 30 June 1819, *ASPMA,* 1:703, 761; Randolph Diary, 1, 2 April 1818.

17. Banks, *Biographical Sketch,* 13; Butler to Parker, 3 May 1818, *ASPMA,* 1:703; Wright, *Creeks and Seminoles,* 204–5; Parton, *Life of Jackson,* 2:450.

18. Butler to Parker, 3 May 1818, *ASPMA,* 1:703; Randolph Diary, 2 April 1818; Gaines to Jackson, 3 April 1818, LRAGO; Banks, *Biographical Sketch,* 12–13.

19. Randolph Diary, 5, 6 April 1818; Hugh Young, "A Topographical Memoir on East and West Florida. . . . ," ed. Mark F. Boyd, *Florida Historical Quarterly* 13 (1935): 144; Banks, *Biographical Sketch,* 13; Jackson to Calhoun, 8 April 1818, Jackson, *Correspondence,* 2:358; Butler to Parker, 3 May 1818, Jackson to Luengo, 6 April 1818, *ASPMA,* 1:703–4.

20. Alexander Arbuthnot to John Arbuthnot, 2 April 1818, Jackson to Luengo, 6 April 1818, Statement of James Gadsden, 19 June 1819, *ASPMA,* 1:704, 722, 761; Franco, *Politica,* 103.

21. Luengo to Jackson, 7 April 1818, *ASPMA,* 1:705.

22. Banks, *Biographical Sketch,* 13; Robinson, *Organization of the Army,* 2:121; Wright, *Creeks and Seminoles,* 205.

23. Some accounts depict Duncan McKrimmon as Josiah Francis's betrayer. See, for instance, Hitchcock, *Diary,* 154. There is, however, no credible evidence to suggest that the Georgia militiaman had anything to do with the capture of the two Red Sticks. He had already been ransomed to the Spaniards at St. Marks by the time McKeever's ships appeared at St. Marks and would not have been able to cooperate with the capture unless he had given away the "British" ships as actually United States naval vessels.

24. Butler to Parker, 3 May 1818; Statement of McKeever, 5 June 1819, *ASPMA,* 1:703, 763; Banks, *Biographical Sketch,* 13; Coker and Watson, *Indian Traders,* 318–19; Jackson to Rachel, 8 April 1818, Jackson, *Correspondence,* 2:357; Wright, *Creeks and Seminoles,* 207; Owsley, "Francis," 288. Some accounts say that Francis was hanged from the yardarm of Arbuthnot's ship, the *Chance,* but this could not have occurred because the Americans did not capture the *Chance* until after the execution of Francis. Likely some writers have confused the execution of Francis with that of Arbuthnot, whom Jackson had hanged from the yardarm of his own schooner. Francis was hanged in the fort at St. Marks and buried outside its walls.

25. *Narrative of a Voyage,* 211; Randolph Diary, 7 April 1818; Young, "Topographical Memoir," 144.

26. Luengo to Jackson, 7 April 1818; Jackson to Luengo, 7 April 1818, *ASPMA,* 1:706; Luengo to Mazot [*sic*], 14 May 1818, *ASPFR,* 4:566.

27. Wright, *Creeks and Seminoles,* 190–91; Craig and Peebles, "Young's Sketch Map," 177; Porter, "The Negro Abraham," 8. Robert Remini erroneously refers to the Seminole headman on the Suwannee as Billy Bowlegs of Second and Third Seminole War fame. Billy could not have been more than a boy in 1818 and was probably King Bowlegs's nephew. See Remini, *Jackson and the Course of American ∟mpire,* 356; also see Porter, "Seminole Wars," 220–21.

28. Robinson, *Organization of the Army,* 122; Jackson to Calhoun, 9 April 1818, *ASPMA,* 1:700; Wright, *Creeks and Seminoles,* 207–8.

29. Butler to Parker, 3 May 1818, *ASPMA,* 1:703; John Banks to Editors, *Columbus Sun,* n.d., Woodward, *Reminiscences,* 51; Paine, "Seminole War," 85; Randolph Diary, 12 April 1818; Banks, *Biographical Sketch,* 14; Covington, "Migration of the Seminoles," 356; McIntosh to Mitchell, 13 April 1818, Telamon Cuyler Collection.

30. Woodward to Banks, 16 June 1858, Woodward, *Reminiscences,* 54; Banks, *Biographical Sketch,* 14; Randolph Diary, 12 April 1818; McIntosh to Mitchell, 13 April 1818, Telamon Cuyler Collection.

31. Banks, *Biographical Sketch,* 14; Thomason, "Acquisition by Foray," 67; Covington, "Migration of the Seminoles," 356.

32. Banks, *Biographical Sketch,* 14; Jackson to McIntosh, 14 April 1818, Jackson Papers, LC; Randolph Diary, 13 April 1818.

33. Jackson to McIntosh, 14 April 1818, Jackson Papers, LC; Testimony of Butler, 3 March 1819, *New American State Papers,* 9:25; Wright, *Creeks and Seminoles,* 205; Coker and Watson, *Indian Traders,* 320; Arbuthnot to John Arbuthnot, 2 April 1818, *ASPMA,* 1:722; Cresson, *Monroe,* 307.

34. Paine, "Seminole War," 85–86; Jackson to Rachel, 20 April 1818, Jackson, *Correspondence,* 2:360; Jackson to Calhoun, 20 April 1818, Butler to Parker, 3 May 1818, *ASPMA,* 1:700–701, 703–4; Banks, *Biographical Sketch,* 14.

35. Jackson to Calhoun, 20 April 1818, Butler to Parker, 3 May 1818, *ASPMA,* 1:701, 704; Banks, *Biographical Sketch,* 14.

36. Paine, "Seminole War," 85–86; Jackson to Rachel, 20 April 1818, Jackson, *Correspondence,* 2:360; Jackson to Calhoun, 20 April 1818, *ASPMA,* 1:701.

37. Paine, "Seminole War," 86–87; Jackson to Calhoun, 20 April 1818; Butler to Parker, 3 May 1818, *ASPMA,* 1:701, 704; Banks, *Biographical Sketch,* 14; James Ambrister to Governor of Bahamas, 29 June 1818, *Niles Weekly Register,* 3 October 1818, 84; Coker and Watson, *Indian Traders,* 320; Randolph Diary, 18 April 1818.

38. James Ambrister to Governor of Bahamas, 29 June 1818, *Niles Weekly Register,* 3 October 1818, 84; Coker and Watson, *Indian Traders,* 320; Wright, "Note on the Seminole War," 572–73; Fairbanks, *Ethnohistorical Report,* 222. Bowlegs and his people apparently also had been warned by a black woman fleeing the attack at Miccosukee. See Porter, "Seminole Wars," 271.

39. Jackson to Calhoun, 20 April 1818, *ASPMA,* 1:701; Coker and Watson, *Indian Traders,* 321.

40. Butler to Parker, 3 May 1818; Jackson to Calhoun, 20 April 1818, *ASPMA,* 1:701, 704; Paine, "Seminole War," 86.

41. Jackson to Calhoun, 20 April 1818; Butler to Parker, 3 May 1818, *ASPMA,* 1:701, 704.

42. Jackson to Calhoun, 20 April 1818, *ASPMA,* 1:701; Paine, "Seminole War," 86–87.

43. Randolph Diary, 21, 25, 26 April 1818; Butler to Parker, 3 May 1818, *ASPMA,* 1:704; McIntosh's Brigade, Creek Indian Warriors, Seminole War, 1817–1818, Box 50822, National Archives; *Narrative of a Voyage,* 211–12, 252–53.

44. The court consisted of Gaines (presiding), Colonel King and Major Muhlenberg of the Fourth Infantry; Major Montgomery and Captain Vashon of the Seventh Infantry; Lieutenant Colonel Lindsay and Major Fanning of the Artillery; Colonel Williams, Lieutenant Colonel Gibson, Colonel Dyer, and Lieutenant Colonel Elliott of the Tennessee Volunteers; and Captain Crittenden of the Kentucky Volunteers. See *ASPMA,* 1:721.

45. Rogin, *Fathers and Children,* 198.

46. The court erroneously referred to the Seminoles as Lower Creeks,

perhaps because they were south of other Creeks. See Minutes of the Proceedings of the Special Court, 26 April 1818, *ASPMA,* 1:721; *Narrative of a Voyage,* 211–12, 252–53, 264–65.

47. Minutes of the Proceedings of the Special Court, 26 April 1818, *ASPMA,* 1:721; *Narrative of a Voyage,* 242, 246–51; Jackson to Calhoun, 26 April 1818, Calhoun, *Papers,* 2:260. Irregularities in Jackson's administration of justice in the cases of Arbuthnot and Ambrister should have surprised no one. In 1815, two months after defeating the British at New Orleans, Jackson had insisted that martial law remain in place in the Crescent City. He also ordered several French-speaking citizens deported from the town, apparently on his own whimsical prerogative. When one of New Orleans's French-language newspapers protested, Jackson ordered the article's author, a Louisiana state legislator, arrested. When federal Judge Dominick A. Hall issued a writ of habeas corpus, Jackson had Hall thrown in jail as well. After it was all settled, Jackson had to pay a $1,000 contempt of court fine. Yet in a manner typical of the way Jackson's civilian superiors would learn to deal with him, Secretary of War Alexander Dallas wrote to Jackson that perhaps he should not have jailed the judge. Still, Dallas quickly assured Jackson that he and the president were certain that the general had good reasons for everything he had done. See Jonathan Lurei, "Andrew Jackson, Martial Law, Civilian Control of the Military, and American Politics: An Intriguing Amalgam," *Military Law Review* 126 (Fall 1989): 135–42.

48. Paine, "Seminole War," 89; Boyd, "Prospect Bluff," 84; *Narrative of a Voyage,* 242, 246; James Ambrister to Governor of the Bahamas, 29 June 1818, *Niles Weekly Register,* 3 October 1818, 84.

49. Arbuthnot to John Arbuthnot, 2 April 1818, *ASPMA,* 1:722; Arbuthnot to Mitchell, 19 January 1818, *ASPFR,* 4:591; Ambrister to Nicholls, 30 January 1818, *Niles Weekly Register,* 3 October 1818, 85.

50. Ambrister to Cameron, 20 March 1818; Ambrister to Nicholls, 30 January 1818, *Niles Weekly Register,* 3 October 1818, 85; Wright, *Creeks and Seminoles,* 193, 205–6.

51. Minutes of the Special Court, 28 April 1818, General Orders, Adjutant General Robert Butler, 29 Apr 1818, *ASPMA,* 1:730, 734.

52. Butler to Park, 3 May 1818, *ASPMA,* 1:704; Wright, *Creeks and Seminoles,* 207.

53. Woodward to Hooper, 20 December 1858, Woodward, *Reminiscences,* 161.

54. Jackson to Calhoun, 26 April 1818, Calhoun, *Papers,* 2:261; Randolph Diary, 28 April 1818; Jackson to Masot, 27 April 1818, *ASPMA,* 1:706–7.

55. Jackson to Calhoun, 5 May 1818, *ASPMA,* 1:701–02.

56. Bibb to Calhoun, 23 January 1818, Bibb to Calhoun, 1 May 1818, Calhoun, *Papers,* 2:88, 270; Southerland and Brown, *Federal Road,* 57–58.

57. Bibb to Calhoun, 27 March 1818, Bibb to Calhoun, 15 April 1818, *ASPMA,* 1:699–700; Bibb to Calhoun, 30 April 1818, Calhoun, *Papers,* 2:268; Bibb to Steele, 30 April 1818, Bibb Papers.

58. *Niles Weekly Register,* 27 June 1818; Waters, "Documentary History of Fort Crawford," 13; Masot to Young, 27 April 1818, Masot to Young, 30 April 1818, Bibb to Jackson, 19 May 1818, *ASPMA,* 1:707, 746.

59. Jackson to Gaines, 5 May 1818, LRAGO; Glascock to Jackson, 30 April 1818, LRSWR.

CHAPTER 7
"Unbecoming a Gentleman and a Soldier"

1. Banks, *Biographical Sketch,* 15–16; *Milledgeville Republican and Reflector,* 15 May 1818; *Columbian Museum and Savannah Daily Gazette,* 9 May 1818.

2. Lee County Historical Society, *Lee County, Georgia: A History* (Atlanta: W. H. Wolfe Associates, 1983), 8–9. Chehaw was situated at the present site of Leesburg, Georgia, near the larger present-day towns of Montezuma and Oglethorpe. See Hart, *History of Laurens County,* 31.

3. *Milledgeville Republican and Reflector,* 5 May 1818. Militiamen later claimed that they had not entered the village under a white flag. See Timothy Rogers to *Georgia Journal,* 15 May 1818; *Niles Weekly Register,* 6 June 1818.

4. Glascock to Jackson, 30 April 1818, LRSWR.

5. Talk of Chehaws to Governor David B. Mitchell, 27 December 1816, William Gibson, Thomas Miller, and William Bailey to Mitchell, 8 February 1817, Telamon Cuyler Collection. There had never been nor would there ever be any question about the friendly disposition of the Chehaws toward the United States. See Timothy Barnard to David Blackshear, 2 December 1815 [*sic,* should be 1814], Barnard to Blackshear, 14 January 1815, Hays, "Letters of Timothy Barnard"; also see Woodward to Hooper, 20 December 1858, Woodward, *Reminiscences,* 156.

6. White, *Historical Collections,* 228; Niles *Weekly Register,* 22 November 1817, 208; Green, *Politics of Indian Removal,* 82. Rabun would not complete his term. He died in office on 24 October 1819.

7. Talk of the Chehaws to Governor Mitchell, 27 December 1816, Telamon Cuyler Collection.

8. Fussell M. Chalker, *Pioneer Days Along the Ocmulgee* (Carrollton, Georgia: By the Author, 1970), 133, 137; Hart, *History of Laurens County,* 28; Cawthon to Rabun, 10 March 1818, Cawthon Loose Paper File, Georgia Department of Archives and History, Atlanta, Georgia; "Creek Letters," 3:903; Powell to Rabun, 14 March 1818, Telamon Cuyler Collection; *Augusta Chronicle,* 4 April 1818. The *Chronicle* reported only five militia killed.

9. *Milledgeville Republican and Reflector,* 24 March 1818; Rabun to Floyd, 16 April 1818, GLB.

10. Dallas to Governors, 14 June 1815, *ASPIA,* 2:8.

11. Calhoun to W. W. Webb [*sic*—should read *Bibb*], Governor of Alabama Territory, 13 May 1818, in Eunice Barber, *Narrative of the Tragical Death of*

Darius Barber, vol. 36 of *The Garland Library of North American Indian Captivities,* ed. Wilcomb E. Washburn. (New York: Garland Publishing Co., 1977), 210.

12. Rabun to Jackson, 25 March 1818, LRSWIA; Rabun to Calhoun, 1 June 1818, GLB; *Historical Collections,* 512; Hart, *History of Laurens County,* 30–31.

13. Rabun to Calhoun, 1 June 1818, GLB. The cavalry companies were commanded by Captains Timothy L. Rogers and Jacob Robinson, the infantry by Captains Dean and Childs, and the miscellaneous groups by Lieutenants Cooper and Jones. See White, *Historical Collections,* 512; Hart, *History of Laurens County,* 30.

14. Wright is described in Rabun's arrest warrant and reward announcement, *Milledgeville Republican and Reflector,* 4 August 1818.

15. Rabun to Calhoun, 1 June 1818, GLB. E. Merton Coulter states that Rabun placed Wright in charge "only after having carefully investigated Wright's record and having received high testimony of his reliability afforded by people of the greatest respectability." See E. Merton Coulter, "The Chehaw Affair," *Georgia Historical Quarterly* 49 (December 1965): 372.

16. Rabun to Calhoun, 1 June 1818, GLB.

17. Chalker, *Ocmulgee,* 138–39. Coulter states that although the commander of Fort Early would not accompany the expedition, he provided it with federal troops. Also, Benjamin Griffith asserts that Rabun authorized Wright to use two companies of United States cavalry to accompany his militia. See Coulter, "Chehaw," 372; Griffith, *McIntosh and Weatherford,* 193.

Aside from the fact that Rabun would not have been able to impress the regular United States Army into Georgia service, there was no such thing as United States cavalry in 1818. Neither Coulter nor Griffith realized that the "federal troops" at Fort Early were actually nationalized Georgia militia, some of whom were designated as cavalry. See "Captain Ebeneezer Bothwell, First Regiment of (Milton's) Georgia Militia, Seminole War, 1817–1818," in Index to Compiled Service Records of Volunteer Soldiers Who Served During the Indian Wars, 1815–1858, Microfilm # 269, Reel 4, National Archives, Washington, D.C. That Bothwell allowed men under his command to accompany an expedition even though he refused to endorse it with his presence is an indication of the muddled nature of authority over militia and regular forces, especially when such regular forces were originally militia.

18. Affidavit of Jacob Robinson to Court, *Georgia Military Affairs,* 4:459.

19. Rabun to Calhoun, 1 June 1818, GLB. Also see *Columbian Museum and Savannah Daily Gazette,* 9 May 1818. Also see Brigade Court Martial Proceedings for Captain Jacob Robinson of Laurens County Troop of Light Dragoons, 12–15 May 1819, Georgia Adjutant General Records, Georgia Department of Archives and History, Atlanta Georgia, hereafter cited as Robinson Court Martial Proceedings. The confusion of the Laurens Troop provides another indication of how haphazard the expedition was.

20. Chalker, *Ocmulgee,* 139. Captain Jacob Robinson of the Laurens County Troop and more or less Wright's principal lieutenant said that most of the cattle

had white settlers' brands. See *Georgia Journal,* 30 April 1818. Of course, Robinson had good reason to justify the attack and his part in it.

21. In one account, the militia rushed into the town firing its weapons. See Glascock to Jackson, 30 April 1818, LRSWR. In another account, Wright's men entered Chehaw under a white flag. See *Milledgeville Republican and Reflector,* 5 May 1818. Whatever the Georgians did, they apparently bewildered the Chehaws, who remained passive throughout the attack.

22. William Mitchell to David Mitchell, 26 May 1818, LRSWIA. Also see Glascock to Jackson, 30 April 1818, LRSWR; *Milledgeville Republican and Reflector,* 5 May 1818; *Columbian Museum and Savannah Daily Gazette,* 9 May 1818.

23. William Mitchell to David Mitchell, 26 May 1818, LRSWIA.

24. Chalker, *Ocmulgee,* 140. Wright also boasted, however, that his 270 men suffered no casualties. See Wright to Rabun, 25 April 1818, *Georgia Journal,* 5 May 1818.

25. Mitchell to Rabun, 6 May 1818, Little Prince to Mitchell, 25 April 1818, Barnard to Mitchell, 30 April 1818, all in *Milledgeville Republican and Reflector,* 26 May 1818; also see Chalker, *Ocmulgee,* 139. Also see Wright's report to Rabun on 25 April in the *Georgia Journal,* 5 May 1818.

26. See the *Milledgeville Republican and Reflector,* 5 May 1818. On the tablet erected in 1912 by the Daughters of the American Revolution, the figure is given thusly: "Here also, in 1818, through misunderstanding, were massacred seven of this tribe by Georgia troops, for which all possible amends were made." See Hart, *History of Laurens County,* 12.

27. McIntosh to Jackson, 5 May 1818, *Niles Weekly Register,* 20 June 1818, 292; Bonner, "McIntosh," 126.

28. Rabun to ?, 29 April 1818, GLB.

29. Mitchell to Rabun, 6 May 1818, Barnard to Mitchell, 30 April 1818, *Columbian Museum and Savannah Daily Gazette,* 1 June 1818.

30. Mitchell to Chehaws, 10 May 1818, LRSWR.

31. Mitchell to Chehaws, 10 May 1818, LRSWR; Mitchell to Rabun, 5 May 1818, Mitchell Papers, Newberry Library.

32. Rabun to Mitchell, 20 May 1818, GLB.

33. Ibid. Rabun's failure to give the source for his information was probably because his source before issuing his orders was Obed Wright.

34. *Milledgeville Republican and Reflector,* 26 May 1818; also see Major Davis to Jackson, 30 May 1818, in *ASPIA,* 2:371 for impressions that Georgians shared the governor's indifference to Chehaw's fate.

35. Jackson to Chehaws, 7 May 1818, LRSWIA.

36. Jackson to Davis, 7 May 1818, LRSWIA.

37. Jackson to Rabun, 7 May 1818, LRSWIA.

38. Remini, *Jackson and the Course of American Empire,* 361.

39. Return J. Meigs to Jackson, 8 August 1816, Meigs to Secretary of War William Crawford, 11 August 1816, *ASPIA,* 2:113–14. Jackson objected to compensating the Cherokees because he said they had not helped in the war against the British. Cherokee Agent Return J. Meigs hotly pointed out that

many Cherokees had been widowed and orphaned by their men having fallen in battle fighting for the United States against the Red Stick Creeks.

40. Rabun to Jackson, 1 June 1818, GLB. Executive Order of Rabun to Wright, 14 April 1818, *Niles Weekly Register,* 23 May 1818, 219.

41. Rabun to Calhoun, 1 June 1818, GLB.

42. Jackson to Calhoun, 7 May 1818, in *ASPMA,* 1:775–76.

43. Davis to Jackson, 30 May 1818, *ASPIA,* 2:371; *Columbian Museum and Savannah Daily Gazette,* 9 June 1818; Rabun to Jackson, 1 June 1818, GLB; Davis to Wright, 24 May 1818, Proceeding of the Court of Baldwin County, 24 May 1818, and Davis to Rabun, 29 May 1818, LRSWIA. Major Davis was reportedly relieved to end his involvement in this matter. See Woodward to J. J. Hooper, 20 December 1858, Woodward, *Reminiscences,* 162. This might account for why Davis took Wright through Milledgeville, a detour from the route to his destination at Fort Hawkins. Coulter was puzzled by this. See Coulter, "Chehaw," 385.

44. Rabun to Jackson, 1 June 1818, GLB; *Columbian Museum and Savannah Daily Gazette,* 9 June 1818.

45. John Clark's relationship with Andrew Jackson grew more intimate as they both found a common enemy in William Crawford. The two would conspire in 1819 to destroy Crawford's reputation. See Jackson to Clark, 20 April 1819, Clark to Jackson, 24 May 1819, Jackson to Clark, 13 July 1819, Clark to Jackson, 18 August 1819, Jackson to Clark, 23 November 1819, Jackson, *Correspondence,* 2:416–18, 419–20, 422–25, 442–43.

46. Butler to Park, 3 May 1818, Jackson to Calhoun, 5 May 1818, Field Report of Jackson's Army, 24 May 1818, *ASPMA,* 1:702, 718.

47. Jackson to Gaines, 5 May 1818, LRAGO.

48. Coker and Watson, *Indian Traders,* 324; Wright, *Creeks and Seminoles,* 208; Ernest F. Dibble, "Captain Hugh Young and His Topographical Memoir to Andrew Jackson," *Florida Historical Quarterly* 55 (1977): 321.

49. Dibble, "Young," 321, 324; Jackson to Calhoun, 2 June 1818, *ASPMA,* 1:708.

50. Jackson to Calhoun, 2 June 1818, *ASPMA,* 1:708; Paine, "Seminole War," 92.

51. Franco, *Politica,* 107; Masot to Jackson, 18 May 1818, *ASPMA,* 1:709; McAllister, "Pensacola during the Second Spanish Period," 318.

52. Masot to Jackson, 23 May 1818, Jackson to Calhoun, 2 June 1818, *ASPMA,* 1:708, 712.

53. Jackson to Masot, 23 May 1818, Jackson to Calhoun, 2 June 1818, *ASPMA,* 1:712–13.

54. Faye, "British and Spanish Fortifications," 290; Jackson to Calhoun, 2 June 1818, *ASPMA,* 1:708.

55. Jackson to Masot, 23 May 1818, *ASPMA,* 1:713.

56. Jackson to Masot, 24 May 1818, Masot to Jackson, 24 May 1818, *ASPMA,* 1:712–13.

57. Masot to Jackson, 24 May 1818, Jackson to Masot, 25 May 1818, ASPMA, 1:713–14.

58. Jackson to Masot, 25 May 1818, *ASPFR,* 4:569–70.

59. Field Report of Jackson's Army, 24 May 1818, Jackson to Calhoun, 2 June 1818, *ASPMA,* 1:718, 708; Paine, "Seminole War," 95; Faye, "British and Spanish Fortifications," 290.

60. Jackson to Calhoun, 2 June 1818, *ASPMA,* 1:708; Paine, "Seminole War," 95; Faye, "British and Spanish Fortifications," 290.

61. Paine, "Seminole War," 95; Masot to Jackson, 28 May 1818, Jackson to Calhoun, 2 June 1818, *ASPMA,* 1:708, 719–20.

62. Jackson to Calhoun, 2 June 1818, *ASPMA,* 1:708; "The Public Buildings of Pensacola, 1818," *Florida Historical Quarterly* 16 (July 1937): 45–47.

63. Proclamation of Jackson, 29 May 1818, Report of Robert Butler, 29 May 1818, *ASPMA,* 1:720.

64. Report of Robert Butler, 29 May 1818, Jackson to Calhoun, 2 June 1818, *ASPMA,* 1:708, 720; Skelton, *American Profession of Arms,* 233.

65. Jackson to Gaines, 2 June 1818, Jackson Papers, LC.

66. Jackson to Calhoun, 2 June 1818, *ASPMA,* 1:708.

67. Jackson to Calhoun, 2 June 1818; Affidavit of William Hambly, 2 June 1818, *ASPMA,* 1:707, 716.

68. Dibble, "Young," 322; Affidavit of George Skeate, 18 September 1818, Affidavit of Charles Le Jeune, 18 September 1818, Affidavit of Santiago Pauphin, 19 September 1818, Affidavit of Joachim Barrelas, 18 September 1919, *ASPMA,* 1:716–17.

69. Paine, "Seminole War," 98; Dibble, "Young," 322.

CHAPTER 8
"There Are Serious Difficulties in This Business"

1. Calhoun, *Papers,* 2:270; Nevins, *Adams Diary,* 4 May 1818, 196.

2. Tyler to Curtis, 19 January 1818, Lyon Tyler, ed., *The Letters and Times of the Tylers,* 3 vols. (1884–96, reprint ed., New York: De Capo Press, 1970), 1:298.

3. Macon to Yancey, 8 February 1818, Bartlet Yancey Papers, Southern Historical Collection, University of North Carolina, Chapel Hill, North Carolina.

4. Calhoun to Forsyth, 24 March 1818, Calhoun, *Papers,* 2:207.

5. Calhoun to John Jackson, 31 March 1818, Calhoun, *Papers,* 2:216.

6. Spiller, "Calhoun as Secretary of War," 90–95.

7. Calhoun to Cass, 6 May 1818, Calhoun, *Papers,* 2:281.

8. Ammon, *Monroe,* 420; Calhoun to Bankhead, 14 May 1818, United States Congress, *Serial Set,* 15th Cong., 2nd sess., serial 22, H. Doc. 117.

9. Crawford to Smith, 23 May 1818, Samuel Smith Family Papers, Library of Congress, Washington, D.C.

10. Calhoun to Bibb, 16 May 1818, Carter, *Territorial Papers,* 18:317.

11. Remini, *Jackson and the Course of American Empire,* 362; Jackson to Rabun, 1 August 1818, Parton, *Life of Jackson,* 2:495. Theodore J. Crackel has argued convincingly that the traditional view of Jeffersonian Republicanism as

antimilitary is too simplified. Jeffersonians did not fear the military; they feared a military controlled by their political enemies. They had as a primary goal the Republicanization of the military. Hence, much of the alarm over a potentially oppressive military was really only political posturing. See Theodore J. Crackel, *Mr. Jefferson's Army: Political and Social Reform of the Military Establishment, 1801–1809* (New York: New York University Press, 1987), 2–3, 14. Crackel's explanation is especially pertinent to the political situation in Georgia.

12. Jackson was quoted in the *Milledgeville Republican and Reflector,* 2 June 1818.

13. Vandeventer to Mitchell, 2 June 1818, LSSWIA.

14. Ammon, *Monroe,* 421; John Niven, *John C. Calhoun and the Price of Union: A Biography* (Baton Rouge: Louisiana State University Press, 1988), 68–69; Calhoun, *Papers,* 2:354; Charles Francis Adams, ed., *Memoirs of John Quincy Adams, Comprising Portions of His Diary from 1785–1848,* 12 vols. (Philadelphia: J. B. Lippincott & Co., 1874–1877), 4:108–14; *Niles Weekly Register,* 27 June 1818, 298; Weeks, *Adams and American Global Empire,* 113.

15. *Niles Weekly Register,* 4 July 1818, 327; 25 July 1818, 369–71; Clay to Tait, 25 June 1818, Clay, *Papers,* 2:580; Anderson Diary, 13 July 1818.

16. Vandeventer to Monroe, 7 July 1818, Calhoun, *Papers,* 2:364; Coker and Watson, *Indian Traders,* 324.

17. Jackson to Monroe, 2 June 1818, James Monroe Papers, New York Public Library, hereafter cited as Monroe Papers, NYPL.

18. Vandeventer to Monroe, 8 July 1818, Calhoun, *Papers,* 2:368.

19. Cresson, *Monroe,* 311; Adams to Monroe, 8 July 1818, Ford, *Writings of Adams,* 6:383; Bemis, *Adams and Foreign Policy,* 308, 313, 317; Weeks, *Adams and American Global Empire,* 113.

20. Monroe to Madison, 10 July 1818, Hamilton, *Writings of Monroe,* 6:54; Jefferson to Monroe, 17 September 1818, Monroe Papers, LC. Responding for both himself and Jefferson, Madison wrote that "both of us think that Genl. Jackson [is] right as we hope he will be sensible of the marked kindness of your letter to him." See Madison to Monroe, 4 August 1818, Monroe Papers, LC.

21. Calhoun to Jackson, 13 July 1818, Calhoun, *Papers,* 2:354, 372.

22. The saga of the missing dispatches was just beginning. Though copies of many of the letters would eventually turn up, some of the contents of the original package were never reproduced. What happened to the original package remains a mystery. See James Gadsden to Calhoun, 31 July 1818, Gadsden to Calhoun, August 1818, Gadsden to Calhoun, 10 August 1818, Bradley to Calhoun, 19 August 1818, Calhoun, *Papers,* 3:12, 19, 41, 42.

23. Paine, "Seminole War," 100–101; Ammon, *Monroe,* 421; Nevins, *Adams Diary,* 6 January, 9 January 1818, 190–91; Weeks, *Adams and American Global Empire,* 114.

24. Nevins, *Adams Diary,* 10 July 1818, 199.

25. Dumas Malone, *Jefferson the President, First Term 1801–1805,* Volume IV of *Jefferson and His Time* (Boston: Little, Brown and Company, 1970), 330–31.

26. Nevins, *Adams Diary,* 6 January, 9 January 1818, 190–91.

27. Paine, "Seminole War," 100–101; Cresson, *Monroe,* 312.

28. Report of the Department of War, 22 February 1818; Monroe to Madison, 27 June 1816, Hamilton, *Writings of Monroe,* 5:323–24; 337.

29. Nevins, *Adams Diary,* 21 July 1818, 200–201.

30. Ammon, *Monroe,* 423–25; Paine, "Seminole War," 100–102; Mooney, *Crawford,* 178–181; Calhoun to Gaines, 14 August 1818, *ASPMA,* 1:696; Adams to Erving, 28 November 1818, Ford, *Adams Writings,* 6:474.

31. Calhoun, *Papers,* 3:85; Calhoun to Tait, 20 July 1818, Tait Family Papers; Merrill D. Peterson, *The Great Triumvirate: Webster, Clay, and Calhoun* (New York and Oxford: Oxford University Press, 1987), 93; Monroe to Jackson, 19 July 1818, Calhoun, *Papers,* 2:400; Cresson, *Monroe,* 315–16; John Spencer Bassett, *The Life of Andrew Jackson* (reprint ed., Hamden, Connecticut: Archon Books, 1967), 275–76.

32. Monroe to Madison, 20 July 1818, Hamilton, *Writings of Monroe,* 6:61.

33. Monroe to Jefferson, 22 July 1818, ibid, 6:63.

34. Monroe to Rufus King, 22 July 1818, in Charles R. King, ed., *Life and Correspondence of Rufus King,* 3 vols. (New York: G. P. Putnam's Sons, 1894–1900), 6:156.

35. Note of 26 June 1818, Adams, *Memoirs of John Quincy Adams,* 6:358–59. The note, in Adams's handwriting, can also be found in the Monroe Papers, LC. See Adams, Wirt, and Crawford to Monroe, 26 June 1818.

36. Adams, *Memoirs,* 6:359; Monroe to Adams, 20 August 1818, Monroe Papers, LC.

37. Rabun to William Davis, 13 July 1818, GLB. Davis was the U.S. District Attorney in Savannah. Also see *Milledgeville Republican and Reflector,* 21 July 1818. The section of the Trade and Intercourse Act of 1802 pertinent to Wright's case read, "If any citizen or other person, shall go into any town, settlement, or territory, belonging to any nation or tribe of Indians, or shall there commit murder, by killing any Indian or Indians, belonging to any nation or tribe of Indians in amity the U. States, such offender, on being thereof convicted, shall suffer death." See *Niles Weekly Register,* 15 August 1818, 416.

38. Rabun to Adams, 29 July 1818, GLB.

39. Robinson Court Martial Proceedings. Robinson was acquitted of any culpability in either the Chehaw massacre or Wright's escape, but he was convicted of padding his payroll and ungentlemanly conduct. Also see *Niles Weekly Register,* 19 September 1818, 63, and the Milledgeville *Republican and Reflector,* 5 January 1819, for the sightings of Wright in Cuba. Coulter indicates that Wright was under detention while in Georgia's custody. See Coulter, "Chehaw," 388. Contemporary accounts, however, corroborate his parole. See Rabun to Jackson, 1 June 1818, GLB.

40. Rabun to Adams, 29 July 1818, GLB. Some accounts mistakenly related that Wright was tried and acquitted. See Remini, *Jackson and the Course of American Empire,* 362; Griffith, *McIntosh and Weatherford,* 194. Obed Wright of Chehaw notoriety was allegedly from Chatham County, although the authors have never been able to determine from city of Savannah or Chatham County

records the documented existence of an Obed Wright. Thomas Woodward perhaps provides a clue as to why Wright does not appear in any Chatham County records. In his *Reminiscences,* p. 162, Woodward calls Wright "a fool Yankee," possibly meaning that Wright was a recent arrival in Georgia and therefore had few, if any, local ties.

41. Rabun to Jackson, 1 September 1818, GLB.

42. Mitchell was able to soothe Creeks' anger over the massacre at a general meeting of the Creek nation on 7 June; see Mitchell to Calhoun, 11 September 1818, LRSWR. Also see *Milledgeville Republican and Reflector,* 7 July 1818. Originally promised $10,000 as compensation, the Chehaws had to settle for the lower figure after government officers estimated the damages accordingly. Calhoun leapt at the revised sum because "the state of the Indian fund requires that the most rigid regard be paid to economy." See Calhoun to Mitchell, 13 July 1818, LSSWIA. Also see Adams, *Memoirs,* 6:359. Calhoun to Mitchell, 9 November 1818, WDLSIA.

43. Parton, *Life of Jackson,* 2:504.

44. Adams to Monroe, 20 July 1818, Ford, *Writings of Adams,* 6:385; Bagot to Castlereagh, 24 July 1818, PRO, Reference F.O. 115, vol. 32, LC.

45. Adams to Rush, 30 July 1818, Ford, *Writings of Adams,* 6:411; Adams to Monroe, 20 August 1818, Monroe Papers, LC.

46. Castlereagh to Bagot, 18 August, 2 September 1818, PRO, Reference F.O. 115, vol. 32, LC; Bemis, *Adams and Foreign Policy,* 278–98; Adams to Rush, 20 August 1818, Ford, *Writings of Adams,* 6:435–36; Rush to Monroe, 13 August 1818, Monroe Papers, LC.

47. Calhoun to Monroe, 1 September, 7 September 1818, Calhoun, *Papers,* 3:87, 108.

48. Planta to Bagot, 5 September 1818, PRO, F.O. 115, vol. 32, LC; Perkins, *Castlereagh and Adams,* 289, 293; Wright, *Creeks and Seminoles,* 213; *Narrative of a Voyage,* 197, 270; *Niles Weekly Register,* 5 September 1818, 32; Sugden, "Southern Indians," 311; Bemis, *Adams and Foreign Policy,* 278–98; Rippy, *Rivalry over Latin America,* 69. Rush grumbled that the British public's "affected indignation at the fate of these two Indian spies, is at once artful and ludicrous." See Rush to Monroe, 13 August 1818, Monroe Papers, LC.

49. Bemis, *Adams and Foreign Policy,* 317; Weeks, *Adams and American Global Empire,* 121.

50. James Chace and Caleb Carr, "The Odd Couple Who Won Florida and Half the West," *Smithsonian* 19 (April 1988): 154; Adams to Onís, 23 July 1818, 24 August 1818, Ford, *Writings of Adams,* 6: 386–87, 444–45; Pizarro to Erving, 29 August 1818, *Narrative of a Voyage,* 282–84; Weeks, *Adams and American Global Empire,* 120.

51. Bemis, *Adams and Foreign Policy,* 323–24; Franco, *Politica,* 106; Monroe to Adams, 17 August 1818, Hamilton, *Writings of Monroe,* 6:64; Langley, *American Mediterranean,* 21.

52. Calhoun to Noble, 1 September 1818, Calhoun to Monroe, 3 September 1818, Calhoun, *Papers,* 3:88, 98; Calhoun to Monroe, 6 September 1818, John C. Calhoun, "Correspondence of John C. Calhoun," in *Annual Report of the*

American Historical Association, ed. J. Franklin Jameson (Washington, D.C.: Government Printing Office, 1900), 2:141; Weeks, *Adams and American Global Empire,* 150–52.

53. Calhoun to Jackson, 2 March 1818, Calhoun to Mitchell, 2 March 1818, Calhoun, *Papers,* 2:169–70.

54. Interrogation of Colonel David Brearley, 19 October 1818, LRSWIA.

55. Gaines to Jackson, 6 June 1818, LRAGO; Jones, *Decatur County,* 152–53; Silver, *Gaines,* 86; Gaines to Calhoun, 29 June 1818, Calhoun, *Papers,* 2:352; Interrogation of Brearley, 19 October 1818, LRSWIA.

56. Smith to Jackson, 30 June 1818, Mitchell to Jackson, 10 August 1818, LRSWR; Jackson to McIntosh, 5 July 1818, Jackson to Mitchell, 8 July 1818, Calhoun, *Papers,* 2:367.

57. Mitchell to Jackson, 10 August 1818, LRSWR.

58. Wright, *Creeks and Seminoles,* 210; Griffith, *McIntosh and Weatherford,* 196–98; Wirt to Monroe, 21 January 1821, *American State Papers: Miscellaneous,* 2 vols. (Washington, D.C.: Gales and Seaton, 1832–1861), 2:959–75.

59. Gaines to Jackson, 8 September 1818, LRAGO; Silver, *Gaines,* 86; Mitchell to Crawford, 12 November 1819, Crawford to Mitchell, 29 April 1820, Crawford to Mitchell, 6 November 1820, Crawford to Mitchell, 2 December 1820, Mitchell Papers, Newberry Library; Calhoun to Mitchell, 31 May 1820, Letters to D. and B. Mitchell, Wisconsin State Historical Society, Madison, Wisconsin. Mitchell later wrote a tract defending himself against the charges leveled by Gaines and Jackson. See Kenneth Coleman and Charles Stephen Gurr, *Dictionary of Georgia Biography,* 2 vols. (Athens: University of Georgia Press, 1983), 2:723; Crawford to Mitchell, 14 March 1822, Mitchell Papers, Newberry Library; David B. Mitchell, *An Exposition of the Case of the Africans, Taken to the Creek Agency by Captain William Bowen on or about the 1st of December 1817* (n.p., 1822).

60. Gaines to Calhoun, 13 June 1818; Gaines to Commander of Fort Scott, 28 June 1818, LRSWR; Twiggs to Gaines, 25 June 1818, Monroe Papers, NYPL; Gaines to Calhoun, 29 June 1818; Calhoun to Bibb, 13 July 1818, Calhoun, *Papers,* 2:352, 372. Throughout the summer, the American military presence in Florida remained substantial, with approximately 300 soldiers stationed at Fort Gadsden, 240 at St. Marks, 400 at Pensacola, and 230 at Amelia Island. See Wesley, *Old Frontier,* 172; Post Returns for Fort Gadsden, Florida, Returns for United States Military Posts, 1800–1916, National Archives, Washington, D.C.

61. Gaines to Jackson, 17 July 1818, LRAGO.

62. Jackson to Gaines, 7 August 1818, *ASPMA,* 1:744.

63. Jackson to Monroe, 10 August 1818, Jackson, *Correspondence,* 2:385.

64. Jackson to Calhoun, 10 August 1818, *ASPMA,* 1:744–45; Gadsden to Jackson, 1 August 1818, James Gadsden, "'The Defenses of the Floridas,' A Report of Captain James Gadsden, Aide-de-Camp to General Jackson," *Florida Historical Quarterly* 15 (April 1937): 242–43, 246–48.

65. Calhoun to Gaines, 14 August 1818; Calhoun to Jackson, 14 August

1818, *ASPMA,* 1:696, 734; Calhoun to Monroe, 15 August 1818, Calhoun, *Papers,* 3:32.

66. Calhoun to Gaines, 14 August 1818, *ASPMA,* 1:696.

67. Calhoun to Gaines, 1 September 1818, *ASPMA,* 1:745; Silver, *Gaines,* 83.

68. Gaines to Calhoun, 8 September 1818, LRSWR; Gaines to Calhoun, 20 September 1818, Calhoun, *Papers,* 3:143.

69. Arbuckle to Gaines, 31 August 1818, Gaines to Calhoun, 16 September 1818, LRSWR; Gaines to Jackson, 16 September 1818, LRAGO; Gaines to Calhoun, 20 September 1818, Calhoun, *Papers,* 3:144.

70. Gaines to Calhoun, 8 September 1818, Gaines to King, 20 September 1818, LRSWR; Gaines to Calhoun, 20 September 1818, Calhoun, *Papers,* 3:144. Roger Spiller asserts that Calhoun's mistrust of militia stemmed from the poor performance of those units in the War of 1812. See Spiller, "Calhoun as Secretary of War," 51. Calhoun, Jackson, and Gaines, however, had not hesitated to utilize them in the Seminole War of 1818. The short duration of their enlistments and the criminal behavior of people like Obed Wright had demonstrated to the administration as well as to officers in the field that militia forces were often unreliable and occasionally dangerous.

71. Calhoun to Jackson, 8 September 1818, *ASPMA,* 1:745; Calhoun to Monroe, 21 September 1818, Calhoun, *Papers,* 3:148.

72. Calhoun to Monroe, 21 September 1818, Calhoun, *Papers,* 3:148.

73. Ibid., 3:148–49; Calhoun to Jackson, 24 September 1818, Calhoun to Gaines, 23 September 1818, LRAGO.

74. Calhoun, *Papers,* 3:3.

75. Calhoun to Lumpkin, 3 September 1818, same to same, 26 October 1818, Calhoun to Rabun, 3 September 1818, Calhoun to Mitchell, 8 October 1818, same to same, 26 October 1818, Calhoun, *Papers,* 96, 99, 193, 235, 236; Little Prince et al. to Gaines, 8 September 1818, Gaines to Little Prince et al., 16 September 1818, Gaines to Calhoun, 16 September 1818, LRSWR.

76. Calhoun to Gaines, 2 October 1818, Calhoun, *Papers,* 3:184–85.

77. Gaines to Calhoun, 8 September 1818, LRSWR; King to Jackson, 15 October 1818, *ASPMA,* 1:751–52; Neel to Calhoun, 22 September 1818, Calhoun, *Papers,* 3:151; Dale to Bibb, 23 September 1818, Creek War Military Records, SPR 359, Alabama Department of Archives and History, Montgomery, Alabama.

78. Gaines to Calhoun, 15 October 1818, Calhoun, *Papers,* 3:205–6.

79. Gaines to Jackson, 22 October 1818, LRAGO.

80. Gaines to Calhoun, 22 October 1818, LRAGO.

81. Calhoun to Gaines, 26 October 1818, same to same, 3 November 1818, Gaines to Calhoun, 7 November 1818, Calhoun to Gaines, 25 November 1818, Calhoun, *Papers,* 3:234–35, 253, 254–55, 299.

82. Jackson to Calhoun, 28 November 1818, *ASPMA,* 1:752.

83. Fred N. Israel, ed., *The State of the Union Messages of the Presidents, 1790–1966,* 3 vols. (New York: Chelsea House Robert Hector Publishers), 1:156–65.

CHAPTER 9
"A Rattling among the Dry Bones"

1. Calhoun to Monroe, 1 August 1818, same to same, 7 August 1818, Gadsden to Monroe, 6 August 1818, Calhoun, *Papers,* 3:4, 12, 14.

2. Calhoun to Meigs, 18 August 1818, Bradley to Calhoun, 19 August 1818, Calhoun to Bradley, 20 August 1818, Calhoun to Jackson, 2 September 1818, McCall to Calhoun, 15 September 1818, Calhoun to Monroe, 29 August 1818, Calhoun, *Papers,* 3:41–42, 57, 81, 92, 131.

3. Calhoun to Tait, 5 September 1818, Tait Family Papers.

4. Crawford to Monroe, 17 August 1818, Calhoun, *Papers,* 3:37.

5. Jackson to Call, August 1818, Jackson Papers, LC.

6. Jackson to Monroe, 19 August 1818, Calhoun, *Papers,* 3:43.

7. Young to Bibb, 1 September 1818, Bibb Papers; Testimony of Joseph Esteeven Caro, 10 September 1818, Testimony of Carlos Baron, 13 September 1818, Deposition of Joachim Barrelas, 18 September 1818, Affidavit of George Skeate, 18 September 1818, Affidavit of Charles Le Jeune, 18 September 1818, Affidavit of Pierre Senac, 19 September 1818, Testimony of Santiago Pauphin, 19 September 1818, *ASPMA,* 1:716–17, 762–63.

8. Monroe to Calhoun, 9 September 1818, 12 September 1818, Calhoun, *Papers,* 3:113, 121.

9. Bibb to Tait, 19 September 1818, Tait Family Papers.

10. Forsyth to Lowndes, 6 October 1818, William Lowndes Papers, Southern Historical Collection, University of North Carolina, Chapel Hill, North Carolina.

11. Jackson to George W. Campbell, 5 October 1818, Jackson, *Correspondence,* 2:395.

12. Monroe to Jackson, 20 October 1818, Jackson to Monroe, 15 November 1818, Calhoun, *Papers,* 3:223, 270; Ammon, *Monroe,* 423–25; Mooney, *Crawford,* 179.

13. Johnson to Desha, 29 October 1818, Joseph Desha Papers, Library of Congress, Washington, D.C.

14. Israel, *State of the Union Messages,* 1:157.

15. Ibid., 158.

16. Ibid., 161.

17. The message only referred to negotiations for the settlement of spoilation claims. See ibid., 157.

18. The first investigation conducted by the House of Representatives had been in 1792 and dealt with Arthur St. Clair's defeat by Indians in the Northwest. The Senate's first major investigation, however, was to be that of the Seminole War in 1819. See James Hamilton, *The Power to Probe: A Study of Congressional Investigations* (New York: Random House, 1976), 5, 63.

19. Ralph Volney Harlow, *The History of Legislative Methods in the Period before 1825* (New Haven, Connecticut: Yale University Press, 1917), 215–16, 224–25.

20. *Annals of Congress,* 15th Cong., 2nd sess., 342, 367–70. Harlow has

pointed out that overlapping committee jurisdiction was an "apparently unavoidable" aspect of the committee system that frequently snarled deliberations. He cites several examples but does not include the dispute between Foreign Relations and Military Affairs in 1818. See Harlow, *History of Legislative Methods,* 229–33.

21. *Annals of Congress,* 15th Cong., 2nd sess., 415. Members of Foreign Relations were Holmes, Philip Barbour of Virginia, John C. Spencer of New York, Henry Baldwin of Pennsylvania, Heman Allen of Vermont, and Joseph Hopkinson of Pennsylvania. Although Hopkinson, in the course of the debates, would disapprove of Jackson's attack on Pensacola and would vote to condemn the act, he did not vote to disapprove of the execution of Arbuthnot and Ambrister. This latter act is most strange, considering that during the debate he had criticized the trials and executions.

22. Paine, "Seminole War," 104–5; Mooney, *Crawford,* 177. Forsyth's biographer has little to say about the incident, but he does declare that Forsyth's motives probably had less to do with Clay than with a sense of the benefits to be derived from possessing East Florida. See Alvin Laroy Duckett, *John Forsyth: Political Tactician* (Athens: University of Georgia Press, 1962), 38–39. William Lowndes, who was quite ill during the Seminole controversy, referred to Forsyth's motion during the debate in Congress, stating that it was incredible that what the House had determined not to take for political reasons, Jackson had resolved to take for military ones. John Tyler also reminded the House of its rejection of the motion. *Annals of Congress,* 15th Cong., 2nd sess., 914, 930. Carl J. Vipperman, *William Lowndes and the Transition of Southern Politics, 1782–1822,* The Fred W. Morrison Series in Southern Studies (Chapel Hill and London: University of North Carolina Press, 1989), 167.

23. Duckett, *Forsyth,* 15–17, 129–30; Rabun to Forsyth, 9 November 1818, GLB; Forsyth to Lowndes, 6 October 1818, Lowndes Papers, SHC. Jackson's friend John Overton later pointed out that Jackson was not the only target, but so were Monroe, Calhoun, and Adams, prefatory to articles of impeachment. See [John Overton], *A Vindication of the Measures of the President and His Commanding Generals in the Commencement and Termination of the Seminole War by a Citizen of the State of Tennessee* (Washington, D.C.: Gales and Seaton, 1819), 8.

24. Duckett, *Forsyth,* 44–45, 64, 129–30; Ammon, *Monroe,* 433–44; Mooney, *Crawford,* 182; George Ticknor, *Life, Letters, and Journals of George Ticknor,* 2 vols. (Boston: James R. Osgood and Co., 1876), 1:212; Walker to Tate [*sic*], 20 December 1819, Tait Family Papers. Forsyth was replaced by John W. Eppes of Virginia on Lacock's Select Committee, much to Jackson's chagrin. See Jackson to Pleasant Miller, 9 June 1823, William Blount Papers, Library of Congress, Washington, D.C.

25. Anderson Diary, 18 December 1818; Niven, *Calhoun,* 92; Eldred Simkins to William Lowndes, 28 October 1821, Lowndes Papers, SHC; Calhoun to Jackson, 7 March 1821, Calhoun, *Papers,* 5:663; Fuller, *Florida Purchase,* 265; Ammon, *Monroe,* 430. Cobb was a Crawfordite, but Crawford's biographer insists that Cobb was acting on his own. Mooney, *Crawford,* 180.

26. *Annals of Congress,* 15th Cong., 2nd sess., 374–75.

27. Anderson Diary, 18 Dec 1818.

28. Eaton to Jackson, 20 November 1818, same to same, 14 December 1818, Monroe to Jackson, 21 December 1818, Jackson, *Correspondence,* 2:401, 403–5; Jackson to Monroe, 7 December 1818, Calhoun, *Papers,* 3:360–61.

29. Jackson to Lewis, 12 January 1819, Jackson-Lewis Letters; Adams to Onís, 31 October 1818, Ford, *Writings of Adams,* 6:455, 457; Onís to Adams, 12 December 1818, *ASPFR,* 4:614.

30. Adams to Erving, 28 November 1818, Ford, *Writings of Adams,* 6:474–500; same to same, *ASPFR,* 4:547; Weeks, *Adams and American Global Empire,* 121.

31. John McIntosh to Mitchell, 2 November 1818, Mitchell Miscellaneous Papers, NYPL; *Niles Weekly Register,* 12 December 1818, 266; Lumpkin to Calhoun, 10 December 1818, *LRSWIA;* Mitchell to Crawford, 30 December 1818, Mitchell Papers, Newberry Library.

32. Gaines to Calhoun, 26 December 1818, 29 December 1818, Calhoun, *Papers,* 3:426, 433; Calhoun to Jackson, 28 December 1818, Calhoun, "Correspondence of Calhoun," 2:150.

33. Gaines to Coppinger, 28 December 1818, same to same, 24 January 1819, Coppinger to Gaines, 3 January 1819, East Florida Papers; Gaines to Calhoun, 2 January 1819, same to same, 16 January 1819, Calhoun, *Papers,* 3:448, 501; Calhoun to Gaines, 19 January 1819, LSSWIA.

34. Calhoun to Mitchell, 5 December 1818, LSSWIA.

35. Nevins, *Adams Diary,* 25 December 1818, 206.

36. Anderson Diary, 25 December 1818.

37. Calhoun to Monroe, 12 December 1818, 30 December 1818, Calhoun, *Papers,* 3:390, 439; Senate Committee, *ASPMA,* 1:739; *Annals of Congress,* 15th Cong., 2nd sess., 37, 70, 74, 76.

38. The Military Affairs Committee consisted of Chairman Richard M. Johnson of Kentucky, Thomas Nelson of Virginia, Joshua Gage of Massachusetts, George Peter of Maryland, James Stewart of North Carolina, Philip Reed of Maryland, and Ebenezer Huntington of Connecticut. Nelson, Stewart, Reed, and Huntington voted for the majority report. *ASPMA,* 1:735.

39. Ibid., 736–39.

40. Anderson Diary, 14 Feb 1819; Johnson to Richard Smith, 29 March 1819, same to same, 30 March 1819, Richard M. Johnson Papers, Library of Congress, Washington, D.C.

41. *Annals of Congress,* 15th Cong., 2nd sess., 588.

42. Those speakers in favor of Jackson's invasion were Richard C. Anderson of Kentucky, Henry Baldwin of Pennsylvania, James Barbour of Virginia, Joseph Desha of Kentucky, James Ervin of South Carolina, John Floyd of Virginia, John Holmes of Massachusetts, Richard M. Johnson of Kentucky, Francis Jones of Tennessee, Hugh Nelson of Virginia, George Poindexter of Mississippi, John Rhea of Tennessee, Lemuel Sawyer of North Carolina, Alexander Smyth of Virginia, George F. Strother of Virginia, James Tallmadge, Jr., of New York, David Walker of Kentucky, and Felix Walker of North Carolina. Those opposed to Jackson's invasion were Henry Clay of Kentucky,

Thomas W. Cobb of Georgia, Edward Colston of Virginia, Timothy Fuller of Massachusetts, James Johnson of Virginia, Charles F. Mercer of Virginia, Thomas M. Nelson of Virginia, Philip Reed of Maryland, Henry R. Storrs of Connecticut, John Tyler of Virginia, and Thomas S. Williams of Connecticut.

43. *Annals of Congress,* 15th Cong., 2nd sess., 663, 835–36, 1108.

44. Nevins, *Adams Diary,* 28 March 1818, 194; Anderson Diary, 22 February 1818.

45. Macon to Bartlett Yancey, 20 June 1820, Kemp P. Battle, ed., *Letters of Nathaniel Macon, John Steele, and William Barry Grove, with Sketches and Notes,* James Sprunt Historical Monograph No.3 (Chapel Hill: University of North Carolina Press, 1908), 73.

46. Charles S. Sydnor, "One-Party Period of American History," *American Historical Review* 51 (April 1946): 439–51.

47. Calhoun to Monroe, 21 January 1819, Calhoun to Clay, 1 February 1819, Calhoun, *Papers,* 32:511, 532–33; Burton Alva Konkle, *Joseph Hopkinson, 1770–1842, Jurist-Scholar-Inspirer of the Arts: Author of Hail Columbia* (Philadelphia: University of Pennsylvania Press, 1931), 211–12; Tyler to Curtis, 19 January 1819, Tyler, *Letters of the Tylers,* 1:305.

48. Hugh Nelson to Charles Everette, 1 December 1818, Hugh Nelson Papers, Library of Congress, Washington, D.C. Ammon, *Monroe,* 430; Cresson, *Monroe,* 318. One of Clay's biographers castigated him for the speech, calling it the "utterance of a factious and ambitious man." Glyndon Van Deusen, *The Life of Henry Clay,* 126. Peterson, *The Great Triumvirate,* 55, described it as "the first of the great oratorical displays in the capital that captivated the age." Robert Remini stated that "it was one of the best speeches of his entire life" but was also "one of the most foolish things Clay had ever done in his life." See Robert W. Remini, *Henry Clay: Statesman for the Union* (New York and London: W. W. Norton and Company, 1991), 163. Alexander Smyth accused Clay of inconsistency on 21 January 1819, the day after Clay's speech. See *Annals of Congress,* 15th Cong., 2nd sess., 679. Clay to Martin D. Hardin, 4 January 1819, Clay to Charles Tait, 25 June 1818, Clay, *Papers,* 2:580, 624.

49. Margaret Bayard Smith, *The First Forty Years of Washington Society,* ed. Gaillard Hunt (London: T. Fisher Unwin, 1906), 146–47. Herman J. Viola, "Andrew Jackson's Invasion of Florida," in *Congress Investigates: A Documented History,* 5 vols., eds. Arthur M. Schlesinger, Jr., and Roger Bruns (New York: Chelsea House Publications, 1975), 1:344, asserts that the galleries were so crowded that some spectators had to be seated on the floor. If he has relied on Smith for this observation (and it would appear he has), he has confused her account of debates in the House on the Seminole War with those in the Senate on the Missouri question. See Smith, *First Forty Years,* 149.

50. *Annals of Congress,* 15th Cong., 2nd sess., 655. Smith, *First Forty Years,* 145.

51. *Annals of Congress,* 15th Cong., 2nd sess., 872–97; Konkle, *Hopkinson,* 211–12.

52. For a representative sample see Richard M. Johnson's speech, *Annals of Congress,* 15th Cong., 2nd sess., 664–65.

53. Clay absolved Monroe of giving Jackson unconstitutional orders because he said there was no evidence of such. See *Annals of Congress,* 15th Cong., 2nd sess., 651, 653.

54. King to C. Gore, 20 January 1819, King, *Life and Correspondence,* 6:194.

55. Smith, *First Forty Years,* 146.

56. *Annals of Congress,* 15th Cong., 2nd sess., 651–53.

57. Ibid., 680–81, 854, 962.

58. Nevins, *Adams Diary,* 23 January 1819, 208; Jackson to Lewis, 25 January 1819, Jackson Papers, LC; Viola makes the assertion about Jackson's manner in "Jackson's Invasion," 345–46.

59. *Annals of Congress,* 15th Cong., 2nd sess., 37, 70; *ASPMA,* 1:739; Abner Lacock to Calhoun, 3 February 1819, same to same, 8 February 1819, Calhoun to Lacock, 20 February 1819, Calhoun, *Papers,* 3:240–41, 556, 596. The members of the Senate select committee were Chairman Abner Lacock (Pennsylvania); John Forsyth (Georgia), who was later replaced by John Eppes (Virginia); Rufus King (New York); James Burrill (Rhode Island); and John Eaton (Tennessee). Lacock, Burrill, and Eppes would vote to condemn Jackson's actions.

60. Viola, "Jackson's Invasion," 1:345–46; Fuller, *Purchase of Florida,* 265.

61. Fuller, *Purchase of Florida,* 264.

62. Jackson to Lewis, 30 January 1819, Jackson Papers, LC; Jackson to Donelson, 31 January 1819, Jackson, *Papers,* 2:408, 4:270–71; Nevins, *Adams Diary,* 3 February 1819, 209–10.

63. *Annals of Congress,* 15th Cong., 2nd sess., 1132–38; Gaines to Calhoun, 14 March 1819, Calhoun, *Papers,* 3:661. Fuller, *Purchase of Florida,* 266–67, cites James Parton for the assertion that Jackson escaped censure because of the faulty tactics of his critics.

64. *Annals of Congress,* 15th Cong., 2nd sess., 699, 849; Ammon, *Monroe,* 430; *ASPMA,* 1:739; Overton to King, 6 January 1819, King, *Life and Correspondence,* 6:187. Prior to King's presentation in the Senate an extended version of the Memorial was published in the fall of 1819 under the title *A Vindication of the Measures of the President and His Commanding Generals in the Commencement and Termination of the Seminole War by a Citizen of the State of Tennessee* (Washington: Gales and Seaton, 1819). Bassett, *Life of Jackson,* 291–92; Weeks, *Adams and American Global Empire,* 168. Also see *ASPMA,* 1:754–60. As John Overton put it, "More has been effected by these measures, in adjusting our differences with Spain, than *thirteen* years negotiation." See Overton, *Vindication,* 97.

65. Cresson, *Monroe,* 320; Rippy, *Rivalry over Latin America,* 69; Fuller, *Purchase of Florida,* 299–307; Langley, *American Mediterranean,* 17–18.

66. Remarks of Clay, 10 February 1819, Clay, *Papers,* 2:667.

67. Monroe to Madison, 7 February 1819; Monroe to Rush, 7 March 1819, Hamilton, *Writings of Monroe,* 6:87–88, 91.

68. Barrett to Holmes, 16 February 1819, John Holmes Papers, New York Public Library, New York, New York; Morrison to Clay, 17 February 1819, Clay, *Papers,* 2:671–72.

69. Monroe to Rufus King, 22 July 1818, King, *Life and Correspondence,* 6:156.

Epilogue

1. Big Warrior to Monroe, 22 January 1819, *LRSWIA.*
2. McIntosh and delegation to Calhoun, 23 February 1819, Calhoun, *Papers,* 3:606.
3. McIntosh and delegation to Calhoun, 9 March 1819, Calhoun to Mitchell, 11 March 1819, Calhoun to Creek delegation, 28 March 1819, Calhoun, *Papers,* 3:646, 654, 700; Mitchell to Calhoun, 7 December 1819, Mitchell to McIntosh, 27 October 1819, *LRSWIA.*
4. Gaines to Calhoun, 18 February 1819, Calhoun to Gaines, 11 March 1819, Calhoun, *Papers,* 3:582, 652.
5. McIntosh to Ross, 21 October 1821, Telamon Cuyler Collection; Green, *Politics of Indian Removal,* 81–88; Griffith, *McIntosh and Weatherford,* 215–17, 224–40.
6. Griffith, *McIntosh and Weatherford,* 248–50; Green, *Politics of Indian Removal,* 96; Southerland and Brown, *Federal Road,* 119; McIntosh to John Ross, 21 October 1821, Telamon Cuyler Collection.
7. Jackson to Lewis, 26 March 1819, Jackson-Lewis Papers.
8. Ibid.; Vanderlyn to Earl, 2 April 1819, John Vanderlyn Letter, Pierpont Morgan Library, New York, New York; Gadsden to Jackson, 2 April 1819, Jackson, *Correspondence,* 2:415; *Niles Weekly Register,* 13 November 1819, 176; Weeks, *Adams and American Global Empire,* 160.
9. Jackson to Atkinson, 15 May 1819, Calhoun, *Papers,* 4:63; Jackson to Calhoun, 24 August 1819, *LRSWIA.*
10. Jackson to William, 25 September 1819, Jackson to Monroe, 22 November 1819, Jackson, *Correspondence,* 2:430, 442; Mitchell to Calhoun, 12 November 1819, *LRSWIA;* Tait to Walker, 9 October 1819, Tait Family Papers.
11. Fuller, *Purchase of Florida,* 310–11.
12. *Niles Weekly Register,* 17 April 1819, 142; Fomentin to Adams, 6 September 1819, William Lowndes Papers, Library of Congress, Washington, D.C.; Forsyth to Monroe, 7 August 1819, Monroe Papers, LC.
13. Jackson to Calhoun, 24 August 1819, *LRSWIA.*
14. Wirt to Coalter, 25 October 1819, William Wirt, "Letter of William Wirt, 1819," *American Historical Review* 25 (July 1920): 693; Fuller, *Purchase of Florida,* 313.
15. Jackson to Monroe, 10 December 1819, Jackson, *Correspondence,* 2:446; Adams to Lowndes, 16 December 1819, 21 December 1819, Ford, *Writings of Adams,* 6:559–63; Calhoun to Adams, 22 December 1819; Adams to Lowndes, 27 December 1819, Lowndes Papers, LC; Calhoun to Jackson, 31 December 1819, Calhoun, "Correspondence of Calhoun," 2:165, 168; Jackson to Calhoun, 21 January 1820, Jackson Papers, LC; Wesley, *Old Frontier,* 173.

16. Fuller, *Purchase of Florida,* 310, 314; Duckett, *Forsyth,* 62; Cresson, *Monroe,* 323.

17. Cresson, *Monroe,* 323–24; Fuller, *Purchase of Florida,* 314.

18. Cresson, *Monroe,* 324–25; Bemis, *Adams and Foreign Policy,* 350–52; Fuller, *Purchase of Florida,* 319.

19. Duckett, *Forsyth,* 62–63; Cresson, *Monroe,* 325; Fuller, *Purchase of Florida,* 323.

20. *Annals of Congress,* 15th Cong., 2nd sess., 630, 634, 742, 853, 1072; Peterson, *Great Triumvirate,* 93.

21. *Annals of Congress,* 15th Cong., 2nd sess., 799, 908–9.

22. Eppes to Legislature of Virginia, 4 December 1819, *Niles Weekly Register,* 25 December 1819, 287; Spiller, "Calhoun as Secretary of War," 5, 6–7, 255; Crawford to Tait, 7 November 1819, Tait Family Papers; C. Edward Skeen, "Calhoun, Crawford, and the Politics of Retrenchment," *South Carolina Historical Magazine* 73 (July 1972): 142.

23. Brown to Joseph G. Swift, 25 January 1820, quoted in Spiller, "Calhoun as Secretary of War," 260.

24. Skeen, "Politics of Retrenchment," 145–47; Crawford to Daniel, 2 May 1821, Crawford Papers, LC; Simkins to Lowndes, 28 October 1821, Lowndes Papers, SHC.

25. Spiller, "Calhoun as Secretary of War," 261; Calhoun to Jackson, 15 March 1820, Calhoun, "Correspondence of Calhoun," 2:171.

26. Spiller, "Calhoun as Secretary of War," 259. Cobb is quoted in Skeen, "Politics of Retrenchment," 145.

27. Richard W. Barsness, "John C. Calhoun and the Military Establishment, 1817–1825," *Wisconsin Magazine of History* 50, No. 1 (Autumn 1966): 52; *Annals of Congress,* 16th Cong., 2nd sess., 367.

28. Russell F. Weigley, *History of the United States Army* (Bloomington: Indiana University Press, 1984), 140; Spiller, "Calhoun as Secretary of War," 280–83; *Annals of Congress,* 16th Cong., 2nd sess., 934–35.

29. Calhoun to Jackson, 8 April 1821, Calhoun, *Papers,* 6:25; Arthur William Thompson, *Jacksonian Democracy on the Florida Frontier* (Gainesville: University of Florida Press, 1961), 1; Nevins, *Adams Diary,* 8 April 1818, 195.

30. Herbert J. Doherty, "Andrew Jackson vs. the Spanish Governor: Pensacola, 1821," *Florida Historical Quarterly* 34 (October 1955): 143–53.

31. John K. Mahon, "The Treaty of Moultrie Creek, 1823," *Florida Historical Quarterly* 40 (1962): 354, 368–70; Mark F. Boyd, "Horatio S. Dexter and Events Leading to the Treaty of Moultrie Creek with the Seminole Indians," *Florida Anthropologist* 11 (September 1958): 65–67; James W. Covington, "White Control of Seminole Leadership," *Florida Anthropologist* 18 (September 1965): 141.

32. Hitchcock, *Diary,* 45.

33. Ibid., 151–55.

Bibliography

PRIMARY SOURCES

Unpublished

Alabama Department of Archives and History, Montgomery, Alabama
    Alabamians at War: War of 1812 and First Creek War
    Alabama Territory, Militia Records
    Governor William W. Bibb Papers, Alabama Territory
    John Coffee Papers
    Creek War Military Records
    Alexander Beaufort Meek Papers
    Mississippi Territorial File, Military Papers
    Mississippi Territory, Governor's Correspondence
    Mississippi Territory, Military Correspondence
    Albert J. Pickett Papers
    Tait Family Papers

Georgia Department of Archives and History, Atlanta, Georgia
    Big Warrior File
    Cawthon Loose Paper File
    John Floyd Papers
    Georgia Adjutant General, Military Affairs
    Governors' Letterbook, May 18, 1814 to October 30, 1827
    Hays, Louise Frederick, ed. and comp. "Unpublished Letters of Timothy
        Barnard."

Indian Files, File 2
Indian Letters, 1782–1839
Young, Hugh. Itineraries, A Record of the Route Followed by Gen. Jackson's army from Hartford to Fort Scott during Seminole War. Georgia Surveyor-General Department

Library of Congress, Washington, D.C.
Richard C. Anderson Diary
William Blount Papers
William H. Crawford Papers
Joseph Desha Papers
East Florida Papers
Andrew Jackson Papers
Richard M. Johnson Papers
William Lowndes Papers
James Monroe Papers
Hugh Nelson Papers
Vincente Sebastian Pintado Papers
Papeles Procedentes de Cuba Archivo General de Indias
Public Records Office, Foreign Office File 115, vol. 31
Samuel Smith Family Papers

National Archives, Washington, D.C.
Diplomatic Instructions, All Countries, vols. VII–X; Dispatches, Great Britain, vols. XVIII–XXX; Dispatches, France, vols. XIV–XXII
Index to Compiled Service Records of Volunteer Soldiers Who Served During the Indian Wars, 1815–1858
Letters Received by the Adjutant General's Office, 1805–1821
Letters Received by the Office of the Secretary of War Relating to Indian Affairs, 1800–1823
Letters Received by the Secretary of the Navy from Captains, 1805–61. Naval Records Collection of the Office of Naval Records and Library
Letters Sent by the Secretary of War Relating to Indian Affairs, 1800–1824
Letters Sent by the Superintendent of Indian Trade, 1806–1823
McIntosh's Brigade, Creek Indian Warriors, Seminole War, 1817–1818, Military Service Records
Records of the Office of the Secretary of War, Letters Received
Returns for United States Military Posts, 1800–1916
Secretary of War, Letters Received, Registered Series
Secretary of War, Letters Sent, Military Affairs

Newberry Library, Chicago, Illinois
David B. Mitchell Papers, Ayer Collection

New York Public Library, New York, New York
    John Holmes Papers
    David Bridie Mitchell Personal Miscellaneous Papers
    James Monroe Papers
    Caesar Rodney and Caesar A. Rodney Papers

Pierpont Morgan Library, New York, New York
    William Harris Crawford, Autograph Letters, Ford Collection
    Andrew Jackson–William B. Lewis Letters, 1817–1845
    John Vanderlyn Letter

Southern Historical Collection, University of North Carolina, Chapel Hill,
North Carolina
    William Lowndes Papers
    Edward Brett Randolph Diary
    Bartlett Yancey Papers

University of Georgia Libraries, Athens, Georgia
    Telamon Cuyler Collection

Wisconsin State Historical Society, Madison, Wisconsin
    Archivo Nacional de Cuba, Legajos 1, 2, 9, Typescripts
    Lyman Draper Manuscript Collection
    Edmund Pendleton Gaines File
    Letters to David B. Mitchell

Published

Adams, Charles Francis, ed. *Memoirs of John Quincy Adams, Comprising Portions of His Diary from 1785–1848.* 12 vols. Philadelphia: J. B. Lippincott & Co., 1874–1877.
American State Papers: Foreign Relations. 6 vols. Washington, D.C.: Gales and Seaton, 1834.
American State Papers: Indian Affairs. 2 vols. Washington, D.C.: Gales and Seaton, 1832.
American State Papers: Military Affairs. 7 vols. Washington, D.C.: Gales and Seaton, 1832–1861.
American State Papers: Miscellaneous. 2 vols. Washington, D.C.: Gales and Seaton, 1832–1861.
Annals of the Congress of the United States. 42 vols. Washington, D.C.: Gales and Seaton, 1834–1856.
Banks, John. *A Short Biographical Sketch of the Undersigned by Himself.* Austell, Georgia: Privately Published, 1936.

Barber, Eunice. *Narrative of the Tragical Death of Darius Barber.* Vol. 36 of *The Garland Library of Narratives of North American Indian Captivities,* edited by Wilcomb E. Washburn. New York: Garland Publishing Co., 1977.

Bassett, John Spencer, ed. *Correspondence of Andrew Jackson.* 7 vols. Washington, D.C.: Carnegie Institute of Washington, 1926–1935.

Battle, Kemp P., ed. *Letters of Nathaniel Macon, John Steele, and William Barry Grove, with Sketches and Notes.* James Sprunt Historical Monograph No.3. Chapel Hill: University of North Carolina Press, 1908.

Calhoun, John C. *The Papers of John C. Calhoun, 1818–1819.* Edited by Robert Meriwether, William Edwin Hemphill, and Clyde Norman Wilson. 20 vols. Columbia: University of South Carolina Press, 1959–1988.

———. "Correspondence of John C. Calhoun." In *Annual Report of the American Historical Association,* edited by J. Franklin Jameson. Washington, D.C.: Government Printing Office, 1900.

———. *Correspondence between Gen. Andrew Jackson and John C. Calhoun.* Washington, D.C.: Duff Green, 1831. LAC 40065.

Carter, Clarence Edward, ed. *The Territorial Papers of the United States.* 28 vols. Washington, D.C.: Government Printing Office, 1934–1975.

Cohen, Myer M. *Notices of Florida and the Campaigns.* N.p., 1836. Reprint edition, Gainesville: University of Florida Press, 1964.

"Creek Letters, Talks, and Treaties, 1705–1839." 4 vols. Georgia Department of Archives, Atlanta, Georgia.

Fisher, Ruth A., ed. "The Surrender of Pensacola as Told by the British." *American Historical Review* 54 (January 1949): 326–29.

Floyd, John. "Letters of John Floyd, 1813–1838." *Georgia Historical Quarterly* 33 (1949): 228–69.

Ford, Worthington Chauncy, ed. *The Writings of John Quincy Adams.* 7 vols. New York: The MacMillan Company, 1913–17.

Gadsden, James. "'The Defenses of the Floridas,' A Report of Captain James Gadsden, Aide-de-Camp to General Jackson." *Florida Historical Quarterly* 15 (April 1937): 242–48.

Georgia Military Affairs. 9 vols. Georgia Department of Archives, Atlanta, Georgia, 1940.

Goldman, Perry M., and James S. Young, eds. *The United States Congressional Directories, 1789–1840.* New York and London: Columbia University Press, 1973.

Hamilton, Stanislas Murray, ed. *The Writings of James Monroe.* 7 vols. New York: G. P. Putnam's Sons, 1898–1903.

Hawkins, Benjamin. *Letters, Journals, and Writings of Benjamin Hawkins.* 2 vols. Edited by C. L. Grant. Savannah: The Beehive Press, 1980.

Hitchcock, Ethan Allen. *Fifty Years in Camp and Field: Diary of Major-General Ethan Allen Hitchcock, U.S.A.* Edited by W. A. Croffut. New York and London: G. P. Putnam's Sons, 1909.

Innerarity, John. "Letters of John Innerarity: The Seizure of Pensacola by Andrew Jackson, November 7, 1814." Edited by Julian C. Yonge. *Florida Historical Society Quarterly* 9 (1931): 127–34.

Israel, Fred N., ed. *The State of the Union Messages of the Presidents, 1790–1966.* 3 vols. New York: Chelsea House Robert Hector Publishers.

Jones, Charles C., Jr. *The Dead Towns of Georgia.* Savannah: Morning News Steam Printing House, 1978.

King, Charles R., ed. *Life and Correspondence of Rufus King.* 3 vols. New York: G. P. Putnam's Sons, 1894–1900.

Latour, Arséne Lacarrière. *Historical Memoir of the War in West Florida and Louisiana in 1814–15.* Facsimile reproduction of the 1816 edition. Gainesville: University of Florida Press, 1964.

Miller, Stephen F., ed. *Memoir of General David Blackshear.* Philadelphia: J. B. Lippincott, 1858. Reprint edition, Louisville, Kentucky: Lost Cause Press, 1981.

Mitchell, David B. *An Exposition of the Case of the Africans, Taken to the Creek Agency by Captain William Bowen on or about the 1st of December 1817.* N.p., 1822.

Moser, Harold D., David R. Hoth, and George H. Hoeman, eds. *The Papers of Andrew Jackson.* 4 vols. Knoxville: University of Tennessee Press, 1980–1994.

Narrative of a Voyage to the Spanish Main, in the Ship Two Friends. Introduction by John W. Griffin. N.p., 1819. Reprint edition, Gainesville: University Presses of Florida, 1978.

Nevins, Allan, ed. *The Diary of John Quincy Adams, 1794–1845: American Political, Social, and Intellectual Life from Washington to Polk.* New York: Longmans, Green and Co., 1928.

The New American State Papers, Military Affairs. 19 vols. Wilmington, Delaware: Scholarly Resources, 1979.

[Overton, John.] *A Vindication of the Measures of the President and His Commanding Generals in the Commencement and Termination of the Seminole War by a Citizen of the State of Tennessee.* Washington, D.C.: Gales and Seaton, 1819.

Parton, James. *Life of Andrew Jackson.* 3 vols. New York: Mason Brothers, 1861.

"The Public Buildings of Pensacola, 1818." *Florida Historical Quarterly* 16 (July 1937): 45–47.

Remsen, Peter A. "Across Georgia and into Alabama, 1817–1818." Edited by William B. Hesseltine and Larry Gara. *Georgia Historical Quarterly* 37 (December 1953): 329–40.

Richardson, James D., ed. *Compilation of Messages and Papers of the Presidents.* Washington, D.C.: Government Printing Office, 1896.

Seager, Robert II, Mary W. M. Hargreaves, and James T. Hopkins, eds. *The Papers of Henry Clay.* 11 vols. Lexington: University of Kentucky Press, 1959–1992.

Smith, Margaret Bayard. *The First Forty Years of Washington Society.* Edited by Gaillard Hunt. London: T. Fisher Unwin, 1906.

Stenberg, Richard R. "Andrew Jackson and the Erving Affidavit." *Southwestern Historical Quarterly* 41 (1937): 142–53.

Ticknor, George. *Life, Letters, and Journals of George Ticknor.* 2 vols. Boston: James R. Osgood and Co., 1876.

Tyler, Lyon, ed. *The Letters and Times of the Tylers.* 3 vols. N.p., 1884–96. Reprint edition, New York: De Capo Press, 1970.

United States Congress. House. *Serial Set.* 15th Cong., 2nd sess. H. Doc. 122.

United States Congress. *Serial Set.* 15 Cong., 2nd sess., H. Doc. 117.

United States Congress. Senate. *Serial Set.* 15th Cong., 2nd sess. S. Doc. 100.

———. *Serial Set.* 15th Cong., 1st sess. S. Doc. 87.

———. *Serial Set.* 15th Cong., 1st sess. S. Doc. 136.

———. *Serial Set.* 15th Cong., 2nd sess. S. Doc. 35.

———. *Serial Set.* vol. 1, 15th Cong., 2nd sess., Senate Journal.

———. *Serial Set,* vol. 14, *Message of the President, 17 November 1818.* 15th Cong., 2nd sess. S. Doc. 1.

Ventura Morales, Juan. "Juan Ventura Morales to Alexandro Ramirez, November 3, 1817." *Boletín del Archivo Nacional* 13 (January–February 1914): 9–21.

White, George, ed. *Historical Collections of Georgia.* New York: Pudney & Russell, Publishers, 1855. Reprint edition, Baltimore: Genealogical Publishing Company, 1969.

Wirt, William. "Letter of William Wirt, 1819." *American Historical Review* 25 (July 1920): 692–95.

Woodward, Thomas S. *Woodward's Reminiscences of the Creek or Muscogee Indians, Contained in Letters to Friends in Georgia and Alabama.* Montgomery, Alabama: Barrett & Wimbish, 1859. Reprint edition, Tuscaloosa: Alabama Book Store, 1939.

Young, Hugh. "A Topographical Memoir on East and West Florida. . . ." Edited by Mark F. Boyd. *Florida Historical Quarterly* 13 (1935): 16–50, 82–104, 129–64.

Periodicals

Athens Gazette
Augusta Chronicle
Augusta Herald
Columbian Museum and Savannah Daily Gazette
Columbus Sun
Georgia Journal
Milledgeville Republican and Reflector
Niles Weekly Register
Savannah Daily Georgian
Savannah Republican

SECONDARY SOURCES

Books

Abernethy, Thomas Perkins. *The Burr Conspiracy.* New York: Oxford University Press, 1954.

————. "Florida and the Spanish Frontier, 1811–1819." In *The Americanization of the Gulf Coast, 1803–1850,* edited by Lucius F. Ellsworth, 88–120. Pensacola: Historic Pensacola Preservation Board, 1972.

————. *The Formative Period in Alabama, 1815–1828.* 2nd ed. University, Alabama: University of Alabama Press, 1965.

————. *The South in the New Nation, 1789–1819.* Baton Rouge: Louisiana State University Press, 1961.

Ammon, Harry. *James Monroe: The Quest for National Identity.* New York: McGraw-Hill, 1971. Reprint edition, Charlottesville and London: University of Virginia Press, 1990.

Bassett, John Spencer. The *Life of Andrew Jackson.* Reprint edition, Hamden, Conn.: Archon Books, 1967.

Bemis, Samuel Flagg. *John Quincy Adams and the Foundations of American Foreign Policy.* New York: Alfred A. Knopf, 1949.

Bonner, James C. "William McIntosh." In *Georgians in Profile: Historical Essay in Honor of Ellis Merton Coulter,* edited by Horace Montgomery. Athens: University of Georgia, 1958.

Braund, Kathryn E. Holland. *Deerskins and Duffels: The Creek Indian Trade with Anglo-America, 1685–1815.* Lincoln and London: University of Nebraska Press, 1993.

Brooks, Philip C. *Diplomacy and the Borderlands: The Adams-Onís Treaty of 1819.* Berkeley: University of California Press, 1939. Reprint edition, New York: Octagon Books, 1970.

Brown, Wilburt S. *The Amphibious Campaign for West Florida and Louisiana, 1814–1815.* University, Alabama: University of Alabama Press, 1969.

Canedo, Lino Gómez. *Los Archivos de la Historía de América, Período Colonial Español.* 2 vols. Mexico, D.F.: Instituto Panamericano de Geografia e Historia, 1961.

Chalker, Fussell M. *Pioneer Days Along the Ocmulgee.* Carrollton, Georgia: By the Author, 1970.

Cline, Howard F. *Notes on the Colonial Indians and Communities in Florida, 1700–1821; Notes on the Treaty of Coweta.* New York: Garland Publishing Co., 1974.

Coit, Margaret L. *John C. Calhoun, American Portrait.* Boston: Houghton Mifflin, 1950.

Coker, William S., and Thomas D. Watson. *Indian Traders of the Southeastern*

Borderlands: Panton, Leslie and Company and John Forbes and Company, 1783–1847. Gainesville: University Presses of Florida, 1986.

Coleman, Kenneth, and Charles Stephen Gurr. *Dictionary of Georgia Biography.* 2 vols. Athens: University of Georgia Press, 1983.

Cotterril, R. S. *The Southern Indians: The Story of the Civilized Tribes before Removal.* Norman: University of Oklahoma Press, 1954.

Covington, James W. *The Seminoles of Florida.* Gainesville: University Presses of Florida, 1993.

Crackel, Theodore J. *Mr. Jefferson's Army: Politicial and Social Reform of the Military Establishment, 1801–1809.* New York: New York University Press, 1987.

Cresson, William P. *James Monroe.* Chapel Hill: University of North Carolina Press, 1946. Reprint edition, Hamden, Connecticut: Archon Books, 1971.

Doster, James F. *The Creek Indians and Their Florida Lands, 1740–1823.* 2 vols. New York: Garland Publishing, 1974.

Dowd, Gregory Evans. *A Spirited Resistance.* Baltimore: Johns Hopkins Press, 1992.

Duckett, Alvin Laroy. *John Forsyth: Political Tactician.* Athens: University of Georgia Press, 1962.

Early County Historical Society. *Collections of the Early County Historical Society.* Vol. 1. Colquitt, Georgia: Automat Printers, 1971.

Fairbanks, Charles H. *Ethonohistorical Report on the Florida Indians.* New York: Garland Publishing Company, 1974.

Franco, José L. *Politica Continental América de España en Cuba, 1812–1830.* Havana: Archívo Nacional de Cuba, 1947.

Fuller, Herbert Bruce. *The Purchase of Florida: Its History and Diplomacy.* 1906. Reprint edition, Gainesville: University of Florida Press, 1964.

Green, Michael D. *The Politics of Indian Removal: Creek Government and Society in Crisis.* Lincoln: University of Nebraska Press, 1982.

Griffith, Benjamin W., Jr. *McIntosh and Weatherford: Creek Indian Leaders.* Tuscaloosa: University of Alabama Press, 1988.

Hamilton, James. *The Power to Probe: A Study of Congressional Investigations.* New York: Random House, 1976.

Harlow, Ralph Volney. *The History of Legislative Methods in the Period before 1825.* New Haven, Connecticut: Yale University Press, 1917.

Hart, Bertha Sheppard. *The Official History of Laurens County, 1807–1941.* Atlanta: Cherokee Publishing Company, 1972.

Henri, Florette. *The Southern Indians and Benjamin Hawkins, 1796–1816.* Norman: University of Oklahoma Press, 1986.

Historic Chattahoochee Commission. *Chattahoochee Trace Historical Markers in Alabama and Georgia.* Eufaula, Alabama: Historic Chattachoocee Commission, 1983.

Horsman, Reginald. *The Origins of Indian Removal, 1815–1824.* East Lansing: Michigan State University Press, 1970.

James, Marquis. *The Life of Andrew Jackson Complete in One Volume.* Indianapolis: Bobbs-Merrill Company, 1938.

Jones, Frank S. *History of Decatur County Georgia.* Spartanburg. S.C.: The Reprint Company, 1980.

Konkle, Burton Alva. *Joseph Hopkinson, 1770–1842, Jurist-Scholar-Inspirer of the Arts: Author of Hail Columbia.* Philadelphia: University of Pennsylvania Press, 1931.

Langley, Lester D. *Struggle for the American Mediterranean: United States–European Rivalry in the Gulf-Caribbean, 1776–1904.* Athens: University of Georgia Press, 1976.

Lee County Historical Society. *Lee County, Georgia: A History.* Atlanta: W. H. Wolfe Associates, 1983.

Lomask, Milton. *Aaron Burr: The Conspiracy and Years of Exile, 1805–1836.* New York: Farrar, Straus, Girous, 1982.

Malone, Dumas. *Jefferson the President, First Term, 1801–1805.* Vol. 4 of *Jefferson and His Time.* Boston: Little, Brown and Company, 1970.

Martin, Joel W. *Sacred Revolt: The Muscogees' Struggle for a New World.* Boston: Beacon Press, 1991.

McGovern, James Robert. *Andrew Jackson and Pensacola.* Hattiesburg, Mississippi: University of Southern Mississippi, 1971.

McLoughlin, William G. *Cherokee Renascence in the New Republic.* Princeton, New Jersey: Princeton University Press, 1986.

Meyer, Leland Winfield. *The Life and Times of Colonel Richard M. Johnson of Kentucky.* Reprint Edition, New York: AMS Press, 1932.

Mooney, Chase C. *William H. Crawford, 1772–1834.* Lexington: University Press of Kentucky, 1974.

Mulroy, Kevin. *Freedom on the Border: The Seminole Maroons in Florida, the Indian Territory, Coahuila, and Texas.* Lubbock: Texas Tech University Press, 1993.

Niven, John. *John C. Calhoun and the Price of Union: A Biography.* Baton Rouge: Louisiana State University Press, 1988.

Northern, William J. *Men of Mark in Georgia.* 6 vols. Atlanta: Caldwell Publishers, 1910. Reprint edition, Spartanburg, South Carolina, The Reprint Company, 1974.

Owsley, Frank Lawrence, Jr. *Struggle for the Gulf Borderlands: The Creek War and the Battle of New Orleans.* Gainesville: University Presses of Florida, 1981.

Patrick, Rembert W. *Florida Fiasco: Rampant Rebels on the Georgia-Florida Frontier, 1810–1815.* Athens: University of Georgia Press, 1954.

———. *Aristocrat in Uniform: Duncan L. Clinch.* Gainesville: University of Florida Press, 1963.

Perkins, Bradford. *Castlereagh and Adams: England and the United States, 1812–1823.* Berkeley and Los Angeles: University of California Press, 1964.

Peterson, Merrill D. *The Great Triumvirate: Webster, Clay, and Calhoun.* New York and Oxford: Oxford University Press, 1987.

Pound, Merritt B. *Benjamn Hawkins, Indian Agent.* Athens: University of Georgia Press, 1951.

Pratt, Julius. *Expansionists of 1812.* New York: Macmillan Company, 1925. Reprint edition, Gloucester, Massachusetts: Peter Smith, 1957.

Prucha, Francis Paul. *A Guide to Military Posts of the United States, 1789–1895.* Madison: The State Historical Society of Wisconsin, 1964.

———. *The Sword of the Republic: The United States Army on the Frontier, 1783–1846.* London: The Macmillan Company, 1969. Reprint edition, Lincoln: University of Nebraska Press, 1986.

Remini, Robert V. *Andrew Jackson and the Course of American Empire, 1767–1821.* New York: Harper and Row Publishers, 1977.

———. *Henry Clay: Statesman for the Union.* New York and London: W. W. Norton and Company, 1991.

Rippy, James Fred. *Rivalry of the United States and Britain over Latin America, 1808–1830.* Baltimore: The Johns Hopkins Press, 1929. Reprint edition, New York: Octagon Books, 1964.

Robinson, Fayette. *An Account of the Organization of the Army of the United States, with Biographies of Distinguished Officers of All Grades.* 2 vols. Philadelphia: Butler and Company, 1848.

Rogin, Michael Paul. *Fathers and Children: Andrew Jackson and the Subjugation of the American Indian.* New York: Vintage Books, 1975.

Schlesinger, Arthur M., Jr. *The Imperial Presidency.* Boston: Houghton Mifflin Company, 1973.

Sheehan, Bernard W. *Seeds of Extinction: Jeffersonian Philanthropy and the American Indian.* Chapel Hill: University of North Carolina Press, 1973.

Silver, James W. *Edmund Pendleton Gaines: Frontier General.* Baton Rouge: Louisiana State University Press, 1949.

Skelton, William B. An *American Profession of Arms: The Army Officer Corps, 1784–1861.* Lawrence: University Press of Kansas, 1992.

Sofaer, Abraham D. *War Foreign Affairs and Constitutional Power: The Origins.* Cambridge, Mass.: Ballinger Publishing Company, 1976.

Southerland, Henry DeLeon, Jr., and Jerry Elizah Brown. *The Federal Road through Georgia, the Creek Nation, and Alabama, 1806–1836.* Tuscaloosa: The University of Alabama Press, 1989.

Sturtevant, William C. "Creek and Seminole." In *North American Indians in Historical Perspective,* edited by Eleanor B. Leacock and Nancy Lurie. New York: Random House, 1971.

Swanton, John R. The *Indian Tribes of North America.* Smithsonian Institution Bureau of American Ethnology, Bulletin 145. Washington, D.C.: Smithsonian Institution Press, 1952.

Thompson, Arthur William. *Jacksonian Democracy on the Florida Frontier.* Gainesville: University of Florida Press, 1961.

Tucker, Spencer C. *The Jeffersonian Gunboat Navy.* Columbia: University of South Carolina Press, 1993.

Turner, Lynn W. "Elections of 1816 and 1820." In *History of American Presidential Elections, 1789–1968,* vol. I, edited by Arthur M. Schlesinger and Fred L. Israel. 1971.

United States Congress. *Biographical Directory of the United States Congress, 1774–1989, the Continental Congress, September 5, 1774, to October 21, 1788, and the Congress of the United States, from the First through the One Hundredth Congress, March 4, 1798, to January 3 1989, inclusive.* Washington, D.C.: Government Printing Office, 1989.

Van Deusen, Glyndon. *The Life of Henry Clay.* Boston: Little, Brown and Company, 1937.

Viola, Herman J. "Andrew Jackson's Invasion of Florida." In *Congress Investigates: A Documented History.* 5 vols., edited by Arthur M. Schlesinger and Roger Bruns, 1:335–49. New York: Chelsea House Publications, 1975.

Vipperman, Carl J. *William Lowndes and the Transition of Southern Politics, 1782–1822.* The Fred W. Morrison Series in Southern Studies. Chapel Hill and London: University of North Carolina Press, 1989.

Waciuma, Wanjohi. *Intervention in the Spanish Floridas, 1801–1818: A Study of Jeffersonian Foreign Policy.* Boston: Branden Press, 1976.

Wallace, Anthony F. C. *The Long, Bitter Trail: Andrew Jackson and the Indians.* New York: Hill and Wang, 1993.

Weber, David J. *The Spanish Frontier in North America.* New Haven, Connecticut: Yale University Press, 1992.

Weeks, William Earl. *John Quincy Adams and American Global Empire.* Lexington: University Press of Kentucky, 1992.

Weigley, Russell F. *History of the United States Army.* Bloomington: Indiana University Press, 1984.

Weisman, Brent Richards. *Like Beads on a String: A Culture History of the Seminole Indians in Northern Peninsular Florida.* Tuscaloosa: University of Alabama Press, 1989.

Wesley, Edgar B. *Guarding the Old Frontier: A Study of Frontier Defense from 1815 to 1825.* Minneapolis: University of Minnesota Press, 1935.

Wilkins, Thurman. *Cherokee Tragedy: The Story of the Ridge Family and the Decimation of a People.* New York: Macmillan, 1970.

Wiltse, Charles M. *John C. Calhoun, Nationalist.* Indianapolis: Bobbs-Merrill, 1944.

Wormuth, Francis D., and Edwin B. Formage. *To Chain the Dog of War: The War Power of Congress in History and Law.* Dallas: Southern Methodist University Press, 1986.

Wright, J. Leitch, Jr. *Anglo-Spanish Rivalry in North America.* Athens: University of Georgia Press, 1971.

———. *Britain and the American Frontier, 1783–1815.* Athens: University of Georgia Press, 1976.

———. *Creeks and Seminoles: The Destruction and Regeneration of the Muscogulge People.* Lincoln: University of Nebraska Press, 1986.

Journal Articles

Amos, Alcione M. "Captain Hugh Young's Map of Jackson's 1818 Seminole Campaign in Florida." *Florida Historical Quarterly* 55 (1977): 336–46.

Barsness, Richard W. "John C. Calhoun and the Military Establishment, 1817–1825." *Wisconsin Magazine of History* 50, No. 1 (Autumn 1966): 43–53.

Boyd, Mark F. "Horatio S. Dexter and Events Leading to the Treaty of Moultrie Creek with the Seminole Indians." *Florida Anthroplogist* 11 (September 1958): 65–95.

———. "Events at Prospect Bluff on the Apalachicola River, 1808–1818: An Introduction to Twelve Letters of Edmund Doyle, Trader." *Florida Historical Quarterly* 16 (October 1937): 55–96.

Brauer, Kinley J. "The United States and British Imperial Expansion, 1815–1860." *Diplomatic History* 12 (Winter 1988): 19–37.

Braund, Kathryn E. Holland. "The Creek Indians, Blacks, and Slavery." *Journal of Southern History* 57 (November 1991): 601–36.

Calkins, Carlos G. "The Repression of Piracy in the West Indies, 1814–1825." *United States Naval Institute Proceedings* 37 (December 1911): 1197–1238.

Chace, James, and Caleb Carr. "The Odd Couple Who Won Florida and Half the West." *Smithsonian* 19 (April 1988): 134–60.

Chamber, Nella T. "The Creek Indian Factory at Fort Mitchell." *Alabama Historical Quarterly* 21 (1959): 15–23.

Coulter, E. Merton. "The Chehaw Affair." *Georgia Historical Quarterly* 49 (December 1965): 369–95.

Covington, James W. "White Control of Seminole Leadership." *Florida Anthropolgist* 18 (September 1965): 137–46.

———. "Migration of the Seminoles into Florida: 1700–1820." *Florida Historical Quarterly* 46 (1968): 340–57.

Craig, Alan K., and Christopher S. Peebles. "Captain Young's Sketch Map, 1818." *Florida Historical Quarterly* 48 (1969): 176–79.

———. "Ethnohistorical Change among the Seminoles, 1740–1840." *Geoscience and Man* 5 (10 June 1974): 83–96.

Davis, T. Frederick. "Milly Francis and Duncan McKrimmon: An Authentic Florida Pocahontas." *Florida Historical Quarterly* 21 (January 1943): 254–65.

———. "McGregor's Invasion of Florida." *Florida Historical Quarterly* 7 (July 1928): 3–71.

Dibble, Ernest F. "Captain Hugh Young and His Topographical Memoir to Andrew Jackson." *Florida Historical Quarterly* 55 (1977): 321–35.

Doherty, Herbert J. "Andrew Jackson vs. the Spanish Governor: Pensacola, 1821." *Florida Historical Quarterly* 34 (October 1955): 142–58.

Doster, James F. "Land Titles and Public Land Sales in Early Alabama." *Alabama Review* 16 (April 1963): 108–24.

Faye, Stanley. "British and Spanish Fortifications of Pensacola, 1781–1821." *Florida Historical Quarterly* 20 (January 1942): 277–92.

"Fort Mitchell, Alabama." *Alabama Historical Quarterly* 21 (1959): 1–14.

Forts Committee, Georgia Department of Archives and History. "Georgia Forts: Fort Early." *Georgia Magazine* (August–September 1968): 24–26.

Grant, C. L., and Gerald H. Davis. "The Wedding of Col. Benjamin Hawkins." *North Carolina Historical Review* 54 (July 1977): 308–16.

Greenslade, Marie Taylor. "John Innerarity, 1783–1854." *Florida Historical Quarterly* 9 (October 1930): 90–95.

Griffin, John W., ed. "Some Comments on the Seminoles in 1818." *Florida Anthropologist* 10 (1957): 41–49.

Hamer, Marguerite B. "John Rhea of Tennessee." *East Tennessee Historical Society Publications* 4 (January 1932): 35–44.

Hassig, Ross. "Internal Conflict in the Creek War of 1813–1814." *Ethnohistory* 21 (1974): 251–71.

Holland, James W. "Andrew Jackson and the Creek War: Victory at the Horseshoe." *Alabama Review* 21 (October 1968): 243–75.

Horsman, Reginald. "The Dimension of an 'Empire for Liberty': Expansionism and Republicanism, 1775–1825." *Journal of the Early Republic* 9 (Spring 1989): 1–20.

Kennedy, Thomas C. "Sibling Stewards of a Commercial Empire: The Innerarity Brothers in the Floridas." *Florida Historical Quarterly* 67 (January 1989): 259–89.

Krogman, Wilton M. "The Racial Composition of the Seminole Indians of Florida and Oklahoma." *Journal of Negro History* 19 (October 1934): 412–30.

Lurei, Jonathan. "Andrew Jackson, Martial Law, Civilian Control of the Military, and American Politics: An Intriguing Amalgam." *Military Law Review* 126 (Fall 1989): 133–45.

Mahon, John K. "British Strategy and Southern Indians: War of 1812." *Florida Historical Quarterly* 44 (1966): 285–302.

———. "The Treaty of Moultrie Creek, 1823." *Florida Historical Quarterly* 40 (1962): 350–72.

McAllister, Lyle N. "Pensacola During the Second Spanish Period." *Florida Historical Quarterly* 37 (January–April 1959): 281–327.

Milligan, John D. "Slave Rebelliousness and the Florida Maroon." *Prologue* 6 (Spring 1974): 4–18.

Mulroy, Kevin. "Ethnogenesis and Ethnohistory of the Seminole Maroons." *Journal of World History* 4 (Fall 1993): 287–305.

Ogg, Frederick C. "The American Intervention in West Florida." *Mississippi Valley Historical Association Proceedings* 4 (1912): 47–52.

Owsley, Frank L., Jr. "British and Indian Activities in Spanish West Florida during the War of 1812." *Florida Historical Quarterly* 46 (1967): 111–23.

———. "The Fort Mims Massacre." *Alabama Review* 24 (July 1971): 192–204.

———. "Jackson's Capture of Pensacola." *Alabama Review* 19 (July 1966): 175–85.

Owsley, Frank L., Jr. "Prophet of War: Josiah Francis and the Creek War." *American Indian Quarterly* 9 (1985): 273–93.

Poitreneau, Abel. "Demography and the Political Destiny of Florida during the Second Spanish Period." *Florida Historical Quarterly* 66 (April 1988): 420–43.

Porter, Kenneth W. "Billy Bowlegs (Holata Micco) in the Seminole Wars." *Florida Historical Quarterly* 45 (1967): 219–42.

———. "Negroes and the East Florida Annexation Plot." *Journal of Negro History* 30 (1945): 9–29.

———. "Negroes and the Seminole War, 1817–1818." *Journal of Negro History* 36 (July 1951): 249–80.

———. "Origins of the St. John's River Seminole: Were They Mikasuki?" *Florida Anthropologist* 4 (1951): 39–40.

———. "The Cowkeeper Dynasty of the Seminole Nation." *Florida Historical Quarterly* 30 (1952): 341–49.

———. "The Negro Abraham." *Florida Historical Quarterly* 25 (1946): 1–43.

Prucha, Francis Paul. "Andrew Jackson's Indian Policy: A Reassessment." *Journal of American History* 56 (December 1969): 527–39.

Shwartzman, Grace N., and Susan K. Barnard. "A Trail of Broken Promises: Georgians and Muscogee/Creek Treaties, 1796–1826." *Georgia Historical Quarterly* 75 (1991): 697–718.

Skeen, C. Edward. "Calhoun, Crawford, and the Politics of Retrenchment." *South Carolina Historical Magazine* 73 (July 1972): 141–175.

Stenberg, Richard R. "Jackson's 'Rhea Letter' Hoax." *Journal of Southern History* 2 (November 1936): 480–96.

Sugden, John. "The Southern Indians in the War of 1812: The Closing Phase." *Florida Historical Quarterly* 60 (January 1982): 273–312.

Sydnor, Charles S. "One-Party Period of American History." *American Historical Review* 51 (April 1946): 439.

Thomason, Hugh M. "Governor Peter Early and the Creek Indian Frontier, 1813–1815." *Georgia Historical Quarterly* 45 (1961): 223–37.

Turner, Lynn W. "Electoral Vote against Monroe in 1820." *Mississippi River Valley Historical Review* 42 (1955): 250.

Usner, Daniel, Jr. "American Indians on the Cotton Frontier: Changing Economic Relations with Citizens and Slaves in the Mississippi Territory." *Journal of American History* 72 (1985): 297–317.

Waselkov, Gregory A., and Brian M. Wood. "The Creek War of 1813–1814: Effects on Creek Society and Settlement Pattern." *Journal of Alabama Archaeology* 32, no. 1 (1986): 1–24.

Waters, Annie C. "A Documentary History of Fort Crawford (Located in East Brewton, Escambia County [Alabama])." *Escambia County Historical Quarterly* 3 (September 1975): 1–24.

Wesley, Edgar B. "The Government Factory System among the Indians, 1795–1822." *Journal of Economic and Business History* 4, no. 3 (1931–32): 487–511.

Wright, J. Leitch, Jr. "A Note on the Seminole War as Seen by the Indians, Negroes, and Their British Advisors." *Journal of Southern History* 34 (1968): 565–75.

Theses and Dissertations

Duffner, Michael Paul. "The Seminole-Black Experience in Florida: An Example of Minority Cooperation." Master's thesis, George Mason University, 1973.

Heidler, Jeanne T. "The Military Career of David Emanuel Twiggs." Ph.D. dissertation, Auburn University, 1988.

Paine, Charles Raymond. "The Seminole War of 1817–1819." Master's thesis, University of Oklahoma, 1938.

Skogen, Larry Clifford. "'To Preserve Peace on the Frontier': Indian Depredation Claims and Native American Policy, 1796–1920." Ph.D. dissertation, Arizona State University, 1993.

Spiller, Roger J. "John C. Calhoun as Secretary of War, 1817–1825." Ph.D. dissertation, Louisiana State University, 1977.

Thomason, Jeffrey Lynn. "Acquisition by Foray." Master's thesis, Austin Peay State University, Clarksville, Tennessee, 1975.

Index